Social Software and Web 2.0 Technology Trends

P. Candace Deans
University of Richmond, USA

INFORMATION SCIENCE REFERENCE

Hershey · New York

Director of Editorial Content:	Kristin Klinger
Director of Production:	Jennifer Neidig
Managing Editor:	Jamie Snavely
Assistant Managing Editor:	Carole Coulson
Copy Editor:	Shanelle Ramelb
Typesetter:	Carole Coulson
Cover Design:	Lisa Tosheff
Printed at:	Yurchak Printing Inc.

Published in the United States of America by
Information Science Reference (an imprint of IGI Global)
701 E. Chocolate Avenue, Suite 200
Hershey PA 17033
Tel: 717-533-8845
Fax: 717-533-8661
E-mail: cust@igi-global.com
Web site: http://www.igi-global.com

and in the United Kingdom by
Information Science Reference (an imprint of IGI Global)
3 Henrietta Street
Covent Garden
London WC2E 8LU
Tel: 44 20 7240 0856
Fax: 44 20 7379 0609
Web site: http://www.eurospanbookstore.com

Library of Congress Cataloging-in-Publication Data

Social software and Web 2.0 technology trends / P. Candace Deans, editor.

    p. cm.

  Includes bibliographical references and index.

  Summary: "This book provides an overview of current Web 2.0 technologies and their impact on organizations and educational institutions"--Provided by publisher.

  ISBN 978-1-60566-122-3 (hbk.) -- ISBN 978-1-60566-123-0 (ebook)

  1. Information technology--Management. 2. Web 2.0. 3. Online social networks. 4. Technological innovations--Management. I. Deans, P. Candace.

  HD30.2.S636 2009

  004.678--dc22

                    2008028571

British Cataloguing in Publication Data
A Cataloguing in Publication record for this book is available from the British Library.

All work contributed to this book set is original material. The views expressed in this book are those of the authors, but not necessarily of the publisher.

To the Spring 2008 MBA Information Technology Class

Robins School

University of Richmond

Kim Baker

Joe Biedenharn

Kostadin Bisharov

Meghan Blake

Kristen Booros

Iryna Butler

Tim Davis

David Esposito

Grant Garcia

Brian Hoade

Cuyler Lovett

Drew Mann

Mike Matthews

Sean-Thomas Pumphrey

Melanie Riera

Jeff Snyder

Kristin Watts

Alex White

Table of Contents

Section I
Introduction to Social Software and Web 2.0

Chapter I

   Peter Burkhardt, IBM, USA

Section II
Business Applications of Web 2.0 Technologies

Chapter II

   David Harrell, Circuit City Stores, Inc., USA

Chapter III

   Samantha C. Bryant, Philip Morris, USA

Chapter IV

   Nadira Ali, University of Richmond, USA
   P. Candace Deans, University of Richmond, USA

Section VI
Glossary and Web 2.0 Tutorial

Detailed Table of Contents

Section I
Introduction to Social Software and Web 2.0

Chapter I
    Peter Burkhardt, IBM, USA

Social networking and Web 2.0 are the hottest words in technology right now; but is there more than just hype? This chapter will define and describe social software and Web 2.0, separate their true concepts from the marketing and buzz, and follow by identifying what might be next for this dynamic technology space. After establishing the social software and Web 2.0 concepts, this chapter identifies the value that they can bring to a company when used in a business context and the shortcomings or pitfalls. Chapter I will set the foundation for subsequent discussions of social software and Web 2.0 for specific industry applications.

Section II
Business Applications of Web 2.0 Technologies

Chapter II
    David Harrell, Circuit City Stores, Inc., USA

Chapter II provides a background on the importance of the Internet in consumer purchases, the development of various forms of consumer feedback, and the implications for multichannel retail businesses.

An analysis of several leading Web 2.0 technologies is provided to clarify key differences. The reader should walk away with a more robust understanding of consumer behavior in today's multichannel retail landscape.

Chapter III

        Samantha C. Bryant, Philip Morris, USA

Emerging Web 2.0 technologies such as wikis, blogs, YouTube, and virtual worlds are not only affecting how companies tactically approach marketing, but also their marketing strategies. Chapter III will explore the impact of Web 2.0 technologies on marketing and brand management and how companies can leverage these technologies to strengthen relationships between their brands and consumers through a Web 2.0 marketing mix. This new Web 2.0 marketing mix supplements the traditional four-p marketing mix (price, product, promotion, and placement) with a new "p" lens: participation. The focus of this analysis is on B2C marketing of products and services only.

Chapter IV

        Nadira Ali, University of Richmond, USA
        P. Candace Deans, University of Richmond, USA

Chapter IV examines the current trends and impact of Web 2.0 on organizations, managers, the workforce, and information exchange within and across companies. This phenomenon is expected to bring another wave of change to organizations that some believe could be on the magnitude of that experienced during the Internet revolution. These technological advancements do not come without challenges. Security, privacy, ethics, and legal considerations all play a major role in how these technologies develop over time. The time has come, however, for companies to begin to determine strategies for utilizing these technologies in order to remain competitive in the global business arena.

Section III
Security and Legal Issues for the Enterprise 2.0 Organization

Chapter V

        Richard T. Barnes, SunGard Higher Education, USA

Chapter V discusses Web 2.0 and its enumerable benefits as well as daunting problems of securing transactions, computers, and identities. Powerful hacker techniques, including cross-site scripting (XSS) and cross-site request forgery (CSRF), are used to exploit applications to reveal and steal, at the worst, confidential information and money, or, at the least, cause trouble and waste time and money for reasons that may be best described as fun or simply possible to do. The people interested in transgressing Web

2.0 applications do so for money, prestige, or for the challenge. An infamous hacker from the early days of the Internet now heads his own Internet security company. A more recent hacker of some infamy has created a stir of concern and consternation as to how pervasive and potentially destructive hacker attacks can be. Securing Web 2.0 applications requires a multifaceted approach involving improved code development standards, organizational policy changes, protected servers and workstations, and aggressive law enforcement.

Companies today face an overwhelming amount of digital information, and many of them are involved at some point in civil litigation. When a company is in the discovery (pretrial) phase of civil litigation, it usually exchanges information, including documents, with the opposing party in the litigation. The Federal Rules of Civil Procedure, which govern civil litigation in federal courts, were amended in 2006 to provide additional guidance to parties with regard to electronically stored information. The management teams of many U.S. corporations are working with their IT departments and lawyers in order to understand the sources of electronically stored information that may be potentially relevant to their litigation. Over the last 20 years, technology has grown increasingly more complex, from the early mainframe and personal computers to sophisticated e-mail and instant messaging applications that enable users to send and receive millions of messages every day. Chapter VI addresses the issues companies may face related to the discovery of electronically stored information as a result of new communication technologies, including Web 2.0 applications.

Section IV
Virtual Worlds

A virtual world is a computer-based simulated environment, usually modeled after the real world, accessed through an online interface, and inhabited by users in the form of avatars. The purpose of this chapter is to explore how these interactive, immersive environments are being used by a variety of organizations. Although various kinds of virtual worlds are introduced, this chapter focuses on the interactive 3-D virtual world of Second Life, describing its demographics and its features. Ways in which Second Life has been used by businesses, educational organizations, and political entities are then discussed. Legal issues associated with virtual worlds in general and Second Life in particular are raised. Chapter VII concludes with some ways this technology is expected to evolve in the future.

In Chapter VIII ethical issues associated with virtual worlds are discussed. Virtual worlds enabled by Web 2.0 technologies are gaining in popularity and use both for recreational and business purposes. Behavioral controls can be regulated through program code restrictions, rules of conduct, and local norms. Most vendor hosts of virtual worlds use code restrictions sparingly, restricting only overtly illegal activities. Otherwise, all worlds publish some form of rules of conduct and rely on the development of in-world local norms to regulate behavior. As a result, many unethical forms of behavior have arisen, including griefing, fragging, and industrial espionage. There is no sure method of solving the unethical forms of behavior unless strong social norms develop; therefore, users must take precautions when acting in virtual worlds to understand how to avoid or deflect virtual attacks of different types.

The purpose of this chapter is to advise developers, content providers, end users, legislators, and business managers about the challenges and ramifications of conducting business in virtual worlds. The chapter examines crime in virtual worlds, as well as evaluates the current status of property rights (real, actual, and intellectual), and suggests changes to the existing legal structure in order to confront virtual crime. Recommendations to the business manager are also included in Chapter IX.

Section V
Theoretical and Educational Perspectives of Web 2.0

This chapter discusses activity theory approaches to authentic online learning through Web 2.0 media tools and practices. With the proliferation of Web 2.0 software, many have access to the tools, but it is more difficult to harness the power in them toward authentic and meaningful action. Activity theory provides a lens to examine the "unit of activity" as a way to describe, analyze, and understand activity en route to learning goals. The first part of this chapter briefly defines activity theory and its main tenets, and the last few sections specifically address learning in authentic situations and developing authentic communities. Web 2.0 tools and practices allow learners to be engaged in content-related challenges using the tools as mediating devices and therefore facilitating more authentic and successful learning trajectories.

Section VI
Glossary and Web 2.0 Tutorial

Foreword

The ability to communicate with anyone anywhere has never been easier than it is today. This is not to say that there are still no boundaries in the world of communications; however, these boundaries are falling fast. The Internet has definitely been a conduit in allowing people to communicate. As the Internet matures, new tools and technologies have evolved earning the label of Web 2.0. The ability for groups of people to truly collaborate is being facilitated by many of the new tools that Web 2.0 has brought to average Internet users. No longer must you be a technology guru to exploit the ability to easily collaborate with others on the Web. This collaboration is occurring in the social, business, and educational environments, and the boundaries between these communities are continuing to be blurred. But, what exactly is Web 2.0 and how does Web 2.0 affect our ability to communicate both in our professional lives and our personal lives?

To see the changes in our communication habits, most of us need to look no further than our own homes. All I need to do is watch my sons communicate to realize that personal communication is no longer bounded by the telephone or the pen and paper. Averaging over 3,500 text messages a month, I am boggled that my 18-year-old son can possibly have time to do anything else. His communication is augmented with the many IM (instant message) conversations he conducts daily. At this time, he uses little e-mail other than for correspondence with vendors and potential colleges. My 20-year-old son recently decided to spend his spring semester volunteering. He used the Web to learn about different volunteer organizations. He subscribed to RSS (really simple syndication) feeds from several organizations to keep abreast of opportunities. Once he decided on volunteering in Costa Rica, he found several blogs to read about other volunteers' experiences in Costa Rica. Off he went. To keep in touch with my son, I simply log on to Facebook and quickly get an update on his volunteer endeavors with the leatherback turtles in Playa Buena Vista. I can view a video on YouTube that shows him learning to surf in his spare time. I quickly read messages left by his friends and know that he is having a good time. Since I am his mother, I do not leave a message on Facebook, but quickly type him an e-mail. He learned in college that many older people use e-mail for communications. He does not have Internet access where he is staying, so the next time he hikes the 4 km to town, he will call home using Skype (much cheaper than the regular phone line). Web 2.0 communication tools are allowing people to keep in touch like never before.

These same Web 2.0 technologies that have changed our personal communications are influencing how businesses communicate internally as well as externally. Methods for gathering and sharing information are having major impacts on businesses' interactions with employees, customers, and vendors. Communication is occurring globally. Organizational structures are changing. Although greater communication is often thought of as a positive influence on organizations, there are new negative consequences that businesses must address. Businesses that do not understand how to capitalize on the use of Web 2.0 tools will definitely find themselves left behind.

Ignorance is not bliss.

This book provides a great foundational structure to learn about Web 2.0 and its influences and impacts on individuals and businesses, making us less ignorant in the world of Web 2.0. The first section of this book introduces social software and Web 2.0. Clear definitions of the many new terms that have exploded around Web 2.0 are introduced. The author provides the reader with the opportunity to explore how communication is changing.

In the second section, understanding how businesses are capitalizing on Web 2.0 is explained. There are case studies that ground the concepts of Web 2.0. Specifically, the interactions of customers with businesses are explored. Special consideration is given to new marketing methods.

In the third section, the legal and security aspects associated with Web 2.0 are explored. Positive and negative impacts associated with Web 2.0 are considered. The issues of privacy, security, and fraud are requiring individuals and businesses to battle new negative consequences. Legislative bodies around the world have been unable to keep up with the changing issues that have arisen with these new technologies. As Internet users, we have questions about not only the use of Web 2.0 products, but our legal obligations associated with the use of these products. Users and businesses must be proactive in protecting data and wisely using Web 2.0 tools.

The fourth section takes the reader into the virtual world. The divide between the physical and virtual worlds continues to blur. Understanding the opportunities in the virtual world is introduced. Businesses are becoming players in the virtual world and individuals need to know how and when to interact. Although the virtual worlds are still in their infancy, much time and expense are being put into this environment.

Finally, the last chapter concludes with exploring how Web 2.0 is influencing education. Clearly, there are many educational areas where Web 2.0 is having an immediate impact. Furthermore, the impact will only continue to expand as education continues to evolve with Web 2.0. Social networking is providing the opportunity to extend knowledge throughout the globe.

The strategic impact of Web 2.0 is only beginning to be understood. Fortunately, the authors in this book provide the reader with a great introduction into the world of Web 2.0. This book is a must-read to learn more about Web 2.0 and the influences on our personal and professional lives.

Gigi G. Kelly
University of Virginia
May 2008

Preface

Enterprise 2.0 is changing the face of business. Social networks are becoming a mainstream means for promoting communication, especially among the younger generations. Web 2.0 technologies that support these changes are evolving rapidly. The ground is shifting under our feet and much will change even before this book is in print. These are exciting times, and at the same time uncertainties creep in as we try to anticipate what these trends mean for our future. These technologies are changing the way we communicate today and possibly forever. Once technology takes us down a certain path, there is no turning back.

Technology makes it possible for information to reach millions of people all over the world at lightning speed. The organization will be the recipient of this massive flood of information and flow of knowledge. The manner in which organizations use this resource will be critical in strategic planning and aligning business objectives. Organizations must prepare for this new wave of communication trends. Social media including blogs, podcasts, social networks, and wikis are becoming a natural component of professional life. The time frame in which companies have to prepare for this change is becoming exponentially shorter. A tipping point will eventually be reached and the way managers, employees, and customers communicate, collaborate, and connect will be forever changed. Organizations that understand the power of these technologies and begin to experiment with applications today will have an easier transition into this emerging era of the social enterprise.

Enterprise 2.0 technologies will not only change communications, but the ripple effects will flow to the work space. Social networks are transforming work models. Innovation is being approached from a community perspective in which ideas are being sought from anywhere, anytime using collaborative technologies. Customer relationships and connectivity are being managed through social networking applications. Facebook, for example, is being leveraged by some companies for sharing documents and communicating information to customers. The development of RSS (real simple syndication) feeds across the enterprise can build communication bridges among people with common interests. Worker productivity may be enhanced and business value improved if platforms are designed to manage the proliferation of RSS feeds. There are limitless ways in which Web 2.0 technologies may impact work, and these are only a few examples.

Social software trends are hard to control because there is a thin line between organizational applications and personal applications. For example, many employees today are members of LinkedIn for personal professional reasons even though there is no involvement from the perspective of the organization. Even though the organization may have no problems with employee membership in LinkedIn, it is an example of how these technologies proliferate with no control and sometimes no knowledge by the organization. Considerable time may be expended by employees on LinkedIn for personal reasons that may not be directly related to work. On the other hand, many employees would argue that LinkedIn has made their work more productive for things such as looking for qualified employees and getting recommendations in a timely manner. Still, this is typically done with no control from the organization. Social software that promotes freedom of expression brings with it a new level of responsibility to manage content creation and monitor access to these resources. Web 2.0 technologies open up new avenues of communication but at the same time present new measures of risk for the company. It is necessary that companies develop social software policies along with their strategic plans for implementing the technologies. This is a new area of policy creation for most companies. These policies, however, will become even more important as information continues to explode and the use of Web 2.0 technologies becomes more prevalent.

Enterprise 2.0 tools are constantly evolving. The technologies are currently at different levels of maturity. It is necessary that companies evaluate the market trends and success factors for implementation by other more experienced companies. Much can be learned from those who have gone before. Most enterprises still struggle to justify the investments in social software and collaborative tools. Making the business case for Enterprise 2.0 technologies is difficult at best. In most cases, a platform solution is necessary to show long-term solutions and benefits. Chief Information Officers (CIOs) must be prepared to make the pitch for longer term benefits even though it is not clear how the technology will evolve over time. Social software and related Web 2.0 technologies pose a challenge for companies to know not only when but how much to invest in these endeavors.

Storage of all this information along with legal and compliance regulations have become huge concerns. Companies were already in the process of implementing systems to manage the content being generated through e-mail and other unstructured information before Web 2.0 technologies appeared on the scene. Now with the explosion of unstructured digitally born data and information, these concerns take center stage as companies struggle to meet legal requirements and compliance standards. These issues will not go away and will likely only become more significant, especially in the short term.

Leaders in organizations will be the agents of change to move their companies through the transition from Enterprise 1.0 to Enterprise 2.0. Determining the appropriate strategy to change the way managers, employees, and customers interact, exchange information, and get work done is a huge undertaking. These changes will not be easy because of the diversity in employee skills. Those in leadership roles are typically not as technologically savvy as the entry-level workforce, and it will be necessary to utilize the talents of younger employees while at the same time bringing seniors in the organization up to speed on this new wave of technology skills. As is typical with every new wave of technology, the challenges fall within the workforce and not the technology per se. Technology implementation is relatively easy compared to the organizational issues and people concerns. Many of these issues are just now beginning to surface and will be key to successful change management.

The purpose of this book is to provide the reader with an overview of the technologies that have become known as Web 2.0. The reader will have a working knowledge of how these technologies are currently being utilized in business, education, and society in general. Current applications and their impact on business will be explored through the various chapters by authors from diverse backgrounds and industries. The value of this book is in its compact coverage of Web 2.0 technologies and applications that are important to know about today. It provides the essential knowledge base from which to proceed and develop more in-depth education or specific skills. All who read this book should walk away with the terminology and basic background to understand the trends that are currently taking place. This provides the reader with a foundation upon which to build.

The book is organized into six main sections. The main theme and content for each section is described following.

Section I: Introduction to Social Software and Web 2.0

The introductory keynote chapter is written by Pete Burkhardt, who has been on the cutting edge of Web 2.0 trends since its inception. This chapter provides the reader with a foundation from which to understand the competing and often confusing terminology that is associated with the phenomenon known as Web 2.0. A distinction is made between terms such as social networking, social software, Web 2.0, and collaboration. These terms are many times used interchangeably. Current issues related to the value of social software and collaboration trends for business are debated in the context of current challenges and opportunities. This chapter provides the reader with a frame of reference from which to evaluate applications for business and education as well as to understand the challenges that may present themselves in this context. These issues make up the discussions for the subsequent chapters in this book.

Section II: Business Applications of Web 2.0 Technologies

The second section focuses on business applications of Web 2.0 technologies. The retail industry has led the way in many respects despite Web 2.0 technologies exploding across all industries and companies both large and small. David Harrell, in Chapter II, addresses applications and examples of the use of these technologies from the perspective of the retail industry. Through the application of Web 2.0 technologies, customer feedback has been transformed. The way consumers approach research and purchase decisions have been changed by Web 2.0 applications. This chapter focuses on consumer-generated content and its impact on customer experiences and behavior patterns. Much experimentation is currently taking place with new possibilities emerging all the time. The concept of the customer relationship is being transformed through the support of these technologies.

In Chapter III, Samantha Bryant presents a conceptual understanding of how the Web 2.0 phenomenon is transforming the marketing mix from a strategic perspective. She argues that the traditional marketing mix represented by the four *p*s—product, pricing, promotion, and placement—are no longer sufficient to adequately describe the marketing mix in the context of Web 2.0. She contends that a new *p*, participation, is necessary to adequately describe how customers are participating in each of the original four *p*s of marketing. She presents some interesting ideas concerning the importance of participation in the marketing-mix concept going forward in this new Web 2.0 world. Traditional marketing has gone through major change since the advent of the Internet and will continue to evolve with the introduction of new technologies.

Finally, Chapter IV takes a more comprehensive approach to how the organization will evolve into the Enterprise 2.0 mind-set and the many challenges and opportunities that will be part of this transformation. Although there is still debate in the literature as to the impact of Web 2.0 and whether this movement is truly transformational for companies, the collaborative and participatory nature of these evolving trends cannot be ignored. Nadira Ali and P. Candace Deans present the premise that Web 2.0 technologies will not only transform the way organizations get work done, but will also transform the roles of leaders, managers, and employees. The implications are much more profound than can probably be imagined today. For one, organizational communication may be changed forever.

Section III: Security and Legal Issues for the Enterprise 2.0 Organization

There are many challenges that will flow out of the implementation of Web 2.0 applications in companies. In Section III, security and legal issues are addressed specifically. Privacy and ethical concerns also play a big role in Web 2.0 technologies and are incorporated into the security and legal discussions of this chapter as well as in the following section focusing on virtual worlds.

In Chapter V, Richard Barnes addresses the security concerns that have emerged with the use of Web 2.0 applications. Many companies have been hesitant to implement Web 2.0 applications because of security issues. The open and participatory nature of Web 2.0 provides an opening for security vulnerabilities that were not as pervasive in the static Web 1.0 world. The details of these security issues are explained in this chapter. Recommendations for how to address these security issues and possible ways to mitigate the potential risks are discussed. Best practices for Web 2.0 security are beginning to emerge and just as with previous technologies, solutions will be found for many of today's pressing problems.

As mentioned previously, the explosion of unstructured information that companies are experiencing as a result of user participation through Web 2.0 technologies is beginning to pose major concerns for companies. These new forms of communication between users will likely become legal records the same way that e-mail messages are defined as legal records. Companies are finding it necessary to implement content-management software solutions to control this massive amount of information and to ensure that search mechanisms are in place to locate relevant information. Litigation can result in insurmountable costs when relevant information cannot be easily located. Bryan Kimes discusses these issues in Chapter VI in particular reference to e-discovery. Web 2.0 has changed the e-discovery landscape and it is important that companies recognize how U.S. laws have recently changed to include electronic data and information and what the implications may be for companies. Hypothetical scenarios are presented to show alternative situations and possible consequences for e-discovery.

Section IV: Virtual Worlds

The concept of virtual worlds has taken off in recent years. Three chapters are dedicated to this topic because it is relatively new and is evolving at a rapid pace. A substantial number of companies and educational institutions have purchased land in *Second Life*, for example, and applications are proliferating. It has become clear that 3-D technologies and virtual worlds will play a big role in the Enterprise 2.0 organizations of the future even though the use of these technologies may be very different from the current applications. These technologies are currently in their infancy. As the technology evolves over time and becomes more user friendly, it will likely become mainstream with an increasing blur between reality and virtual worlds.

In Chapter VII, Carolyn Jacobson provides a comprehensive overview of virtual worlds, focusing specifically on *Second Life*. This chapter serves as a seminal piece that pulls together the current literature and state-of-the-art technology as it exists today. A discussion of the technology and features of *Second Life* as well as business and educational applications are presented. After reading this chapter, the reader should have an understanding of how virtual worlds developed over time and have evolved in such a short time frame to encompass applications for both business and education.

Sue Conger extends the discussion of virtual worlds in Chapter VIII to focus on the emerging ethical issues and unethical forms of behavior that have become part of this virtual environment. The complexity of issues in virtual worlds mirrors that of the real world. Controls to regulate virtual behavior are only now beginning to emerge and this has become an area of much interest for companies and educational institutions as liability issues and other risks are increased.

In a discussion of legal concerns in Chapter IX, Hunter Jamerson builds on this discussion from the previous two chapters. This chapter addresses the array of legal issues that have emerged out of this virtual-world concept. Legal issues raised in Chapter VII are more extensively discussed here. Property rights and inappropriate behavior including stealing, murder, rape, and other acts of violence have become huge concerns. The U.S. legal system is not currently designed to address legal concerns in a virtual context. Virtual worlds have their own code of conduct and service agreement terms that currently govern participant actions. There is much debate as to how conflicts and disputes should be resolved. As virtual worlds continue to merge with real-world operations, legal matters will take on greater significance. An interesting discussion of these current issues and emerging areas of concern is presented in this chapter.

Section V: Theoretical and Educational Perspectives on Web 2.0

In the final section, a theoretical perspective on Web 2.0 technologies is presented. Tom Reinartz provides a convincing argument for the evolution of new learning environments that are supported by Web 2.0 tools. He uses theoretical underpinnings to support the link between Web 2.0 technologies and their contribution to more authentic and meaningful learning outcomes. These technologies provide the impetus for a paradigm shift from an instructor-centered process for learning to a more co-collaborative and participatory model. The younger generations today are embracing social networking opportunities such as Facebook, MySpace, and Flickr. This represents a new way of interacting and participating within environments of learning. Educational processes in the business context as well in the academic setting will out of necessity move from linear to more collaborative interactions.

This chapter emphasizes the significance of Web 2.0 trends for education that will in turn have tremendous implications for business. It will be essential that businesses understand this evolution and the learning styles and instinctive ways of communicating that will be part of the future generations entering the workforce. The Web 2.0 movement is expected to have a significant impact on how education is delivered and subsequently on how students learn. This evolution is currently in its infancy but the potential impact is already unfolding. Businesses will need to embrace this change in ways that provide positive results. Although the challenges are many, so are the opportunities for those who seize the possibilities and act.

Section VI: Glossary and Web 2.0 Tutorial

The final section of the book includes a glossary of terms and a Web 2.0 tutorial. These will benefit the reader who is less familiar with the terminology of Web 2.0 and the uses of the various tools. The tutorial provides some background and perspective as well as a concise guide to using the technologies for basic applications. Although an extensive number of how-to books exist, most of these provide more than most readers want or need in order to have a general understanding of the basics. In addition, the tutorial provides coverage of the major Web 2.0 technologies in one document. For those who only need a good overview, this tutorial serves that purpose well. It may be beneficial to read the tutorial first. The chapter content may be easier to follow and may spark more creative ideas when read after the tutorial.

The tutorial is divided into sections based on the major Web 2.0 technologies. These include blogs, podcasts and videocasts, wikis, virtual worlds, social networks, social bookmarks, social photo sharing, social tagging, mashups, and Web conferencing. Each section follows a similar format. The outline for each section includes historical perspectives, current trends, business applications, educational applications, hands-on descriptions, future trends, and additional relevant resources. This tutorial provides a valuable resource and reference for the reader who needs a simple hands-on explanation of the technologies. It should be noted that this tutorial also has value as a stand-alone component.

CONCLUSION

Content updates have been incorporated in this work to the extent possible in the final revisions. It should be noted that there may still be some overlap in content across chapters and with the content of the tutorial. It is difficult to completely avoid this given that each author is to some degree writing in a vacuum. In an ideal world where deadlines are met and time frames are adhered to, there is time for numerous revisions. In the real world, it is sometimes necessary to live with some imperfection, especially when technology is changing so rapidly. It is possible that in the future, all writing will be done using a wiki-type format so that the content is continuously being updated and there is continuous revision and oversight by many participants. It is the intention here that the reader find value in this work today since its life span is likely to be short lived.

Acknowledgment

My sincere gratitude goes to the chapter authors who contributed their time and expertise to this project. Countless hours went into the completion of this manuscript by these writers from both the business community and academic institutions. The reviewers also play an important role in strengthening the presentation of content for the final version. Their work is greatly appreciated. A special thank you goes to Pete Burkhardt from IBM who provided valuable insights and wrote the keynote introductory chapter and glossary.

A special word of thanks is extended to Hunter Jamerson, a May 2008 graduate of the University of Richmond's T.C. William's School of Law and current MBA student. He currently serves as law clerk to the Honorable Michael C. Allen, judge of the 12th Judicial Circuit of Virginia. Hunter contributed many hours of help with writing, editing, and providing suggestions and feedback throughout every phase of the manuscript preparation process. His research interests focus specifically on the legal aspects of the topics covered in this book. His contributions are greatly appreciated.

Appreciation also goes to the spring 2008 Robins School MBA information technology class (MBA 550) at the University of Richmond for their combined contributions to the tutorial section of the book. Their names are listed with their contributions in the tutorial. We learned firsthand that "no one of us can write what all of us can write." It was truly one of the rewarding experiences of my professional career. Without their help this book would not have been possible.

In addition, thank you to Ryan Hill and Jordan McGhee, both undergraduate students in the Robins School who worked for me as student assistants during the year this book was being prepared. Their willingness to do whatever was required to get things done is appreciated.

Dean Jorge Haddock and Senior Associate Dean Richard Coughlan of the Robins School provided necessary resources.

Last, but not least, thank you to Heather Probst, editor at IGI Global, who was very helpful during the publication process.

P. Candace Deans, Virginia, USA
May 2008

Section I
Introduction to Social Software
and Web 2.0

Chapter I
Social Software Trends in Business:
Introduction

Peter Burkhardt
IBM, USA

ABSTRACT

Social networking and Web 2.0 are the hottest words in technology right now; but is there more than just hype? This chapter will define and describe social software and Web 2.0, separate their true concepts from the marketing and buzz, and follow by identifying what might be next for this dynamic technology space. After establishing the social software and Web 2.0 concepts, this chapter identifies the value that they can bring to a company when used in a business context and the shortcomings or pitfalls. This chapter will set the foundation for subsequent discussions of social software and Web 2.0 for specific industry applications.

INTRODUCTION

Social software is the hottest topic in the technology space right now. It is nearly impossible to avoid hearing about Web 2.0 and social networking in mainstream media publications and broadcast news—and it is not just technology magazines or TV shows either. For example, just about every recent issue of *Time* magazine has had an article on Web 2.0, social networking, or something related to those buzzwords.

It is not just the mainstream media that are picking up on this hot topic. The technology itself is being used to tout both its unmatched potential and its less-often-mentioned shortcomings. Web 2.0 is providing the ability for evangelists and skeptics across the globe to weigh in and have equal voice on the very platform they are using to deliver their opinions and thoughts. For those not in the know, this seems like an opportunity that can only be missed at one's own peril.

Every new Web site is clamoring to be known as a Web 2.0 or social networking site and be the next big buzz. Gone are the days when it was good enough to provide a store front on the Internet and generate millions of dollars in sales. These days, you have to have the ability to connect people, provide consumer ratings systems, and allow everything to be tagged and commented on. Users have become more fickle and will quickly move on to another Web site that enlists more Web 2.0 feel and functionality. Casual Internet users have evolved and do not want to just browse for information; they want to project themselves, get connected to others, and interact or collaborate.

Likewise, traditional corporations are clamoring to put Web 2.0 and social software to work for their own benefit as well. Many managers and executives have said that they need to implement Web 2.0 and social software to have a competitive advantage and not be left behind by the competition. However, many will also admit that they are not quite sure what Web 2.0 really is or what social software really does for their business.

As a result of all this recent press and the amazing amount of hype surrounding Web 2.0 and social software, there are many who believe that these are new concepts (which they use interchangeably), have only recently come to fruition, and have been made available in the last few years. However, like most things, the application of social networking in software is just a new application of a concept that has existed for quite some time. Web 2.0 has been more of a gradual evolution than the instantaneous explosion that the hype would have one believe.

To help one understand where the social software market trend is going, it is extremely important to remove the hype and understand its underlying concepts and history. Only after understanding the foundation concepts of social software can one truly define its value in the marketplace and what social software means to a corporation. The remainder of this chapter will answer the question "What is social software?" and discuss its value to businesses. Subsequent chapters will proceed to examine the relevance

of social software and its value as applied in the context of specific business and educational applications.

BACKGROUND

One of the most common issues that leads to confusion in this space and obfuscates the ability to see the value in social software is the interchangeable usage of terms. Just about everyone who talks and writes about this technology space freely and openly substitutes terms such as *Web 2.0*, *social networking*, and *collaboration* as though they all mean the same thing. This only serves to make this market space appear more nebulous than it needs to be and confuses those who are not already knowledgeable on the topic.

Perhaps all of this confusion should be an indicator that there is more marketing hype than substance in the social software trend. However, there are also examples and data to substantiate the validity of the use of social software for the benefit of business. The reality of the situation is that it is quite a bit of both. While there is true business value to be derived from social software, it takes the ability to see through the "buzzword bingo" that regularly occurs.

This is not to say that all terms have been clearly defined to date either. There are many experts in this space who still cannot seem to reach agreement on what certain terms, such as *Web 2.0*, really mean. Therefore, it is important to establish some definitions in order to build our social software foundation of understanding and to see the business benefits of social software.

Social Networking

Contrary to recent technology hype, social networking is a sociology concept that has evolved from sociology studies in the late 1800s and continues to mature even today. While the first studies of social networks may not have been deemed as such, the coining of the term *social network* and the analysis thereof became more mainstream and evolved rapidly within the sociology field in the 1950s to 1970s.

A social network is a grouping of personal relationships that each of us establishes. As opposed to other types of networks, the value of a social network is not in the nodes on the network, which in this case are people, but are in the relationships themselves. Social networking, therefore, is the act of building one's social network. People rely heavily on these relationships to help them with everyday tasks, such as making decisions, forming opinions, and/or finding information:

Our heavy reliance on other people for information and learning is one of the most consistent and robust findings in the social sciences. It also matches our intuition and lived experience in organizations: other people are critical to our ability to find information, learn how to do our work, and develop professionally. (Cross, Abrams, & Parker, 2004, p. 152)

As a result, one of the many uses of a social network is in conjunction with, and as a precursor to, collaboration. Leveraging one's social network vastly improves the ability to collect the right people and information upon which to collaborate toward a common goal. While social networking is a strong precursor for collaboration, the same cannot be said for the relationship when examined in the inverse order.

Social Software

Building upon this definition then, social software is about using technology, and more specifically computer software, to support the process of social networking. It is important to note that the software itself is not performing the activity of social networking. The software is simply being leveraged to support and facilitate the creation and maturation of relationships between individuals, otherwise known as social networking.

The value of social software lies in its ability to do two things. First, it helps to cross traditional barriers that keep individuals from creating relationships. In a corporate environment this could be departmental organization, where people in different departments do not normally talk to each other. The purpose of the software is not to overcome the department structure, but to acknowledge the boundaries and then cross them in order to connect people.

Second, social software assists people to better leverage their existing relationships in order to find knowledge. By exposing contextual relationships between individuals, it can assist in helping to streamline the process of identifying who should be included in a collaborative effort or who knows where to find the knowledge that is being sought. Many people easily confuse this area of value with expertise management. In reality, this may lead to someone eventually locating an expert; however, it is not expertise location in itself because the determination of the expert qualifications is inferred, at best, in social software.

Social Network Analysis

Social network analysis (SNA) is a way of identifying and understanding social linkages and relationships between people. Through the understanding of these relationships, we can then assess information flows and communication breakdowns in a social network. When applied to a business, this information can then be leveraged to identify where talent and expertise could be better applied, how work gets done in a company, and where bottlenecks exist for processes, decision making, and information flow.

SNA starts with gathering relationship information through a series of interviews, questionnaires, and company communication data. After the information has been gathered, it is analyzed to uncover the relationships that exist within an organization. More specifically, the analysis examines the nodes or actors that are in the network, the relationships between the actors, and the attributes that may be affecting those relationships. As a result of the analysis, an organization will have a better understanding of how things happen and can take actions to increase productivity, efficiency, and/or innovation. Corporate mergers and acquisitions are a prime example of how SNA can benefit a business. After performing an SNA, the two businesses can be organized and melded together in a way that takes advantage of the most efficient processes and people in each business.

Collaboration

Collaboration is defined by Merriam-Webster's Online Dictionary ("Collaboration," n.d.) as "to work jointly with others or together especially in an intellectual endeavor." Collaboration is about more than one person (a team, a group, etc.) working together toward a common goal. There have been many types of software in the past that support collaboration, mainly in the business environment. However, the fault of these applications was that they assumed that the identification of the people being brought together to collaborate had already been conducted. While the tools facilitated the collaboration, they did not ensure that the teams had the right people involved in the collaboration or all of the most appropriate information to collaborate upon. Recent increased focus on social networks has demonstrated their importance as a precursor to collaboration and helped to exponentially increase the value of collaboration.

While collaboration software has been available in the corporate or enterprise space for quite some time (e.g., Lotus Notes, Domino), it has not been prevalent in the public domain and available to end users independent of organizational affiliation. As a result, individuals have had a tough time leveraging the Internet for collaboration in the public domain. That trend is starting to change as new technologies like wikis provide individu-

als with the ability to organize and collaborate toward a common goal in the public domain. The impact of domains is discussed in greater detail later in this chapter.

Web 2.0

Web 2.0 is the most commonly heard term in the social software trend and the most confusing. Even the experts disagree on the definition. O'Reilly Media is accredited with the creation of the term *Web 2.0* during a conference brainstorming session in 2004 between O'Reilly Media and MediaLive International (O'Reilly, 2005).

In short, Tim O'Reilly (2006, p.1) states, "Web 2.0 is the business revolution in the computer industry caused by the move to the internet as platform, and an attempt to understand the rules for success on that new platform." It is meant to refer to the second generation of the Internet and is composed of seven core principles.

1. The Web as a platform
2. Harnessing collective intelligence
3. Data as the next Intel Inside
4. End of the software release cycle
5. Lightweight programming models
6. Software above the level of a single device
7. Rich user experiences

Web 2.0 has, without a doubt, become the hottest buzzword today in the technology space and has just about every company and Web site clamoring to claim that they are or use Web 2.0. However, there is also a great deal of misunderstanding, or lack of understanding, as to what Web 2.0 really means when you start to boil down the term.

Critics have stated that Web 2.0 is merely a buzzword, skips over important evolutionary changes to the Web by declaring itself the second generation, does not really have much substance to it, and has yet to produce any meaningful or truly important results. One important critic is Tim Berners-Lee, the inventor of the World Wide Web. In an interview in July 2006, Berners-Lee was asked if it was fair to say that "Web 1.0 was about connecting computers and making information available; and Web 2 is about connecting people and facilitating new kinds of collaboration." His response was

Totally not. Web 1.0 was all about connecting people. It was an interactive space, and I think Web 2.0 is of course a piece of jargon, nobody even knows what it means. If Web 2.0 for you is blogs and wikis, then that is people to people. But that was what the Web was supposed to be all along. And in fact, you know, this Web 2.0, quote, it means using the standards which have been produced by all these people working on Web 1.0. (Laningham, 2006, p. 1)

In clarifying the definition of Web 2.0, Tim O'Reilly (2006, p. 1) subsequently had this to say: "Ironically, Tim Berners-Lee's original Web 1.0 is one of the most 'Web 2.0' systems out there—it completely harnesses the power of user contribution, collective intelligence, and network effects." So, to summarize the attempts at Web 2.0 definition, O'Reilly coins the concept of Web 2.0 as the next generation of the Internet, gets challenged on that statement, and then clarifies it by saying that the first generation of the Internet is the perfect example of the second generation of the Internet. If that does not confuse people, nothing will.

While there may never be a solid definition for this nebulous concept, for the sake of argument, I will define how Web 2.0 fits into the Internet today in order to discuss it in the context of business. Web 2.0 is a technology concept, unlike social networking (which is a sociology concept). Web 2.0 refers to a style or method for combining existing technologies to empower people. A list of the technologies commonly combined under the Web 2.0 banner is discussed in the next section of this chapter.

The idea is to make the usage of software applications and Web sites faster, easier, and more intuitive for users. This is accomplished through three general thrusts. First, Web 2.0 leverages the power of end users' computers to improve the responsiveness of the user interface (UI) of Web applications. As opposed to previous Web application architecture, where all layers of an application were combined on centralized servers, Web 2.0 moves some of the application logic and management of the UI to the client on the end user's computer. Second, by separating the content from the UI design, users can focus on the publishing and exchange of information without having to know the UI programming required to publish the information. Third, by improving the UI to be more dynamic and responsive, users' attention is drawn to the application and their experience is greatly improved.

These improvements to software applications and Web sites did not happen overnight, though. Many software applications use numbers to indicate versions of the software, with newer versions meant to replace older versions through an installation process. This is where Web 2.0 is very misleading. By using the *2.0* nomenclature associated with software product releases, one might think that Web 2.0 is meant to replace Web 1.0 or is the next version of the Web. This could not be further from the truth. There have been many significant milestones in the evolution of the Web since its inception. The Web continues to change on a regular basis as a result of new ways for combining technologies and concepts, not in a disjointed, iterative manner, but in a smooth evolution.

In reality, Web 2.0 is really nothing new. It is simply a way of recombining and repackaging existing technologies that have been around for quite some time. There are no truly fundamental differences between the technologies used in Web

1.0 and Web 2.0. A brief examination of the most common technologies that are associated with the Web 2.0 banner is included below.

Technologies within Web 2.0

The hypertext markup language (HTML) has been around since the creation of the Internet. This language is used to create and format the content that is included on Web pages.

The extensible markup language (XML) is a programming language that allows a developer to define content and specific tags that surround the content. Like HTML, the content can be formatted through the use of tags. However, XML also allows the programmer to create his or her own tags and then find and manipulate content through the tags that are associated with the content.

Cascading style sheets (CSS) are used to describe the presentation of a document written in HTML or XML. For each style that is defined in the markup language, CSS tells the client how to display that style. For example, CSS would define that the Header style should be displayed in a bold 12-point font.

JavaScript is a cross-platform scripting language that can be used in a server or client environment to manipulate data and objects. It is most commonly used for client-side Web development to create a more dynamic user experience with a Web page.

Asynchronous JavaScript and XML (AJAX) is a development technique used on Web sites that combines the use of JavaScript and XML to create a more interactive user experience. The concept is to separate the user interface from data in order to be able to exchange data with the server without having to refresh the entire user interface. As a result, the Web page becomes more responsive. AJAX is a key part of Web 2.0 because of its ability to greatly improve the user interface of applications and make them more dynamic.

Really simple syndication (RSS) is a method for publishing information in a structured feed format (usually in XML). This allows clients and other software applications to subscribe to and receive timely information updates. Many people use feed readers to subscribe to a number of Web sites and have the updates aggregated into a single interface. RSS is part of Web 2.0 because of its ability to exchange data in a structured but easily consumable manner between applications.

ATOM is another publishing format that is similar to RSS, but is more robust and flexible. It is based on XML and, while not as widely used as RSS, is gaining market adoption. Like RSS, ATOM is part of Web 2.0 because of its ability to exchange data in a structured but easily consumable manner between applications.

JavaScript object notation (JSON) is a lightweight computer data interchange format. It is a subset of the JavaScript programming language and is commonly used within AJAX as an alternative to using XML.

Tags are keywords that users of a particular application can associate with a piece of content in that application. For example, if a user is posting a blog entry about what he or she ate for breakfast, that entry might be tagged with the keywords *orange juice*, *toast*, *breakfast*, and *eggs* so that other users searching on those keywords will find the blog entry. Users can also tag content created by others.

A folksonomy is a taxonomy where the tags and categorization of data are created and updated in a dynamic way by the consumers of the content. Folksonomies are part of Web 2.0 because they give the responsibility of creating the tags and associating them with the content to the users of the system.

A weblog (blog) is a Web site that is essentially a journal posted on the Web. The most common uses for the journal are either personal publishing, or commentary or news on a particular topic. Blogs are part of Web 2.0 because they enable common users to publish their thoughts and have their voices heard without the need to know how to program Web pages.

Wikis are server software that allows for one or more users to work together to create and edit content. Many wikis serve as a place for multiple people or communities to come together to collaborate on a particular topic. Wikis are part of Web 2.0 because of their ability to facilitate collaboration between users.

A podcast is a radio-style broadcast that is recorded and made available for users to download onto their computers, iPods, or MP3 players. Users generally find and subscribe to podcasts from Web sites as a method to keep up with the information being disseminated on the site. Podcasts are a very valuable tool to both mobile and office workers because they provide the ability to access audio information (e.g., presentations) at the convenience of the listener. Podcasts are part of Web 2.0 because of their ability to be easily created and disseminated by users without costly equipment or extensive experience.

Mashups are Web sites or applications that take multiple data sources and bring them together to provide specialized or situational value. Mashups are part of Web 2.0 because of their ability to let regular users create valuable situational applications without having to perform extensive application development.

Enterprise 2.0

Enterprise 2.0 is a recently identified term that is used to refer to the application of Web 2.0 and social networking concepts in an enterprise business context. First coined by Andrew McAfee (2006b, p. 1), "Enterprise 2.0 is the use of emergent social software platforms within companies, or between companies and their partners or customers."

McAfee (2006a) opines that these new Web 2.0 and social software may replace traditional communications methods in companies because of their ability to make tacit knowledge available to more employees. While it is still too early to tell if this will come to pass, there are some businesses that have taken advantage of them in addition to traditional communications methods.

Anything 2.0

In perpetuating the Web 2.0 moniker, many have started taking the *2.0* label and using it on the end of anything that they wish to express as exciting, new, and/or cutting edge (i.e., Media 2.0, Manufacturing 2.0, etc.). Due to the Web 2.0 buzz, this tactic certainly brings attention where desired. However, like Web 2.0, it does still leave people wondering what the differences from the previous version are and what is so new and great. In a way, this also detracts from the Web 2.0 concept itself because it further reinforces the notion that anything *2.0* is more hype than results.

DO YOU BELIEVE THE HYPE?

With all of the excitement surrounding the Web 2.0 and social software phenomenon, many businesses are in the position of deciding whether they should jump on the Web 2.0 and social software bandwagon or sit this one out. It is not an easy choice when you are a business. The stakes are high and a gamble in the technology space that does not pay off can have quite an effect on the company's bottom line. On the other side of the coin, if the company decides to sit it out and then its competitors can leverage the trend, the company is at a competitive disadvantage in the marketplace and could be equally penalized on the bottom line of the fiscal reports. So, what is a company to do? Should it buy into the hype and take the risk? Is there really something to this social software trend or is this just an example of the emperor's new clothes?

Social software is not a panacea or silver bullet. It will not solve all problems that a business entity has and instantly make things run smoothly while adding millions of dollars to the company's bottom line. It will not instantly resolve tensions in the organization between groups or make people instantly start talking to everyone that they should be talking to. It will not unravel issues with a supply chain or instantly create a distribution network for a product, and it will not result in all of the corporate knowledge being made available online so the company can do more with less people.

Social software can be used to help surface innovative ideas, respond to customers more dynamically, and cross departmental and organizational boundaries where appropriate to get things accomplished. It can assist in rapid growth, the hiring of new talent, and employee retention. It can reduce the loss of tacit corporate knowledge through natural attrition and retirement. It can also improve productivity and allow employees, partners, and customers to do more, faster.

Interestingly enough, there are some teams sometimes found in businesses that may seem like they would be ripe to quickly adopt social software and leverage its capabilities. Contrary to what one might assume, these teams may have the hardest time accepting and adjusting to social software. Two examples of this situation might be with the research and development (R&D) and knowledge management (KM) teams.

Research and development teams have been the staple of innovation in many organizations for the last century. Business entities hire the brightest and most creative minds and give them the funding and freedom to come up with the next set of great innovations that will make the company a success. It is probably not surprising that when the opportunity is created to have others provide innovation and exercise their creativity, R&D may feel a bit like its mission is threatened. However, this is not really the case as experience has shown that R&D is still greatly needed, but its role might slightly change. Instead of being the source of all innovation, it may now participate in the innovation instead of lead, and take on the greater importance by proving the innovation.

Likewise, a knowledge management team may also feel a bit threatened by social software. The reason for this is that the KM team has a wealth of experience in organizing and managing corporate knowledge. Members probably have a rich background in working with knowledge management and collaborative software, and lots of experience in creating information taxonomies. So, the concept of folksonomies may seem to go against everything on which they have worked for the past decade. Again, social software does not make the team obsolete, though; it simply changes the team's role. Social software will allow users to connect and leverage relationships, but it is not a replacement for knowledge management and does not address important aspects of knowledge management, such as the storage and availability of information. Instead, it is a compliment to knowledge management.

Social software is currently in the peak-of-inflated-expectations phase of its hype cycle (*Understanding Hype Cycles*, n.d.). It is not the be-all, end-all in the technology space that some make it out to be. However, it can bring very real results to a business. A business will most likely not use it in all of the ways that it is being used on the social networking Internet sites. If a business takes the time to understand the fundamental concepts behind Web 2.0 and social software, the underlying value propositions associated with each, and select the ones that are appropriate, it can put them to work for the business.

While the benefits are undeniable, many will struggle with measuring those benefits. Most businesses today use objective numbers to measure success. Companies look at things such as revenue, profit, and expenses at the macro level, and sales quotas, wages, product volume delivered, hours worked, and other measurements at the micro level to measure and track progress. In the case of social software, though, the focus is the human element, not finances or output measured.

The problem with measuring the value of social software and social networking is the extreme difficulty of putting an objective measure on a subjective topic. It is just not possible to put a direct measurement on human elements, like relationships or tacit knowledge. For example, a company may deploy a social software environment to help with recruiting new employees. The system will help new employees to grow their network more quickly, which they can, in turn, use to locate knowledge faster. But how does the company measure that? Any attempt to quantify that value into a dollar amount will need to include a number of assumptions and mostly fictional, best-guess estimates. Inevitably, this is an inaccurate method of measurement, at best, and is usually fraught with skewed data and meaningless results.

Social software may have a direct effect on the company's bottom line, but the direct correlation between social software and items in the general ledger may never be numerically established. Social networking is about personal relationships and personal relationships are about people. In order to make the investment in social software, a company has to value their employees, partners, and customers and be ready to make an investment in people.

FINDING AND APPLYING THE VALUE OF SOCIAL SOFTWARE FOR BUSINESS

It is a good first step to identify that there is value in using social software to support daily interactions and relationships between individuals working at or with a business. However, that is not quite enough to harness that value and put it to work for the business. Not all aspects or implementation methods of social software are appropriate for a business. Likewise, not all existing social networking applications that are available on the Internet are appropriate for use in a business environment. Some sites like LinkedIn (http://www.linkedin.com) offer some value to

employees by allowing them to make contacts in other businesses for sales or marketing reasons. Others require more examination and may not necessarily be appropriate.

The very first area of examination must be the concept of, for lack of a better word, what I will call *domains*. In this area of examination, the individual's use of the Internet will be referred to as the public domain; the business IT environment, including use of the Internet to work with customers and partners, will be the enterprise domain. It is extremely important to understand the differences between these domains, the nuances of each domain, and the behavior and motivation of users in each domain. These differences and characteristics will have a profound impact on leveraging social software in a business.

The public domain can largely be characterized as having recreational users with minimal affiliations. Most users will be independent individuals using the Internet for personal use. While many voluntarily identify themselves appropriately, anonymity is entirely possible and is leveraged by some. Their purpose for use will most likely be associated with serving self-interests. This is the domain where many of the most popular social networking sites are currently active. Sites like MySpace (http://www.myspace.com), Facebook (http://www.facebook.com), Flickr (http://www.flickr.com), and others are focused on serving the self-interests of individuals by providing services to connect with each other on an independent, individual level.

The enterprise domain can be characterized as having professional users associated or affiliated with businesses or professional organizations. This association of user with business or professional organization is usually readily indicated in the identity that is used online. The purpose of use will most likely be associated with serving either the associate business or the professional life (e.g., career) of the user and is expected to be used in a professional manner. This is the domain where the traditional business IT communications, financial, sales, marketing, and similar systems are located. Applications such as company e-mail, financial software, collaboration software, portals, supply chain management, and intercompany applications are focused on providing value to the business by facilitating business functions.

The purpose of social software remains the same independent of domain, but the way that social software is valued and, as a result, leveraged is quite different in each domain. Public-domain users value social software for its ability to facilitate relationships that are self-interest focused. Businesses value social software for its ability to facilitate relationships that benefit the needs of the business. Therefore, businesses do not see a lot of value in having users join MySpace to create a profile and keep up with people's hobbies, likes, and dislikes, but public-domain users do. However, businesses do see a lot of value in using this same concept to provide profiles of their employees that identify their skills, professional affiliations, areas of expertise, and tags for the purpose of locating people with particular skills or knowledge.

To get the most value from social software, businesses should not try to duplicate the most popular Web sites that exist in the public domain and bring them into the enterprise domain. Instead, businesses need to examine the social software and Web sites in the public domain, understand why they are popular and what functions they offer that could be useful to the business, and then implement those functions in areas of their business that will provide the greatest benefit.

For example, podcasting got its start as a way for an audio blog to be taken off line and listened to on personal media devices. This was quickly adopted by the media industry and leveraged to provide audio files such as radio broadcasts and audio journalistic articles for subscribers to listen to on their personal media devices while disconnected. Since then, many businesses have taken a close look at the concept of podcasting as a way to use audio and sometimes video files to deliver

information in a quick and asynchronous way to users. As a result, businesses have been able to leverage the concept to accommodate increasingly time-constrained employees, partners, and customers with important presentations, training, recorded meetings, and even sales and marketing materials that are available when they want, where they want. It is even being used to overcome language and cultural barriers by allowing people the ability to pause and listen multiple times to a recording that may be in a second language to them. This greatly increases comprehension and the effectiveness of the information being delivered.

Most importantly, businesses need to understand that all of the individual added value social software brings to the table roll up under one umbrella. The social software trend is about empowering people. Through this empowerment, a business achieves the maximum potential from social software. Freeing people from traditional business control of information and organization and giving them tools that they need to make their voices, thoughts, and ideas heard while transcending boundaries is the value that social software brings to the table.

If a business is satisfied with its current business process and thinks there is no room for improvement, social software is not for it. If it is not interested in improving customer services and does not care about suggestions for cutting operating costs, social software is not for it. If a business is not concerned about employee morale or overcoming communication and cultural barriers, it need not examine social software for its business. If it has all of the innovation that it needs and does not want to find new sources of ideas or better know what its customers need, social software is unnecessary.

However, if a business does care about all of these things, and arguably every business should, then social software brings a great deal of value to the initiatives, not by traditional formal programs or structured initiatives, but through unstructured approaches to tapping into normally unheard ideas. Every company has employees with ideas about how to refine processes that they work with on a daily basis to be more efficient or how to cut wasteful spending. There are plenty of customers and business partners that are willing, and even anxious, to tell a business exactly what they need, how to improve a product, or even become involved with the design and innovation process in order to contribute their experience and requirements. It is through empowering the people and letting their contributions be heard that the great advances are made.

Fostering innovation in a company is one of the most highly touted uses for social software in business. Empowerment through social software can have a profound effect: "Research and development projects fail more often than they succeed. In fact, out of every 10 R&D projects, five are flops, three are abandoned and only two ultimately become commercial successes" (Rizova, 2006, p. 49). Traditional business approaches to R&D put the source and responsibility for innovation squarely on the shoulders of a single structured department. The brightest minds would be hired to work in this department—people with master's and doctorate degrees and a history of researching, being innovative, and capturing their results in academic papers and prototypes.

Does it not seem that there is something fundamentally wrong with this approach? It is not reasonable to assume that only the people who work in the R&D department can be creative or should be allowed to be creative. Most businesses would agree that there are other people in a company or who work for business partners and customers who are creative. In the overwhelming majority of cases, most businesses do not have the capacity, tools, or methods in place to hear and capture the innovation from those additional sources. That is where social software can support the process. As a rudimentary example, if a business were to implement blogs for their employees and allow them to start expressing their thoughts, frustrations, wishes, ideas, and more, there is plenty of innovation that could be harvested from the blogs and ultimately turned into valuable business assets.

Another major area of benefit under the empowerment umbrella is the ability to provide easier access for users to find, use, and integrate data sources. For example providing RSS or ATOM feeds to key business systems allows a user to aggregate that information to a place that is easy to scan and keep up with (much like scanning the headlines of a newspaper). This makes users more aware and knowledgeable about the business as a whole and makes them more effective in their tasks relating to the business. It also increases their efficiency because what once took an hour of time to seek out multiple data sources and review or interact with them now takes a fraction of the time because they are summarized in a single location. Another example would be to provide users with the ability to create a mashup so that they can generate reports or create situational applications that are context sensitive and specific to their task at hand. By putting this capability in the users' hands, a business removes the shackles of having to request and wait for the IT department to create the needed application or reports.

Additionally, many of the Web 2.0 technology aspects of social software trends provide for a more interactive and responsive user experience in working with data. By improving the user experience of interacting with the data, two things occur. First, users are comfortable using the software and prone to use it more extensively. Second, as power users leverage the software more, additional users will be drawn into using the software through both necessity and word of mouth. This is known as "viral" adoption of the social software system because usage spreads like a virus instead of through traditional IT mandate or formal marketing.

CONCERNS ABOUT SOCIAL SOFTWARE IN THE ENTERPRISE

By removing the traditional business structure and empowering people through such an open solution, most businesses will be legitimately concerned about corporate information security. This is yet another aspect of social software in the enterprise domain that is not an issue or consideration in the public domain. The very thought of accidentally exposing internal confidential information is something that will immediately send business IT security departments into a full panic. Realistically, there is a balance to be struck between providing openness and ensuring that truly confidential information does not wind up freely available to all.

This balance is struck by understanding which boundaries are going to be crossed by using social software, recognizing the implications of crossing each boundary, and putting the proper guidance and security in place for each. Most businesses already have corporate information guidelines that can be easily extended to cover social software. For example, users should understand that there are different conduct guidelines that apply to blogs only available on a business's internal network vs. blogs available on the company's public Web site. On the internal blog location, the boundaries being crossed are internal (e.g., between departments), with users having the same association (the business) and therefore needing less rigorous guidelines because all users are business employees and working toward the same general business goal. Users should be able to post almost any content with a few exceptions (i.e., no customer names, no personal attacks, etc.). As a result, there may be plenty of blog entries that complain about business processes or strategy, share ideas for new products or solutions, and share personal information.

However, this type of content would not be appropriate to be posted on the business' public Web site. Externally available social software crosses the boundaries between the business and partners, customers, and the general public. As a result, there are additional guidelines that should be applied to address the different associations and affiliations of users of the social software. In this situation, blogs or wikis might be used to publicize new or little-known information about products or solutions and work together with customers and partners on advancing nonconfidential business ideas. Additionally, guidelines will need to be established to deal with information posted by those with negative intentions. These guidelines do not include constructive criticism, but instead are directed toward malicious content and spam.

Most users will intuitively realize what content is appropriate to be posted in social software based on the boundaries that are being crossed. This does not mean that there is no need for a business to deal with exceptions. For example, what happens when someone creates a blog entry that negatively talks about another department in the organization? That is probably not so bad if it is an individual's blog and is expressing the thoughts of the individual. It helps bring an issue to the surface so that it can be addressed and resolved, and everyone can move on. However, what happens if this same entry were to appear in a group or team blog? The author's name posting the entry is explicit, but how does this reflect on the entire team that owns the blog? Members might not all feel this way about the other department, but now these negative thoughts are projected as coming from the entire team. Perhaps in this situation, it is not appropriate and the author should move the entry to his or her personal blog or remove the posting altogether. There is no right answer to these types of scenarios, but some guidelines for working with these situations should be established and publicized to the users of the social software.

Social software also raises privacy concerns in the enterprise domain, but not in the public domain. Most social software solutions work based on a voluntary participation basis, empowering the user to contribute, but not mandating participation in the usage of the software. While this type of opt-in participation does eliminate many of the privacy issues that might be associated, there are some social software (more specifically, social network analysis) tools that analyze corporate communications data to extract social relationship data and make that available. Some would consider this an invasion of privacy and even have the feeling of the business's "big brother" watching.

However, there is another perspective that data in corporate communications tools belongs to the corporation and not the individual. Additionally, most of these types of social software will analyze only cursory information in the communications data (e.g., e-mail headers, but not the body) and store or transmit only the analysis itself, not the data being analyzed. Businesses have to comply with national employee privacy laws that address the types of employee data that can be made available and used by the business. It is important to always make sure that the business is in full compliance with these laws.

In many businesses, social software is viewed by some as a way for employees to waste time. Initially, some do not see the inherent value in social software, but instead think that it will make the company less productive because users will spend all their time working on things of no value to the business. Those same people are starting to have a realization that they need to use this technology, but are not quite sure just what should be done about it.

This is nothing more than a case of history repeating itself. This same opinion was voiced by many when e-mail first emerged as a new communication tool. It was often viewed by many as a way for people to waste their time sending each other frivolous messages. This same opinion was then applied to the Internet, where users would presumably while away their hours surfing the Internet. Most recently, this same approach has been applied to instant messaging. Many view

it as a kid's toy and a way for people to waste time chatting with their friends about nothing in particular. In each of these cases, the naysayers have been proved wrong and each technology has become an integral part of the way business is done on a daily basis. In fact, all of the previous technologies mentioned here have moved into the critical path for businesses and many do not know how they ever operated without them. Social software is destined to follow this same path and become an integral part of doing business.

FUTURE TRENDS

Is there a Web 3.0? Will Web 2.0 one day go the way of Web 1.0? The real question is not whether Web 2.0 will be usurped, as it is only natural that the evolution of the Web continues. The real question is what will be next. At this point, there are two concepts that look to be the most promising and are gaining a large amount of interest. However, they are only conceptual at this point and there has not yet been any real traction in making the concepts into a reality.

The Semantic Web refers to a vision for the Web to become a medium for machines to be able to understand, relate, and compile information without human intervention: "It is envisaged to smoothly interconnect personal information management, enterprise application integration, and the global sharing of commercial, scientific and cultural data" (W3C [World Wide Web Consortium] Advisory Committee, 2007, p. 1). The current configuration of the Web supports the linking and interaction of Web sites, but requires human interaction to interpret the data that is on the Web site. In the Semantic Web, individual pieces of data that are available on the Web are surrounded by descriptive tags that allow computers to understand relationships between pieces of data, as well as the properties of those pieces of data.

By making individual pieces of data readable and understandable to computers, the Semantic Web will truly transition the Web as we know it today from a collection of interacting Web sites to an unbelievable mass of data that is free to be combined and integrated. Allowing machines the ability to combine individual pieces of data will lead to the ability for machines to begin to perform tasks on behalf of humans. For example, a human currently has to submit a query on Google and then review the results to find the result that best fits the context with which they are interested. In the Semantic Web, a machine would be able to query and review the results for the appropriate context to return to the human.

While the Semantic Web has been discussed as early as 1999, critics have cited that there has not been a great amount of progress made on the Semantic Web coming to fruition over the past 9 years. Also, concerns of privacy and censorship would have been raised because of the ability for machines to understand the data that they are communicating. If this understanding were in place, computers could be made to more rigidly filter or display that data without human approval.

Another direction for the future centers on opening up the individualized social networking Web sites. Many sites now require users to register and then maintain their connections to others within the site. This causes a lot of frustration and extra work when users move to a different social networking site and have to reenter all of their information and connections to friends. Not to mention that their friends might not even be part of the new site; then they have to convince their friends to move over as well. This is a very Web site focused approach to social networking and only a fraction of how true social networking works outside of computers.

To address this issue, there has been much discussion about the Social Graph. The Social Graph refers to a visual mapping of all of our social interactions and connections as human beings. As opposed to having connections to others maintained on a Web-site-by-Web-site basis, it has been proposed that there be one open Social Graph created to manage connections between anyone and everyone. The Social Graph would also take care of maintaining a single identity for a user. The identity and connections could then be mapped to and leveraged by any Web site without having to recreate and store this information in a proprietary way.

This Social Graph further evolves the Internet from a space of interconnected Web sites to a space for interconnected people. After all, users may care about information or knowledge in a contextual and periodic nature (for business use, for personal use, etc.), but care about relationships to others (family, friends, colleagues, etc.) on a constant basis.

In both the Semantic Web and the Social Graph, it is proposed that the Internet move away from a set of connected Web pages and documents and focus connections more on people and data. This shift in direction will prove to be another powerful evolution because it will expose data and relationships at a much more granular level, thereby paving the way for a new level of contextual application. It would not be surprising to see some combination of these two notions in the future.

CONCLUSION

Social software and Web 2.0 are the hottest topics on the Internet. As they continue to draw an incredible amount of attention through the media and online traffic, there is also a great amount of confusion being perpetuated. The intermixing and interchangeable use of terms is, at best, confusing people and leaving others thinking that the social software trend is all smoke and mirrors. While some of the hype surrounding Web 2.0 and social software is just that, there is value in the concepts that underlie the trend.

Just like the value of the social network lies in the relationship between people, instead of the people themselves, the value of defining the terms associated with the social software trend lies in their relationships. Social networking is about the relationships between people. It is about bringing people and knowledge together and better leveraging what you know about who you know. Collaboration is about formalizing the group established through a social network into a team to work toward a common goal. Web 2.0 is the technology that is being used to empower and facilitate the social networking and, in some cases, the ensuing collaboration.

Many businesses are starting to examine the social software and Web 2.0 trend in order to see how it can add value to their business:

Much like late 1997, when technology specialists were getting asked by senior executives "What is the Internet, exactly, why is it a big deal, and what's our Internet strategy?" The question now is "What's Web 2.0/Enterprise 2.0/social media, exactly, why is it a big deal, and what's our W2.0/E2.0/social media strategy?" (McAfee, 2007, p. 1)

Social software is about relationships and relationships are about people. In order to fully leverage the social software trend, a company needs to value its human resources and be prepared to invest in people. There may never be a direct correlation between the deployment of social software and the bottom line of the ledger sheet (without a few bits of creatively fictional logic), but the company will surely see the value reflected in subjective measures, like customers' satisfaction, increased productivity, enhanced cost cutting, improved employee morale, and more. All of these factors will translate to an improved financial bottom line.

Businesses will need to apply the concepts behind the social software trend to areas of their business where they can be effectively used to unlock and open up the business and provide a voice to users. By empowering users, social software will allow for new sources of innovation and collaboration. According to a 2006 IBM Global CEO study (IBM Global Services, 2006), only 17% of CEOs ranked internal R&D as a source for new ideas. This means that overwhelmingly, businesses will be looking to customers, partners, and other company sources for the ideas and innovation that will power the future of their business.

Unlocking all of this value will not come without some challenges. It is encouraging, however, to know that those challenges can be overcome. Issues of security, privacy, and adoption of social software will emerge within businesses. Nevertheless, these issues have emerged with previous technologies, such as e-mail or the Internet itself, and have been addressed accordingly.

Now that we have had a look at how social software trends can impact businesses, subsequent chapters will examine how elements of social software are being adopted by businesses in different industry segments.

REFERENCES

Collaboration. (n.d.). *Merriam-Webster's Online Dictionary*. Retrieved December 15, 2007, from http://www.m-w.com/dictionary/collaboration

Cross, R., Abrams, L., & Parker. (2004). A relational view of learning: How who you know effects what you know. In M. L. Conner & J. G. Clawson (Eds.), *Creating a learning culture: Strategy, technology, and practice* (pp. 152-168). Cambridge University Press.

IBM Global Services. (2006). *Expanding the innovation horizon: Global CEO study 2006*. Retrieved December 15, 2007, from http://www-935.ibm.com/services/us/gbs/bus/html/bcs_ceostudy2006.html

Laningham, S. (2006). *developerWorks interviews: Tim Berners-Lee*. Retrieved December

15, 2007, from http://www.ibm.com/developer-works/podcast/dwi/cm-int082206.html

McAfee, A. (2006a). Enterprise 2.0: The dawn of emergent collaboration. *MIT Sloan Management Review, 4*(3), 21-28.

McAfee, A. (2006b). *Enterprise 2.0, version 2.0.* Retrieved December 15, 2007, from http://blog.hbs.edu/faculty/amcafee/index.php/faculty_amcafee_v3/enterprise_20_version_20

McAfee, A. (2007). *How to hit the Enterprise 2.0 bullseye.* Retrieved December 15, 2007, from http://blog.hbs.edu/faculty/amcafee/index.php/faculty_amcafee_v3/how_to_hit_the_enterprise_20_bullseye

O'Reilly, T. (2005). *What is Web 2.0?* Retrieved December 15, 2007, from http://www.oreillynet.com/pub/a/oreilly/tim/news/2005/09/30/what-is-web-20.html

O'Reilly, T. (2006). *Web 2.0 compact definition: Trying again.* Retrieved December 15, 2007, from http://radar.oreilly.com/archives/2006/12/web_20_compact.html

Rizova, P. (2006). Are you networked for successful innovation? *MIT Sloan Management Review, 47*(2), 49-55.

Understanding hype cycles. (n.d.). Retrieved December 15, 2007, from http://www.gartner.com/pages/story.php.id.8795.s.8.jsp

W3C (World Wide Web Consortium) Advisory Committee. (2007). *Semantic Web activity statement.* Retrieved December 16, 2007, from http://www.w3.org/2001/sw/Activity.html

Section II
Business Applications of Web 2.0 Technologies

Chapter II
The Influence of Consumer–Generated Content on Customer Experiences and Consumer Behavior

David Harrell
Circuit City Stores, Inc., USA

ABSTRACT

The purpose of this chapter is to inform retail business managers about the amplification of consumer voices through new forms of Internet media. Candid, real-time feedback through various forms of Web 2.0 have revolutionized the way consumers research, purchase, and enjoy products and services in today's world of commerce. The chapter provides a background on the importance of the Internet in consumer purchases, the development of various forms of consumer feedback, and the implications for multichannel retail businesses. An analysis of several leading Web 2.0 technologies is provided to clarify key differences. The reader should walk away with a more robust understanding of consumer behavior in today's multichannel retail landscape.

INTRODUCTION

Marketers have long believed that consumers trust the opinions of others more than they trust the communications of companies and advertisers (see Appendix A for justification). Web 2.0 technologies have redefined word-of-mouth communication, empowering individual customers by enabling them to reach millions of people through online media such as threaded message board conversations, blog posts, collaborative wikis, video posts, social networking, tagging, and customer ratings and reviews. The rapid growth of consumer-generated content is having a significant impact on customer experiences for multichannel shoppers by equipping them with relevant information supplied by peer consumers. The collaborative intelligence generated by customer communities provides unbiased, mutual opinions and advice that other consumers can utilize as they move through the entire purchase funnel: from research decisions to after-the-sale enjoyment.

Many companies in the retail landscape are already leveraging online customer communities to improve their overall marketing, merchandising, and customer service efforts. Leading retailers are generating additional payback by analyzing customers' information preferences and shopping behaviors, and leveraging this knowledge to develop multichannel strategies that deliver on customer expectations and enhance lifetime customer value. Insights gained from social retailing initiatives can inform innovation priorities, provide real-time feedback on marketing programs, and, in many cases, even provide predictive input on demand for key products and services. This raw source of customer insight allows retailers to identify internal opportunities to continuously improve online and off-line efforts in areas such as Web site experience design and store experience design as well as full life-cycle planning of assortments, pricing, and promotions across multiple channels.

Additionally, retailers have the opportunity to strengthen partnerships with value chain members, such as product vendors and third-party service providers, by sharing customer-driven insights that accentuate wins in the marketplace or present opportunities to deliver improved products and services with more customer-driven features. The growing practice of using customer insights to affect the upstream decisions of value chain partners will improve retailers' abilities to exceed consumer expectations by continuously improving product information, selection, and availability and enhancing service execution after the sale.

The potential to segment geographic observations in order to create tailored offerings that address regionalized demand differences is one of the ultimate goals of complex retail organizations. At the end of the day, a retailer's goal is to understand and more effectively serve specific consumer needs so that it can build lifetime customer value and deliver profitable growth. However, before new players attempt to leverage online consumer communities to improve their businesses, they need to develop a careful understanding of the unique potential benefits of the different Web 2.0 technologies and the challenges that come along with the territory.

LITERATURE REVIEW

Throughout the world, the Internet is becoming an increasingly important factor in the overall customer experience of investigating and actually purchasing goods and services. According to researcher comScore, e-commerce rates continue to rise at double-digit rates as Americans spent US\$24.6 billion shopping online in the most recent holiday season (Kharif, 2007). In 2006, 63% of some 67,000 households surveyed by consultancy Forrester Research investigated purchases online (Kharif). Both of these findings suggest there is a significant opportunity to capture sales and influence consumer behavior through a variety of media and information available on the Internet. In the November 2006 Touchpoints survey by DoubleClick, now a Google company, researchers came to the following powerful conclusions:

The Internet—in its various forms of websites, search engines, advertising, email, and professional and consumer reviews—is highly influential at every stage of the process, from first awareness to final decision making. In fact, the web influences purchase decisions—online and offline—more than any other factor. (Row, 2006)

While this certainly illuminates the prominent role of the Internet in modern consumer commerce, it is imperative that managers dig deeper in order to develop actionable plans and reasonable goals that reflect differences between product categories and the behaviors of different customer segments. The DoubleClick study also found that in hard asset categories, such as home products and apparel, physical retail stores remain the most important touch point for all three stages of the purchase decision-making process (initial awareness, information gathering, and purchase decision). However, the study revealed that in more service-oriented verticals, such as investments or telecommunications, word of mouth is extremely important in the first-learning and final-decision stages (Row, 2006). Finally, for categories such as air travel, hotels, and rental cars, the study found that the Web "overwhelmingly dominates" as the most influential factor for consumer decision making (Row). These results demonstrate the fact that consumer behavior varies greatly by product or service vertical, and it is important for marketers to be keenly aware of consumers' information needs in each stage of the purchase process.

Since it is clear that the Internet is a key resource for consumers as they research product categories, compare items, and make purchases, it is also relevant to understand how executives are viewing the importance of the online channel for information and purchases. A March 2007 McKinsey Global Survey *How Businesses are Using Web 2.0* found that executives across the world are showing "widespread but careful" interest in Web 2.0 technologies (Bughin & Manyika, 2007). Of the 2,847 corporate-level executive respondents, more than half said they are pleased with the results of their investments in Internet technologies over the last 5 years, and nearly three quarters say that their companies plan to maintain or increase investments in Web 2.0 technologies in coming years (Bughin & Manyika). Executives from some industries and regions that were slow to invest during the past 5 years are poised to make more aggressive investments. For example, retail executives, whose companies were more likely

than the average company to invest cautiously in the past, now overwhelmingly say they will boost investment in Web 2.0 technologies in the near future. Executives say they are using Web 2.0 technologies to communicate with customers and business partners and to encourage collaboration inside the company. Seventy percent say they are using some combination of these technologies for communicating with their customers. For example, about one fifth of them say they are using blogs to improve customer service or solicit customer feedback (Bughin & Manyika).

THE RETAIL INDUSTRY

While Web 2.0 technologies present opportunities for many, if not all, business sectors, this work will focus specifically on how consumer-generated content through these technologies can be leveraged within the retail industry. Retailers know that customers, especially the younger and more Net savvy, want to be heard, and they also want to hear each other. Consumer-generated content stimulates customers who are knowledgeable advocates of your brand to share their passion with other consumers through a variety of online media. It also creates an opportunity for disgruntled customers to voice their opinions and warn other customers of potential issues with a product or service. This phenomenon allows other customers to tap the minds and experience of millions of experts and peers, giving them access to a tremendous amount of additional information during the course of their shopping experience. Dr. David Reibstein, a distinguished marketing professor at The Wharton School, made the following statement on shop.org's blog Word-of-Mouth Wisdom:

There is a common belief that consumers trust other people's opinions and content more than they trust that of advertisers....It is an unbiased view that carries some greater degree of trust....

Advertisers' motivations are to represent their products/services in the best light. Other consumers are less biased....It is the case that consumers can probe and interact with other consumers in a way that they have previously never been able to with companies. Companies, in general, have not been able to figure out how to deal with the multitude of customers and address each of their questions, yet given a large number of customers, it is likely that customers could ask very specific questions and find user-generated answers. (Reibstein, 2007)

Consumer reviews and consumer-generated content, in general, have become mainstream to the point where they can successfully influence browsers to become buyers. The effect of consumer-generated content on the customer experience is likely to vary by industry since research behaviors vary in time and intensity. The retail industry can be broken down into many categories, such as food and beverage, auto, furniture, fashion, electronics, home improvement, books, toys, and so forth. Based on current literature, it appears that the retail sectors in which consumers spend more time researching purchases online will be most affected by the growing trend of consumer-generated content. This makes logical sense because these shoppers need more information and time to make decisions on more expensive items. However, as the prominence of consumer-generated content is amplified, it may become a requirement for almost any purchase decision. Whether customers are buying a big-screen TV or a new gadget for the kitchen, they are beginning to crave more feedback from customers who have already moved through the purchase process and gained insights along the way. This desire to more thoroughly research purchases through social commerce is being filled in many big-ticket categories such as home improvement (Home Depot, Lowes), consumer electronics (Circuit City, Best Buy, Amazon.com), and automobiles (CarMax), among others. Many of the leading

players are also incorporating reputation systems and social networking features that can enhance the reliability of the information within the site as well as the overall experience from research to purchase to enjoyment.

To take advantage of this social commerce loyalty opportunity, more retailers across the landscape are increasingly opening up their Web sites to customers, letting them rate products, write reviews, and in some cases post relevant photos and videos. "In the past, people could just share information with their neighbors, but now people can influence the global village by sharing their experiences on the Internet," says Brett Hurt, founder and CEO of Austin, TX based Bazaar Voice, which manages customer reviews for several leading retailers (Gogoi, 2007). Companies that do not even have a Web presence are also being affected by emerging metareview sources such as Yelp.com, an online review site for local service businesses. Consumers can post reviews on their recent experiences at any service business from hair parlors to restaurants to medical specialists. The site has evolved into a review-oriented social network in large cities, where established reviewers develop a rapport with fellow "Yelpers" and therefore have an incredible amount of influence. Localized metareview sites are a new manifestation of consumer-generated content that allows for visitors to new cities to be equipped with the wisdom of the most experienced local residents by quickly searching for their service needs within the relevant geographic area. Small retail businesses can especially benefit from getting exposure on third-party metareview sites because positive mindshare and Web exposure does not require IT infrastructure or Web content management. This phenomenon could level the playing field with larger, national retailers in some cases because brand experiences can be broadcasted in detail to interested consumers. At the same time, strong national and international retailers are more likely to have the expertise and resources to provide hosted experiences on their

Web sites that are customized to target unique customer-segment needs. With the customer voice being amplified and delivered in a variety of new ways, retail executives need to develop a keen understanding of the risks and benefits of each Web 2.0 technology in order to align their efforts with their firms' overall business strategies.

MAJOR WEB 2.0 TOOLS IN THE RETAIL INNOVATION LANDSCAPE

Customer Reviews on Message Boards

Retailers across nearly every product category are capturing primary marketing research by encouraging customers to provide opinions and ratings on products and services they have purchased. Threaded message board conversations have developed into a virtual exchange of advice on product categories—an exchange most powerfully exhibited when it takes place between novices and enthusiasts. Participating customers help create a body of content that enriches the experience of other customers and gives the retailer's Web site a competitive advantage. In addition, many retailers are bringing more integrity to reviews on their site by allowing visitors to rate the quality of product reviews in addition to the products themselves. By the end of 2006, 43% of e-commerce sites offered customer reviews and ratings, almost double the 23% figure at the end of 2005, according to New York research firm MarketingSherpa (Gogoi, 2007). In a survey of more than 1,300 people, MarketingSherpa also found that as much as 50% of customers aged 18 to 34 have posted a comment or a review on products they have bought or used. These trends facilitate innovation in the retail industry in two main areas: the customer experience and merchandising.

Customer reviews become an essential piece of information in the consideration phase of the purchase experience. Community participation in reviewing products allows consumers to have more confidence in their purchase decisions because they are provided with information that enhances the detail and credibility of what the retailer and manufacturer have already provided. PETCO.com launched customer reviews in October 2005, and within weeks noticed that visitors who clicked on the highest-customer-rated products were 49% more likely to buy something. PETCO.com also found that they spend 63% more than shoppers who clicked on options like "top-sellers" or "lowest-priced" (Gogoi, 2007). These increases in conversion and spending levels are likely a result of customers' price-value perceptions changing as they receive helpful information from customers much like themselves.

Customer reviews can also play an important role in making merchandising decisions. One reason that some retailers dragged their feet in letting customers post comments and reviews was a fear of negative feedback. However, Sucharita Mulpuru, a senior retail analyst at Forrester Research, found that 80% of all customer reviews on e-commerce sites are positive (Gogoi, 2007). Furthermore, even negative reviews provide the retailer with insights on how it can improve by adjusting assortments, modifying pricing, and tweaking multichannel execution. In a 2005 survey of 137 retailers conducted by Forrester Research and the National Retail Federation, just 26% of participating retailers offered customer ratings and reviews on their Web sites, but 96% of those who did rated the merchandising tactic as effective or very effective at increasing online conversion rates (Barton, 2006). Customer feedback accelerates managers' insights about expected sales velocity of recently launched products and can be a leading indicator for emerging mind share and popularity for new product categories. Merchandising decisions go from managers pushing their instincts out to the market to customers pulling in the products and services that deliver the most value to a given customer segment. Coupled with customer zip codes, aggregations of customer opinions could be integrated into assortment localization strategies across different stores to capitalize on regional market differences.

Buying Guides: Wikis and Videocasts

Customers interested in becoming more informed about a product category often look to buying guides published by experts from sites on the Internet just as they use *Consumer Reports* and other publications. A trend is on the horizon to invite selected customers to provide detailed input that helps strengthen existing content or create something entirely new. ShopWiki.com, a comparison shopping search service, encourages users to contribute their expertise to guides that are originally written by a team of editors at the company. The company clearly recognizes the benefits of collaborative intelligence in producing valuable content that aligns with consumer needs, but they also ensure that contributions to the guides are valuable by having their editing team monitor all user input. Leading retailers could also begin to encourage users to contribute content needed after the purchase experience, such as usage tips and how-tos. For this application, wikis have an advantage over blogs and message boards because they encourage user contribution to a single document rather than promoting a continuous stream of back-and-forth messaging. In addition, ShopWiki.com has motivated several hundred users to create video guides for a variety of product categories. While promoting individual customers to upload videos onto corporate sites presents potential problems, a carefully controlled initiative could lead to increased customer engagement and satisfaction by allowing passionate, expert shoppers to share their knowledge with the rest of the world through a more vivid medium.

Customer Experience Weblogs (Blogs)

In the retail context, blogs are often channels of communication where individual consumers can post diaries of their experiences with a particular company. Postings are displayed in reverse chronological order and comments are posted to specific articles that are published by the blogs' administrators. Many customers might want to share their retail experiences when a company has disappointed or angered them to the point that they feel others should know about it. It is also possible that brand advocates want to share their positive experiences with a given company by broadcasting their satisfaction across the Internet. No matter what content bloggers decide to post, retailers should certainly keep their eyes and ears open for anything that is being said about their companies. Quick responsiveness to customer complaints could soften the impact of negative experiences that are being shared. Likewise, identifying wins in the marketplace where customers are providing positive feedback about recent experiences allows companies to incorporate recent learning into initiatives that are in the pipeline.

RSS Newsletters, Catalogs, or Offers (Really Simple Syndication)

Retailers are using RSS (really simple syndication) feeds to provide their more tech-savvy customers with relevant information such as news, sales promotions, and featured products. It is very comparable to a customized virtual flyer that is delivered to the e-mail inboxes of millions of RSS subscriber customers on a user-controlled basis. Retailers might send special deals to loyal customers who have achieved special spending milestones, or they might send new customers promotional deals that complement recent purchases. Burpee, an online gardening retailer, decided to incorporate customer reviews in the Featured

Products section of its RSS feeds. Burpee found that RSS feeds containing a single customer review had a 43% higher number of click-throughs on average than RSS feeds that did not include customer reviews (Barton, 2006).

Other Web 2.0 Technologies

There are several other technologies that could potentially become more influential in the interaction between retailer and customer experience. Social networking, podcasts, and mashups are all high-potential trends that have not yet made a large appearance in retail. While videocasts offer a deeper level of content than podcasts, there could potentially be a use for podcasts when users need to access information on the go (using portable audio devices). Social networking could come more into effect when users want to ask their peers about a particular purchase they are considering. One person could post content about a potential purchase on a social networking page and allow their friends to provide opinions on what they should do. This differs greatly from the collaborative intelligence of blogs, wikis, and customer reviews because it involves direct friends rather than total strangers. While there are few, if any, firms who are implementing this capability on their Web sites today, it is easily imaginable how this would be applicable to retail sectors that are prone to social interaction, such as fashion.

IMPLICATIONS FOR RETAIL

Participant Input

As more and more retailers open up their Web sites to different forms of consumer-generated content, millions of customers will have the ability to listen in on conversations that were previously one on one. At the end of the day, it is the collaboration of a variety of online customer feedback sources that will end up affecting consumer decisions of

tomorrow. As more people participate in these forms of social communication, companies will see that engaging customers in online communities will be critical for gathering new insights. Customer feedback will continue to fuel new ideas across industries, revolutionizing the way businesses market, merchandise, and manufacture. Retailers who prove most effective at encouraging more customers to make e-commerce community contributions are likely to gain a customer experience advantage over their competitors. However, there is a potential bias in the information that is provided on these Web sites. Are all comments that the retailer receives being displayed on the site? Are negative comments being hidden? Do the comments being posted reflect the viewpoints of the various customer segments a given retailer serves? Or do they represent a biased population of customers who might be more inclined to share their experiences? Getting to the bottom of these very practical issues is critical for the customer experience because the value of collective intelligence is much higher when input is received by representatives from all segments of a retailer's customer base. By having more knowledge about participants' likes and dislikes, it is possible to integrate useful information and product offerings into other customers' purchase experiences.

Customer Experience

While online shopping and content contribution might be more popular with younger generations, many retailers are learning how to expose additional segments to this valuable information by moving it into off-line formats as well. Leading retailers are not only integrating customer feedback into RSS feeds and subscriber e-mails, they are also integrating it into weekly circulars and seasonal catalogs that reach a much wider audience than searchable parts of corporate Web sites. As customers become more accustomed to integrating collective intelligence into difference phases of the shopping experience, companies who deliver this information in the most useful and relevant way will receive further praise from brand advocates and ultimately recruit new customers. By providing rich, in-depth content from a large base of knowledgeable consumers, individual customers will feel more confident in evaluating purchase options and making their final decisions. Business managers must develop communities in which customers give credence to the content consumers find relevant to their purchasing experience. Amazon.com has already built a powerful recommendation engine based on customer transaction history, but incorporating their vivid customer reviews and ratings equips customers to make even more informed decisions. Customers of different age, sex, or geographic location might demand a different set of product or service attributes that best satisfies their needs, so it might be worth considering a segmentation strategy that addresses the uniqueness of distinct customer groups. Myriad opportunities are presenting themselves every day to help businesses better understand how consumers would prefer to interact with information throughout the purchase and enjoyment process, and it is the eager retailers that strive to create a perpetually evolving community that will win in their industry.

Integrating Feedback into Business Functions

In the digital age and the world of Web 2.0, more channels than ever are available to engage and communicate with customers. While this presents an extraordinary opportunity for organizations of all kinds, managers must develop unique approaches to facilitate a consistent end-to-end experience that is representative of their brands' values. In the past 2 years, companies like Bazaarvoice and PowerReviews have emerged as leaders among companies that build customer review functionality for retailer Web sites and manage the entire process. Newcomers to the world of consumer-generated content should reflect upon what other retailers have learned in the marketplace to beware of the risks of taking certain courses of action. For example, retailers that have been caught seeding comments on their own customer forums will have a hard time regaining the trust of their customers. It is better to learn from negative reviews than to try to avoid them. Retailers should take advantage of the tremendous opportunity to learn more than they ever have about their customers' needs and concerns; companies can correct problems faster than ever before by developing a community of customers who actively want to improve their businesses.

Leveraging the power of customer communities allows retailers to gauge consumer concerns about a wide variety of things: product preferences, price thresholds, service quality, and the quality of new initiatives. Products and services that are clearly winning in the marketplace could potentially deserve higher premiums rather than being given deep promotional discounts to drive demand. By developing concepts and product lines that consumers will embrace, companies can increase overall satisfaction and loyalty instead of competing on the proposition of price. Consumers in the consideration stage are in need of becoming more educated about the overall product category, and retailers who can strengthen their marketing arsenal with deep customer insights will certainly leave others behind. Meaningful dialogue before and after the purchase helps consumers enjoy the entire experience, which eventually leads to retaining them for future sales.

OPPORTUNITIES FOR FUTURE RESEARCH

There is a great deal to learn about how consumers use various forms of consumer-generated content at the different phases of the purchase process. When would customers want to see blogs that offer chronicles of customer experiences with a certain retailer or brand? At what point do consumers want to see how others have rated a particular product? How should these pieces of information be effectively integrated into online and off-line retailing tactics, such as newsletters, catalogs, and brick-and-mortar store environments?

The biggest area of opportunity related to future research is developing an understanding of how consumer-generated content actually affects results. How are consumers' price-value perceptions influenced by the addition of consumer-generated content? Are they inclined to spend more for high quality or are they inclined to search further for lower prices? How are conversion rates affected across all industries? One would be inclined to think that big-ticket, high-consideration items that are researched for greater lengths of time would be most impacted by the advent of consumer-generated content in the purchase experience. However, is it just as likely that purchase behavior for low-consideration products could be greatly affected by consumer-generated content? Ultimately, firms should take it upon themselves to answer these questions rather than relying on industry-wide market research. Customer segments of different retailers could have varying behavior, and it is therefore important to understand the intentions and behaviors of your own customers. By encouraging customers to contribute their feedback through a variety of tools, retailers can develop a better understanding of what drives their customers in a variety of situations. In doing so, leading retailers will be able to drive profitable behavior by adjusting various activity-level strategies and tactics that can be customized to deliver upon customer needs.

REFERENCES

Barton, B. (2006). Ratings, reviews, and ROI: How leading retailers use customer word of mouth in marketing and merchandising. *BazaarVoice.* Retrieved April 15, 2008, from http://www.jiad.org/vol7/no1/barton/bv-wom-wp-oct06.pdf

Bughin, J., & Manyika, J. (2007). *How businesses are using Web 2.0: A McKinsey global survey.* Retrieved April 19, 2008, from http://www.mckinseyquarterly.com/article_page.aspx?ar=1913&pagenum=1

Gogoi, P. (2007). Retailers take a tip from MySpace. *Business Week.* Retrieved April 15, 2007, from http://www.businessweek.com/bwdaily/dnflash/content/feb2007/db20070213_626293.htm?chan=search

Kharif, O. (2007). Retail 2.0. *Business Week: Innovation.* Retrieved April 15, 2007, from http://www.businessweek.com/innovate/content/jan2007/id20070131_360739.htm?chan=search

Reibstein, D. (2007). *Word of mouth wisdom.* Retrieved April 15, 2008, from http://blog.shop.org/index.php?s=Reibstein

Row, H. (2006). *DoubleClick touchpoints survey IV: How digital media fit into consumer purchase decisions.* Retrieved April 19, 2007, from http://www.doubleclick.com/insight/pdfs/dc_touchpointsIV_0611.pdf

APPENDIX A

Quotes from Thought Leaders in the Field

➤   *"As a co-founder and board member of BizRate/Shopzilla, I, from the beginning, have believed that consumers want to hear from other consumers about their product and merchant experiences. It is an unbiased view that carries some greater degree of trust. The first opportunity this provides to the marketer is the feedback from the marketplace about how consumers perceive their offerings. The opportunity is to listen to it, not just to cringe from the bad ratings. It will also be the opportunity to observe what seems to matter. Is something poorly rated on certain dimension, yet still capture sales? There is information in these ratings."*

-Dr. David Reibstein, marketing professor from Wharton http://www.wharton.upenn.edu/faculty/reibsted.html

➤   *"Amazon.com, with its NPS (net promoter score) of 73 percent, has also nurtured a creative community, notably by encouraging book reviewers to comment and grade the publications that the company offers for sale. These customers help create a body of content that enriches the customer experience and is tough for the competition to match....Then it enabled customers to rate the quality of the book reviews as well as the book themselves....Now the volunteer book-reviewers compete for the attention of millions of Amazon.com customers—and especially for the status of becoming a 'Top 10' reviewer. The reviewers' reputation is established by community voting—and once they have earned this recognition, they have an even greater incentive to maintain a steady stream of high-quality content."*

- Fred Reichheld, author of *The Loyalty Effect: The Hidden Force Behind Growth, Profits and Lasting Value* (HBR Press, 1996), and *The Ultimate Question: Driving Good Profits and True Growth* (HBR Press, 2006)

➤   "Pierre Omidyar, founder of eBay, likes to remind audiences that it wasn't eBay's first mover advantage that accounted for its success. Plenty of others saw the potential of electronic auctions. What propelled eBay ahead of the pack, he argues, was its capacity for rapid innovation. During the day, Omidyar would carry on daily message-board conversations with his customers. Each night, those conversations would guide programming changes to the site. The next day, Omidyar could learn from the ongoing conversations which solutions were working and where he still had more to do. This rapid-response loop between conversation and innovation is what separated eBay from the competition.

To this day, eBay continues to tap the power of community through message-board dialogue. When eBay decided to revamp its 'collectibles' category, it solicited advice from site users. It got nearly ten thousand suggestions. The result was a portal that was well tailored to the needs and interest of individual collectors. CEO Meg Whitman describes eBay users as a crucial component of the company's product development process:

'Their involvement multiplies the strength of our own management team. One of our users suggested a way to speed up auctions for impatient bidders, so we introduced "Buy It Now," a feature that lets bid-

continued on following page

APPENDIX A CONTINUED

ders end an auction at a set price. Now 45 percent of listings use this feature...We rely on the feedback of our users for almost all changes to the site.'"

-    Fred Reichheld, author of *The Loyalty Effect: The Hidden Force Behind Growth,*
     Profits and Lasting Value (HBR Press, 1996) and *The Ultimate Question: Driving Good Profits and True Growth* (HBR Press, 2006)

➢   *"Even if your firm distributes through retailers and you don't know your end customers, you can still use the power of the Internet to tap into and build customer communities. Hallmark, for example, engaged Communispace Corporation, the Watertown, Massachusetts, online community software and solutions vendor, to recruit 250 to 300 target customers to facilitate an ongoing dialogue about ways to generate more customer promoters....These communities deliver real-time insights that are deeper and richer than those provided by traditional customer feedback tools. Some executives became more informed about why some cards worked so well compared to others. Other executives tap these communities for immediate reactions to new concepts as well as for brainstorming....Hallmark leaders say they have been amazed by the time and creative energy community members willingly invest in shopping the competition and providing relevant comparisons and suggestions....Executives compare the tool to having a roomful of target customers camped out in the corner conference room, always ready to comment on a new idea, evaluate new pricing, or contribute creative ideas. Hallmark execs call their online customer community a focus group on steroids."*

-    Fred Reichheld, author of *The Loyalty Effect: The Hidden Force Behind Growth,*
     Profits and Lasting Value (HBR Press,1996) and *The Ultimate Question: Driving Good Profits and True Growth* (HBR Press, 2006)

Chapter III
A Strategic Framework for Integrating Web 2.0 into the Marketing Mix

Samantha C. Bryant
Philip Morris, USA

ABSTRACT

Marketing strategy set by the marketing mix has remained fundamentally the same through years of other business disciplines being significantly disrupted by emerging technologies. Emerging Web 2.0 technologies such as wikis, blogs, YouTube, and virtual worlds are not only affecting how companies tactically approach marketing, but also their marketing strategies. This chapter will explore the impact of Web 2.0 technologies on marketing and brand management and how companies can leverage these technologies to strengthen relationships between their brands and consumers through a Web 2.0 marketing mix. This new Web 2.0 marketing mix supplements the traditional four-p marketing mix (price, product, promotion, and placement) with a new "p" lens: participation. The focus of this analysis is on B2C marketing of products and services only.

INTRODUCTION

Marketing has gone through a number of evolutions and technology has revolutionized a number of disciplines. New generations of consumers are consuming media in a different fashion than before. Gone are the days of the 30-second Super Bowl advertisements and here are the days of Facebook, Flickr, and MySpace. Collaborating and participating on the Internet is the preferred entertainment.

Web 2.0 technologies such as wikis, blogs, YouTube, and *Second Life* are changing the behavior of consumers like never before.

- Empowering them with knowledge from a myriad of sources
- Enabling them to self-organize around brands and share their passion (or dissatisfaction) for a brand
- Enabling them to act as marketers of brands

Marketing strategy set by the marketing mix has remained fundamentally the same through years of other business disciplines being significantly disrupted by emerging technologies. However, Web 2.0 is not only affecting how companies tactically approach marketing, but also their marketing strategies.

This chapter will explore the impact of Web 2.0 technologies on marketing and brand management and how companies can leverage these technologies to strengthen relationships between their brands and consumers through a Web 2.0 marketing mix. The focus of this analysis is on business-to-consumer (B2C) marketing of products and services only.

BACKGROUND: WEB 2.0 TECHNOLOGIES AND MARKETING

Web 2.0 technologies, also known as social software technologies, are a second generation of Web-based communities and services that facilitate collaboration and sharing between users. Web 2.0 does not refer to an update to any technical specifications of the Web but to changes in the way it is being used. These technologies are built on an architecture of participation ("Web 2.0," 2007).

Little has been published about Web 2.0 technologies, particularly about their effect on marketing. In 2004, *High Intensity Marketing* explored the effects of a new emerging stream of networked technologies on marketing. However, these technologies were the mere beginning of what was to explode a few years later as Web

2.0. (Mootee, 2004). *Wikinomics: How Mass Collaboration Changes Everything* discussed Web 2.0 technologies, with examples of companies' use to interact with their consumers and improve their product offerings (Tapscott & Williams, 2006). The American Marketing Association (AMA) is one of the largest professional organizations for marketers and is trusted to provide relevant marketing information to experienced marketers. One channel through which it educates its members is conferences. The AMA has just begun to acknowledge how Web 2.0 is disrupting traditional marketing theory. In 2008, the AMA hosted its first conferences on Web 2.0 (social media) and marketing. The conferences focused on how companies need to recognize the impact social media has on their brands and how they can benefit from using social media as new marketing tools (American Marketing Association, 2007a).

Not surprisingly, the most written about this relationship between Web 2.0 technologies and marketing has been via Web 2.0 technologies themselves, particularly blogs. Blogs, also known as weblogs, are shared online journals or diaries where people can post entries via the Web. Live-Journal, Blogger, and WordPress are examples of online blog services where users can post their thoughts with an emphasis on user interaction within the community. LiveJournal is one of the most popular, with currently over 14 million journals and communities. Numerous individuals blog daily about what they are witnessing and hearing about in the marketing world. These same individuals then harness the power of Web 2.0 by linking to each other's blogs and commenting on the author's thoughts. What results is insightful speculation about trends emerging as a result of Web 2.0's impact on marketing and brand management.

THE TRADITIONAL MARKETING MIX (FOUR *P*S)

With such revolutionary technologies disrupting consumers' lives, many businesses wonder what the implication is to the marketing of their products and brands.

The marketing mix, invented in the 1950s, is the mix of controllable marketing variables that a company uses to pursue the desired level of sales in the target market. The most common model of these factors is the four-factor classification called the four *P*s. Optimization of the marketing mix is achieved by assigning the amount of the marketing budget to be spent on each element of the marketing mix so as to maximize the total contribution to the firm (American Marketing Association, 2007b).

The four *P*s of the traditional marketing mix are product, pricing, promotion, and placement.

- **Product:** The product aspects of marketing deal with the specifications of the actual goods or services, and how it relates to the user's needs and wants. Generally, this also includes supporting elements such as warranties, guarantees, and support.
- **Pricing:** Pricing refers to the process of setting a price for a product, including discounts. The price need not be monetary; it can simply be what is exchanged for the product or services, such as time, energy, psychology, or attention.
- **Promotion:** Promotion includes advertising, sales promotion, public relations, and personal selling, and refers to the various methods of promoting the product, brand, or company.
- **Placement:** Placement or distribution refers to how the product gets to the customer, for example, point-of-sale placement or retailing. This *p* is also the place, referring to the channel by which a product or service is sold (e.g., online vs. retail), to which geographic region or industry, and to which segment (young adults, families, professionals; American Marketing Association, 2007b).

While effective for setting marketing strategy since its creation, the traditional marketing mix lacks relevancy when it comes to Web 2.0. A new term coined Marketing 2.0 is being used to describe the impact Web 2.0 has had on the discipline of marketing. Companies are finding many uses of Web 2.0 technologies to successfully connect with their consumers. These are discussed in the next section.

ISSUES AND EXAMPLES: THE EFFECT OF WEB 2.0 TECHNOLOGIES ON MARKETING AND BRAND MANAGEMENT

Numerous companies are integrating Web 2.0 technologies into their portfolio of marketing channels. Let us explore some Web 2.0 technologies and how they are affecting marketing strategy.

Second Life (Virtual World)

A virtual world is a computer-based simulated environment intended for its users to inhabit and interact, usually represented in the form of graphical representations of avatars. *Second Life* is an Internet-based virtual world developed by Linden Research, Inc. that is a massive multiplayer online game. *Second Life* enables its users to interact with each other through motional avatars, providing an advanced level of a social network service. Residents can explore, meet other residents, socialize, participate in individual and group activities, and create and trade property and services with one another.

Second Life has received much media attention regarding its benefits to the business world, most significantly from a cover story in *Business Week* in April 2006 that brought the virtual world to the attention of the masses, including a number of business leaders. The unique avatar population in the virtual world *Second Life* topped 7 million in 2007, with about 4 million distinct individuals participating in the online world (Rose, 2007).

Second Life has been recognized to have so much marketing potential that new companies have been established to assist companies with establishing their presence. For example, Millions of Us, an agency specializing in virtual worlds, designs and measures marketing programs for clients across a wide spectrum of platforms, especially *Second Life* (*Millions of Us*, 2007). Another company, The Electric Sheep Company, is the largest company in the world dedicated to designing experiences and add-on software for 3-D virtual worlds and has implemented major projects in both *Second Life* and There (another virtual world) technologies (Carter, 2007).

In addition to Millions of Us and The Electric Sheep, REPERES has formed as the first market research institute in *Second Life*. REPERES performs quantitative research by surveying avatars and qualitative research via private interviews with avatars. REPERES assists companies in the development of their products and offers in *Second Life* using the following:

- A panel of avatars that are representative of the overall population of *Second Life* in terms of nationality, gender, and age; this panel is called upon to address issues faced by brands seeking to establish themselves or develop an offer on *Second Life*
- An understanding of behaviors, innovations, and trends in *Second Life*
- A space for tests and cocreation projects to be tried and evaluated (*REPERES Second Life*, 2007)

In mid-2006, Scion sensed an opportunity to engage the technology and design-oriented communities of *Second Life*. Millions of Us and

Scion collaborated to create Scion City, a *Second Life* island that housed the first virtual-world car dealership, representing the first time a major auto manufacturer created a presence in a virtual world. *Second Life* residents had the opportunity to not only purchase all three Scion models in the dealership, but also customize them to make them their own. This is consistent with Scion's approach to allow buyers to customize numerous aspects on real-world cars as well. This launch was such a success that Scion and Millions of Us have continued to work together to extend Scion's presence in *Second Life* through the following:

- The expansion of Scion City into a full-fledged urban environment where residents are able to develop their own homes and businesses around the Scion dealership
- A simultaneous real and virtual launch of Scion's 2008 line at the Chicago Auto Show, meaning the new vehicle was launched in both *Second Life* and the real world at the same time
- Free expert-led customization classes in *Second Life* for consumers to learn how to personalize their virtual Scions; consumers can then showcase their designs in a Scion gallery in *Second Life*

The Scion xB launch received substantial media attention, and the buzz only grew with each subsequent release and event. Scion City has organically developed its own culture and loyal base of residents; one even created a MySpace page chronicling the evolution of this community, which shows the convergence and power of Web 2.0 technologies working together (*Millions of Us*, 2007).

While Scion was the first major automobile manufacturer with a significant presence in *Second Life*, numerous car companies have followed suit, including Pontiac, Mercedes, BMW, Nissan, and Toyota. Mercedes-Benz operates a car dealership that sells virtual cars and gives away branded racing suits to avatars. BMW even allows avatars the opportunity to test drive their vehicles.

At the 2007 Food Marketing Institute Supermarket Convention and Educational Exposition, Kraft Foods, Inc. unveiled more than 70 new products. Kraft chose to showcase these new offerings at a virtual supermarket in *Second Life*. Online, consumers and convention attendees could interact with Kraft's latest products and take part in online forums with Kraft experts. By having new products introduced online, consumers could see, "touch," and learn about the product before it was able to hit physical supermarket shelves (Kraft Foods, 2007).

In addition to Scion and Kraft, numerous other brands have built a presence in *Second Life*, including Adidas, Dell, Reebok, Sony BMG, Vodaphone, Sun, Sears, AOL, and Circuit City.

Reebok opened a virtual store that is an extension of its real-world RBK custom campaign. The store sells plain white sneakers by size and then features coloring machines for avatars to customize their shoes. Reebok grounds also contain a basketball court for avatars to play on.

Adidas owns an island that features branded video clips and billboards. Avatars who purchase Adidas shoes at the store may then bounce on a trampoline next to the store, demonstrating Adidas' shoes' bounciness.

Wired magazine reports that at least 50 major companies have a *Second Life* presence (Rose, 2007). YouTube is a video-sharing Web site where users can upload, view, and share video clips. So many brands and products have moved in that a YouTube video of brands in *Second Life* has been developed (Hayes, 2007).

Widgets

A widget is a small application that can be embedded on different Web pages. Widgets represent a new indirect marketing channel that enters consumers' lives via other Web 2.0 technologies and effectively promotes a brand, product, or service and generates awareness. A widget can be placed by users onto their personalized home pages, blogs, or other social networking pages. The widget is not intrusive advertising as a consumer must actively choose to add the widget.

The content on widgets can include blogs, live discussions, bookmarks to other Web sites, webcasts, video, games, and more. Companies are already capitalizing on widgets to market their brands, products, and services. On its traditional Web site, CBS lets consumers select widgets to embed in their social networking profiles or blogs to allow them (and everyone else who views their pages) to see advertising about the shows. For example, CBS launched a constantly updating rich-media widget to promote a new series. Consumers can watch full episodes directly on the widget, get short mini clips of some of the stars, send the widget to a friend, link out to download ring tones, and more. The widget is designed to stand out on any site it is placed on ("CBS Mobile Launches Widget to Promote New Animated Series," 2007).

Sony promoted the film *Zathura* via widgets vs. a traditional online option like banner ads. Widgets enabled Sony to provide an application related to the movie and more importantly allowed users to interact with it. The widget was offered via Freewebs, a Web site that enables consumers to easily create their own Web sites at no cost. The 11 million Web site owners of Freewebs were able to embed the widget within their Web sites, and 11,000 Web sites took this up within 6 weeks. The widgets were viewed 600,000 times, and long after the original movie was out of theaters, thousands of widgets were still delivering content (Jaokar, 2006).

To enable PC users to experience a game offered on a different gaming system (Xbox), interactive agency AKQA created a weather widget to promote the *Microsoft Flight Simulator X* game for the Xbox. The widget allows users to virtually fly and find out the weather at any airport through a live feed from the National Weather Service. In the first 2 months, users downloaded the widget more than 150,000 times, spending an average of 23 minutes with the flight simulator, the agency says (Steel, 2006).

Numerous other companies are using widgets to market their products and services. Reebok created a widget that allows users to display customized pairs of RBK shoes for others to critique. Radio stations are offering widgets that stream a station's broadcast live. Airlines including American Airlines and Air France offer a ticket purchasing widget that allows a consumer to purchase a ticket through the widget without having to visit the airlines' Web sites. (Guiragossion, 2007).

Having a user add a widget to a personalized site that is visited by individuals who share similar interests is an effective way to share your marketing message with those who would find it most relevant. By adding the widget to his or her page, the user is showing endorsement for the brand, making others trust the brand.

Flickr (Tagging)

Tagging is the assignment of descriptive contextual tags to data, such as Web links stored with memorable words for easy future access. An example is Flickr, an online photo-management and -sharing application that allows users to collaboratively organize their photos by tagging them with descriptors that are searchable.

On Flickr, users can post pictures and tag them with words that describe the photo so others can search and view the photos. One quick search on Flickr reveals 88,923 pictures tagged with Coke, 4,650 with Crayola, 3,472 for Vitamin Water, and 32,367 for Heineken. One user posted a picture entitled "Just been to the Heineken Experience," described as a photo taken of the photographer's friend after an exciting trip to the Heineken Experience tourist attraction housed in the former Heineken brewery on the Stadhouderskade in Amsterdam. The administrator for a group entitled

Got Heineken? contacted the user and invited them to join the Heine group. The Heine group invites members to post pictures of themselves holding a nice ice-cold Heineken or simply a photograph of anything related to Heineken. There is no official indication that Heineken is sponsoring it. Currently, the group has 363 photos posted by 212 members.

Eurostar, the United Kingdom's high-speed train, recognized that moving from Waterloo to St. Pancras International Station was a significant event in the brand's life. Eurostar set up an account with Flickr, EurostarForTomorrow, to promote the move to a new station. Eurostar posted a number of photos of the new station, and collected a number of photos other users have taken and saved them as favorites. This was an effective way to generate interest about the Eurostar brand and promote a significant event in the brand's history. It also recognized Eurostar consumers who had taken photos of Eurostar and shared them with others on Flickr (Terret, 2007).

Social Networks

Social networks are another Web 2.0 technology disrupting traditional marketing strategy. Social networks are Web sites designed to allow multiple users to publish content. Users are able to connect with those sharing similar interests and to exchange public or private messages. Facebook and MySpace are popular examples. Facebook is a social utility that connects users with other people by enabling them to publish profiles with text, photos, and videos; to review friends' profiles; and to join a network. MySpace allows users to create a community and share photos, journals, and interests with a growing network of mutual friends. Some marketers are making their own social networking sites such as Coke's mycokerewards.com and USA Network's Characters Welcome Web site.

For those brands that have not created their own social networking site, existing social networks enable consumers to create brands for themselves and assist others with creating their brands. At MySpace, brands have member profiles and make friends with other MySpace members. At Facebook, members join Facebook brand groups, just like they join Facebook fraternity or hobby groups, and can even display brand logos on their personal profiles.

Social branding may prove to be the ultimate product placement strategy. Companies can create a page for their brand or product. For example, Big Sky Brands, maker of Jones Soda, created its own page. In addition to company information and a list of retailers carrying the Big Sky Brand's products, its MySpace page contains a blog with discussions about the new Jones Activated Energy Boosters, the latest extension to the brand family. The blog also talks about promotions, such as the Hot Topic and Jones Soda Carbonated Candy Summer Promo. Currently, Big Sky Brands has 495 friends who, in the comments section of the page, engage in discussions about how much they love the brand and which products are their favorites. The site also links to Big Sky Brands Music MySpace page, another site dedicated to empowering their consumers with Big Sky Brands' enthusiasm through the medium of music (Big Sky Brands, 2007).

In addition to this official Big Sky Brands Web site, a number of unofficial MySpace pages have been developed to support Jones Soda. The majority of these page owners have become MySpace friends of Big Sky Brands. In contrast, Swiffer WetJet also has a number of MySpace pages, but none are sponsored by Procter & Gamble.

Virtual worlds, widgets, tagging, and social networks are Web 2.0 technologies offering opportunities for companies to integrate them into their marketing mix. The next section provides a simple framework to help leverage Web 2.0 to supplement and enhance their marketing efforts.

SOLUTIONS AND RECOMMENDATIONS: A REVISED MARKETING MIX TO MAXIMIZE THE BENEFITS OF WEB 2.0 TECHNOLOGIES

A characteristic of Web 2.0 is an architecture of participation that encourages users to add value to the application as they use it. Tapscott and Williams (2006) argue in their book *Wikinomics: How Mass Collaboration Changes Everything* that the economy of Web 2.0 is based on mass collaboration that makes use of the Internet. Companies can leverage the collective power of their consumers by leveraging Web 2.0 technologies to enable the consumers to participate in the marketing of the brand.

Idris Mootee (2004) in his book *High Intensity Marketing* examines the role of strategic marketing in the network economy, which is relationship driven, network centered, technology enabled, and information intensive. Mootee developed an analytical model supplement to the traditional marketing *p*s called "The New 4P's." Mootee's new four *p*s are participation, peer-to-peer communities, predictive modeling, and personalization. Participation focuses on allowing consumers to choose their products, providing valuable insights to companies about consumers' needs and wants. Mootee cites Dell, Procter & Gamble, and Levi's as examples. Mootee also briefly touches on consumers playing a role in defining and owning brands, such as Burton snowboards.

Participation is more relevant than ever with the Web 2.0 revolution, but it is more than a supplemental *p* to the marketing mix. Participation should now encompass all of the four *p*s as a lens through which the *p*s should be approached. The previous section explored a number of examples of B2C companies successfully leveraging Web 2.0 technologies to market their products. Applying a participation lens to the marketing mix can lead similar companies to similar success.

To be more successful at marketing using Web 2.0 technologies, the traditional four-*p* marketing mix discussed earlier (price, product, promotion, and placement) should be approached with a new *p* lens: participation. This is the Web 2.0 marketing mix.

In this new marketing mix, each of the four elements is approached by enabling consumers to participate in it. Let us explore how consumers are currently participating in each *p* of the marketing mix and the steps a company can take to capitalize on that interaction and encourage more.

Web 2.0 technologies provide a medium for consumers to directly participate with companies and their brands. Consumers can write blogs about their favorite brands, define themselves and create communities in social networks like Facebook and MySpace by associating themselves with brands, develop their own commercial advertisement for brands and post them on YouTube, and tag pictures they have uploaded of their brands on Flickr.

In addition, Web 2.0 technologies enable companies to more readily identify brand evangelists: those consumers that are devoted to a brand or product and preach their devotion to the world.

Companies can make it even easier for consumers to participate in their marketing by evaluating each *p* in their marketing mix and fostering involvement by their consumers via Web 2.0 technologies. Let us specifically examine each marketing mix element.

Product

The product aspects of the marketing mix are the specifications of the actual goods or services, and how they relate to the user's needs and wants. The scope of a product generally includes supporting elements such as warranties, guarantees, and support.

In *Wikinomics: How Mass Collaboration Changes Everything*, Tapscott and Williams (2006) explore a new generation of "prosumers" who treat the world as a place for creation, not consumption. These prosumers can be engaged to participate in all aspects of a product, from identifying consumers' unmet needs to the development of a new product to supporting the product once in a consumer's hands. Companies need to encourage consumers to participate in their products and recognize the contributions that are made. There is an allure of prestige and sense of social belonging that develops within prosumer communities (Tapscott & Williams).

Web 2.0 provides immediate feedback about products. Companies do not need a Web site to harness the power of the numerous discussions of products on Web sites beyond the control of the company. Blogs are a great tool to identify latent consumer needs and wants. Communities are free focus groups of very raw, unscripted feelings not tainted by groupthink, or the act of reasoning or decision making by a group that often occurs in traditional focus groups. Companies can also learn more about the total product life cycle beyond just the physical product, and identify additional uses for it. Companies can gain valuable customer insight and interaction via Web 2.0 in a quicker and cheaper fashion than traditional market research.

Flickr can be an avenue for trend spotting. Trend spotting is a relatively new consumer research methodology that seeks to anticipate what consumers will desire in the future and to keep existing products relevant. For example, on Flickr, a company can search for what consumers are carrying in their purses. Companies can ask consumers to participate in identifying product trends by sending out a call to action to post photos of what is in their purses. Maybe Capital One with their "What's in your wallet?" campaign could ask consumers to post Flickr photos of what is in their wallets, including a Capital One credit card. While a company may not know a lot about the consumer, Web 2.0 enables it to reach into consumers' lives and learn more about their behaviors (Brighton, 2005).

Lego fostered an early prosumer community. Lego's Mindstorms enables users to build working robots out of programmable bricks. Users reverse-engineered the products and shared feedback with Lego. Lego developed a Web site for users to share their discoveries and inventions with other enthusiasts and the company. Users can even virtually develop their own models and then order the bricks to physically build it. This enables Lego's consumers to become a decentralized virtual design team, far larger than the number of the in-house designers (Tapscott & Williams, 2006).

Procter & Gamble is also successfully leveraging the powers of Web 2.0 to enhance its research and development efforts for new products. The research and development team had a success rate of less than 20%, below industry standards of 30%. Via the Web, Procter & Gamble turned to the outside world for new and better ideas, and now more than 35% of the ideas come through the Web, resulting in success for 80% of Procter & Gamble's new product launches.

One example was the discovery of a way to put edible ink pictures on potato chips. The solution came from an Italian professor at the University of Bologna who had invented an ink-jet method for printing edible images. This technology helped the company get the new Pringles Prints potato chips out in a single year, about half the normal time for such a process (Stephens, 2007).

Cadbury brought back the discontinued Wispa chocolate bar after a campaign on Web sites like Facebook, MySpace, and YouTube demanded its return. The chocolate company says that it is frequently contacted by consumers asking for old favorites to be reintroduced, but said the numbers that had joined the Internet campaign to relaunch Wispa were unprecedented (Wallop, 2007).

In the support stage of the product life cycle, brands have an opportunity to engage with consumers during a crisis using Web 2.0. Consumers are pretty responsive to companies and brands who engage, especially when there is a problem.

Speaking at Nielsen Business Media's Next Big Idea Conference, EVP of strategic services at Nielsen Online Pete Blackshaw focused his remarks on brand intelligence as he explained how companies can "defensively" market their products by turning negative trends in the marketplace to their advantage. Blackshaw noted the surge in the blog traffic surrounding consumer crises, such as the Mattel toy lead paint and poisonous pet food recalls from brands including Alpo and Mighty Dog, are opportunities for brands to have a touch point with consumers. Companies, said Blackshaw, should learn to "manage around the spikes, listen, react," and move money out of mass media and into online channels, asking consumers to participate in the support of a product, even during a recall (Kiley, 2007).

Pricing

The pricing *p* of the marketing mix refers to the process of setting a price for a product, including discounts. The price need not be monetary; it can simply be anything exchanged for the product or services, including time, energy, psychology, or attention.

Companies can leverage Web 2.0 to learn more about value that consumers perceive about brands and what consumers perceive they are paying for a product beyond just the monetary value. For example, online Web services such as eBay and craigslist let the consumer (or market) determine the price for products.

Consumers are able to discuss prices online via blogs or social networking sites for plane tickets, HDTVs, furniture, cars, and so forth. They can even let other consumers know where to find the best discounts.

A mashup is a Web page or application that integrates complementary elements from two or more sources. The most popular mashups include Google Maps as a source to identify certain things on a map. For example, one mashup shows secret fishing holes in the United States via a Google map. Mashups help locate the best price, such as CheapGas.

Beyond monetary value, companies can also get see what consumers are forfeiting other than money by choosing their brands or products. For example, a number of loyal Starbucks consumers are concerned about the impact they are making to the environment by enjoying Starbucks coffee in a new cardboard cup everyday with a cardboard sleeve. These consumers found a Web site that sold inexpensive reusable cloth holders to protect hands from the hot coffee cup and were elated to share it with one another. Starbucks could learn about this concern of its consumers and address it, possibly by offering this reusable cloth sleeve product in stores or developing one of their own.

Promotion

Promotion is the element of the marketing mix where consumers can most readily participate and add value to the marketing of a brand. This includes advertising, sales promotion, public relations, and personal selling, and refers to the various methods of promoting the product, brand, or company.

Consumers can develop an advertisement for a product or brand and then publish that ad for free on YouTube, tagged with keywords to inform others of the ad.

Companies may also use Web 2.0 to promote their brands with an advertisement. Smirnoff developed a viral marketing video for the launch of their new Raw Tea product. The video was placed on YouTube and at this time had over 4 million views (Iamigor, 2006). The Web 2.0 technology enabled consumers to access the video on YouTube and then participate in disseminating the information by informing their friends about the video. The launch of Raw Tea also included a Web site with the videos and a sharing capability. By placing the advertisement on a Web 2.0 site, Smirnoff made it easier for their consumers to

participate by rating and sharing the video on a site they already frequent.

A wiki is any collaborative Web site that users can easily modify via the Web, typically without restriction. A wiki allows anyone using a Web browser to edit, delete, or modify content that has been placed on the site, including the work of other authors. One popular wiki is Wikipedia, a free encyclopedia that anyone can edit. Wikipedia is updated every second by thousands of active contributors, making it an up-to-date reference source vs. a printed encyclopedia that is updated monthly or yearly.

Wikis capture the knowledge of the collective whole. Consumers can define your product or brand on Wikipedia. Consumers define what a brand stands for or describe a product, including its intangible intrinsic value. Companies should check for accuracy but not stifle the participation by their consumers to define the brand.

A key to enabling consumers to participate in promotion is to make it easy to search and find areas where other consumers talk about your brand, product, or service, or create your own site where consumers can talk about what you are interested in learning more about. Procter & Gamble developed a social networking site for women called Contessa. The intention of the social network is not about selling products, but for P&G to learn more about its women consumers and learning about their needs and habits (Ives, 2007).

Placement

Placement or distribution refers to how the product gets to the customer, for example, point-of-sale placement or retailing. This fourth *p* of the marketing mix has also sometimes been called *place*, referring to the channel by which a product or service is sold (e.g., online vs. retail), to which geographic region or industry, and to which segment.

Companies can distribute their products via Web 2.0. American Apparel operates a clothing store in *Second Life* that sells virtual clothing for avatars. American Apparel has run promotions in *Second Life* where after purchasing a clothing item in *Second Life*, a consumer receives a coupon for a discount on the same or similar item at an American Apparel store in the real world (Jana, 2006).

Coke established the Virtual Thirst Pavilion in *Second Life*. It sponsored a contest to develop a Virtual Thirst vending machine. The winning vending machine will be rolled out throughout *Second Life*, making this real-world distribution channel as ubiquitous in *Second Life* as it is in the real world. Coke did not intend for consumers to merely replicate an existing real-world vending machine but to

create a portable device for Second Life's in-world digital society that unleashes a refreshing and attention-grabbing experience, on demand. Our goal is to enable individual creativity in pursuit of a "vending" machine that can exist only in your wildest imagination. Virtual worlds make it possible for such innovations to occur, and we selected Second Life as the most conducive to this experiment,

says Michael Donnelly, director of global interactive marketing (Coca-Cola, 2007). This *Second Life* contest establishes a new distribution channel for the brand in a virtual world, but also taps into consumers' creativity for ideas for real-world distribution mechanisms.

On Flickr, in addition to tagging photos, a user may add notes that are visible when someone viewing the photo scrolls over a particular aspect of it. For new product introductions, such as a new pair of Nike shoes, a photo of the shoe may be uploaded to Flickr with associated tags (Nike, new, shoe, blue, limited edition, New York store) and notes that can link to a Web site where the shoe may be purchased.

Companies can even create a mashup using Google Earth to locate products that are not widely distributed such as specific shoe sizes. Online retailers such as Amazon.com and Travelocity are building widgets that can drive traffic to their sites for consumers to make purchases.

CHALLENGES

The consumer defines the brand; a brand is not what a company defines it as, but what a consumer says it is. Via Web 2.0, consumers have numerous avenues to add their interpretation of brands, for better or worse. Brands need to relinquish control to get influence. Two barriers to adoption are regulation of content and security.

One of the reasons Web 2.0 technologies like YouTube and Flickr are successful is because they are authentic: "The lack of corporate polish adds to the feeling that there are real people behind the idea" (Moore, 2006).

What does it say about a brand to have a presence or be communicated via these technologies? Before embracing participation in Web 2.0, a company must determine if a brand is compatible with the spirit of Web 2.0. Web 2.0 is more about spirit, concepts, and principles than definition. It is imperative that a brand be in accordance with that spirit before launching an initiative. If a brand is incompatible with this experience of openness and exchange, it is advised to create or use another brand or subbrand as a workaround for Web 2.0 initiatives to protect the integrity of the core brand (Smagg, 2007).

The best action for a company to take may be no action at all as long as it is recognized that Web 2.0 technologies are having an effect on marketing. In summer 2007, *Wired* magazine exposed *Second Life* for not achieving the commercial potential that was initially expected. A trip to Starwood Hotels' Aloft Hotel in *Second Life* was described as creepy due to the entire place being deserted, compared to the movie *The Shining*, where a tenant at a deserted hotel goes psycho due to the isolation—not exactly the reputation Starwood wanted for its new hotel chain brand.

The NBA sought to capitalize on Web 2.0 for its marketing efforts by developing both an island in *Second Life* and a channel on YouTube. The YouTube channel saw over 14,000 subscribers with 23 million views, while the *Second Life* island had a mere 1,200 visitors. Those numbers are not as surprising when it is revealed that the traffic in *Second Life* is slightly more than 100,000 Americans per week (Rose, 2007).

In late 2007, IBM broadcast a television advertisement featuring two employees of an unknown company talking about avatars from a virtual world. The dialogue is as follows:

"This is my avatar. It's all the latest rage. I can do business, I even own my own island! It's innovation!" "But...can you make money?" "Um... virtual or real money?" "Real money. The point of innovation is to make real money." "Oh. My avatar doesn't know how to do that." (Vielle, 2007)

While the advertisement is mocking the value of Web 2.0 technologies, in a roundabout way, IBM is capitalizing on Web 2.0 to market its "Stop Talking. Start Doing." campaign. Yet, in mid-2007, IBM established a presence in *Second Life*, the virtual IBM Business Center staffed by real IBM sales representatives from around the world. In the press release for the launch of this virtual center, IBM boasts it has over 4,000 employees active in *Second Life*. The question remains: Is IBM not seeing the value from this investment in a Web 2.0 technology, or did it create the advertisement mocking avatars merely to generate interest for the IBM brand because avatars are popular at the moment? It also could have been buzz for its own presence in *Second Life* (IBM, 2007).

IMMEDIATE ACTION FOR COMPANIES

Companies should use Web 2.0 to assist with keeping a pulse on their brands' and products' involvement in Web 2.0 technologies. Most brands already have a Web 2.0 presence, and most likely, it is not officially endorsed by the brand.

Web 2.0 technologies make it very simple for a marketer to quickly and easily learn about what consumers are saying about a brand or product. RSS or real simple syndication is any of various XML (extensible markup language) file formats suitable for disseminating real-time information via subscription on the Internet. RSS has become a popular technology for bloggers and podcasters to distribute their content. NewsGator is a free Web-based RSS news reader that consolidates news and updates from the Web, blogs, premium content providers, and internal applications and systems and automatically delivers them to users.

RSS feeds can be set up to find and aggregate information about a brand or product from blogs, podcasts, and so forth, and be sent out via e-mail every morning to keep a marketer updated. Technorati is an RSS service that searches and organizes blogs and other forms of user-generated content (photos, videos, voting, etc.). Technorati is currently tracking over 110 million blogs and over 250 million pieces of tagged social media. The home page will immediately update you on "what's percolating in blogs now," but a quick search of your brand's name will share what is hot about your brand at the moment. It is an easy way to monitor the brand's image (*Technorati*, 2007).

Quick monthly visits to Web 2.0 Web sites can also keep marketers up to do date about their brands (and the competition). Visit Flickr and type in your brand name. Cheerios returns over 8,000 images, many showing how Cheerios plays a role in the everyday life of a child. Marketers will be happy to find this is consistent with the brand's image, values, and positioning.

Visit YouTube and type in your brand name. A McDonald's marketer may be interested to find that some commercials are tagged as creepy and racist and are not positively portraying the megabrand. However, a video containing the McDonald's menu song has had over 1.5 million views. The McDonald's menu song was a song listing all of McDonald's menu items from a promotion in 1989. Reviewing the thousands of comments about the video reveals that consumers are excited to view this video on YouTube and remember memorizing the song in 1989 when it was advertised during television commercials. This is definitely some valuable insight available for McDonald's.

Visit MySpace and type in your brand name or visit http://www.myspace.com/brandname. Mountain Dew does not have an official page, but a 21-year-old from Southern California owns http://www.myspace.com/mountaindew. JC from Newport Beach, California, owns Nike. In addition to learning about consumers' thoughts on your brand, this exploring can also result in insights about your loyal consumers who add your brand to their MySpace pages.

Visit Wikipedia and type in your brand name. Wikipedia's American Express entry has a wealth of historical information, including advertising. The entry is up to date with AmEx's most recent promotions, including its Member's Project. Anyone can contribute to a wiki, so periodically verifying information is correct and adding updates can benefit a brand ("Web 2.0," 2007).

With Web 2.0 technology, companies can quickly and inexpensively make things happen. You can have your advertising messages spread on the Web like a wildfire with social bookmarking sites, RSS, and other Web 2.0 methods, and without having to pay anything for it, have thousands of people coming to your Web site in a matter of days. What would have cost you millions of dollars in investment and a dedicated team of developers may now be accomplished with these Web 2.0 tools by a couple of guys in a garage in just a few days (Beaudoin, 2007).

Web 2.0 technologies intermingle with each other as well, so a presence in one Web 2.0 technology can give you a presence in others. For example, MySpace allows its members to blog on their pages and add YouTube videos.

FUTURE TRENDS

The Web is not going anywhere and will only continue to evolve. More Web applications will be developed and compete for consumers' time and attention. As consumers become accustomed to communicating and collaborating on the Web, they may choose to take marketing your brands into their own hands. Companies should be delighted at this occurrence. It is best to identify and monitor these actions as they transpire, but not take actions to impede them. If a consumer is passionate enough to devote energy toward positively marketing your brand, you can be sure that once disgruntled they will also take action, only this time it could be detrimental.

CONCLUSION

Web 2.0 technologies will not replace traditional marketing such as direct mail or TV advertisements, but instead are new complementing marketing channels that many consumers will expect their brands to communicate through.

Companies that feel Web 2.0 technologies are a right fit for their brands should take action to market their brands using the Web 2.0 marketing mix as a guide. Enabling consumers to participate in each aspect of the marketing mix will help brands remain relevant in today's changing world.

REFERENCES

American Marketing Association. (2007a). *Beyond Marketing 2.0: Harnessing the power of social media for marketing campaign results.* Retrieved December 28, 2007, from http://www.marketingpower.com/aevent_event1221988.php

American Marketing Association. (2007b). *Dictionary of marketing terms.* Retrieved October

15, 2007, from http://www.marketingpower. com/mg-dictionary-view1876.php

Beaudoin, J. (2007). *Web 2.0 for marketers ebook review on Web 2.0 portals*. Retrieved November 26, 2007, from http://www.web20portals.com/web-20-marketing/web-20-for-marketers

Big Sky Brands. (2007). *MySpace*. Retrieved November 26, 2007, from http://www.myspace. com/bigskybrands

Brighton, G. (2005). Flickr kills trendspotting. *PSFK*. Retrieved September 27, 2007, from http:// psfk.com/2005/03/flickr_kills_co.html

Carter, B. (2007, October 4). Fictional characters get virtual lives, too. *The New York Times*. Retrieved November 12, 2007, from http://www. nytimes.com/2007/10/04/arts/television/04CSI. html?_r=1&ex=1192161600&en=6994ec8ad88a b2d8&ei=5070&oref=slogin

CBS mobile launches widget to promote new animated series. (2007). *MuseStorm*. Retrieved December 28, 2007, from http://www.musestorm. com/site/jsp/spotlight/1042.jsp

Coca-Cola. (2007, April 16). *Coca-Cola launches competition to design online "virtual thirst" coke machine*. Retrieved October 14, 2007, from http://www.virtualthirst.com/virtualthirst-social-mediarelease.html

Guiragossion, L. (2007, October 29). A thousand ways to widget in the age of Web 2.0 marketing. *Web 2.0 Marketing*. Retrieved December 28, 2007, from http://web2pointzeromarketing. blogspot.com

Hayes, G. (2007). *A video comp of major brands in Second Life*. Retrieved December 28, 2007, from http://www.youtube.com/watch?v=tEGHJuCbGdo

Iamigor. (2006, August 2). *Tea partay*. Retrieved October 15, 2007, from http://www.youtube. com/watch?v=PTU2He2BIc0

IBM. (2007, May 15). *Live IBM sales people to staff new virtual IBM business center*. Retrieved October 15, 2007, from http://www-03.ibm.com/press/us/en/pressrelease/21551.wss

Ives, B. (2007, December 1). More Web 2.0 stories, part two: Procter and Gamble embraces the wisdom of the Web for new product ideas. *The FASTForward Blog*. Retrieved December 28, 2007, from http://www.fastforwardblog. com/2007/12/01/more-web-20-stories-part-two-proctor-gamble-embraces-the-wisdom-of-the-web-for-new-product-ideas

Jana, R. (2006, June 27). American Apparel's virtual clothes. *Business Week*. Retrieved September 26, 2007, from http://www.businessweek.com/innovate/content/jun2006/id20060627_217800. htm

Jaokar, A. (2006, October 25). *Ajit Jaokar's mobile Web 2.0 blog: The widget widget Web*. Retrieved October 12, 2007, from http://www.web2journal. com/read/289798.htm

Kiley, D. (2007). Using bad news to a brand's advantage. *Business Week*. Retrieved November 14, 2007, from http://www.businessweek.com/the_thread/brandnewday

Kraft Foods. (2007). *Kraft foods goes digital to unveil more than 70 new products in first-ever virtual supermarket in Second Life*. Retrieved October 12, 2007, from http://www.kraft.com/mediacenter/country-press-releases/us/2007/us_pr_04192007.htm

Millions of Us. (2007). Retrieved October 12, 2007, from http://www.millionsofus.com

Moore, J. (2006). *Five reasons why...* Retrieved October 16, 2007, from http://brandautopsy. typepad.com/brandautopsy/2006/08/five_reasons_wh.html

Mootee, I. (2004). *High intensity marketing*. Canada: SA Press.

REPERES Second Life. (2007). Retrieved October 12, 2007, from http://www.reperes-secondlife.com

Rose, F. (2007). How Madison Avenue is wasting millions on a deserted Second Life. *Wired Magazine*. Retrieved November 12, 2007, from http://www.wired.com/techbiz/media/magazine/15-08/ff_sheep?currentpage=all

Smagg, C. (2007). *15 golden rules for Web 2.0*. Retrieved October 12, 2007, from http://visionarymarketing.wordpress.com/2007/07/03/web20

Steel, E. (2006). Web-page clocks and other "widgets" anchor new Internet strategy. *Wall Street Journal*. Retrieved November 12, 2007 from http://marcomm201.blogspot.com/2006/11/marketing-widgets-you-saw-it-here-first.html

Stephens, R.(2007). *P&G Web 2.0 success story*. Retrieved December 27, 2007, from http://www.rtodd.com/collaborage/2007/11/pg_web_20_success_story.html

Tapscott, D., & Williams, A. (2006). *Wikinomics: How mass collaboration changes everything*. New York: Portfolio.

Technorati. (2007). Retrieved December 28, 2007, from http://technorati.com

Terret, B. (2007). Brand in good Web 2.0 project shock. *Noisy Decent Graphics*. Retrieved December 28, 2007, from http://noisydecentgraphics.typepad.com/design/2007/11/brand-in-good-w.html

Vielle, T. (2007). IBM avatar commercial. *SL Universe*. Retrieved December 31, 2007, from http://sluniverse.com/php/vb/showthread.php?t=2797

Wallop, H. (2007). Cadbury plans Wispa revival. *Telegraph*. Retrieved November 28, 2007, from http://www.telegraph.co.uk/news/main.jhtml?xml=/news/2007/08/18/nwispa118.xml

Web 2.0. (2007). *Wikipedia*. Retrieved September 15, 2007, from http://en.wikipedia.org/wiki/Web_2.0, http://en.wikipedia.org/wiki/American_Express

Chapter IV
The Enterprise 2.0 Organization

Nadira Ali
University of Richmond, USA

P. Candace Deans
University of Richmond, USA

ABSTRACT

The implementation of Web 2.0 technologies in organizations ushers in a new era of collaboration and communication for enterprises. Enterprise 2.0 is the term that has emerged to describe the organization's embrace of Web 2.0 technologies. This chapter examines the current trends and impact of Web 2.0 on organizations, managers, the workforce, and information exchange within and across companies. This phenomenon is expected to bring another wave of change to organizations that some believe could be on the magnitude of that experienced during the Internet revolution. These technological advancements do not come without challenges. Security, privacy, ethics, and legal considerations all play a major role in how these technologies develop over time. The time has come, however, for companies to begin to determine strategies for utilizing these technologies in order to remain competitive in the global business arena.

INTRODUCTION

The introduction of the Internet brought a new wave of technology to the world that has made communication easier than even the telephone. By impacting businesses, education, and social life, the Internet has shrunk the world and made it easier to communicate at a macro level. A new wave of Web 2.0 technologies promises to provide another layer of change in the way we communicate and interact socially as well as how we conduct business. These technologies are changing the world outside the realm of business, especially for the younger generation who has grown up using these technologies as a normal part of life. Businesses cannot expect this generation to give up the tools that have become part of their established lifestyle when they enter the workforce. Therefore, businesses must make strategic decisions now as to how they will incorporate these collaborative tools into the normal activities of the organization.

Enterprise 2.0 represents the next "edition" of the Internet creating an atmosphere that welcomes mass communication. Within this realm, there are many new applications that are impacting policy and organizational norms. This new collaboration method is creating an environment where knowledge, power, and productive capability will be more dispersed. It is a place where ideas and knowledge will be shared at a very rapid pace and the only hope for survival is to be connected (Tapscott & Williams, 2006). Contributors will be of all ages and races each providing their own perspectives to the advancement of novel ideas and knowledge.

Business implementation of Web 2.0 technologies is being observed across industries through a variety of applications. Some of these have been discussed in previous chapters. Educational institutions are also recognizing the usefulness of social software in the context of student learning as well as to prepare students for the business world they will enter. Businesses and educational institutions must work hand in hand to promote Enterprise 2.0 effectively and efficiently in the future. Enterprise 2.0 organizations will be dependent on leadership from educational institutions to prepare the work force for this evolving business environment. The changes, however, will go beyond technological advancement and will impact the assumptions upon which organizations have previously operated.

What is this Enterprise 2.0 organization and how does it work? The journalist A. J. Liebling once said that "freedom of the press is limited to those who own one" (McAfee, 2006, p. 1). In essence, Web 2.0 creates a printing press for every individual. These individual printing presses are

changing the dynamics of the world and business in particular.

In this chapter, we will provide the reader with some thoughts on the future for organizations as they embrace Web 2.0 technologies and evolve in this context. These emerging Web 2.0 technologies are already transforming the landscape of forward-thinking businesses. As best practices and success factors become more prevalent, more organizations will begin to move in this direction with the same determination as happened with the Internet revolution. This second wave of the Internet promises to be as exciting and far reaching as the first wave.

EVOLUTION FROM ENTERPRISE 1.0 TO 2.0

The primary difference between Enterprise 1.0 and Enterprise 2.0 is the type of communication. The first phase of the Internet was stated facts. Users would go to Web sites and gather information that was provided to them by a third-party source that was given the authority to release the information. In Web 2.0, all users are the authoritative source, which allows more viewpoints to be heard. It is a union of consumer and enterprise applications and a forum where "everybody is somebody" (MacKinnon, 2005).

Enterprise 2.0 harnesses the true potential of the Internet. Users can simultaneously communicate and collaborate with other users. Web 2.0 technologies shape the way users interact with information and the way work is accomplished. The shift is toward the user of the information who now has access to other users around the world through collaborative participation. The user experience is richer as data can be shared across the Web using a variety of tools. Sharing becomes the norm and collective intelligence is highly valued.

As stressed by Tapscott and Williams (2008), it is mass collaboration that is the key to the changes corporations will experience. Collaboration is not new; it is the magnitude and scale of the collaboration made possible by Web 2.0 technologies that will make the difference. This shift will require pioneers to pave the way. Sharing secrets and collaborating with competitors and consumers are all foreign to most companies today. This technological shift must be accompanied by a mind-set shift at the top. Transparency and openness will be the norm. This is the path to growth and innovation in the Web 2.0 world. The Web 2.0 CEO and CIO must prepare their companies, managers, and employees for this mind-set change. First, these leaders must prepare themselves for a different way of leading and operating in the world economy.

THE ENTERPRISE 2.0 ORGANIZATION

As companies seek to find value through Web 2.0 technologies, the organization will evolve to meet user participation needs and workplace demands. These changes taking place in organizations are a result of several trends coming together simultaneously. The mobile technology revolution and the trend toward increased telecommuting work hand in hand with Enterprise 2.0 technologies to further support online collaboration that promotes work from anywhere, anytime. Web 2.0 technologies enhance the workplace environment, offering more options and opportunities for the individual. Organizational power shifts to the user who now has greater control and more alternatives for getting work done. Collaboration technologies further enhance communication across companies and countries.

Enterprise 2.0 applications are changing the way organizations are managed. Ideas and people are moving up the ladder much more quickly. Additionally, businesses are increasingly focused on the team and the end product of the sum of all the parts. Instead of individual recognition, the focus is now on team achievements. This is leading to more emphasis on the training of employees to be more team oriented while improving communication and collaboration skills. Additionally, innovation is increasingly being created through team efforts.

Web 2.0 thrives off of social networking and relationship building. This new concept is often referred to as peer production or "peering." Peering involves masses of people openly collaborating to drive innovation and growth in industries. The greatest impact of Web 2.0 will be felt in how relationships between the enterprise and its constituents will revolutionize organizations (Rangaswami, 2006). Andrew McAfee, an associate professor at Harvard, believes that the impact of Enterprise 2.0 technologies will be tremendous because it gives a voice to employees who typically do not have a corporate voice, thus increasing the source of ideas (Gaudin, 2007).

There are those who are skeptical about the whole phenomenon of Enterprise 2.0 and its impact on organizations. Tom Davenport, a professor at Babson College, states,

I have yet to see any major example of how capitalist organizations make more money because of Enterprise 2.0 or any example of corporate culture being transformed by Enterprise 2.0. I have no problems with using Web 2.0 technologies in organizations, but I do have some problem with the idea that it means a radically new version of enterprises. (Gaudin, 2007, p. 1)

Even though he disagrees on the extent of the impact of Web 2.0, he does not disagree that it has the possibility of bringing a great return when he stated, "I'm an agnostic about this and not an atheist." He added, "I don't pretend to know for sure" (Gaudin, p. 1).

So the question becomes, will organizations, managers, and employees embrace this new phenomenon in ways that will transform their operations? Many argue both sides; however, neither can deny that Enterprise 2.0 and its technologies are changing the way business is done and the way we communicate. If and how it will transform organizations is still to be seen. In the following sections, we suggest possible outcomes and ways these changes are beginning to unfold in organizations.

ENTERPRISE 2.0 MANAGERS

The traditional management style no longer excels in the Enterprise 2.0 world. Web 2.0 provides a platform for more open communication and enhanced sharing of information. The Web 2.0 manager has the flexibility to be more fluid in actions and communications with subordinates. It will be the responsibility of the Web 2.0 manager to keep direct reports focused in order to ensure that individuals are productive and collaborative teams are effective and efficient. Organizing and overseeing an Enterprise 2.0 workforce is difficult at best because Web 2.0 tools allow information to be passed to multiple people quickly and in different formats. Evaluating an employee's contributions, productivity, and overall value to the organization becomes more difficult when compared to the more traditional measures associated with Enterprise 1.0. New metrics for employee compensation may be necessary and will involve charting new ground for many organizations. Attributes such as seniority and authority will be replaced with characteristics such as creativity, speed, and diversity of opinion. This will require a mind-set change for many managers. The focus shifts to communities and open relations rather then companies and secrecy. With more transparency comes more autonomy for employees. Employees will set deadlines, determine tasks, and provide input and insights in policy discussions. Successful outcomes will require that everyone understand the new rules of the game and how they apply to their particular organization.

Enterprise 2.0 managers will not have a script or mentor to follow. As this era is new, they will have to pave their own paths and learn from their own mistakes as they go along. These managers can no longer be content with job status and title or position in the organization. They have to constantly strive to innovate and make their companies and employees better.

Being an Enterprise 2.0 manager means being connected 24 hours per day. Always being connected to work has both its positives and negatives. While giving managers more flexibility to be away from the physical office, there are trade-offs in terms of having enough quality time away from all responsibility. Having direct reports that also struggle with these issues requires specific guidelines in terms of expectations. Managers who work through these issues successfully will have much to gain in terms of future opportunities and career enhancements.

One of the biggest challenges facing Enterprise 2.0 managers is the diversity of the employee base. Employees are increasingly diverse in both age and background as well as in geographical dispersion. The differences between the generations are more pronounced than ever with respect to technological awareness and the ability to easily adapt to new technological trends. Due to their technological skills, young employees may get a promotion ahead of more senior employees in the organization. As a result, possibilities for tension amongst coworkers must be managed. It will be necessary to create an atmosphere where everyone thrives and enjoys his or her work. This will represent a challenge to managers who have been around for many years and have established their own management style. Enterprise 2.0 will necessitate changes in management skills in order to gain the greatest benefits.

Cultural differences will also test the managerial abilities of Enterprise 2.0 managers who are inexperienced with a culturally diverse workplace that may span the globe. These issues are exacerbated in the context of technological changes. Many will not have had cultural diversity experiences or even the opportunity to explore other parts of the world, thus creating a huge learning curve. Additionally, the ability to manage employees located in different countries can be very challenging. Given limited face time with these employees, managers will have to utilize technologies such as videoconferencing to deliver their message to employees. The hardest part may be monitoring the progress employees make on projects without actually seeing the product. How will these managers monitor deadlines, know when employees may actually be swamped with other work, or know if they are just not doing their work? These are all challenges Enterprise 2.0 managers will face. A balance between face-to-face and virtual meetings will be necessary in order to obtain maximum productivity from workers.

ENTERPRISE 2.0 EMPLOYEES AND THE WORKFORCE

There are many unanswered questions as to how the workforce will change in the future. Mass communication has increased the pace of globalization and is quickly changing the dynamics of the business world. One of the important issues Enterprise 2.0 raises is the relationship between the manager and employee. As companies become more decentralized, the hierarchy of experience becomes less important. Employees are no longer promoted based on the amount of time they have served the company, but rather on the content and skill of their work. This dynamic has allowed young people to move up quickly in the workforce even though they may lack experience that is often carried by older employees. With employees all over the globe and the occurrences of physical meetings rare, employees have to adapt to managers they rarely see. Additionally, cultural

and language barriers exist that often hinder the completion of projects on a timely basis.

Web 2.0 is changing the way that work gets done in companies. Through the Internet, employers are now able to have a much larger employee base. As long as employees have Internet access, they may work for a company. Now, employees are hired on a need or project basis. This creates fewer permanent employees for companies, making it less expensive for companies to operate. Furthermore, the applicant pool is larger and more competitive because prospects are competing with individuals worldwide. This is especially prevalent in the research field where companies such as Merck are posting research opportunities. Researchers worldwide are given the opportunity to work on the project, and the researcher who is able to find a solution will be rewarded the benefits. This is good for companies because they are able to utilize all their options, but it is often not as beneficial for individuals because the sense of job security no longer exists and employees are constantly competing with others for jobs.

The greatest change, perhaps, are the employees themselves. Coming in, college graduates are more connected than previous generations. Having developed in a more online-based community, these individuals are more Internet savvy than previous generations. However, this trend also poses challenges for many businesses. Although these individuals are very good at staying connected through the Internet, their interpersonal skills and one-on-one communication skills in meetings may be deficient. Along those same lines, communication has allowed businesses to expand globally and work together even in different locations; but again, how does this affect work if employees are working closely with people they have never met? How is communication affected when these individuals finally do meet? Does it create an awkward setting where no party feels comfortable or do individuals feel as if they have known the other person for years? The answers to these questions will unfold with experience and time.

ENTERPRISE 2.0 COMMUNICATION AND PARTICIPATION

One of the major hallmarks of Web 2.0 is the participation of all individuals. Increased consumer participation is creating more economic opportunities and is helping to boost the economies of many countries. It is hard to avoid not joining a collaboration network because of the pure number of people participating on these sites. In 2007, there were over 34 million active users on Facebook and 22,000 more join daily (http://www.wikipedia.org). If nothing else, the networking connections these social sites create are vast because people are able to get in touch with individuals and carry on conversations without ever physically meeting.

In a similar manner, the use of blogs, instant messages, and e-mails has made the workforce more connected no matter where employees are globally. Blogs have allowed CEOs to communicate internally with their employees and externally with their customers. These interactive blogs allow CEOs to be in direct contact with staff employees that they typically would not have regular communication with. Furthermore, these blogs allow for employee feedback no matter what their rank in the office.

Web 2.0 applications allow employees internally to be more aware of what is happening within the company, thus creating a smarter environment. Furthermore, these applications have changed the hierarchal structure into a more horizontal structure because employees at all levels are allowed to participate in the activities of the company. Additionally, it also expands the location of companies because it is now easier for businesses to join partners with companies around the world. This creates a greater competitive advantage for companies. Simultaneously, by joining hands with other companies, it is often more cost efficient because employers are able to choose from a larger employee base and select the best employees for their company.

Both written and oral communication has become less formal. Blogs for example, are personal thoughts typed into words. E-mails are often written without proper grammar or punctuation. Communication in general has become less formal. Web 2.0 technologies only add to the informal nature of corporate communications. Whether positive or negative, Web 2.0 further encourages less personal interaction. It appears that a transformation in corporate communication may be taking place as a direct consequence of advancements in collaborative technologies.

ENTERPRISE 2.0 INFORMATION EXCHANGE

One of the biggest impacts Enterprise 2.0 will have on the world will be the rate at which information will travel. Almost instantaneously, information can be available to millions of people. In addition, the introduction of Enterprise 2.0 applications has overwhelmingly increased the amount of information exchanged between people. YouTube, an Enterprise 2.0 technology, serves as a site for many amateur recorders to upload their videos. Many of these videos have become primary sources of information for the rest of the world. In places struck by war or turbulent times, it is these videos that relate information to the rest of the world because they are released before newspeople are able to make it to the scene. These unscreened reports are unbiased and often leave a huge impact on viewers. In addition to relating news, these videos can also relate messages, ideas, and views because Internet regulations are not very strict on the type of information that can be posted. It encourages individuals to openly express their ideas. These technologies are being used increasingly by companies to get their message out whether to consumers or inside the organization to employees.

Besides videos, the electronic written word is also more prevalent. International magazines and newspapers are available from all over the world. This mass information exchange allows users to be able to expand their knowledge. As Internet information becomes more and more popular, the threat comes to the published written word. On average, newspaper sales have steadily decreased over the past few years as more and more people use other Internet methods to receive their news. Additionally, books are now available online or on disk, and podcasts are readily available on many topics. No doubt, books will still be published, but the number of people reading them may decrease as individuals find it easier to use Web 2.0 technologies to read information sources digitally.

The increased use of collaboration threatens to create chaos through the mere amount of information that will be available. In addition, the accuracy of information may be more difficult to determine. Since Web 2.0 is so interactive, often times, information is opinion rather than fact. Wikipedia, the online encyclopedia available in over 30 languages, strives off of user input because any user can input or delete information. This has created a new dynamic within the enterprise world for official rules for providing information. Although unwritten rules exist, there is no assurance that all users will abide by them. This presents two issues—one being that users often have to be wary of what they read on wikis since it is hard to regularly monitor these sites given the pace at which entries are made. In the future, rules and regulations may have to be established in order to preserve the accuracy of information, but will that not defeat the purpose of a wiki? Additionally, the question may also arise as to how a fact differs from an opinion. Before Web 2.0, users were taking information from the Internet as fact although that information was only coming from one source: those who

held power. In the Web 2.0 world, these problems only become more pronounced.

ENTERPRISE 2.0 PROJECT MANAGEMENT

Enterprise 2.0 technologies will also provide opportunities for change in the realm of project management. Project management can be improved using collaborative tools that enable better productivity and efficiency across the organization. Change management is an important key to success for project managers. Collaborative technologies allow for enhanced communication, greater user buy-in, and a means for interactive input as the project progresses, thus providing a means to better manage change. Geographical boundaries no longer pose obstacles to participation by all members of the organization no matter where they are located. If employed wisely, Organization 2.0 tools can be used to create value for the organization through project management applications.

The traditional assumptions of project management life cycles are being tested in this new context. Many companies are experimenting with an agile project management team approach that replaces the traditional systems analysis and design with new methods and more efficient operations. A middle ground will likely be found that addressees the needs of the evolving organization as well as the requirements of the traditional systems approach. Web 2.0 technologies will play an important role in this progression.

Web 2.0 provides project managers with more options. Those who are creative can change the dynamics of how they interact with their teams. In the agile environment, team members make the decisions on timelines and budgets, and negotiate solutions to project issues. Collaborative technologies make this shift possible. Companies must pay attention to these emerging trends in order to remain competitive and understand how the technologies are potentially being used by their competitors.

ENTERPRISE 2.0 OPEN INNOVATION

Enterprise 2.0 creates an innovative atmosphere as more of the world's population now becomes part of the general exchange of ideas. As more people across countries participate in this open forum of ideas, more choices are available to people. It creates an atmosphere where people are more comfortable expressing their individualized thoughts because with more people participating, there are more who agree with the traditionally unpopular ideas. It also may lead to a trend where there is no norm because everybody will be able to express themselves individually and openly.

Perhaps the greatest benefit of Enterprise 2.0 technologies is the quality of ideas and innovation that comes when masses of people are connected. When ideas are openly shared and communicated, it becomes increasingly possible to solve complicated problems. Mass collaboration can help people unite in the fight for a greener planet or to protect the ozone layer. It opens the door for people with similar interests and passions to come together and discuss world issues. Forums and blogs create open discussions and debates as to how to find solutions to world problems. It also allows for creativity and innovation to be established from collaborative thought.

InnoCentive is a company that was founded in 2001 in Massachusetts and is a leading example of how Enterprise 2.0 technologies are being used to help solve company problems. InnoCentive is a site where challenges are listed in fields such as chemistry biology, business, and math. A cash reward is given to the one person who can find the best solution to a given problem. Those who strive to find a solution are termed *solvers*, while companies that present the issues are *seekers*. Some of the companies that have participated on

this site include Procter & Gamble and Rockefeller Foundation. The idea behind it is to create a site where any researcher can go and try to help solve problems and issues that companies may be facing. Since only the best solution receives the award, seeking companies are receiving free consultation and are able to choose their preferred solution. Currently, there are over 125,000 solvers registered on the Web site. Often times, the Web site is referred to as the world's first "open innovation marketplace" as it strives to unite the innovative thinkers of the world. To join the network, there is no charge unless you are a seeking company. As a seeking company, you must be able to pay a reward between US$5,000 to US$1 million for the solution to your challenge (InnoCentive, 2008). InnoCentive does have a few competitors including NineSigma, yet2.com, and YourEncore (http://www.wikipedia.org).

Collaborative technologies will likely continue to play a huge role in organizations as they seek to find new ways to innovate.

ENTERPRISE-TO-ENTERPRISE COLLABORATION

Public access to information has tightened competition but at the same time has brought competitors together. For the past decade, companies have used the theory "bigger is better"; thus, the late '90s and early 2000s saw a stream of mergers and acquisitions as companies tried to acquire talent and innovation to beat out their competition. However, many mergers and acquisitions were unsuccessful because of cultural and strategic differences between companies. Through collaboration, large companies are actually divesting parts of their company and creating equal partners with suppliers and peers to enhance the productivity of the business. Mike Blair from Boeing uses this approach and believes "[this] way we get the best ideas from everybody, as opposed to just ours." Amazon.com provides another example of openly sharing information with competitors in order to improve their own services. As stated on the Amazon.com site, "the more data that we're able to put in the hands of developers, the more interesting tools, sites, and applications will be built, and the more of those that exist the greater return to Amazon" (Tapscott & Williams, 2006, p. 196). Thus, the new era of collaboration is removing the hierarchal dimensions throughout businesses and in turn creating horizontal associations amongst competitors.

VIRTUAL WORLDS AND THE IMPACT ON THE ENTERPRISE 2.0 ORGANIZATION

Virtual worlds such as *Second Life* and *Kaneva* are also transforming enterprise operations. *Second Life* will be discussed briefly here and in more detail in Section IV of this book. *Second Life*, a virtual world that was initially started as a game, is made up of fictitious characters who lead normal lives but in a virtual context. Users create characters, possibly what they would like to be in real life, and control their daily moves. In essence, users are able to live a second life through this application.

However, in addition to creating another social networking scheme, *Second Life* has created an investment ground for corporations. Companies are able to utilize the virtual world as a testing ground for introducing products. David E. Stone, a research fellow, created a simulation in 3 days for $350, which in the real world would have taken 6 months and $60,000 (Mollman, 2007). The currency in *Second Life* is Linden dollars, and the exchange rate is roughly 275 Linden dollars for US$1 (http://secondlife.com).

Second Life creates investment opportunities even at the individual level. It has a monthly economy of about US$50 million (Carpenter, 2007). Recently, Anshe Chung created the *Second Life* character Ailin Graef for a US$9.95 investment

and has become the first millionaire on *Second Life* (Hof, 2006). Thus, there are financial benefits in addition to the social benefits. There are numerous accounts of individuals on *Second Life* who have quit their real-world jobs because they make enough money by specializing in a particular trade in the virtual world. It is also a huge investment opportunity as individuals, businesses, and universities are racing to buy property.

Companies such as Reebok, Adidas, and Calvin Klein have opened stores in this virtual realm. IBM, for example, tests certain products through the *Second Life* community in order to get a feel for the success of the product since they can get feedback from users all over the world (Harkin, 2007). Computer-savvy companies are conducting preliminary interviews through *Second Life* to see if interviewees are competent with the technology. Additionally, it allows for videoconferencing and instant messaging, making it easier for company employees to communicate with each other.

As *Second Life* nears its tipping point, the effects and impact are still unsure; however, it has already proven that it can impact the world in many ways. It has been shown that it is very beneficial to businesses as it creates efficiencies unmatched in the real world, and it is proving profitable for many individuals. As the technology evolves over time and more people become part of the world of *Second Life*, it will be interesting to see what opportunities the virtual world will provide for organizations in the future.

ORGANIZATIONAL CHALLENGES FOR ENTERPRISE 2.0

Opportunities usually come with challenges, and this is no different for Enterprise 2.0. As will be discussed in a subsequent chapter (Chapter V) devoted to security issues, security is a huge challenge for companies implementing Web 2.0 technologies for the first time. This was the same with previous technologies such as wireless in the early days of implementation. Solutions had to be found for the early problems, and this will be no different for Web 2.0 as the problems are exposed and solutions are determined. With any new technology, there is an evolution as people adapt and the technology becomes mainstream.

An array of issues has emerged that will need to be addressed as companies move forward to embrace these trends. Privacy and ethical concerns are becoming important. As companies become more connected, protection of information and individuals is a huge concern. Likewise, legal issues have also emerged due to the unique problems presented by this explosion of information.

In order for Enterprise 2.0 to be successful, the culture of the work environment must change as well. Upper management must be aware of the benefits and impact of Enterprise 2.0 as well as be willing to change its methods of managing. It must lead the initiative so that employees will willingly follow and adjust to the new changes. Although having management adjust to these changes can be a challenge, it is also one of the biggest solutions for successful implementation. History has shown numerous examples of company failures when companies become complacent and lag behind in research, innovation, and technology. Often times, it can cost the entire company its reputation if leaders become content with their status at the top.

IMPLICATIONS OF ENTERPRISE 2.0 FOR INTERNATIONAL BUSINESS

Tapscott and Williams (2006) identify four pillars of mass collaboration: openness, peering, sharing, and acting globally. The first three are fulfilled through Enterprise 2.0 technologies; however, acting globally is based on a shift in mind-set and ideology. History has shown through time that different empires such as the Romans and the British have economically and politically ruled the world. During the past century, the United States has been the global economic powerhouse. Currently, the global shift is moving toward countries like China, India, Russia, and Brazil. As these countries develop into economic powerhouses, their dominance will be different from the empires before them because their survival will rely on the global economy and all the countries they interact and trade with. No longer can an empire be the sole economic provider. Every country must be connected on a global scale in order to benefit from the sharing of ideas and products. Efficiency, productivity, and innovation are being created on a global network, and this network is allowing individuals and companies to compete and succeed at new levels.

Global companies have offices in numerous countries and some U.S. companies have moved their headquarters to countries other than the United States. These global companies now have a more diverse and talented employee base and face new challenges as company leaders try to manage offices around the world. At the same time, benefits accrue to these companies because ideas are being generated from a greater number of employees as well as employees with various backgrounds. This helps companies benefit from the ideas of others and learn from their mistakes. It also expands the employee applicant pool by making it more competitive. In essence, global companies are incorporating the openness, sharing, and peering ideas discussed by Tapscott and Williams (2008).

Web 2.0 technologies unite the world. As people of different races and backgrounds work side by side, cultural awareness is heightened by all involved. In the Enterprise 2.0 world—from Blackberries to laptops to iPods—individuals are always connected. Proof of the rapid growth in mass communication is more evident in many other countries than in America. For example, in countries such as Syria or Dubai, most children under the age of 10 have cell phones. Furthermore, these cell phones are not only world phones, but they are adaptive to their region. For instance, to adapt to the predominant religion in the Middle East, phones have programs where prayer times are set and the call to prayer comes on the phone. All the major cities within the Middle East are programmed for this feature. Additionally, there is a compass guiding the direction to which people need to pray. This is only one example of trends taking place around the world.

Acting globally has many benefits, but it also has its risks and issues. Communication is vital to the Enterprise 2.0 organization. Communication can be hindered through cultural differences. A global economy also means global awareness. Benefiting from business practices in other countries requires an understanding of the differences in culture and an understanding of how to communicate. Some cultures are much more formal than others, and it is a challenge to maintain the respect of others without unconsciously insulting the leaders or managers from different backgrounds. This problem can be solved as long as people are formally trained in these differences.

The language of communication also comes into question. Until now, English has been considered a global language and numerous countries teach English as a second or third language. However, as the global power shifts toward Asia, will the language of trade also shift with it? Even if the language does not officially change, it may serve as a benefit to many people doing trade in these countries to learn Chinese or Russian in order to fully capitalize and benefit from these countries. It also may give those who do try to learn these languages greater respect amongst the civilians of the country.

Government involvement and regulations can also play a significant role in the implementation of Web 2.0 technologies across borders. China, for example, is a communist state, and its government has strict regulations and laws that may require that information be censored, thus resulting in restriction to the free flow of information. A more connected world means greater dependence on one another. For companies, the value chain is broken when one link in the chain is affected. Political strife in countries may also impact the success of collaboration across borders.

The digital divide across countries is another issue that comes into play. The options companies have in some countries are limited due to the lack of technological capabilities and basic infrastructure. Before the world can truly be considered global, every country needs to be connected on this network of collaboration.

WHY ENTERPRISE 2.0?

In an ever-flattening world, communication and collaboration are vital for success. Companies, business, and individuals that do not stay continuously connected will become isolated and fall behind. In the corporate world today, those companies that are globally connected and continuously striving to stay connected will be more likely to be successful.

The emergence of MySpace, Facebook, You-Tube, and numerous other social networking companies over a short time frame is evidence enough that a major shift is taking place that companies cannot ignore. Just as with the Internet, there is no turning back the clock once technological advancement has reached a tipping point. Companies must carefully evaluate how to incorporate these technologies and determine what works and does not work for their businesses or industries. Embracing the technology and confronting change are always difficult, but the alternative of ignoring the trends is high risk in today's fast-paced business environment.

Enterprise 2.0 provides many benefits and opportunities that are only now beginning to surface. Innovative and creative companies will seize these opportunities for competitive gain and long-term advantage. Others will fall behind if they are not educating themselves and evaluating the opportunities and obstacles for their operations. In a globally connected world, technology will continue to rule as long as companies are able to find the competitive edge.

CONCLUSION AND FUTURE TRENDS

A more global workforce, flexible work space, and more efficient communication are all characteristics of Enterprise 2.0, and each will impact organizations differently. Enterprise 2.0 is about agility, efficiency, and productivity. It is about using social software in ways that provide quicker access to information, better and far-reaching access to ideas, and an increase in distributed work and decision making. In addition, global teams can derive added value and more effective communication across the world. As Enterprise 2.0 technologies continue to permeate the workplace, organizations will find it necessary to respond to these changes. Organizations that do not take a leadership position on these emerging trends could fall behind in their industries and their positions in the world.

Collaborative technologies as we know them today will evolve. Companies must find ways to embrace these technologies today in order to evolve as these technologies change in the future. Companies must create the collaborative space that moves organizations toward more organic and dynamic structures. These changes will not come easily, and leaders will need to tread carefully as they move in these directions.

As mentioned previously, security, privacy, ethics, and legal concerns must be considered as they will each play a significant role in the success of organizational endeavors with Web 2.0. Innovative solutions to these problems will be required because they are not going to disappear. Those who find solutions to these potential obstacles and risks stand to gain much in this rapidly changing global business world.

Even though Web 2.0 has not been fully implemented, there are talks of Web 3.0 and what the future may hold. Many predict it will be the Semantic Web where users will be able to request information rather than have to search for it. However, many argue that this type of Web would involve a structural change in the current way information is stored on the Internet, and it is not probable that it will occur in the near future (Jerney, 2007). A more realistic prediction for Web 3.0 is that users can easily consume and produce programs and content like they create blogs in Web 2.0 (Jerney, 2007). The advantage of this type of Web is that information is stored on a user's personal computer, not on a network; thus, information is not as public. Online dweller Jason Calacins comments that "Web 3.0 is the creation of high-quality content and services produced by gifted individuals using Web 2.0 technology as an enabling platform" (Lilley, 2007). Web 3.0 will use cognitive deduction to relay information that users request (Markoff, 2006). In essence, users will be relying more heavily on artificial intelligence as machines and technologies get smarter. It is too early to say exactly what Web 3.0 may entail; however, if artificial intelligence does not succeed in this version of the Web, it is not far fetched to say users will see it sometime in the near future.

This new era represents an exciting time—a time where problems may be solved and new ideas are created more readily. It may be looked at as a time in history where "the nature of the game was changed" (Tapscott & Williams, 2006). The theory of mass collaboration and the spread of globalization combine to impact the nature of business and society in ways we have never seen. *Virtual work spaces* and *global managers* are terms that are taking on new meanings. We can no longer sit and watch as the world changes; we much each pick up our printing press and join the global team.

REFERENCES

Carpenter, P. (2007). *The current and future state of Second Life.* Retrieved February 15, 2008, from http://www.computerworld.com/blogs/node/5426

Gaudin, S. (2007, June 18). *Rivals face off in Enterprise 2.0 debate.* Retrieved February 15, 2008, from http://www.informationweek.com/news/showArticle.jhtml?articleID=199905148

Harkin, F. (2007). *Virtual style? In another life.* Retrieved February 15, 2008, from http://www.ft.com/cms/s/0/733d2398-05a6-11dc-b151-000b5df10621.html

Hof, R. (2006). *Second Life's first millionaire.* Retrieved February 15, 2008, from http://www.businessweek.com/the_thread/techbeat/archives/2006/11/second_lifes_fi.html

InnoCentive. (2008). Retrieved February 15, 2008, from http://www.innocentive.com

Jerney, J. (2007, January 23). Even experts have difficulty understanding Web 3.0. *The Daily Yomiuri (Tokyo),* p.18.

Lilley, A. (2007). *Is Web 3.0 a brand relaunch just like Kylie's new look?* Retrieved April 28, 2008, from http://www.guardian.co.uk/media/2007/oct/15/mondaymediasection8

MacKinnon, R. (2005). *Chinese bloggers: Everybody is somebody.* Retrieved February 15, 2008, from http://rconversation.blogs.com/rconversation/2005/11/chinese_blogger_1.html

Markoff, J. (2006). *Entrepreneurs see a Web guided by common sense.* Retrieved April 28, 2008, from http://www.nytimes.com/2006/11/12/business/12web.html?_r=1&oref=slogin

McAfee, A. (2006). *The trends underlying Enterprise 2.0.* Retrieved February 15, 2008, from http://blog.hbs.edu/faculty/amcafee/index.php/faculty_amcafee_v3/the_three_trends_underlying_enterprise_20

Mollman, S. (2007). *Second Life's 2nd value: Testing ideas.* Retrieved February 15, 2008, from http://edition.cnn.com/2007/BUSINESS/09/16/second.life

Rangaswami, M. R. (2006). *The birth of Enterprise 2.0.* Retrieved February 15, 2008, from http://sandhill.com/opinion/editorial.php?id=98

Second Life. (2008). Retrieved February 15, 2008, from http://secondlife.com/whatis/economy-market.php

Tapscott, D., & Williams, A. D. (2006). *Wikinomics: How mass collaboration changes everything.* New York: Penguin Group.

Tapscott, D., & Williams, A. D. (2008). *Wikinomics: How mass collaboration changes everything.* New York: Penguin Group.

Wikipedia. (2008). Retrieved February 15, 2008, from http://www.wikipedia.org

Section III
Security and Legal Issues for the Enterprise 2.0 Organization

Chapter V
Security in a Web 2.0 World

Richard T. Barnes
SunGard Higher Education, USA

ABSTRACT

Web 2.0 has brought enumerable benefits as well as daunting problems of securing transactions, computers, and identities. Powerful hacker techniques, including cross-site scripting (XSS) and cross-site request forgery (CSRF), are used to exploit applications to reveal and steal, at the worst, confidential information and money, or, at the least, cause trouble and waste time and money for reasons that may be best described as fun or simply possible to do. The people interested in transgressing Web 2.0 applications do so for money, prestige, or for the challenge. An infamous hacker from the early days of the Internet now heads his own Internet security company. A more recent hacker of some infamy has created a stir of concern and consternation as to how pervasive and potentially destructive hacker attacks can be. Securing Web 2.0 applications requires a multifaceted approach involving improved code development standards, organizational policy changes, protected servers and workstations, and aggressive law enforcement.

INTRODUCTION

With the multitude of benefits derived from the various Web 2.0 technologies, it is unfortunate that this book needs a chapter on security. Although the collaborations, synergies, and transformations of the collective Web technologies (known as Web 2.0) have immeasurably changed society in a good way, there is a bad element that we must recognize, understand, and defend against.

The relatively open and participative nature of Web 2.0 is, at once, a strength and weakness. Opening sites to user content and comment creates synergies that would not exist had the sites been restricted to a select few. However, it is difficult to restrict user input to only positive discourse; various motivations compel some to poison this well we know as Web 2.0.

Collectively, the responsibility and burden falls on organizations and individuals to share in constraining the enablers to minimize the damage to our 2.0 Web sites. Although it is helpful to understand the motivations behind the various (and growing) attacks, it is more important to follow best practices in code development and security design (Evers, 2007). The adage "the best defense is a good offense" does not apply well to Web 2.0 security. We cannot proactively prosecute and punish someone before they commit a Web attack; we may be on the road to a changing world, but constitutional rights cannot be trampled upon.

It is likely that some are dissuaded by the possibility of punishment if caught; but if only a few carry out Web attacks, our best approach, still, is to mount our best defense. It is of course equally important to prosecute security offenses. The threat of punishment has to be more than theoretical: Offenders must know that if they are caught, there will be consequences.

This chapter will explore the motivations, methods, and defenses against the malicious behaviors that cost time and money, and lessen the positives that can come from these technologies. There have been notable attacks to prominent Web sites; a few of these will be examined for their causes and associated effects. The evolution of the World Wide Web into version 2.0 has had social impacts, too. What are these impacts, and are there trends evident that may help us predict where security attacks and defense strategies will go in the future? Some possibilities are explored here and in subsequent chapters.

There is an old adage that says those who forget the past are condemned to repeat it. This idea cannot be forgotten in Web 2.0 security. We must remember how attacks happened before so we can avoid similar attacks in the future. By examining the trends, analyzing our mistakes, and understanding our needs, we can improve on Web 2.0 and make it better. That is how we got to version 2.0 from 1.0. Perhaps, as the Web evolves into what some in the community are calling Web 3.0, the lessons learned here will not be forgotten.

BACKGROUND

It is perhaps ironic that the following definition for application security comes from one of the best known wikis, Wikipedia. Application security encompasses measures taken to prevent exceptions in the security policy of an application or the underlying system through flaws in the design, development, or deployment of the application. This definition is an excellent start in addressing a very large problem. However, it does not really tell us why; that is, why is it necessary to prevent exceptions to security policy?

A broader definition may help. There are several definitions of the word *security*: The freedom from danger or the freedom from fear and anxiety are two variants that tell us why application security is so important to Web 2.0 applications. Identity theft, corporate espionage or sabotage, and/or simple maliciousness are certainly enough to give most of us some pause or anxiety. Application security, as it relates to Web 2.0, is now an area of great attention because of our collective need to be free of these dangers.

A confluence of factors has complicated our lives as Web 2.0 becomes a more significant presence. The graphics-rich functionality, collaboration, and opportunities have not only yielded "serendipitous innovation" (Tapscott & Williams, 2006), but less desirable consequences, too.

Consequences such as cross-site scripting (XSS) and cross-site request forgeries (CSRFs) were not anticipated when foundational Web 2.0 technologies were created. Asynchronous JavaScript and XML (extensible markup language), or AJAX, is a set of Web development techniques that enable Web sites to be interactive and rich with features that make the static Web pages of a few years ago seem, well, static. However, it is through AJAX and other technologies that Web attackers have created innovative ways to, at the least, cause mischief, and at the worst, cause severe harm.

The subject of Web 2.0 security has a number of important acronyms; AJAX is one. Others include XML, RSS (really simple syndication), and SOAP (simple object access protocol; Shah, 2006). This chapter is not necessarily intended to define and explain these terms, but more to put them in context with the larger problem (and challenge) of Web 2.0 security. Much of the recent literature talks of where the burden lies: with the developers, with the companies, and with the users. The reality, however, is that at least some of the burden falls on each of us.

Developers can build security into the applications they write instead of adding security later as an afterthought. Companies can elevate security to an enterprise-level initiative and build it into the products they sell. Although companies have been victims of security incursions, especially of late, the user has often been victimized, and it is often at the user level where good security hygiene is easiest and best applied.

A comprehensive approach to securing Web 2.0 applications stands the greatest chance for success. It is not enough to say that developers need to do a better job or companies cannot rush products to market when everyone can contribute to better security. How ironic that one of the great strengths of Web 2.0, collaboration, can, in effect, help solve one of its greatest weaknesses!

SECURITY PROBLEMS AND WEAKNESSES

AJAX in this context is not a cleanser made famous by a television jingle, nor is it a reference to the Greek who out of madness quite literally fell on his sword. AJAX in this context is a programming technique that employs a few other successful technologies including, as the acronym implies,

XML and JavaScript (O'Reilly, 2005). Seen as an essential enabler of the Web 2.0 era, AJAX serves as the technical nexus for the development of the rich, interactive Web sites that we now take for granted. Capable of making direct communication with the Web server, AJAX Web sites can request server data without reloading the Web page. These behind-the-scenes data exchanges occur without the user's knowledge and provide a transparency to applications that make them distinctly more advanced than their Web 1.0 predecessors.

This direct communication between the Web server and Web application also provides an opening for application security transgressions (Enright, 2007). One method of attack, known as XSS, involves the injection of malicious code into a Web page viewed by others. The silent (i.e., hidden) execution of the AJAX code is perhaps one of the biggest areas of concern for IT security experts. Because transactions are occurring in the background without the user's knowledge and input, the potential for the execution of malicious code running unimpeded is large. This code may run on the computers of unsuspecting Web site visitors, exposing the visitors to the possible theft of sensitive information (e.g., banking information, authentication credentials, etc.). There are several types of XSS attack methods; however, the common denominator in the end result is that the user's browser always executes code that is, at least, not authorized, and at worst, destructive or compromising (McMillan, 2007).

Attacks using the CSRF method have been less common, but a large unrealized potential exists for more attacks (and more harm) in the future. The *cross-site* in CSRF is derived from the XSS method explained above and denotes some of the similarities between the two methods. Where the two methods are most different can be denoted in the *forgery* part of the name. According to Merriam-Webster Online, a forgery is defined as an imitation passed off as genuine. This is quite literally what the CSRF attack method does: Unauthorized (or forged) commands from a user are transmitted to or from a trusted Web site. The reliance and trust on an established (authenticated) identity is how the Web has worked, and the CSRF method exploits this common characteristic by imitating the authenticated user (Waters, 2007).

XML poisoning is another method of attack. Web 2.0 applications transmit XML data between the client and server as part of their normal operations. Although poisoning may sound a bit overstated, the method will corrupt (or poison) the XML data in such a way as to disrupt the processing of the information. The effect of this poisoning can range from denial of service (DoS), where the targeted server is bombarded with spurious requests that will, in effect, bring the server down or render it nonfunctional, to compromised confidential information.

RSS is a method and an XML 1.0-compliant format that aggregates disparate sources of Web information into a feed for the user. The user subscribes to the feed and sets the criteria for what information should be included (or excluded) in the feed. While this may sound like an incredible time saver for the user, what it also can do is expose the user to malicious code embedded in the source information. This code may also be aggregated along with the legitimate information, and the user will not necessarily know anything is amiss. This RSS injection method, as it is known, can install and launch software on the user's computer, potentially compromising confidential information.

Web services can be a fertile ground for Web 2.0 security intrusions. SOAP is the common protocol used for Web services remote procedure calls, and is therefore an often-used method for attack. Parameter manipulation and node exploitation are common techniques used in Web-services-related attacks. In parameter manipulation, the variables that are passed in services calls can be manipulated to suit the attacker's needs. If a site has insufficient validation of received parameters, the site is open to attack and compromise. Nodes on the Internet cannot be assumed to be secure:

If a node is compromised, a SOAP message en route can be intercepted and modified as part of an attack. Although there are several variations on the Web services theme, these types of attacks are less prevalent than the JavaScript-based attacks.

WHO ARE THE ATTACKERS, AND WHAT ARE THEIR MOTIVATIONS?

Just as Web applications have evolved from the static, even boring presentation of webmaster-defined content, so too have the people who stage attacks on the Web. Because *evolution* may imply betterment, perhaps it is incorrect to say that attackers have evolved; what has really happened is that their methods have become more sophisticated as the Web infrastructure has become more complex. But, who are the attackers and why do they do what they do?

There are no clear definitions or labels for these Web attackers. While the word *hacker* has been generally used in a pejorative sense by the media, there are other words that may be more precise. The word *cracker*, also known as a black hat, refers to a person who illegally compromises the security of a computer system or network to reach a malicious end. A white hat will (attempt to) compromise security, but will also have valid permission from the system or network owners; the objective, of course, is to locate security holes and plug them before they are exploited. Not to imply a standard curriculum has been established, but to acquire the necessary skills to be a cracker, one should first be a hacker (Walker, 2005). The usage of the word *hacker* has changed over the years. Its etymology has mostly had a creative connotation. However, since the movie *Wargames* in 1983, the general (public) meaning has been to creatively manipulate computer code or procedures to achieve a desired outcome, generally a mischievous or malicious one. For purposes of brevity, the word *hacker* will be used in this chapter not to be imprecise, but more specifically to be consistent with the general connotation of the word.

The rebellious, antiauthority teenager may still exist, but the harm that erstwhile person can do is now less than before, mostly thanks to much higher numbers of installed security software. While it is certainly not ubiquitous, the awareness of computer viruses and worms is higher than what it was, therefore leading to a greater number of protected computers. There are exceptions, of course, but the days are mostly passed when a lone and unassisted teenager can cause significant harm (without a significant response) from his basement computer. However, the problem will never go away. As new, more complex applications are deployed, new exploitable vulnerabilities are found.

Perhaps one of the earliest and best known hackers who had the mind-set, skills, and intelligence for finding vulnerabilities is now out of jail. Having satisfied all penalties levied against him, he now has his own security consulting company and has published more than a few books. According to a recent interview, Kevin Mitnick's original motivation was "fun and entertainment." There was a thrill to gaining access to confidential or proprietary information (Brandon, 2007).

A hacker of more recent fame, the creator of the infamous Samy worm that forced MySpace off line after an XSS attack, created it as a prank according to an interview shortly after the incident. Despite the greater prevalence of security software, the Samy worm raised awareness to the increased risks associated with applications under the Web 2.0 umbrella. When it became known that Samy's very first AJAX project created the Samy worm, business and security leaders took note; if this is his first, what could be next? It may seem a bit perverse that Samy, the perpetrator of the attack, did not fault himself or MySpace for the worm's success, but instead blamed the client browsers for making it easy to run unauthorized JavaScript code on them (Lenssen, 2005).

Like Mitnick who preceded him, but perhaps to a lesser degree, Samy may have gained more than he has lost from his exploit. Although Samy Kamkar was sentenced to probation, community service, and a certain amount of restitution, his reputation has been indelibly etched into Web history. One online news source even referred to his exploit as "cunning" (Orlowski, 2005).

The motivations behind Web 2.0 attacks have changed. While it may have been a prank or an adventure a few years ago, the development of new Web exploits is now the stuff of nationalism, social castes, and real money. A denial-of-service attack that hit Estonia in early 2007 is suspected to be rooted in Russian nationalism, although some security experts dispute the nationalism claim (Brenner, 2007), saying it was motivated by anger over a government decision to move a revered monument. Despite the lingering issue of why the Estonian attack happened, Russia is thought to be a proverbial hotbed of malware (malicious software) engineering (Brenner). Other than the booming petro economy, the Russian "other" economy is bleak, and programmers not only see malware as a money opportunity, they also do not believe developing malware is wrong. Still, the nationalist bent cannot be discounted; a small Russian newspaper reportedly praised the local perpetrators of a hacking attack for their accomplishment at the capitalists' expense (Claburn, 2007). With a report that a Russian Web server was found to be hosting approximately 400 malware applications (Brenner), and a report that China's production of malware exceeds Russia, how long will it be before nationalist Web attacks are directed to the Western hemisphere?

In the West, a social order has developed among the people who develop and/or deploy malware on the Web (Claburn, 2007). Even though Kevin Mitnick has a legitimate career now after paying his dues to society, he is held in reverence and awe by young and aspiring hackers. Samy Kamkar is substantially younger, but his "Samy is my hero" prank on MySpace is still admired by people in their teens, 20s, and even 30s. Even though they are legitimate now because of their admiring fans, both Mitnick and Kamkar are certainly near the high end of the hacker social order.

The lure of an income, perhaps a large income, is a major motivator in both the West and in Asia. No longer is malware just written by and for the exclusive use of its writer. Malware kits, that is, kits for developing malware, are readily available for sale on the Internet. Originators of malware programs or kits are at or near the top of the hacker social order. These are the people who stand to earn the greatest amount of money from their actions, and the money can be considerable. Lower in the hacker social order are the people who buy these kits to develop their own malware, but that does not mean they are of lesser significance; the availability and the use of malware kits are a significant factor in the proliferation of malware on the Internet. Though the road can be tough (Kevin Mitnick was arrested several times), the hope of a lucrative hacking career and the high status it may bring can be compelling.

Malware kits are one source of income. Another money-earning method involves renting botnets. Botnets are networks (or groups) of security-compromised computers known as zombies. Botnets are also used in spamming (mass junk e-mail distributions), focused attacks to steal data, and denial-of-service attacks as client-naïve instruments. They have even been used to extort money under threat of a DoS attack.

Depending on the size of the botnet, that is, how many zombie computers are part of the botnet, the weekly rental income can be several hundred dollars. More income can be earned with the sale of an unpublished security vulnerability, perhaps up to US$1,000 or more (Evers, 2007). What is less known, but feared more, are the markets for identity-related data such as credit card numbers, social security numbers, and company-related confidential information to be used in espionage.

Phishing scams are relatively new, but their impact cannot be understated. With Web sites that look legitimate, but are in fact facades developed to acquire credit card numbers, passwords, social security numbers, and other personal data, phishing is proving to be a lucrative criminal method of cyber attack. Security firms such as Symantec have included phishing protection in their software, and Microsoft has phishing filter functionality included in Internet Explorer 7 to help minimize the dangers phishing can pose to the unwitting user.

WHAT CAN WE DO?

What can be done to mitigate the security risks and minimize the problems that have evolved from Web 2.0? We cannot eliminate the problem of cyber attacks on Web 2.0 applications or otherwise. The best we can hope for is to minimize the probability of an attack, or if attacked, minimize the damage done.

The field is a rapidly changing one, where hackers find a weakness, companies or individuals respond, and society slowly incorporates and adapts to the changes over the long term. During the 1980s, few could have imagined what the Internet in general and Web 2.0 in particular could have become in 2007, but what was unimagined then is reality now: Society will continue to adapt. One constant, though, is that hackers will exploit a weakness, and the rest of us will respond. Society's innovation will always be challenged by the hacker's innovation.

Many blame the rush-to-market mentality of companies in getting their Web 2.0 applications up and running. In their haste to meet deadlines, developers forego what few best practices there are to complete their tasks. There are two things that can be done to address this part of the problem. In 1996, Alan Greenspan, the Federal Reserve chairman, used the term "irrational exuberance" to characterize the overinflated values of the stock market; perhaps companies venturing into Web 2.0 territory need to tamp down their exuberance to a level where their developers can properly include security into their Web 2.0 applications. Secondly, Web security is a rapidly changing field; to keep up with the changes, developers should be continually trained on threats, techniques, and best practices. As mentioned before, there is not one answer to the security problem, but as companies work toward a whole solution, they should concentrate on two of the biggest threat sources: cross-site scripting and cross-site request forgeries.

There is more that companies can do to address Web security issues. Widely acknowledged as a problem, company confidential or proprietary data can appear in Web 2.0 weblogs (blogs) that may eventually become known to the company's competitors. This is not caused by hackers, but more likely company employees, disgruntled or simply naïve. Companies need to develop (better) data policies: Their data need to be identified, managed, and controlled (Vijayan, 2007). Knowing what data the company has and where they are located is an essential first step. Also essential to know is who has access to data; that is, companies should know who should have access and put controls in place to enforce company policy on data.

A more problematic approach is determining if and how to limit employee access to blogs. Whether deliberate or accidental, when an employee puts company data on a blog, they become public and potentially compromise the position of the company. An outright ban on company computers is certainly possible. Web sites can be blocked, firewall rules can be stringently applied, and so forth (Fanning, 2007), but how can a ban be enforced on noncompany computers? The short answer is it cannot, so the likely answer for companies is to take a middle position; develop, apply, and enforce a comprehensive data policy that can extend beyond the company's parking lot.

The onus should not be completely on companies to address Web security problems. Organizations are generally more strident about security, and individuals should learn from their employers and become more security conscious. Personal data should be guarded as closely as company data. Home computers can be current on the latest security software just as work computers are (usually). Individuals should recognize the public nature of the Internet and the Web, and realize that *public* does not mean *safe*. Web 2.0 has enabled the Web to become more of a conversation than a billboard; that conversation will have questionable and nefarious participants, and individuals have to remember that.

WHAT IS ON THE HORIZON FOR WEB SECURITY?

As suggested in the previous section, companies and individuals are reacting to the Web security issues that have been exacerbated with Web 2.0 technologies. Some believe there really is one magic solution, while others embrace the idea that a comprehensive strategy and solution is the best approach.

One notable and positive trend is the telltale movement to thin-client applications and hardware. Thin clients are essentially input and output devices only; the applications, heavy processing, and data reside on a server. With the advent of fast corporate and broadband networks, thin-client computing is more possible than ever. In 1995, Oracle founder Larry Ellison presaged a future where network computers replaced the personal computer (Bock, 2006). Though his reasoning was based on the growing complexity of personal computers during the 1990s and not the security concerns raised in the 2000s, his prediction was nevertheless prophetic. Microsoft now has in beta a server-based version of Office that will further the trend of thin-client applications. With computing power and data moving to more protected Web servers, opportunities for intrusion are lessened and malware attacks will be reduced.

The best practices for Web security are developing and becoming better known. When Web 2.0 applications began to appear, the best practices had not caught up to the technology, but that is changing now. Control Objectives for Information and Related Technology (COBIT) is both a format and forum for governance of all things IT. As practices become established and accepted by the IT community, COBIT-codified practices are updated and disseminated through traditional channels such as conferences and published standards. Web 2.0, podcasts, blogs, and wikis, though perhaps nontraditional channels now, are becoming evermore important in communicating best practices to the people and organizations that need them.

There may be a developing trend with negative consequences for Web security, at least in the short term. An increasing number of acquisitions of Web security specialty firms have some security experts concerned. With IBM's acquisition of Watchfire and HP's recent acquisition of SPI Dynamics, will the products of those companies be less available to the general market? These smaller companies, before their acquisitions, were autonomous leaders in Web 2.0 security. However, with their independence gone, it is unclear whether their products will be directly available to the market at large, or limited as offerings from the acquiring companies. This should be a short-term problem because their technology, and technology from other similarly acquired companies, will eventually make its way to the market (Germain, 2007).

CONCLUSION

Where are we now with Web security? This chapter has examined the background and evolution of where we were. It is evident now that with the advent of Web 2.0, the security technology for

Web applications lagged behind the technology for the social software embodied in Web 2.0.

This gap in technologies created an opportunity for makers of mischief, maliciousness, espionage, and profit. However, the market has responded and will continue to respond.

In the context of Web security, terms such as AJAX and SOAP may never become well-known outside IT circles, however the impact they have (and will) have on all of us cannot be understated.

This is certainly not to suggest or imply support of hackers, their social order, or the nationalistic motivations behind Web security incursions and attacks, but what is the underlying net effect of hackers, nationalists, IT, and security companies? Is the net effect positive, negative, or neutral? Besides the obvious inconveniences and annoyances, the negative side includes companies sabotaged, extorted, and coerced out of uncounted sums of money. IT departments have had to divert resources to the security problem in order to plug the leaks known and identify the holes not yet known, and individuals have had identities stolen and bank accounts drained.

Is there a plus side? Perhaps yes—more companies have been created that specialize in Web security, IT department budgets have been increased to augment their security staffs and tools, and while of questionable value, some (formerly unemployed) people in Asia and elsewhere are now working to help meet the burgeoning demand for malware.

From a dispassionate viewpoint, one might argue that the plusses outweigh the minuses; that is, the response to Web security problems has been more beneficial to the many than harmful to the few. A victim of identify theft or the CEO of a company that was impacted by an attack or extortion will surely disagree.

It should be clear that there will always be concerns over Web security. A certain trend is that knowledge of the security threats arising from Web 2.0 is spreading, and users, developers, and companies are responding with education, new products, and new strategies to mitigate the risks. In this Web 2.0 world of podcasts, blogs, and wikis, there is an unfortunate but real repeating process that helps keep IT security managers employed. As security awareness increases, knowledge increases; as knowledge increases, the potential for new security threats increases. Although security is fleeting, the field of IT security is forever.

REFERENCES

Bock, W. (2006). *Larry Ellison and the network computer that wasn't*. Retrieved December 30, 2007, from http://www.mondaymemo. net/031103feature.htm

Brandon, J. (2007). *Q&A with the forefather of hacking*. Retrieved December 24, 2007, from http://www.pcmag.com/print_article2/ 0,1217,a=213916,00.asp

Brenner, B. (2007). *Black hat 2007: Estonian attacks were a cyber riot, not warfare*. Retrieved December 30, 2007, from http://searchsecurity. techtarget.com/originalContent/0,289142,sid14_ gci1266728,00.html

Brenner, B. (2007). *How Russia became a malware hornet's next*. Retrieved December 30, 2007, from http://searchsecurity.techtarget.com/ originalContent/0,289142,sid14_gci1275987,00. html

Claburn, T. (2007). *Hacker profile becomes more social, adds women*. Retrieved December 24, 2007, from http://www.informationweek. com/shared/printableArticle.jhtml?articleID=2 05101618

Enright, G. (2007). *Web 2.0 vulnerabilities to watch for*. Retrieved July 22, 2007, from http://www. computerworld.com/action/article=9027342

Evers, J. (2007a). *Hacking for dollars*. Retrieved December 24, 2007, from http://www.news. com/2102-7349_3-5772238.html

Evers, J. (2007b). *The security risk in Web 2.0*. Retrieved July 17, 2007, from http://news.com. com/2102-1002_3-6099228.html

Fanning, E. (2007). *Editor's note: Security for Web 2.0*. Retrieved July 17, 2007, from http://www. computerworld.com/action/article=283283

Germain, J. M. (2007). *IT security and the no good, very bad Web app nightmare*. Retrieved December 24, 2007, from http://www.technews- world.com/story/60208.html

Lenssen, P. (2005). *Samy, their hero: Interview*. Retrieved December 29, 2007, from http:blogo- scoped.com/archive/2005-10-14-n81.html

McMillan, R. (2007). *Researchers: Web 2.0 security seriously flawed*. Retrieved December 24, 2007, from http://www.pcworld.com/print- able/article/id,131215

O'Reilly, T. (2005). *What is Web 2.0: Design patterns and business models for the next generation of software*. Retrieved July 1, 2007, from http: www.oreilly.net.com/lpt/a/6228

Orlowski, A. (2005). *Web 2.0 worm downs MySpace*. Retrieved July 17, 2007, from http:// www.theregister.co.uk/2005/10/17/web20_ worm_knocks_out_myspaces/print.html

Shah, S. (2006). *Top 10 Web 2.0 attack vectors*. Retrieved July 17, 2007, from http://www.net- security.org/article.php?id=949&p=1

Tapscott, D., & Williams, A. (2006). *Wikinomics: How mass collaboration changes everything*. New York: Portfolio.

Vijayan, J. (2007). *Six ways to stop data leaks*. Retrieved July 17, 2007, from http://computer- world.com/action/article=285138

Walker, A. (2005). *How and why hackers want to get inside your machine.* Retrieved December 24, 2007, from http://www.informit.com/articles/printerfriendly.aspx?p=425380

Waters, J. K. (2007). *Web 2.0 entails "sleeping giant" security risk.* Retrieved December 24, 2007, from http://www.adtmag.com/print.aspx?id=21499

Chapter VI
Web 2.0 and E-Discovery

Bryan Kimes
Altria Client Services, Inc., USA

ABSTRACT

Companies today face an overwhelming amount of digital information, and many of them are involved at some point in civil litigation. When a company is in the discovery (pretrial) phase of civil litigation, it usually exchanges information, including documents, with the opposing party in the litigation. The Federal Rules of Civil Procedure, which govern civil litigation in federal courts, were amended in 2006 to provide additional guidance to parties with regard to electronically stored information. The management teams of many U.S. corporations are working with their IT departments and lawyers in order to understand the sources of electronically stored information that may be potentially relevant to their litigation. Over the last 20 years, technology has grown increasingly more complex, from the early main-frame and personal computers to sophisticated e-mail and instant messaging applications that enable users to send and receive millions of messages every day. This chapter addresses the issues companies may face related to the discovery of electronically stored information as a result of new communication technologies, including Web 2.0 applications.

INTRODUCTION

Companies today are dealing with new technologies and a growing amount of digital information. Each year, the global information growth is larger than any previous year, and that trend is not showing any signs of slowing down. In 2002, an estimated 5 exabytes of digital information were created worldwide. For reference, 5 exabytes is the equivalent of 37,000 libraries the size of the Library of Congress (University of California at Berkley, 2003). The annual growth is roughly doubling each year, and U.S. corporations are contributing to this trend. Electronic communication technologies, including e-mail as well as next-generation Web 2.0 social technologies (e.g., instant messaging [IM], blogs, and wikis), are also contributing to this rapid growth. For example, Cellular-News reported that Gartner predicts that an estimated 1.9 trillion instant messages were sent worldwide in 2007 ("SMSs to Surpass 2 Trillion Messages in Major Markets in 2008," 2007). These new technologies are transforming modern organizations and their employees. Corporate technology managers are assessing the potential benefits of these new technologies relative to the burden and risk they present to the organization, including that from litigation.

This chapter is not intended to be a comprehensive review of the phases of civil litigation or the Federal Rules of Civil Procedure (FRCP). In addition, the author of this chapter is not a lawyer and the information in this chapter is generalized and not intended for specific situations, and should not be substituted for the advice of a lawyer. The following is an overview of the business issues related to managing electronically stored information that may be required in litigation. By way of background, many companies will face civil litigation, which is when one individual or organization sues another seeking relief, oftentimes for money damages.

E-DISCOVERY BACKGROUND

The *United States v. Microsoft* case, which was tried in 1998, is a famous civil case in which the United States Department of Justice (DOJ) filed an antitrust claim against the software giant alleging it used its monopoly power of the Windows operating system to bundle its Internet Explorer Web browser. The government claimed that other Web browsers, such as Netscape, were not able to compete in the Web browser market due to Microsoft's positioning of Internet Explorer within the Windows operating system. The DOJ won in the trial court, but an appeals court overturned the decision and the case later settled. The Microsoft case was full of headlines and was an example of a case where e-mail played a critical role. The DOJ trial lawyers used internal Microsoft e-mails, many authored by senior executives, including Bill Gates, to demonstrate the company's alleged

strategy to "cut off Netscape's air supply" (United States Department of Justice, 1999).

Civil litigation follows specific procedures. Cases in United States federal courts follow the Federal Rules of Civil Procedure. The Federal Rules define the rules into different categories, including Commencement of Action, Pleadings and Motions, Parties, Deposition and Discovery, Trial, and Judgment. The remainder of this chapter will focus on the discovery phase of civil litigation. During the discovery phase of a case, thousands or even millions of documents may be collected, reviewed, and produced from the files of either party in the lawsuit.

Let us use a hypothetical example to illustrate the process. The Acme Corporation, a fictional product manufacturer, is involved in civil litigation. The case involves a former employee, John Doe. John filed a lawsuit against Acme alleging he was terminated as a result of age discrimination. John Doe, who is the plaintiff, hired a lawyer to represent him in his suit against Acme, the defendant. Acme also hired a law firm to represent it in the case. When the case reached the discovery phase, John's lawyer asked Acme for documents that related to John's termination. Acme's management, working with its lawyers, determined which employees had documents that related to his termination. It instructed specific employees to not discard the documents that related to the issues in the case. Acme's IT director worked with his management to determine the locations where electronic documents that related to the case were stored.

Now, let us walk through three variations of the Acme example at different points in time. In the first variation, Acme terminated John in 1990. In 1990, most companies did not have company-wide e-mail accounts or network servers. Wireless cellular telephones were just getting started and smart phones were still a science fiction concept. The computer systems at Acme, including those used by John and his management, were probably running MS-DOS or Windows 2.0 (the classic

286 PC). If Acme was on the cutting edge of computer technology in 1990, it may have had Windows 3.0, which ran on the 386 powerhouse. In order to respond to the John Doe lawsuit, Acme's management contacted the employees that may have had records that related to John's termination, including the personnel files from John's manager, the human resources (HR) files that related to John and Acme's employment policies. In order to find the electronic documents, Acme's management went to the IT director who managed all of Acme's computer systems. The IT director managed a relatively small system that included a mainframe computer system. The IT director worked with management to find material regarding John's case.

Now let us assume Acme terminated John in 2000. In 2000, Acme had been using e-mail for several years now and employees regularly use e-mail to correspond with each other to get their work done, including personnel matters. Acme had Windows 98 running on employees' desktops, which allowed employees to save documents, for example, in Microsoft Word, to their computers. Employees saved documents to the computers' desktops, local drives, and some network file servers. Acme's management followed a similar process for collecting the documents as it did in 1990. However, because the electronically stored information at Acme has multiplied since 1990, Acme's job to identify the relevant documents has become more complicated. Acme management asked various employees that worked with John, including his manager, to identify the documents that related to the case. It also worked with the IT director to understand how the computer systems were managed and how employees used those systems. Acme's cost associated with the discovery phase of the case has likely grown due to the increased volume of documents that Acme's lawyers needed to review and potentially produce to John's lawyers.

Finally, let us assume that Acme terminated John in 2007. Since 2000, Acme implemented several new technologies to help its employees be more productive and communicate faster. In 2007, Acme used Microsoft Vista with SharePoint. It had Microsoft Exchange 2007 with unified messaging (voice mail integrated into users' e-mail account). Many senior employees have wireless handheld devices that integrate into their e-mail accounts as well as instant text messaging. Acme employees use these new technologies and create more documents on their desktops and rely on electronic communication tools, including e-mail and instant messaging. In 2007, the IT director has to address a more complicated network of computer systems to help management identify those systems that contain documents that relate to John's lawsuit. As a result of the increase in the number of documents, Acme's costs associated with the discovery phase of the case is likely to be even more expensive and time consuming in 2007 than in 2000 due to the higher volume of electronically stored information.

Acme is certainly not alone. Companies all over the world are facing a new generation of technology as new employees, who have been teething on instant messaging, MySpace, and Facebook, join the workforce. For example, many companies convene meetings using Web-based electronic rooms, for example, WebEx, with shared desktops. These next-generation meeting rooms allow participants to attend meetings without ever leaving their desks, and many participants may never meet each other face to face.

Technology managers, like the IT director at Acme, may have a difficult task when they are asked to identify systems and electronically stored information that may contain documents relevant to a lawsuit. Additionally, the technology generation gap is often short relative to the time it takes for courts and litigators to deal with these new issues in actual cases. It can take years for a dispute to make its way into a courtroom. Technology managers are faced with making decisions about how to implement new technology tools without knowing what, how, or when they will have to produce documents in the future.

FEDERAL RULES OF CIVIL PROCEDURE

Companies that find themselves involved in civil litigation follow certain rules. If the case is in a federal court, they use the FRCP; if the case is in a state court, the parties follow the state's rules of civil procedure, which often follow, if not verbatim, the FRCP. Again, this chapter will not be an exhaustive review of the FRCP, but it will touch on a few rules that relate to electronically stored information.

On December 1, 2006, amendments to the Federal Rules of Civil Procedure were submitted by Congress and approved by the Supreme Court. The amended rules specifically address electronically stored information. Let us start with a rule that was not amended, FRCP 26(b)(1), which defines the scope and limits of Discovery.

- **Rule 26(b)(1): Discovery Scope and Limits**
  In General. Parties may obtain discovery regarding any matter, not privileged, that is relevant to the claim or defense of any party, including the existence, description, nature, custody, condition, and location of any books, documents, or other tangible things and the identity and location of persons having knowledge of any discoverable matter. For good cause, the court may order discovery of any matter relevant to the subject matter involved in the action. Relevant information need not be admissible at the trial if the discovery appears reasonably calculated to lead to the discovery of admissible evidence. All discovery is subject to the limitations imposed by Rule 26(b)(2)(i), (ii), and (iii). (U.S. House of Representatives Committee on the Judiciary, 2006)

Now let us return to the Acme example. Why is Acme's IT director's job more complicated in 2007 than in 1990? I suggest to you that it is the result of the explosion of electronic documents, specifically e-mail and other documents stored on Acme's computer systems.

Below is a summary of the electronic-discovery amendments to the Federal Rules of Civil Procedure that this chapter will discuss.

- **Rule 26(a)(1)(B): General Provisions Governing Discovery; Duty of Disclosure; Required Disclosures; Methods to Discover Additional Matter**
  A copy of, or a description by category and location of, all documents, electronically stored information, and tangible things that are in the possession, custody, or control of the party and that the disclosing party may use to support its claims or defenses, unless solely for impeachment. ("Law Library/Court Rules," n.d.)

What Might this Mean for Acme? When Acme's IT director reviewed this amended rule with management and outside lawyers, they discussed, among other things, the computer systems at Acme and thought about a summary of the electronically stored information, such as in databases, servers, and electronic archives, that may be relevant to John's case against Acme.

- **Rule 26(b)(2)(B): General Provisions Governing Discovery; Duty of Disclosure; Discovery Scope and Limits; Limitations**
  A party need not provide discovery of electronically stored information from sources that the party identifies as not reasonably accessible because of undue burden or cost. On motion to compel discovery or for a protective order, the party from whom discovery is sought must show that the information is not reasonably accessible because of undue

burden or cost. If that showing is made, the court may nonetheless order discovery from such sources if the requesting party shows good cause, considering the limitations of Rule 26(b)(2)(C). The court may specify conditions for the discovery. ("Law Library/Court Rules," n.d.)

What Might this Mean for Acme? When Acme's IT director reviewed this rule with management and lawyers, they discussed, among other things, what sources of potentially relevant electronic information that they thought were not reasonably accessible and that they did not intend to search. If John's lawyer wanted Acme to provide documents from one of the sources that Acme disclosed as not reasonably accessible, then John's lawyer could serve a motion to compel the production of information from the sources identified as not reasonably accessible. Acme will then have to explain why the information that John's lawyer is seeking would require undue burden or cost to obtain.

Now let us look at another hypothetical exchange. John's lawyer wants Acme to provide information from an old HR computer system that is no longer active, and Acme considers the old system not reasonably accessible because it would require the IT director to hire a specialized vendor to restore the old system. John's lawyer files a motion to compel in order to obtain the information contained within the computer system. Acme's IT director explained to the court that the request is unduly burdensome; specifically, it will cost Acme US$500,000 to restore the legacy computer system. Acme feels that the burden is excessive relative to the amount John's lawyer is seeking in the case, which is only US$100,000 in money damages. The court will have to weigh these factors when determining whether to permit discovery.

- **Rule 34(a) & (b): Production of Documents, Electronically Stored Information, and Things and Entry Upon Land for Inspection and other Purposes; Procedure**
(a) SCOPE: Any party may serve on any other party a request (1) to produce and permit the party making the request, or someone acting on the requestor's behalf, to inspect, copy, test, or sample any designated documents or electronically stored information—including writings, drawings, graphs, charts, photographs, sound recordings, images, and other data or data compilations stored in any medium from which information can be obtained—translated, if necessary, by the respondent into reasonably usable form, or to inspect, copy, test, or sample any designated tangible things which constitute or contain matters within the scope of Rule 26(b) and which are in the possession, custody or control of the party upon whom the request is served;
(b) PROCEDURE: The request shall set forth, either by individual item or by category, the items to be inspected, and describe each with reasonable particularity. The request shall specify a reasonable time, place, and manner of making the inspection and performing the related acts. The request may specify the form or forms in which electronically stored information is to be produced. Without leave of court or written stipulation, a request may not be served before the time specified in Rule 26(d). The party upon whom the request is served shall serve a written response within 30 days after the service of the request. A shorter or longer time may be directed by the court or, in the absence of such an order, agreed to in writing by the parties, subject to Rule 29. The response shall state, with respect to each item or category, that inspection and related activities will be permitted as requested, unless the request is objected

to, including an objection to the requested form or forms for producing electronically stored information, stating the reasons for the objection. If objection is made to part of an item or category, the part shall be specified and inspection permitted of the remaining parts. If objection is made to the requested form or forms for producing electronically stored information—or if no form was specified in the request—the responding party must state the form or forms it intends to use. The party submitting the request may move for an order under Rule 37(a) with respect to any objection to or other failure to respond to the request or any part thereof, or any failure to permit inspection as requested. Unless the parties otherwise agree, or the court otherwise orders:

(i) a party who produces documents for inspection shall produce them as they are kept in the usual course of business or shall organize and label them to correspond with the categories in the request;

(ii) if a request does not specify the form or forms for producing electronically stored information, a responding party must produce the information in a form or forms in which it is ordinarily maintained or in a form or forms that are reasonably usable; and

(iii) a party need not produce the same electronically stored information in more than one form. ("Law Library/Court Rules," n.d.)

What Might this Mean for Acme? When the Acme IT director reviewed this rule with management and lawyers, they likely discussed, among other things, the options regarding how they would produce documents for John's lawyers. They discussed an upcoming meeting between their lawyers and John's lawyers, during which they would discuss the form of the document production. The Acme IT director has already met with some vendors that provide specialized tools to assist with document productions. The IT director understands that John's lawyer may specify a form of production and if he does not, then Acme will have to produce the documents in the form they are ordinarily maintained at Acme or in a reasonably usable format. Let us assume John's lawyer agreed to accept a production of the relevant documents in Adobe's Portable Document Format (PDF). In addition, Acme provided an accompanying index of metadata including the date, title, author, recipient, document type, and extracted full text.

The amended federal rules have provided organizations and their IT departments with more instruction regarding electronically stored information. However, complying with the obligations associated with electronic discovery can be very difficult for organizations, even those with a modest technology portfolio. Organizations with newer generation technologies may find themselves in a much more complicated situation when faced with discovery in civil litigation.

In a recent *Richmond Journal of Law & Technology* article, Doug Rogers, citing the Sedona Principals,[1] stated "it is unreasonable to expect parties to take every conceivable step to preserve all potentially relevant electronically stored information":

For instance, a party should not have to preserve all possible sources of e-mail simply because it is possible that an existing or former employee, who claims she was harassed, may have forwarded an e-mail from her supervisor to other employees, or because one of the e-mails may have been exported into a .pst file outside of the e-mail folders in the cache of a computer.

Comment 5a to Sedona Principle 5 explains: The obligation to preserve relevant evidence is generally understood to require that the producing party make reasonable and good faith efforts to identify and manage the information that it has identified as reasonably likely to be relevant. Satisfying this obligation must be balanced against the right of a party to continue to manage its electronic information in the best interest of the enterprise, even though some electronic information is necessarily overwritten on a routine basis by various computer systems. (Rogers, 2008, p. 25-26)

Companies like Acme are not alone when working through these issues. Over the past few years, many specialized litigation support vendors have emerged that offer a variety of technology and process solutions to assist organizations and their IT departments in managing the discovery process. In July 2007, one such vendor, Autonomy, acquired another company, Zantaz, which is an e-mail archiving firm, for US$375 million. Soon after the Zantaz acquisition, Autonomy reported a US$70 million deal with an unspecified customer. The customer is believed to be a large global bank that is preparing for a wave of civil litigation in the wake of the subprime mortgage lending crisis. The value of this transaction, which is Autonomy's largest, is reported to be almost double Autonomy's average transaction with a single customer. If this type of transaction is any indication of future business, Autonomy could see a return on the Zantaz acquisition much faster than many anticipated (Mellor, 2008).

Companies and organizations around the world are evolving their technology footprints. Many commentators believe the volume of documents that employees create on new applications are also increasing at a rapid rate, some say exponentially. The legal environment is also evolving and new cases are emerging that deal with new issues regarding electronically stored information. One case that has gained some notoriety is the Columbia Pictures case (*Columbia Pictures Indus. v. Bunnell et al.*). In this case, Columbia Pictures was ordered to capture and preserve data stored in temporary random access memory (RAM), which is very volatile and can be overwritten by the computer system when shutting down, starting up, or simply opening and closing applications.

Some commentators have stated that the judge's holding is limited to the specific facts at issue in this case and generally considered data in computers' temporary RAM to be excluded from discovery because they are so transitory (Jacoby, 2007). Some commentators have expressed that Rule 34, which describes "other data or data compilations stored in any medium from which information can be obtained," would not apply because the RAM data were not easily obtainable. In this case, however, the judge stated that the data stored in this computer system's RAM was "extremely relevant and may be key," and that it was not available anywhere else (Jacoby).

A notable distinction of the temporary, or ephemeral, data at issue in the Columbia Pictures case is the way the specified computer system was configured. Many computer systems use RAM as a memory buffer that will randomly (hence the name *random access*) write some data to help support the application. For example, take an ordinary desktop computer. When a user turns the computer on, the computer will allocate some RAM to support the operating system. If the user then opens Microsoft Word, the computer will allocate more RAM for the application and the associated documents that are open. If the user then opens Excel and closes Word, the RAM assigned to Word is sometimes overwritten in order for the computer to run Excel. The computer, during normal operation, will recycle RAM memory to whatever application(s) needs it. The information stored in RAM, if viewed by a human, would most likely appear as gibberish as it is bits and bytes of computer code that the computer uses to function properly.

Nevertheless, the computer systems at Columbia Pictures, based on its own testimony, had a logging feature that was turned off. The court ordered Columbia to prospectively activate the logging feature and that the prior deletion of RAM was not a violation of the preservation order in the case (Jacoby, 2007).

Instant Messaging is now a ubiquitous technology across grade schools, college campuses, shopping malls, and movie theaters (much to my chagrin). Instant messaging took off in the mid-1990s with the popular ICQ ("I seek you"). This was followed by AOL's Instant Messenger in the late 1990s. Today, there is a variety of open-source instant messaging, or text messaging, applications that run on desktop computers, mobile phones, and other wireless devices. Many instant messaging applications, especially those on mobile phones, are similar to RAM in that many of them do not keep a permanent log of past messages. Many mobile messaging devices keep messages for a short period of time, sometimes only minutes or hours, before they are overwritten or deleted.

IM is slowly invading the workplace. Instant messaging allows employees to communicate faster than e-mail and slightly slower than a real-time phone call. Users can carry on several conversations at the same time. They can create buddy lists, which allow for quicker communication as well as the ability to see if someone is online or not. In a *Wall Street Journal* online article, Mamberto (2007) cites a 2006 study of the American Management Association and the ePolicy Institute that found roughly one third of employees are using IM, many of them without their employers' knowledge. Many corporations and organization are reluctant to deploy IM systems due to security concerns, loss of productivity, and inappropriate use. Despite these reservations, Gartner, an IT research firm, predicts IM will dominate 95% of the workforce of large companies within the next 5 years (Mamberto).

Desktop-computer-based IM applications are slightly different than mobile-phone-based systems, notably with regard to storage. Many desktop-based IM applications provide options for longer term storage, similar to conventional e-mail systems. When Acme's IT director implemented desktop IM, he or she may have worked with the records, compliance, and law department to determine whether Acme needed to include a storage component in the event it would need to save some messages for a longer term purpose, either for business or litigation purposes.

Web 2.0 technologies, including IM, offer employees at large organizations instant access to colleagues across the organization. These technologies flatten out the hierarchical structure of many organizations. Andrew McAfee, associate professor at Harvard Business School, states employees "increasingly react to situations and problems on the fly, not solely by hierarchy" (Mamberto, 2007, p. 2).

The American Bar Association (ABA; American Bar Association Legal Technology Resource Center, 2008) cited a January 2008 *Detroit Free Press* report (Wendland, 2008) that IM text messages obtained from the offices of Detroit Mayor Kwame Kilpatrick suggested he had a 2-year affair with his chief of staff Christine Beatty. Over 14,000 text messages between Kilpatrick and Beatty, who were both married at the time, were exchanged that allegedly illustrated a sexual affair including during official business trips. The lawsuit, which was filed by a former police officer, alleged that he and another officer were fired in retaliation because of their role in an internal investigation that would potentially expose the mayor's affair. Mayor Kilpatrick testified that he did not have an affair with his chief of staff and that he did not retaliate by firing two police officers. The City of Detroit tried to avoid producing the damaging IM text messages, but eventually they were disclosed. The case eventually settled for US$8 million.

The ABA article (2008) further reported that an estimated 20 billion IM text messages are sent each month in the United States alone. The article cited a Gartner report, which estimated that 1.9 trillion text messages were sent worldwide in 2007. The report predicted a 19% increase to 2.3 trillion text messages in 2008. When Acme's IT director implemented desktop IM, he or she worked with the records, compliance, and law department to consider how to train employees on the proper use of IM, similar to the corporate e-mail system.

Blogs (Web logs), wikis (collaborative Web sites), and RSS (really simple syndication) are also on the rise within companies and organizations. These new technologies can offer significant advantages to organizations. Most of the advantages are in response to the limitation of e-mail. For example, a user can subscribe to relevant work sites using RSS feeds as opposed to relying on e-mails from colleagues. E-mail can be a very inefficient way to keep employees updated on a given topic because many employees will overuse the carbon copy (CC) function as a way to inform people on the distribution list. There are two problems with this technique. First, the person sending the message may not know all the people that really need to be informed of the topic. Second, many people on the distribution list may not even care about the message.

One of the advantages of RSS as a communication tool is that users can decide what they are interested in and will subscribe to those topic areas. The RSS technology will notify users of updates and direct them to the source of the information. Many of the RSS sites will keep track of the pages viewed so users do not need to worry about reading articles twice because it is tracked by the system ("The Logic of Blogs and Wikis in the Enterprise," 2005).

Now, let us return to the Acme example, specifically, a project to develop a new product. The Acme project team created an electronic workroom where project team members could save and update important documents related to the product. The workroom had several blogs and wikis for employees to discuss current issues related to the project, including materials, sales strategies, and budgets. Managers who were not working on the project day to day could use the RSS tool to subscribe to the workroom. The manager would be notified when new content had been added to the workroom on a specific topic.

Blogging is still a relatively new technology and companies are still learning and assessing the security risks related to employee blogging. John Browning (2007) of the *Houston Business Journal*, citing a 2006 survey of the Employment Law Alliance, found that about 5% of Americans have a personal blog, while only 15% of their employers have a blogging policy. Additionally, Browning stated that an estimated 27% of adults read blogs according to the Pew Internet and American Life Project. Employees may make seemingly innocent statements on a public blog that can put a company, and the employee, at great risk. For example, if one of the Acme employees working on the new product was at home spending time on a personal blog, he or she may post an entry about how great Acme is and that it has a great future—referencing the new product without actually mentioning it by name. The employee is a hardworking and dedicated individual who really believes in Acme and is proud to work there. The employee may not even have to mention the new product by name but could indirectly disclose trade secrets or forward-looking financial information that could be damaging to Acme. Before the lightening fast World Wide Web, an innocent comment to a neighbor in the driveway presented some risk to the company, but in the days of online blogs, where users from all over the world can easily search and find just about anything on anything, a seemingly innocent comment is now within infinitely greater reach. Again, the employee probably had no intention of making a public statement about Acme's financial future. Many companies have existing policies that govern employee communication, which would generally cover employee blogging. However, the Society for Human Resource Management reports that a small number (3%) of firms have implemented blogging policies specifically (Browning).

CONCLUSION

Employees are faced with new technologies every year, and the current wave of Web 2.0 technologies will soon be replaced with a new generation of tools that will enable employees to share information faster and easier. Information technology managers must make decisions regarding these changing technologies and must work with their management to assess the pros and cons of implementing them. Many IT managers realize that employees will create and store documents on these new systems and those documents may be needed for future litigation. Furthermore, as the overall volume of documents increases as a result of newer technologies, the overall cost to organizations will also likely increase due to the time and expense for lawyers to collect, review, and produce these documents in litigation. As the volume of discoverable electronically stored information grows, the real winners may be the specialized vendors, like Autonomy, that offer specialized document management and litigation support services to companies dealing with huge volumes of data. If the current data-growth trends continue, coupled with increased user adoption of Web 2.0 technologies, then companies, including their management, IT managers, and lawyers, will have a lot of work ahead of them.

REFERENCES

American Bar Association Legal Technology Resource Center. (2008). *Text messaging and the importance of a records retention policy.* Retrieved February 25, 2008, from http://meetings. abanet.org/ltrc/index.cfm?&data=20080204#E6 AADE50-02C7

Browning, J. (2007). Adopting a blogging policy could limit your exposure to legal risk. *Houston Business Journal.* Retrieved February 25, 2008, from http://houston.bizjournals.com/houston/sto-ries/2007/05/28/smallb2.html

Jacoby, C. J. (2007). E-discovery update: Discovery of ephemeral digital information. *Law and Technology Resources for Legal Professionals.* Retrieved February 25, 2008, from http://www. llrx.com/columns/fios19.htm

Law library/court rules. (n.d.). *LexisNexis Applied Discovery.* Retrieved February 25, 2008 from http://www.lexisnexis.com/applieddiscovery/ lawLibrary/courtRules.asp

The logic of blogs and wikis in the enterprise. (2005). *The Gilbane Report, 12*(10). Retrieved February 25, 2008, from http://gilbane.com/ gilbane_report.pl/104/Blogs__Wikis_Technolo-gies_for_Enterprise_Applications.html

Mamberto, C. (2007). Instant messaging invades the office: Companies say it spurs broader collaboration—and scares some bosses. *Wall Street Journal Online.* Retrieved February 25, 2008, from http://online.wsj.com/article/ SB118523443717075546.html

Mellor, C. (2008). Sub-prime crisis god news for legal discovery software. *Techworld.* Retrieved February 25, 2008, from http://www.techworld. com/storage/news/index.cfm?newsid=11042

Rogers, D. (2008). A search for balance in the discovery of ESI since December 1 2006. *Richmond Journal of Law & Technology.* Retrieved May 5, 2008, from http://law.richmond.edu/jolt/ v14i3/article8.pdf

SMSs to surpass 2 trillion messages in major markets in 2008. (2007). *Cellular-News.* Retrieved February 25, 2008, from http://www.cellular-news.com/story/28126.php

University of California at Berkeley's School of Information Management and Systems. (2003). *How much information?* Retrieved January 2, 2008, from http://www2.sims.berkeley.edu/re-search/projects/how-much-info-2003/execsum. htm

United States Department of Justice. (1999). *U.S. Department of Justice proposed findings of fact.* Retrieved February 25, 2008, from http://www. justice.gov/atr/cases/f2600/2613-1.htm

U.S. House of Representatives Committee on the Judiciary. (2006). *Federal rules of civil procedure.* Retrieved February 25, 2008, from http://judiciary. house.gov/media/pdfs/printers/109th/31308.pdf

Wendland, M. (2008). Most text messages just vanish. *Detroit Free Press Online.* Retrieved February 25, 2008, from http://www.freep. com/apps/pbcs.dll/article?AID=/20080125/ COL11/801250422/1081/COL

ENDNOTE

[1] The Sedona Principals: Best Practices, Recommendation & Principles for Addressing Electronic Document Production is a project of The Sedona Conference Working Group on Best Practices for Electronic Document Retention and Production. The Sedona Conference is a non-profit organization of lawyers, consultants, academics and jurist.

Section IV
Virtual Worlds

Chapter VII
Virtual Worlds and the 3–D Internet

Carolyn McKinnell Jacobson
Mount St. Mary's University, USA

ABSTRACT

A virtual world is a computer-based simulated environment, usually modeled after the real world, accessed through an online interface, and inhabited by users in the form of avatars. The purpose of this chapter is to explore how these interactive, immersive environments are being used by a variety of organizations. Although various kinds of virtual worlds are introduced, this chapter focuses on the interactive 3-D virtual world of Second Life, describing its demographics and its features. Ways in which Second Life has been used by businesses, educational organizations, and political entities are then discussed. Legal issues associated with virtual worlds in general and Second Life in particular are raised. The chapter concludes with some ways this technology is expected to evolve in the future.

INTRODUCTION

The Internet is continuing to evolve, and the second phase promises to be as revolutionary as the first. In the early 1990s, the World Wide Web project led to widespread public interest in the Internet as a source of what would become massive amounts of interlinked, hypertext documents and applications. For about the first 10 years, interaction mainly consisted of a person accessing content on the Web. Since the beginning of the 21st century, the Internet has provided a much more dynamic platform, becoming more visual and allowing users to interact with each other in communities and share information in real time. The new Internet is a social medium, and online communities are taking on a new dimension, quite literally, in the form of immersive 3-D virtual worlds.

A virtual world is a computer-based simulated environment, usually modeled after the real world and accessed through an online interface. It is inhabited by users in the form of avatars: two- or three-dimensional graphic characters that may resemble humans, animals, or imaginative creatures that take on fanciful names. These digital doppelgangers can then walk or fly around this virtual world, meeting other avatars, playing games, attending concerts and other events, and carrying on conversations through text chat.

Virtual worlds, sometimes also called digital worlds, have a number of characteristics in common (*What is a Virtual World?*, n.d.). Multiple users share a common space that is depicted visually, ranging in style from 2-D cartoon-like imagery to a more immersive 3-D environment. Any number of users may participate at the same time and interact in real time. These users are able to create, modify, and submit customized content. The virtual world permits and encourages the formation of in-world social groups, which may take the form of clubs, guilds, communities, sports teams, and so forth. The virtual world continues to exist whether or not an individual user is logged on.

THE DEVELOPMENT OF VIRTUAL WORLDS

A Variety of Worlds

A major influence in the development of virtual worlds was Neal Stephenson's science fiction classic *Snow Crash*, published in 1992. The novel is set in two worlds: Los Angeles in the 21st century and the Metaverse, Stephenson's concept of how an online virtual space might evolve in the future. Written before the concept was technologically feasible, the novel has inspired many online virtual worlds today. *Cybertown*, with its futuristic science fiction theme, perhaps comes closest to recreating the Metaverse that Stephenson envisioned.

One of the early visual virtual worlds was Lucasfilm's *Habitat*, a technologically influen-

tial multiparticipant online virtual environment launched in 1985 and designed for Commodore 64 machines. Although it was neither 3-D nor immersive, its graphical user interface (GUI) and a large user base have led to its being regarded as the precursor to today's online communities ("Habitat", n.d.; *VZones*, n.d.).

Virtual worlds come in a variety of forms. Perhaps the largest category is massively multiplayer online role-playing games (MMORPGs), in which the participants assume the role of a specific predefined character, are restricted by rules, and progress through a series of competitive events to a predefined goal. MMORPGs, such as *World of Warcraft* and *EverQuest*, are usually based on a fantasy theme, and players progress through a series of events (e.g., slaying dragons) that require interactions, and perhaps even teaming up, with other players. These games are defined by the large number of players at any given time, and the continued existence of the world in which they interact, even if a given player is logged off.

At the other end of the spectrum are virtual worlds that are more community focused and emphasize socializing rather than gaming. These worlds offer a more unrestricted experience and are more comparable to the cultures associated with text-based chat rooms. Although participants may engage in small-scale, casual games, the focus of these worlds is on socializing in an environment similar to the real world. The participants, represented by avatars, may create this environment and the objects in it. Participants may design and alter their avatars at will, customizing such features as height, weight, skin color, eye color, hairstyle, and dress. Users generally create idealized versions of their real-world appearance, with the avatar being a little thinner, a little taller, or a little more "hip" than its real life counterpart.

Avatars are controlled through keyboard commands and act out a dynamic, unscripted role that reflects their personal motivations. Conversation appears in a bubble above the avatar's head, and interaction takes place in a personal space that the user may choose to create and decorate. The human (real world) sees everything from the perspective of the avatar (in-world): speaking, hearing, and interacting with other "residents" who are nearby. Until recently, communication was restricted to text, although some virtual worlds are now using real-time voice communication through voice over Internet protocol (VoIP).

Virtual Worlds Review (http://www.virtualworldsreview.com) identifies about 30 online virtual worlds, including some 2-D chat communities. One virtual world, *Sora City*, is unique in that it can only be visited with a mobile phone. Most virtual worlds are designed for teens (e.g., *Habbo Hotel*), although some target young children (e.g., *Whyville*, *Virtual Magic Kingdom*) and others target young adults in their 20s and 30s (e.g., *Virtual Ibiza*, *Sora City*). Virtual worlds such as *Moove* and *Traveler* are frequently visited by those in their 40s, 50s, and even 60s. Of course, in-world you can be any age you want to be.

National borders do not restrict virtual worlds. *Dreamville* is based in Malaysia, *Moove* allows for interaction in German or English, and *Playdo* provides graphical chat in English or Swedish. China has its own version of the popular English-language-based *Second Life*. *HiPiHi* is customized for China and targets Internet users less than 40 years of age who are not very tech savvy (McKenzie, 2007). *Habbo Hotel*, created by a company in Finland, has international versions for residents of 19 countries, including Australia, Singapore, Brazil, Canada, the United States, and many European countries.

Admission to some virtual worlds is free, while others may have a free trial period before requiring a monthly fee. Although some of these virtual destinations are strictly for socializing, others have developed in-world economies with their own currencies (e.g., *Gaia Online*, *There*, *Second Life*). These currencies, for which each has its own exchange rate, can be purchased with real-world money and then used in-world to pay for such items as virtual cars, clothing, furniture,

houses, and land. In-world currency can also be converted back to real money. In addition to accepting credit cards online, *Habbo Hotel* offers prepaid cards through Target stores. These cards can then be redeemed online for Habbo coins.

A Variety of Purposes

Virtual worlds may serve a variety of purposes, including social, educational, organizational, political, or just pure entertainment. Social worlds allow participants to meet people and interact in a way that may be viewed as the next step beyond texting. *IMVU* (http://www.imvu.com), for example, describes itself as a chat site that goes "beyond instant messaging," where participants can create a 3-D self, make new acquaintances, and demonstrate their creativity. Rather than simply chatting online, users create avatars that may reflect their real-life personality, or that may provide an opportunity to explore various aspects of their persona (Noguchi, 2005) as users may choose to represent themselves as a butterfly or a mythical animal.

Educational worlds may take numerous forms, including a 3-D replication of a museum, library, or university. Sponsors may include an academic institution, a nonprofit organization, or a corporation. Active Worlds, Inc. has created *The Active Worlds Educational Universe* (AWEDU), a platform that allows teachers and students to explore "new concepts, learning theories, creative curriculum design, and discover new paradigms in social learning" through applications of Active Worlds' technology (*Active World's Educational Universe*, n.d.). Among the more than 80 participants are the Boston Museum of Science, NASA Ames Research Laboratory, the Oslo School of Architecture, and the United Nations.

Some organizations establish their own virtual worlds for business purposes. IBM has purchased several dozen islands in *Second Life* for virtual training and simulations of key business processes (Evans-Correia, 2007). It has also developed its own product, Innov8, to teach business process management and technology skills to university students and young professionals. Players enter a 3-D virtual environment where they may be required to redesign a call center or process an insurance claim (McConnon, 2007a). Johnson & Johnson Pharmaceutical Research and Development has developed a 3-D world called *3DU* (*U* for university) to orient nearly 1,500 new employees to the company's health benefits and ethics policies (McConnon, 2007c). McKinsey & Co. runs an online simulation called *CEO of the Future*, in which players from around the world may be asked to launch a new product and manage it against competitors. Players who increase the value of the company by the largest margin are invited to present their strategies to a panel of McKinsey partners and CEOs from other companies sponsoring the competition (McConnon, 2007c). A 2007 survey of 1,500 members of the eLearning Guild found that over 50% of accounting, banking, and finance companies are investigating the use of some form of immersive-environment video game for work (McConnon, 2007c).

Few virtual worlds are designed specifically for political purposes, although political issues can arise in other worlds as well. One example of a virtual world with a political focus is *AgoraXchange*, based on Thomas More's *Utopia*. In this "large scale interactive social system," participants are challenged to develop a new social environment founded on utopian incentives and rewards in order to see "what kinds of behaviors will emerge" (http://www.agoraxchange.net).

All of these purposes—social, educational, business, political, entertainment, and more—come together in one virtual world that has been attracting a lot of attention.

SECOND LIFE

Dominant among the community-focused 3-D virtual worlds is *Second Life* (http://www.

secondlife.com). Inspired by Neal Stephenson's *Snow Crash* and created by Linden Lab of San Francisco, *Second Life* was launched in June 2003 with several thousand users and nowhere to go: The virtual world was empty (Bell, Pope, Peters, & Galik, 2007; Kirkpatrick, 2007c). Founder and CEO Philip Rosedale wanted to provide a platform rather than a game, allowing the *Second Life* denizens to invent their own world. After 5 months, only about 1,000 users were regularly logging in, but they were starting to create cities, games, jungles, clubs, and imaginative avatars. Three years later, the population hit the 1 million mark. By April 2007, *Second Life*'s population was growing at a rate of 20 to 30% per month (Bell et al.), and according to the *Second Life* Web site, in November 2007, the population surpassed 11 million registered users. Estimates are, however, that only about half a million registered users are active.

Demographics

Who are these people who are logging in? *Second Life* demographic data are not yet well established. However, it is clear that this is truly a global community, with Europeans making up 61% of total users. As of the first quarter of 2007, the fastest growing segment was from the United States, accounting for 16% of total log-ins. The third largest group is Asian Pacific at 13%, with the Middle East and Africa providing only 2% of total active residents (Burns, 2007).

Residents of *Second Life* are not the stereotypical teenage males that one would expect to find on gaming sites. Forty-five percent of *Second Life* participants are women. The median age of residents is 36, and the mean age is 32. You must be at least 18 years old to join; for those younger (13-17 years old), there is a separate *Teen Second Life Grid*. *Second Life* represents a demographic "that is savvy to multiple communication technologies and highly selective in how it receives information" (*Second Life lets CDC be Every-*

where—All at Once, n.d.). One can find college professors teaching classes and librarians setting up information islands. A survey of 150 CIOs found that 12% of them are personally logging in to virtual worlds (Alter, 2007).

The Technology of Second Life

Logging in to *Second Life* requires the proper hardware and software. *Second Life* can be accessed from either a PC or a Mac, and current system requirements can be found on *Second Life*'s Web page (http://secondlife.com/corporate/sysreqs. php). Users can simply sign up at the *Second Life* Web site, create a password, and then download and install client software from Linden Lab.

In contrast to MMORPGs such as *World of Warcraft*, in which much of the graphical content is delivered to the user on a CD-ROM, *Second Life* uses streaming 3-D graphics over the Internet. This streaming media technology makes it possible to deliver live events through *Second Life*. This virtual world runs on 1,800 Debian Linux servers, with multiple copies of the simulation software on each server. As of early 2007, 6,400 simulator software devices, each representing 16 acres of virtual land, tracked activity in this virtual world. A simulator, the equivalent of a Web server, works in conjunction with MySQL databases to track activities on each 16-acre parcel of land. Linden Lab runs four simulators per server, and more than 120 racks of servers were being added weekly in 2007 to accommodate the demand for new land (Carr, 2007).

Active participants represent only a small fraction of registered members. This may be partially explained by the fact that a number of users have found that the technology is difficult to learn, hard to use, and not particularly intuitive. Designing an avatar can take more than an hour (Hillis, 2007). One user commented that she has spent her first hour on *Second Life* "wearing both sneakers and high heels, because [she] couldn't figure out how to discard one pair" (Dell, 2007, p. 49). Help is

available in the form of the Knowledge Base, Orientation Island, and Help Island.

The Knowledge Base (http://www.secondlinfe.com/knowledgebase) consists of guides and how-to articles that explain how things work. Glancing through the topics that are included can help the newcomer solve a problem or simply become familiar with the range of possibilities. The Knowledge Base is supplemented by the *Second Life* wiki, which contains tutorials and general information on writing scripts in the Linden scripting language (LSL). Scripts are short programs that animate objects in *Second Life*. It is not necessary to write scripts to be able to have fun in *Second Life*, but scripting does allow the user to be more creative. For help with a specific issue, go to one of the Linden Lab-sponsored forums (http://forums.secondlife.com/index.php). The Linden blog (http://blog.secondlife.com/) provides information about the latest developments.

The new user first enters *Second Life* on Orientation Island where a short tutorial teaches the basics. The new resident is issued a basic avatar, an attractive young male or female in jeans and a T-shirt. The next stop is Help Island with more tutorials and demonstration areas as well as mentors: longtime residents who volunteer to help new arrivals. At the Freebie Store, one can select outfits and hair types. New residents also receive a number of welcome gifts, including a small house, a drivable vehicle, and landscaping items. Once you are comfortable that you have learned what you need to know, you are off to the mainland where you will also be able to find more mentors and more tutorials, and also decide what kind of virtual life you want to live (Rymaszewski, Au, Wallace, Winters, Ondrejka, & Batsone-Cunningham, 2007).

Features of Second Life

Three features make *Second Life* particularly representative of virtual worlds: the ability to model human behavior through avatars, the development of an in-world economy, and a new platform for almost any kind of application, limited only by one's imagination. As digital versions of real people, avatars allow participants to be whomever they want to be, creating alternate and even fanciful personae while the real-life identity remains hidden. Disguises and masks are not new, having been part of various cultural traditions for centuries. One need only think back to the masquerade balls that were popular in 15th century Italy, the tradition of Mardi Gras, or even Halloween. What is interesting, however, is how people behave when they assume these new identities (Gillen, 2007). Some have suggested that people care about their online identity being trusted (Noguchi, 2005). The playwright Oscar Wilde wrote, "Man is least himself when he talks in his own person. Give him a mask, and he will tell you the truth" (Wilde, 1921, p. 185). Virtual worlds provide a platform for exploring these issues. Unlike anonymous chats and webcasts, virtual worlds allow the participant to interact with a wider audience. It is this feature that makes virtual worlds of particular interest to marketers (Gillen).

Second Life has its own economy and a currency called Linden dollars that can be bought and sold on the LindeX, the official exchange in *Second Life*. The average rate of exchange is approximately 270 virtual Linden dollars (270L$) to one real U.S. dollar. The Linden dollar is a floating currency, and a small fee is charged for currency transactions. Millions of Linden dollars change hands every month in payment for goods and services. In October 2007, nearly 23 million resident transactions took place, ranging from 1L$ to 500,000L$, with 95$ of transactions less than 500L$ (see the *Second Life* Web site for current economic data). Residents can construct, sell, or trade anything from jewelry to office buildings, earning real money for virtual goods and services. In November 2003 Linden Lab made the unprecedented policy decision of allowing users to retain complete ownership of the content they create (Hof, 2006). As the *Second Life* Web site declares, "You create it, you own it—and it's yours to do with as you please."

In-world occupations range from gardener to gunsmith and publicist to private detective. Nathan Keir, a 32-year-old programmer, known in-world as Kermit Quirk, invented a game called *Tringo*. It became so popular in *Second Life* that he has licensed it for use on Nintendo's Game Boy Advance (Hof, 2006; Kirkpatrick, 2007c). An avatar named Janie Marlowe has been so successful with her digital clothing store that her real-life counterpart has quit her day job as a dispatcher and reportedly quadrupled her previous salary (Craig, 2006).

Even virtual possessions need to be put somewhere, so Linden Lab began selling virtual land. What started as 64 acres in 2003 has expanded to over 65,000 acres and is still growing rapidly. Residents can buy a piece of the mainland or a 16-acre private island, which sells for US$1,675 and costs US$295 per month to maintain. The buyer has a choice of various topologies and can place the island in any vacant space. Need more space later? The owner can buy a second island and join it to the first, creating a contiguous space. IBM, for example, owns 24 islands. According to Kirkpatrick (2007c, ¶ 23), "In essence, customers are renting space on the 1,800 servers that store the digital representation of the land" (Carr, 2007).

Land can be rented, subdivided, and even sold at a profit (Bell et al., 2007; Kirkpatrick, 2007c). Unlike the real world, Linden can simply create more digital real estate to meet demand. Ailin Graef, known by her avatar's name of Anshe Chung, has reportedly amassed real-world assets of over US$1 million by buying and developing *Second Life* real estate and then renting or selling it (Carr, 2007). Be prepared, though. Someone may build on an adjoining piece of land and block your view, or additional digital waterfront property can be created, adversely impacting your real estate value. It is estimated that over US$1 million is spent daily on all products and services, generating a GDP (gross domestic product) of about US$220 million, according to *Second Life*'s Web site.

The creation of this new economy has attracted attention, although no one knows just yet how to make the best use of this new interactive world. What is clear is that this new phenomenon goes beyond the realm of online video games, typically involving one or two players, to a world of about 40,000 inhabitants logged in at any given time. It is also clear that *Second Life* is not just a destination, but also a venue for interaction. According to Pierre M. Omidyar, eBay Inc. founder and chairman and an investor in Linden Lab, "This generation that grew up on video games is blurring the lines between games and real life" (Hof, 2006, p. 74).

As of August 2007, 65 real-world companies and dozens of universities had moved into the virtual world of *Second Life*, according to the *Second Life* Web site. The following section takes a look at some of the opportunities and challenges created by this 3-D virtual world for business, education, and political entities.

Business in Second Life

The corporate world has used *Second Life* for a variety of purposes, including marketing, building relationships with customers and partners, recruiting new employees, holding conferences, and creating business value. Most of these initiatives have been experimental attempts to discover how to best use this new medium, and some of them have been quite successful, however one might define that. Because the hard sell goes against the social mores of *Second Life*, organizations are focusing on softer goals centered on activities, educational events, and an attractive environment (Robinson, 2007). In May 2007, *Computerworld* identified eight top corporate sites worth visiting: IBM, Pontiac, Sun Microsystems, Dell, Reuters, Cisco, H&R Block, and Best Buy (Brandon, 2007).

At the top of the list is IBM, which has established a separate corporate unit for 3-D Internet and is spending millions of real-life dollars developing what it believes will be the next big thing. Hoping to establish itself as the leading consultant for virtual worlds, IBM announced a US$100 million initiative in November 2006 to fund 10 projects, including the creation of a 3-D Internet of virtual worlds for businesses and consumers (Nichols, 2006). IBM chairman and CEO Sam Palmisano made the announcement through his online avatar in a virtual-world replica of China's Forbidden City (*IBM CEO Sets Sights on the 3-D Internet*, 2006). Three key areas that IBM is exploring are virtual commerce and applying virtual worlds to business problems, new models of collaboration and education, and new ways to interact with the broader community in virtual worlds (Charlesworth, 2006). IBM regularly uses *Second Life* for global conferencing with many of its executives represented as avatars (Villafania, 2007). Big Blue has developed an extensive list of virtual-world guidelines for its employees, covering such topics as appropriate behavior and appearance as well as intellectual property issues.

IBM partnered with Circuit City to open a prototype online store to try to understand what 3-D virtual worlds might mean for multichannel retailing. The Circuit City store allows customers to browse the aisles, pick up products, and examine them. Other immersive features allow customers to test all the functions on a new digital camera or camcorder, and to create a model of their living rooms so they can choose the optimal screen size for a television (Charlesworth, 2006).

Educationally, IBM has developed a new interactive 3-D business simulator called Innov8, designed to teach a combination of business and information technology skills to university students and young professionals who have grown up playing video games. Players enter a virtual world where they can "visualize how technology and related business strategies affect an organization's performance. Together, users can visualize business processes, identify bottlenecks, and explore 'what if' scenarios before the technology is deployed" (*IBM Introduces Video Game to Help University Students Develop Business Skills*, 2007). Corporate customers will be charged for the game based on the amount of customization required for a particular client. However, Innov8 is available free to universities through IBM's Academic Initiative. As of November 2007, more than 30 colleges and universities have incorporated the game into their curricula.

IBM also envisions the 3-D world as a different way to think about work and collaboration. With 40% of IBM employees working off-site, the company is studying ways to prepare managers to lead a global workforce, gathering information and assessing risk (McConnon, 2007a), and has already hosted meetings in the virtual world: "More than 320 IBM researchers, developers, and consultants are already working with dozens of customers in virtual worlds to see how these future 3-D Internet environments can change business and society" (*IBM CEO Sets Sights on the 3-D Internet*, 2006). In the words of IBM strategist Irving Wladawsky-Berger, "Could we be at the onset of v-business?" (Baker, 2006).

Second only to IBM in terms of encouraging innovation in virtual worlds is Pontiac, which opened a *Second Life* dealership to sell customizable versions of its Solstice GXP. Although Pontiac only offers the one model, the customer can have it in any color he or she wants, to include stripes, polka dots, or plaid. Within the first 5 months, the Pontiac dealership had sold 7,000 virtual cars—no small feat in a culture where everyone can fly and teleport (Sponder, 2007). Proceeds are donated to the nonprofit Electronic Frontier Foundation (Morath, 2007). The dealership is surrounded by 96 virtual acres known as Motorati Island. Pontiac offered free land to 30 carefully selected entrepreneurs to develop anything related to cars. Car fans had soon built a monster truck course,

a radio-controlled car racetrack, a movie drive-in, and an area called AskPatty.com for women car enthusiasts. Pontiac also sponsors multiple entertainment events to bring an audience to the island (Morath, 2007; Wagner, 2007a).

Two of Pontiac's Japanese competitors are also in *Second Life*. Scion offers three models (the xA, xB, and tC) that can be fully customized and sell for about 300L$. At the current exchange rate, that is a little more that US$1 . One resident customized the boxy xB by turning it into a toaster on wheels (Morath, 2007). Nissan offers its Sentra free of charge to residents. Someone named Toast Alicious gives you a token, which you deposit in a vending machine the size of an office building, and out pops your virtual car. In the first few weeks, Nissan distributed about 2,500 virtual Sentras (Valdes-Dapena, 2006).

A third top site is Sun Microsystems, Inc., which hosted the first Fortune 500 press conference in *Second Life* in October 2006. One of the speakers was Sun chief researcher John Gage, who appeared in avatar form. After the event, attendees were invited to tour the Sun Pavilion, which includes "an outdoor theater, meeting spaces, and kiosks that exhibit videos highlighting recent Sun innovations, events, and Sun customer projects" (*Sun Microsystems Takes a Leap into Virtual World Second Life*, ¶ 2). Although the company has no plans to sell its products directly on *Second Life*, it does provide a forum for Java code developers to "try out code, share ideas, and receive training" (Needle, 2006, ¶ 2).

Dell, fourth on the list of top corporate sites, offers a number of attractions on Dell Island, including a replica of the Dell factory. Residents may sit down at a drafting table to configure their own XPS 1710 PCs. Linden dollars can be used to purchase a virtual PC, but if you want one delivered to you in real life, a link will take you to a secure Web site that will require your real name and U.S. currency. Dell Island also has a museum with a walk-through model of a Dell computer and a mock-up of the dorm room at the

University of Texas at Austin where Michael Dell began his now multibillion dollar company (Del Conte, 2006; Krazit, 2006).

One might not expect a venerable news outlet known for its financial and business reporting to have a presence in *Second Life*, yet Reuters is number five on the *Computerworld* list of top sites. Reuters' goal is two-fold: to bring real world news to the virtual world, and to bring financial and cultural stories from *Second Life* to the real world. Adam Pasick, a Reuters media correspondent and the first virtual bureau chief, stated that editorial rules from the real world will still hold, although one might question a conflict of interest between writing about a virtual world and establishing a presence there (Glaser, 2006): "Being unbiased, being accurate, being fast, all the things that Reuters strives for, they hold true in just about any environment in which you would want to report the news" ("All the Virtual News that Fits," 2006, ¶ 13). There is one major difference: *Second Life* participants who read a story of interest will be able to teleport immediately to the Reuters Atrium to discuss headline news with other residents ("All the Virtual News that Fits"; Brandon, 2007; Terdiman, 2006).

Other media organizations have opened virtual news bureaus as well. CNN has opened the I-Report hub where it hopes to gather reports from residents about events in the virtual world: "When Second Life residents observe an in-world event they deem newsworthy, they can take snapshots, shoot video, or write a report about the event and submit to CNN" (*CNN Enters the Virtual World of Second Life*, 2007, ¶ 6). Reports selected for publication can be viewed in both the virtual and the real worlds. The CNN in-world hub consists of a news desk for editorial discussions and an amphitheater for larger audience events, including appearances by CNN anchors and correspondents (*CNN Enters the Virtual World of Second Life*).

Perhaps it is not surprising that *Wired* magazine and CNET, publications that cover technology, would have a presence in a virtual world as well. The overall architecture of *Wired*'s offices defy Newtonian physics and once inside, suggest that one is inside a computer as the visitor is surrounded by circuit boards, serial ports, and graphics cards. The amphitheater offers various lectures and events. CNET's structure is a facsimile of its real-life headquarters and includes an amphitheater, office space, and an outdoor patio where CNET reporters can talk about stories they have written (Glaser, 2006).

Sixth on the list is Cisco, which has constructed a virtual campus in *Second Life* designed to build community. More interactive than Dell's site, Cisco's presence consists of two private islands and four islands that are open to the public, each having a different focus. The marketing island, named Cisco Systems, has three amphitheaters for large classes and a model of the future real-world field for Oakland Athletics. The island is designed to educate the customer, focusing on product information, product launches, and streaming video. Demonstrations allow potential customers to learn about network switches and see how they fit into a data center. Another island, named Cisco Island, is geared toward community interaction and customer support, and consists of areas where people can sit and talk. Cisco Networking Academy, which offers networking classes in nine languages and 150 countries in the real world, now offers its training in one of two private classrooms on Cisco Island (Brandon, 2007; Holden, 2006; LaPlante, 2007; Wagner, 2007a).

More recently, Cisco has launched its own version of a 3-D world modeled after a trade show and designed to provide a place for the company's "40,000 global channel partners to meet and exchange information with application providers and device manufacturers" (Hamblen, 2007, ¶ 1). Labeled the Industry Solutions Partner Network (ISPN), the site is not open to the public, and users do not have to design an avatar or purchase Cisco dollars. However, they can chat with one another.

Where there is money, even the virtual kind, there is a need to manage it, and H&R Block appears in seventh place on *Computerworld*'s list of top corporate sites in *Second Life*. Looking for new ways to connect clients with tax professionals, H&R Block provided real-life tax professionals in avatar form to answer tax questions free of charge during the height of the 2007 tax season (March 13-April 17). Visitors are also able to watch a video about H&R Block's new tax preparation product, Tango, which sells for 100L$ (less than US$1) and retails for US$70 in the real world. The Tango product bundle includes a variety of virtual scooters to tour H&R Block Island, virtual dancing shoes that allow the wearer to do a tango-style dance, as well as other Tango apparel. The company also hosts various events and activities outside of tax season (*H&R Block Launches First Virtual Tax Experience in Second Life*, n.d.). Tax implications of virtual-world transactions are discussed later in this chapter.

Other financial organizations have gotten into the act as well. Wells Fargo has created a virtual community called Stagecoach Island to involve 18- to 24-year-olds with the brand and teach them personal finance (Hoover, 2007). Set up as a game, visitors are given $50 (virtual) to spend on such things as snowboarding. By answering financial questions and developing their financial knowledge, they can win more money (Robinson, 2007). The Dutch bank ABN AMRO opened a virtual office that is an exact copy of its real-life building. When avatars (controlled by real people using keyboards and mice) had difficulty maneuvering through the small door, the bank made the walls permeable so they could fly through—probably not a good idea for a bank in the real world. On ABN AMRO's Young Professionals Island, 25- to 35-year-olds can receive training on how to interview for a job or how to finance a first home. At biweekly investment seminars, the audience can pose questions to avatars representing real-life investment professionals.

For assistance in purchasing a new home, a resident can visit the virtual offices of Coldwell Banker, one of the largest real estate brokerage firms in the Untied States. The virtual offices are staffed with avatars of real-world real estate professionals who sell virtual real estate and also answer questions about the real world. One outcome the brokerage firm had not anticipated was the number of people who stopped by to ask about employment opportunities. Some wanted to be virtual realtors, but others were interested in jobs in the real world (Capps, 2007; Kirkpatrick, 2007a).

Last on *Computerworld*'s list of top sites is Best Buy, which opened Geek Squad Island. Avatars representing real-world technical support staff wear short-sleeve button-down shirts, black pants, and a badge. During regular office hours (6 p.m. to 3 a.m. EDT, 7 days a week), Geek Squad agents dispense free computer advice. Real-world product purchases are handled via phone or e-mail. The island also features a future home that includes an interactive exhibit of new home technology. Best Buy plans to add other events and offerings as the island evolves (Brandon, 2007; Freed, 2007).

Although not on the *Computerworld* list, at least one other site merits mention for the innovative ways it is soliciting customer feedback. Starwood Hotels, owner of the Westin, Sheraton, and W chains, has tested a virtual prototype of a moderately priced loft-style hotel in *Second Life*, called aloft. Hotel prototypes usually consist of a single room displayed at a trade show, and this is the first time a company has created a complete version of a hotel to act as a laboratory: "Staffers will observe how people move through the space, what areas and types of furniture they gravitate towards, and what they ignore" (Jana, 2006, ¶ 4). Visitors to aloft are also encouraged to share ideas on a blog. The virtual hotel is both a testing ground and a marketing strategy, with the ultimate goal being to attract young, tech-savvy customers to the aloft brand. The first aloft hotels are planned for Lexington, Massachusetts; Tucson, Arizona; Cherry Creek, Colorado; and the San Francisco and Philadelphia airports (Jana).

A final *Second Life* business application, which cuts across a number of organizations, is the recruitment event. Some employers are experimenting with virtual job fairs for interviewing entry- to junior-level professionals. CMP Technology held a 7-day professional development conference, with keynote speakers, panels, and networking breakfasts for about 1,000 senior program developers, represented by avatars. Hewlett-Packard, Microsoft, Verizon Communications, and Sodexho Alliance all participated in a virtual job fair hosted by TMP Worldwide Advertising & Communications in May 2007. The process works very much as it does in the real world. Applicants, who must be registered on *Second Life* and have an avatar, upload a resume to a TMP Web site and request an interview. Participating companies are assigned a specific location on TMP Island where they meet with and interview job seekers. The recruiter screens the resumes and schedules interviews. TMP's first virtual job fair boasted 872 registered job seekers and 750 requested interviews. Two hundred and nine registrants were interviewed and at least three hires could be traced to the event (Athavaley, 2007; Evans-Correia, 2007).

Virtual recruiting events are not without their mishaps, some of which relate to learning how to maneuver an avatar (Athavaley, 2007; Evans-Correia, 2007). One job applicant flew into the interview room instead of walking. Another, not knowing how to sit in a chair, ended up sitting on top of it. Still a third reached into his virtual inventory for his resume and accidentally handed the Hewlett-Packard recruiter a beer can instead (Athavaley). Recruiters are not immune to such glitches, either. During one interview, Bain & Co., the global management consultancy, witnessed a partner's avatar unintentionally slump over and appear to be asleep (Athavaley). Then there was the challenge of knowing what time to show up,

as the real-life counterparts to the avatars lived in different time zones (Athavaley). Glitches aside, such events allow companies to reach a wider audience in an international job market.

Education in Second Life

Universities from around the globe have also planted their flags in the virtual world. More than 150 colleges from the United States and 13 other countries have established a presence in *Second Life* (Foster, 2007c). Activities represent various levels of involvement, ranging from building virtual models of campuses to teaching, conducting research, and supervising student projects. (See http://simteach.com/wiki/index.php?title=Institutions_and_Organizations_in_SL#UNIVERSITIES.2C_COLLEGES_.26_SCHOOLS for a complete list of institutions from around the world that have a site in *Second Life*.)

Several universities have built virtual versions of their campuses in *Second Life*. Case Western Reserve University built a replica of its 550-acre campus to provide tours for those unable to travel to Cleveland. Prospective students are able to see buildings from the outside and also to go into a virtual dormitory and look out the window at the athletic fields. Current students conduct the tours—as avatars, of course. One freshman tour guide at first designed her avatar to look like she does in real life. Later she changed her hair color to purple and then to green. One visitor showed up as a frog, hopping around the virtual campus. Although the university has no statistics on the impact of this project, it certainly conveys an image of an institution that is at the forefront of technology (Young, 2007).

The Massachusetts Institute of Technology (MIT) uses *Second Life* to help incoming freshmen select a dormitory that best matches their lifestyle. MIT is using part of their in-world island to represent the various campus residence halls: the artsy dorm, the jock house, the dorm for computer geeks, and a number of others. The models were created as part of a university-sponsored competition in which 47 students participated. The winning team received US$500 (Foster, 2007b).

Not all projects have such happy endings. Woodbury University in Burbank, California, established an island to allow communications students to experience novel forms of human interaction. Linden Lab, the company that runs *Second Life*, closed the island after administrators at Woodbury reportedly ignored warnings that avatars affiliated with the school were allegedly attacking other sites and behaving in a racist and harassing manner, behavior known in-world as "griefing." Although the island was removed, no Woodbury faculty or student avatars were apparently exiled. Linden Lab requires all new users to agree not to act in a harassing manner and not to damage digital property or computer systems while in world. It also reserves the right to close accounts and remove islands without prior notice and without compensation for any loss incurred (Foster, 2007a).

Other institutions have also had problems with troublemakers. On Ohio University's island, a user with a virtual gun entered a building and began shooting at bystanders. The university closed its island until the virtual gunman could be removed (Carnevale, 2007).

Behavior policies are common in virtual worlds. When Steve Taylor, the director of academic computing services at Vassar College, created a digital replica of the Sistine Chapel on the college's island, he also created a code of conduct for anyone wanting to visit the site. The code requested that avatars behave with the respect due for what many consider a sacred place in the real world. Based on the positive feedback, the college is now considering adopting a similar policy for anyone visiting Vassar's island (Carnevale, 2007).

Faculty and students at a number of universities are also teaching and conducting research in *Second Life*. In spring 2007, the New Media Consortium, a not-for-profit consortium of learning-focused organizations that explores uses of new media and technologies, surveyed educators to learn about their activities, attitudes, and interest related to *Second Life*. Fifty-four percent of the 209 respondents reported they were involved with some type of education-related activity in the virtual world. Among the most commonly reported activities were taking a class (43%) or teaching in *Second Life* (29%), supervising real-life educational class projects and/or class activities in-world (24%), or conducting research (24%). Eighteen percent reported that they had held virtual office hours in-world (*Spring 2007 Survey: Educators in Second Life*, 2007).

Faculty conducting educational activities in *Second Life* represent almost all disciplines. Among 104 faculty responding, about one third were engaged in some type of faculty development, training, or support activity. Considering the relative newness of this medium, this figure is not surprising. Twelve percent of those engaging in educational activity are in technology or computer science. Other disciplines represented include social sciences, art, theater, English, healthcare, sciences, and business. The diversity of disciplines represented suggests that the possibilities are limited only by the imagination (*Spring 2007 Survey: Educators in Second Life*, 2007).

In the technology and computer science category, respondents reported activities in digital entertainment, educational technology, and media. Social sciences applications included cultural studies (a field trip in *Second Life* for a sociogeography assignment), women's studies, media psychology, political philosophy, global issues, and criminology and substance abuse (*Spring 2007 Survey: Educators in Second Life*, 2007). A professor in Bradley University's multimedia program chose the culturally diverse *Second Life* as the medium for his ethnography class to conduct field research rather than the riskier environment of downtown Peoria, Illinois. Students meet regularly in-world as avatars in a "boardroom in the sky," and on Saturday nights, Professor Beliveau (his in-world name) can be found playing guitar and singing before an online audience (Foster, 2007c).

Art, theater, and performance activities are also common. *Second Life* has been used for classical music and orchestral performances, digital storytelling, and a graphic-design history course. Music industry students have had assignments to promote, market, and produce concerts in *Second Life* (*Spring 2007 Survey: Educators in Second Life*, 2007). Architecture students at Montana State University have used the virtual world to brainstorm and create rough prototypes of buildings prior to developing complete architectural specifications (Carr, 2007). Steve Taylor, Vassar College's director of academic computing services, created a replica of the Sistine Chapel in about 8 weeks. Taylor, known in-world as Stan Frangible, used electronic images he found on the Internet to construct his representation of the famed chapel. In *Second Life*, visitors can view the ornate interior of the chapel and fly up to the barrel-vaulted ceiling to get a closer look at Michelangelo's frescos. Taylor hopes that his project will inspire others to create additional educational venues in *Second Life*, whether they be outdoor environments to study ecology or replicas of famous buildings (Foster, 2007c).

Survey respondents suggested several activities for English, writing, languages, and the liberal arts. The study of foreign languages certainly lends itself to in-world activities, providing the platform for avatars from around the globe to practice a second language and discuss cultural differences. Literature can also be brought to life through the creation of virtual worlds. An English instructor at Lehigh Carbon Community College has created three-dimensional in-world models of various literary locations, including the abyss in Dante's *Inferno*, depicted as a half-frozen, half-fiery pit lined with steps. Students in a contemporary fiction class were assigned to place photos of well-known figures on the steps,

based on their assessment of the appropriate level of hell for that person. At Montclair State University, students can immerse themselves in a setting from Gloria Naylor's novel *Mama Day* or walk along a sylvan trail from Nathaniel Hawthorne's short story *Young Goodman Brown*. Central Missouri State has a grant to recreate Harlem, New York, from the 1920s era, including cabarets and other activities. A freshman English composition class at Ball State University writes about their observations in *Second Life*, including how avatars form communities and a comparison of in-world and real-world identities. The instructor is a pink-haired avatar known as Intellagirl Tully (Bell et al., 2007; Foster, 2007c).

Healthcare and social services also lend themselves to virtual-world applications. Atlanta-based Centers for Disease Control and Prevention (CDC) has entered *Second Life* to share real-world information about public health. Represented by Hygeia Philo (named after the Greek goddess of health), the CDC is using the medium to learn "how people seek, find, and use public health information" (*Second Life lets CDC be Everywhere—All at Once*, n.d., ¶ 4). It will use this information to structure its Web sites and improve responses to questions from the public. The National Library of Medicine is also providing healthcare information on their HealthInfo Island. Other health-related organizations using this platform include the following:

- The University of California at Davis Medical Center developed virtual clinics to train emergency medical workers. The CDC funds the project.
- The American Cancer Society offers support group meetings, virtual lectures delivered by avatar doctors, and other events. A recent fundraising marathon brought in more than US$115,000 in real money.
- The March of Dimes is building a virtual neonatal intensive care unit for education about preterm births.

- Stanford University built virtual operating and emergency rooms to train doctors.
- Britain's National Health Service constructed a complete digital hospital.
- A University of California psychiatrist created a virtual psychiatric ward complete with disembodied voices to help medical personnel better understand schizophrenia (Craig, 2006; Stein, 2007).

Individuals have also caught on to the concept, forming in-world support groups for cancer, cerebral palsy, cystic fibrosis, strokes, and other maladies. After suffering a stroke, Susan Brown was unable to walk in real life, but in the virtual world, she could run, dance, and even fly. John Dawley, who has a form of autism, has begun learning how to interact with others by practicing with avatars. Recent experiments in Japan are even showing how electrical changes in the brain can be used to control a keyboard or a mouse, allowing people with severe paralysis to maneuver an avatar through the virtual areas in *Second Life* without moving a muscle (*Disabled Could Think Their Way Around "Second Life,"* 2007). Researchers warn that these virtual-world experiences may not work for everyone, but that is to be expected (Stein, 2007).

In the sciences, students can immerse themselves in a virtual world to study astronomy, biology, geoscience, or nanotechnology. Jean-Claude Bradley, a chemistry professor at Drexel University, uses *Second Life* to show his class molecules in three dimensions, allowing the students to walk around the molecule as they discuss it (Sussman, 2007). Another instructor reported building virtual ecological educational environments. A class can also visit the in-world International Spaceflight Museum.

Business activities can include entrepreneurship and starting a virtual business without the need for venture capital. Students can study the principles of economics in a virtual economy with a currency exchange, where waterfront property can be created when there is a demand. Economists at the University of Chicago are studying whether people behave differently in a virtual world than they do in a real laboratory. People will participate in a test known in economics as the public-goods game to assess their altruistic tendencies (Foster, 2007d).

Libraries are also an important part of *Second Life*. The 259-member Alliance Library System rented a small building in the virtual world to see what role libraries might play in that environment. Other potential partners approached them almost immediately about developing library services and resources. As of 2007, the *Second Life* library, known as the Information Archipelago, consists of a collection of 17 islands that comprise a virtual library. Ten of these islands are virtual libraries, averaging 5,000 visitors per day. The remaining seven islands are library partners: sites for special events and projects (Bell et al., 2007).

Residents request books, reference services, and access to resources. Books are available in several formats. Several publishers, including Penguin Books and Bantam Dell, have established a presence, displaying their publications and providing links to their real-world Web sites for actual sales. Reference service can be provided either face to face (avatar to avatar), virtually, through e-mail, or by instant messaging. OCLC (Online Computer Library Center) has made Question-Point and WorldCat available in-world through June 2008. Twenty librarians each volunteer 2 hours a week to staff the reference desk. Patron queries are evenly divided between questions about *Second Life*, the Information Archipelago, and traditional library questions. Residents are referred to their real-world libraries for access to commercial databases due to the cost involved (Bell et al., 2007). As for library fines for overdue books, one library in North Carolina has set up a fines paying machine in *Second Life* that accepts Linden dollars (Basiat, 2007).

Politics in Second Life

Politics has also found its way into the virtual world, and it will no doubt have a role to play in the U.S. presidential elections of 2008. John Edwards launched his presidential campaign in *Second Life* in February 2007. Edwards' campaign sees this as an appropriate venue to address such issues as Net neutrality, which the candidate supports, and the digital divide. It is also a way to reach a broader audience for issues such as the environment, which are both national and global. Residents can e-mail Edwards with comments and questions (Werribee, 2007).

Edwards is not the first politician—nor is he expected to be the last—to create an avatar of himself in *Second Life*. Former Virginia Governor Mark Warner had a digital double when he thought he might be running for president (Maney, 2007). Philippines President Gloria Macapagal-Arroyo activated her avatar to launch the Philippine National Innovation Strategy in the National Innovation Summit in Makati. Her secretary of science and technology, Estrella Alabastro, joined her in-world. They can be found in the IBM Innovation Center, one of the sponsors of the Innovation Summit.

Avatars are known to support political and charitable events. On January 27, 2007, more than 120 *Second Life* residents from all over the United States and seven other countries showed up on the steps of a virtual Capital Hill in Washington, DC, to support the national peace march. In the spirit of a true political rally, some carried placards reading "Avatars Against the War" and others displayed the peace sign reminiscent of demonstrations in the 1960s. Another group, calling itself Midnyte Childs, sponsored an in-world event to raise money for Coats for Kids, a real-world organization that provides warm winter coats for those who cannot afford to buy them.

Several countries have set up embassies in *Second Life*. The Maldives opened the first virtual embassy, referred to as Diplomacy Island. The island includes an academy that holds forums relating to modern diplomacy. It also hosts conferences on Internet issues regarding privacy, security, and the digital divide. Visitors to the embassy are able to ask an avatar ambassador about visas and trade issues. The Maldives Foreign Ministry sees this virtual world as a new means "for diplomatic representation and negotiation, especially for small and developing countries that have limited diplomatic outreach in the real world" (Page, 2007, ¶ 8).

Other countries that have opened virtual embassies include Serbia and Estonia. Serbia's goal is not so much to create a virtual embassy as it is to connect with the estimated 2 to 4 million Serbs who live outside of their homeland, especially the Internet-savvy youth (Kimban, 2007). Also planned is a museum in honor of Nikola Tesla, Serbian inventor and engineer, known for his work in the study of electricity and magnetism. In addition, many large companies, tourist agencies, and banks are expected to develop sites on Serbia Island. Telekom Srbija, the national telephone and Internet provider, is one of the main sponsors of the project (Kimban).

Estonia, the Eastern European nation that was formerly a Soviet Republic, wants to use its presence in *Second Life* to promote the country to those not able to travel there in the real world. Housed in a virtual postmodernist building that includes artwork and meeting spaces, Estonia's virtual embassy hopes to use its presence in *Second Life* to encourage communication with countries where it has no real-world representation (Riley, 2007).

Legal Issues and Second Life

Virtual worlds, like the real world or any other client application, involve legal issues as well as the usual risks associated with IT security, access management, confidentiality, and corporate image (Broersma, 2007). *Second Life*, with its in-world economy and a policy that allows residents to legally own their virtual creations, gives rise to issues covering in-world commerce, taxation, gambling, crime, and even law enforcement. According to Jorge Contreras, Jr., an intellectual property attorney in Washington, DC, "Virtually every aspect of real life is getting duplicated" (Davis, 2007, ¶ 13).

Philip Rosedale, chief executive of Linden Lab and creator of *Second Life*, has resisted policing the online community that has been developed by users. According to the "Terms of Service," Linden Lab has the "right but not the obligation" to resolve disputes. Of particular interest is the following clause, which can be found on its Web site:

As a condition of access to the Service, you release Linden Lab (and Linden Lab's share-holders, partners, affiliates, directors, officers, subsidiaries, employees, agents, suppliers, licensees, distributors) from claims, demands and damages (actual and consequential) of every kind and nature, known and unknown, suspected and unsuspected, disclosed and undisclosed, arising out of or in any way connected with any dispute you have or claim to have with one or more users of the Service. (*Second Life*, http://secondlife.com/corporate/tos.php)

Legal issues came to the forefront when about 100 residents came together in 2006 for a virtual town meeting to discuss a crime wave. They wanted to know what Linden Lab was going to do about a program, referred to as Copybot, which lets users copy various unique objects and buildings that residents had created. They were also concerned about viruses that could allegedly steal members' identifying information. Some residents were calling for an official system of law and order (Holohan, 2006).

What would a system of justice look like in a virtual world? How would such a system handle political, legal, and economic issues? What kinds of punishments would be imposed and by whom? What about issues such as intellectual property, taxes, fraud, competition, defamation, privacy,

and even employment? (Yes, some in-world avatar-run businesses employ other avatars.) How would the virtual world's system reconcile the perspectives of various legal systems from around the world? The country of Portugal set up an arbitration center in *Second Life*, although the center has no legal authority to enforce its decisions (Davis, 2007).

One of the basic issues is that of identity. Avatars generally assume fanciful names, thus hiding the true identity of the persons controlling the digital representations. Linden Lab must reveal the programming code for the images that users create so that other users can see those images and interact with them. However, personal information regarding the identity of those users is protected on Linden's own servers (Holohan, 2006). Even in cases such as the political figures referred to earlier, how does one know that the avatar who shows up is actually the person it claims to be?

Another fundamental challenge in-world is the protection and infringement of intellectual property rights: "Virtual world residents can make, buy, and modify digital replicas of most major real-world branded products, from Ferraris to football kits" (Naylor, 2007, ¶ 3). Residents can also purchase media screens preloaded with infringing copies of music videos, television programs, and movies (Naylor, ¶ 4). One resident created and copyrighted a virtual sex device (essentially software code written in Linden scripting language) for sale in-world. He has now filed a copyright infringement lawsuit against the unknown owner of an avatar named Volkov Catteneo, alleging that Catteneo began selling unauthorized copies of the object (Davis, 2007). While such lawsuits have unique challenges (e.g., obtaining the real-world identity of the avatar's owner; Bugeja, 2007a), there are also some advantages. Everything that happens in *Second Life* is captured on computer servers. Assuming the logs are retained, events can be replayed, as they happened, to provide evidence (Davis).

Financial issues represent an area of concern and fuzziness, and taxes fall into that area. Under United States tax law, any earnings of real U.S. dollars that occur within virtual worlds are reportable to the Internal Revenue Service (IRS). However, it is not clear if transactions that occur in Linden dollars and do not involve any real-world currency are taxable. Some would argue that profits that are generated in, and remain in, a virtual world are taxable because there is an exchange of items of economic value. Bartering, for example, involves trading goods or services without the exchange of real money, and that is a taxable event in the United States. Others suggest that as long as the activity stays in the virtual world it should not be taxable. A spokesperson for the IRS offered the following perspective: "Any time someone wins a tangible prize or award, the value is reportable as taxable income. An accumulation of 'points' would not result in tax consequences, but redeeming or selling them for money, goods, or services would" (Wong, 2007, ¶ 12). Considering the interest of the Joint Economic Committee of Congress in *Second Life*'s economy, it is anticipated that this tax question will be resolved, at least in the United States, in the not-too-distant future.

Gambling was also a significant activity in *Second Life*, representing 5% of the virtual world's economy (Naone, 2007). Numerous casinos provided poker, slot machines, and blackjack. Seeking guidance on virtual gaming activity, Linden Lab invited the FBI to visit *Second Life* and take a look around. Shortly after, in August 2007 the company announced that it was banning gambling, citing "conflicting gambling regulations around the world" (Konrad, 2007, ¶ 3). Linden Lab also threatened to report violators to authorities. It is not yet clear what effect this might have on the economy, although numerous users have complained that the ban was "a heavy-handed move to restrict freedom" (Konrad, ¶ 6).

Virtual worlds can also take a toll on interpersonal relationships. Marriage, divorce, and cybersex are common in *Second Life*. This can become an issue when someone in a real-world relationship also becomes involved with someone in a virtual world. Researchers have only begun to study virtual relationships, but according to Byron Reeves, a professor of communication at Stanford University, they are finding "people respond to interactive technology on social and emotional levels much more than we ever thought. People feel bad when something bad happens to their avatar, and they feel quite good when something good happens" (A. Alter, 2007, ¶ 5). On a neurological level, researchers are finding that our brains may not distinguish between virtual worlds and real ones (A. Alter). Although cyber affairs are not legally defined as adultery unless they cross over into the real world, they may be cited as grounds for divorce and can affect alimony and child custody decisions in some states in the United States (A. Alter).

Although islands can be designated as private and visitors to those islands can be restricted, there is still a great deal of violence, assault, and sexual content in *Second Life*. Academics who are considering using *Second Life* with their students should consider carefully whether they are willing to accept responsibility for anything that might happen between avatars. Linden Lab has acknowledged that assault and harassment are the two most common violations in *Second Life* (Bugeja, 2007b). Harassment can include a number of behaviors, including "impeding movement through the use of primitives [the fundamental building blocks of all *Second Life* objects], continuous instant messaging and other unwanted contact, sexual harassment [and] verbal abuse" ("What is Online (or 'Cyber') Harassment?" 2006). According to Linden Lab, there is an added "creep factor" when the harasser is an anonymous avatar ("What is Online (or 'Cyber') Harassment?").

Who is responsible if a student files a complaint for being exposed to virtual shootings or offensive behavior by other avatars? In its "Terms of Service," Linden Lab describes itself as a distributor of content that "has very limited control, if any, over the quality, safety, morality, legality, truthfulness, or accuracy of various aspects of the Service" (*Second Life* Web site, "Terms of Service," ¶ 1.2). Would professors take their students on a field trip to that kind of a neighborhood in the real world (Bugeja, 2007b)? Add to that the anonymity of users, and the situation becomes more complicated.

Michael Bugeja, director of the School of Journalism and Communication at Iowa State University, suggests that there may be a conflict between Linden Lab's "Terms of Service" and freedom-of-information laws that govern public universities. He asked Robin Harper, Linden Lab vice president for marketing and community development, if her company would provide the identity of a *Second Life* resident if a code violation occurred on the university's virtual campus. She replied that the information would not be provided without a subpoena (Bugeja, 2007a). Paul N. Tanaka, general counsel for Iowa State University, describes the potential conflict as follows:

Even though the records created by avatars may not be part of a university activity and therefore are not public records, the fact that the activity occurs in the university's virtual space will result in instances in which we would want to have access to information, such as the identity of avatars to investigate misconduct affecting a member of our university community. The lack of ability to have access to such information should give administrators reason to reconsider using such services. (Bugeja, 2007a, ¶ 10)

Bugeja (2007a) raised a number of other issues addressed through Peter Gray, an account executive at Lewis Global Public Relations, which represents Linden Lab. Specifically, the company pointed out that the "Terms of Service" forbids harassment and the vast majority of residents

adhere to these standards. In cases where it does occur, residents can mute an object or avatar that is bothering them and/or use one of the built-in tools to prevent, discourage, or report abuse. Disputes between residents are best settled between residents, although Linden Lab does "participate in dispute resolution to the extent that is appropriate for a platform provider" (Bugeja, 2007a). Gray points out that educational organizations can create private campuses that are accessible only to registered students and faculty. Educators can also take advantage of the resources provided by the *Second Life Grid* (http://secondlifegrid.net) and the *Second Life* education mailing list (http://secondlifegrid.net/programs/education).

FUTURE DIRECTIONS

In 2007, Linden Lab announced it would release open-source versions of its client software for Windows, Mac OS, and Linux while retaining control of the proprietary software code for its back-end services. This release will allow independent programmers to modify the software used to control avatars, communicate with other users, and conduct transactions in the virtual economy. Users create most of *Second Life*'s in-world content, and Linden executives estimate that over 15% of users are currently producing 7 million lines of code per week in the Linden scripting language. "We feel we may already have a bigger group of people writing code than any shared project in history, including Linux," said Linden CEO Philip Rosedale (Kirkpatrick, 2007b, ¶ 7). Many in that group are professional programmers at companies such as IBM, Sun, and Autodesk. It is anticipated that the move to open source will foster further innovation and growth (Kirkpatrick, 2007b).

One of the newer features in *Second Life* is voice, added in August 2007 using Vivox technology. Within a few months, about one third of residents were using voice (Wagner, 2007b).

Previously, avatars could only communicate through text chat. This new feature is expected to lead to new forms of in-world entertainment, including karaoke and comedy clubs. Voice has been rather controversial among current residents. On the one hand, *Second Life* has communities of users who are deaf or autistic, and it is feared that those who choose not to use it will be considered second-class citizens. On the other hand, it will open the community to those who may have physical challenges that limit their ability to use a keyboard (Wagner, 2007c). Early in 2008, avatars will be able to get real-world phone numbers and receive phone calls from real-world phones. Other voice-related plans include "voice fonts," which will allow residents to create "realistic and intelligible" sounds (Wagner, 2007b).

New technology is also anticipated that will eventually allow avatars to migrate from one virtual world to another. The time and effort required to create an avatar is seen as a barrier to growth since few users are expected to want to repeat this process in multiple worlds. For avatars to be able to move freely among worlds would require that companies agree on standards. One need only to think of similar battles over standards (e.g., HD DVD vs. Blu-ray DVD) to realize what a challenge it might be to agree on what those standards should be (Hillis, 2007; McConnon, 2007b).

Several organizations are already working on such open technologies. The Multiverse Network Inc. has developed avatars that can migrate among worlds that are created using Multiverse software tools. To encourage experimentation, the company gives away its tools. Another group, the Web3D Consortium, is working to develop an open-standards file format called X3D for developing 3-D objects and scenes. The result would be an Internet that allows the user to move among Web sites and virtual worlds in much the same way that we currently move from reading online text to watching a video clip on YouTube. Gartner Research estimates that by 2011, "80 percent of Internet users and major companies will have

avatars, or digital replicas of themselves, for online work and play" (McConnon, 2007b, ¶ 4).

CONCLUSION

Virtual worlds represent a relatively immature technology, and organizations are still exploring how these 3-D worlds might be used to serve real-world purposes. Just as the Web evolved from "a medium for academics and hobbyists to one that supports corporate commerce and marketing" (Carr, 2007, ¶ 6), Sandy Kearney, director of the virtual-worlds program at IBM, forecasts that virtual worlds may be the next big thing, and that new businesses will be created in 3-D worlds just as they were on the Web (Carr). As of 2007, however, there are still occasional problems with slow software and communications links that sometimes fail, problems that must be overcome if virtual worlds are to become an economic platform for business (Carr). Despite these challenges, larger companies such as IBM, Sun, and Intel have become seriously engaged in virtual worlds (Broersma, 2007), and Kearney suggests companies that experiment with this technology now may have an advantage later on (Carr).

To be successful in this brave new world of 3-D requires thinking differently about the Web. As we have seen, organizations tend to enter *Second Life* by replicating the kinds of activities they undertake in the real world. In most cases, this has met with limited success, as indicated by deserted venues with little traffic (*Gartner Says 80 Percent of Active Internet Users Will Have a "Second Life,"* 2007). To attract residents, venues must incorporate ways to interact and engage with people and avatars (Wagner, 2007a). "The quickest way to become a ghost town in Second Life is to set up shop in a virtual world 'just to be there,'" says Giff Constable, VP of Electric Sheep, a virtual-world media company and designer of a number of corporate sites in *Second Life* (Capps, 2007, ¶ 3). When Cisco Systems launched its *Second*

Life site, it started with static displays providing information about its products. When the displays did not attract residents, Cisco replaced them with meeting rooms and coffee shops, and had to expand from one to three amphitheaters to accommodate the increased traffic (Wagner, 2007a).

Offering a product is not enough; there has to be some value to the community (Wagner, 2007a). Rather than simply replicating a hearing aid, for example, Constable suggests building a community of people with a hearing disability and allowing them to share their experiences (Capps, 2007). Campfire, a marketing agency, developed the very successful Motorati Island for Pontiac by giving away land to residents to develop automotive-related sites and activities. "This is not the kind of place where you have a salesperson avatar trying to collect leads...you have to stand back and let them explore you," says Mark-Hans Richer, marketing director for Pontiac (Capps, sidebar).

Mitch Wagner (2007a), writing for *InformationWeek*, recommends ignoring both the hype and the backlash in the business press about *Second Life*, pointing out that *Wired* magazine had first praised and then bashed the virtual world. Adult-oriented areas have received a lot of coverage for their strip clubs and outlandish behavior, but according to CEO Philip Rosedale, they comprise less than 18% of the land in *Second Life*. Rather than focus on some of the negatives, which might be found anywhere on the Web, look at the demographics of the residents. Half a million people log in regularly, a number that continues to grow rapidly (Wagner, 2007a). That is equivalent to a small city—bigger than Atlanta, Georgia, and smaller than Washington, DC. Many of the residents are software developers and IT managers with money to spend on high-end computers and fast Internet connections. They tend to be early adopters and have time to spend exploring a virtual world. They spend more than US$1 million in-world every 24 hours, paying for land, objects, clothing, or experiences. Considering that in-world site

development costs start at around US$20,000 to US$30,000, with annual costs averaging between US$100,000 and US$300,000, the risk of failure is minimal when compared to marketing budgets of major advertisers (Capps, 2007; Wagner, 2007a). In fact, the risk of not getting into *Second Life* may be much greater than the risk of jumping in too soon (LaPlante, 2007).

Serious risks exist related to IT security, access management, confidentiality, and corporate reputation (Broersma, 2007), and anyone planning to develop an in-world presence should make use of the tools available on *Second Life* to control access to one's land. Griefers have been known to attack prominent sites and events including Toyota's Scion Island and John Edwards' presidential campaign site. The Toyota attack involved a collection of suspended missiles appearing on Scion Island, accompanied by loud machine noises. John Edwards' site was plastered with Marxist and Leninist slogans, and griefers harassed visitors (Wagner, 2007a). Such incidents can be minimized through proper use of the software tools Linden Lab provides. University campuses, for example, can establish lists of approved visitors to their private islands.

Although *Second Life* has been officially out of beta since 2003, it still has bugs, and software updates are issued several times a month. The user interface can be confusing and difficult to learn. *Second Life* servers can only handle a maximum of 78 avatars in one location, although alternate arrangements can be made to accommodate larger crowds. However, consider the evolutions, or perhaps revolutions, that we have already seen: from command-line interfaces to GUIs, from Gopher to Google, and from static Web-based documents to dynamic hyperlinks. It will take some time to work out all the problems, but the potential is there. As Michael Monello, a partner at Campfire, phrased it, "The fact that so many people are willing to engage with [virtual worlds], despite the problems, demonstrates how powerful they are" (Wagner, 2007a).

At its Gartner Symposium/ITxpo 2007: Emerging Trends event, Gartner Consulting predicted "the majority of active Internet users and major enterprises will find value in participating in this area in the coming years" (*Gartner Says 80 Percent of Active Internet Users will Have a "SecondLife,"* 2007). However, Gartner also cautions their corporate clients to limit their investments in virtual worlds "until the environments stabilize and mature," suggesting that business use will lag behind individual consumer use. The consulting firm offers five laws for those participating in virtual worlds (*Gartner Says 80 Percent of Active Internet Users will Have a "Second Life"*):

- Virtual worlds are not games, but neither are they a parallel universe (yet).
- Behind every avatar is a real person. Expectations for behavior and culture are still developing, and corporate users must consider corporate image.
- Be relevant and add value. So far, companies have not been successful in creating an "effective, profitable sales channel" in a virtual world.
- Understand and contain the downside. In a world with adult content, activities in public areas could tarnish corporate image or brand.
- It will take some time before market pressures lead to a merging of virtual worlds into fewer open-source environments that permit assets and avatars to move easily from one to another.

Virtual worlds are still in the early experimental stages. Their potential is not fully understood and appropriate business models have not yet been developed. In spite of the concerns, this trend is predicted to have a significant impact in the next 5 years (*Gartner Says 80 Percent of Active Internet Users will Have a "Second Life,"* 2007).

REFERENCES

Active World's educational universe. (n.d.). Retrieved November 26, 2007, from http://www.activeworlds.com/edu/awedu.asp

All the virtual news that fits. (2006, October 16). *Wired.* Retrieved September 1, 2007, from http://www.wired.com/techbiz/media/news/2006/10/71954

Alter, A. (2007, August 10). Is this man cheating on his wife? *Wall Street Journal,* p. 1.

Alter, A. E. (2007, August 23). A second life: 10 Web 2.0 Apps CIOs personally use. *CIO Insight.* Retrieved August 27, 2007, from http://www.cioinsight.com/print_article2/0,1217,a=213943,00.asp

Athavaley, A. (2007, June 20). A job interview you don't have to show up for. *The Wall Street Journal,* p. D1.

Baker, S. (2006, November 15). IBM on Second Life: More than PR. *BusinessWeek.* Retrieved September 1, 2007, from http://www.businessweek.com/the_thread/blogspotting/archives/2006/11/ibm_on_second_1.html?chan=search

Basiat, S. (2007, November 4). *Library allows students to pay fines in Second Life.* Retrieved November 28, 2007, from http://www.slnn.com/article/library-fine-paying-machine

Bell, L., Pope, K., Peters, T., & Galik, B. (2007, July/August). Who's on third in Second Life? *Online, 31*(4), 14-19.

Brandon, J. (2007, May 2). The top eight corporate sites in Second Life. *Computerworld.* Retrieved November 19, 2007, from http://www.computerworld.com

Broersma, M. (2007, August 12). *Virtual worlds pose business risks.* Retrieved October 11, 2007, from http://www.washingtonpost.com/wp-dyn/content/article/2007/08/13/AR2007081300007.html

Bugeja, M. J. (2007a, November 12). Second Life, revisited. *The Chronicle of Higher Education.* Retrieved November 12, 2007, from http://chronicle.com/weekly/v54/i12/12c00101.htm

Bugeja, M. J. (2007b, September 14). Second thoughts about Second Life. *The Chronicle of Higher Education.* Retrieved September 14, 2007, from http://chronicle.com/weekly/v54/i03/03c00101.htm

Burns, E. (2007, May 4). *Second Life users top 1.3 million in March.* Retrieved December 6, 2007, from http://www.clickz.com/3625769/print

Capps, B. (2007, May 28). How to succeed in Second Life. *Advertising Age, 78*(22), 6.

Carnevale, D. (2007, July 13). Colleges find they must police online worlds. *The Chronicle of Higher Education*, p. A22.

Carr, D. F. (2007, March 1). Second Life: Is business ready for virtual worlds? *Baseline.* Retrieved March 4, 2008, from http://www.baselinemag.com/c/a/Projects-Management/Second-Life-Is-Business-Ready-For-Virtual-Worlds

Charlesworth, A. (2006, December 19). Circuit City and IBM launch 3-D Web store. *ITNews.* Retrieved December 7, 2007, from http://www.itnews.com.au/Tools/Print.aspx?CIID=70445

CNN enters the virtual world of Second Life. (2007, November 12). Retrieved November 12, 2007, from http://www.cnn.com/2007/TECH/11/12/second.life.irpt/index.html?iref=newssearch

Craig, K. (2006, February 8). Making a living in Second Life. *Wired.* Retrieved November 12, 2007, from http://www.wired.com/gaming/virtualworlds/news/2006/02/70153

Davis, P. (2007, August 10). "Second Life" avatar sued over virtual sex device. *USA Today.* Retrieved December 7, 2007, from http://www.usatoday.com/tech/webguide/internetlife/2007-08-10-virtual-sex-lawsuit_N.htm

Del Conte, N. T. (2006, November 14). *Dell to see PCs on Second Life.* Retrieved December 8, 2007, from http://www.pcmag.com/article2/0,1895,2059016,00.asp

Dell, K. (2007, August 20). Second Life's real-world problems. *Time, 170*(8), 49.

Disabled could think their way around "Second Life." (2007, November 27). Retrieved December 8, 2007, from http://www.news.com

Evans-Correia, K. (2007, August 23). *Second Life job fairs boost IT prospects.* Retrieved December 8, 2007, from http://searchcio.techtarget.com/originalContent/0,289142,sid19_gci1269191,00.html?trac=NL-48&ad=601108&asrc=EM_NLN_2046654&uid=3195005

Foster, A. L. (2007a, July 13). The death of a virtual campus illustrates how real-world problems can disrupt online islands. *The Chronicle of Higher Education*, p. A22.

Foster, A. L. (2007b, June 11). MIT's virtual dormitories for freshmen. *The Chronicle of Higher Education.* Retrieved December 8, 2007, from http://chronicle.com/wiredcampus/index.php?id=2143?=atwc

Foster, A. L. (2007c, September 21). Professor Avatar. *The Chronicle of Higher Education*, pp. A24-A26.

Foster, A. L. (2007d, July 6). Virtual worlds as social-science labs. *The Chronicle of Higher Education*, pp. A25-A27.

Freed, J. (2007, April 4). Best Buy offers help in "Second Life." Retrieved December 9, 2007, from http://www.msnbc.msn.com/id/17953078

Gartner says 80 percent of active Internet users will have a "second life" in the virtual world by the end of 2011. (2007, April 24). Retrieved December 6, 2007, from http://www.gartner.com/it/page.jsp?id=503861

Gillen, P. (2007, May 7). Giving Second Life a first chance. *B to B, 92*(6), 13.

Glaser, M. (2006, October 23). *Wired, CNET, Reuters agog over Second Life.* Retrieved December 8, 2007, from http://www.pbs.org/mediashift/2006/10/virtual_journalismwired_cnet_r.html

Habitat. (n.d.). *Wikipedia.* Retrieved November 21, 2007, from http://en.wikipedia.org/wiki/Habitat_(video_game)

Hamblen, M. (2007). *Second Life for a Cisco virtual press conference: Fly on over!* Retrieved November 21, 2007, from http://blogs.computerworld.com/node/6496

Hillis, S. (2007, October 10). Open borders sought for virtual worlds. *Boston.com Business.* Retrieved October 11, 2007, from http://www.boston.com/business/technology/articles/2007/10/10/second_life_ibm_in_open_borders_for_virtual_worlds/?rss_id=Boston+Globe+--+Technology+stories

Hof, R. D. (2006, May 1). Virtual world, real money. *BusinessWeek*, pp. 72-82.

Holden, R. (2006, December 6). *Cisco gets a Second Life.* Retrieved December 8, 2007, from http://www.thestreet.com/pf/newsanalysis/second-life/10326341.html [Note: Virtual reporter Robert Holden is known in the real world as Robert Holmes.]

Holohan, C. (2006, November 21). The dark side of Second Life. *BusinessWeek.* Retrieved December 8, 2007, from http://www.businessweek.com/print/technology/content/nov2006/tc20061121_727243.htm

Hoover, J. N. (2007, May). Wells Fargo taps Web 2.0. *Wall Street & Technology, 25*(5), 25.

H&R Block launches first virtual tax experience in Second Life. (n.d.). Retrieved December 9, 2007, from http://www.hrblock.com/presscenter/articles/secondrelease.jsp

IBM CEO sets sights on the 3-D Internet. (2006, November 14). Retrieved December 7, 2007, from http://www-03.ibm.com/press/us/en/photo/20632.wss

IBM introduces video game to help university students develop business skills. (2007, November 6). Retrieved March 2, 2008, from http://www.03.ibm.com/press/us/en/pressrelease/22549.wss

Jana, R. (2006, August 23). Starwood Hotels explore Second Life first. *BusinessWeek.* Retrieved December 9, 2007, from http://www.businessweek.com/innovate/content/aug2006/id20060823_925270.htm

Kimban, D. (2007, November 19). *Small country has big plans for Second Life.* Retrieved November 29, 2007, from http://www.slnn.com/article/serbia-island

Kirkpatrick, D. (2007a, March 23). Coldwell Banker's Second Life. *Fortune.* Retrieved December 9, 2007, from http://money.cnn.com/2007/03/22/technology/fastforward_secondlife.fortune/index.htm

Kirkpatrick, D. (2007b, January 8). Second Life to go open source. *Fortune.* Retrieved September 3, 2007, from http://money.cnn.com/2007/01/07/technology/secondlife.fortune/index.htm

Kirkpatrick, D. (2007c, January 23). Second Life: It's not a game. *Fortune Small Business.* Retrieved September 3, 2007, from http://smallbusiness.aol.com/start/startup/article-partner/_a/second-life-its-not-a-game/20070130134209990001

Konrad, R. (2007, August 2). Second Life bans gambling. *ABC News.* Retrieved December 7, 2007, from http://abcnews.go.com/Technology/wireStory?id=3438941

Krazit, T. (2006, November 14). Dell sets up "Second Life" shop, offers PCs to residents. Retrieved December 8, 2007, from http://news.zdnet.com/2100-9595_22-6135497.html

LaPlante, A. (2007, February 3). Second Life lessons: Cisco, IBM pace corporate push into virtual worlds. *InformationWeek*. Retrieved December 8, 2007, from http://www.informationweek.com/news/showArticle.jhtml?articleID=197001839&pgno=1&queryText=

Maney, K. (2007, February 4). The king of alter egos is surprisingly humble guy. *USA Today*. Retrieved November 19, 2007, from http://www.usatoday.com/tech/news/2007-02-04-second-life-rosedale_x.htm

McConnon, A. (2007a, June 14). IBM's management games. *BusinessWeek*. Retrieved September 26, 2007, from http://www.businessweek.com/print/technoloyg/content/jun2007/tc20070613_838152.htm

McConnon, A. (2007b, August 13). Just ahead: The Web as a virtual world. *BusinessWeek*, pp. 62-63.

McConnon, A. (2007c, August 13). The name of the game is work. *BusinessWeek*. Retrieved March 5, 2008, from http://www.businessweek.com/innovate/content/aug2007/id20070813_467743.htm

McKenzie, H. (2007, April). Hype sparks rash of 3-D world launches in Asia. *Media*, p. 5.

Morath, E. (2007, January 26). Automakers connect with hip, young buyers in virtual world. *Detroit News Online*. Retrieved January 29, 2007, from http://www.detnews.com/apps/pbcs.dll/article?AID=20070126

Naone, E. (2007, November/December). Financial woes in Second Life. *Technology Review, 110*(6), 13.

Naylor, D. (2007, May 17). Virtual environments create their own legal problems. *New Media Age*, p. 17.

Needle, D. (2006, October 11). *Sun finds a home in Second Life*. Retrieved December 7, 2007, from http://www.internetnews.com/dev-news/article.php/3637411

Nichols, S. (2006, November 14). IBM to fund "3-D Internet" project. *ITNews*. Retrieved December 7, 2007, from http://www.itnews.com/au/Tools/Print.aspx?CIID=68316

Noguchi, Y. (2005, November 22). Self 2.0: Internet users put a best face forward. *Washington Post*, p. A01. Retrieved December 6, 2007, from http://www.washingtonpost.com/wp-dyn/content/article/2005/11/21/AR2005112101787.html

Page, J. (2007, May 24). *Tiny island nation opens the first real embassy in virtual world*. Retrieved November 22, 2007, from http://technology.timesonline.co.uk/tol/news/tech_and_web/article1832158.ece

Riley, D. (2007, December 5). *You're not in the USSR any more: Estonia opens an embassy in Second Life*. Retrieved December 8, 2007, from http://www.techcrunch.com/2007/12/05/youre-not-in-the-ussr-any-more-estonia-opens-an-embassy-in-second-life

Robinson, K. (2007, September 1). Virtual worlds: Another world, another business. People are using avatars to develop businesses and have fun in virtual worlds such as Second Life. *The Banker*. Retrieved November 12, 2007, from http://proquest.umi.com.proxymu.wrlc.org/pqdweb?index=0&did=1334571311&SrchMode=1&sid=1&Fmt=3&VInst=PROD&VType=PQD&RQT=309&VName=PQD&TS=1197220110&clientId=31813

Rymaszewski, M., Au, W. J., Wallace, M., Winters, C., Ondrejka, C., & Batsone-Cunningham, B. (2007). *Second Life: The official guide*. Hoboken, NJ: John Wiley & Sons, Inc.

Second Life. (n.d.). Retrieved from http://www.secondlife.com

Second Life lets CDC be everywhere—all at once. (n.d.). Retrieved December 6, 2007, from http://www.cdc.gov/about/stateofcdc/everywhere/secondLife.htm

Sponder, M. (2007, March 29). *Pontiac Second Life case study*. Retrieved December 7, 2007, from http://www.webmetricsguru.com/2007/03/pontiac_second_life_case_study.html

Spring 2007 survey: Educators in Second Life. (2007). Retrieved November 27, 2007, from http://www.nmc.org/news/nmc/sl-educator-survey

Stein, R. (2007, October 6). Real hope in a virtual world. *Washington Post*, p. A01.

Sun Microsystems takes a leap into virtual world Second Life. (2006, October 10). Retrieved December 7, 2007, from http://www.sun.com/smi/Press/sunflash/2006-10/sunflash.20061010.2.xml

Sussman, B. (2007). Teachers, college students lead a Second Life. *USA Today*. Retrieved December 7, 2007, from http://abcnews.go.com/print?id=3439059

Terdiman, D. (2006, October 26). Reuters' "Second Life" report talks shop. *CNET News.com*. Retrieved December 8, 2007, from http://www.news.com/Reuters-Second-Life-reporter-talks-shop/2008-1043_3-6129335.html

Valdes-Dapena, P. (2006, November 18). *Real cars drive into Second Life*. Retrieved December 7, 2007, from http://www.cnn.com/2006/AUTOS/11/17/2nd_life_cars/index.html

Villafania, A. (2007, November 26). *Arroyo activates virtual self in Second Life*. Retrieved December 7, 2007, from http://technology.inquirer.net/infotech/infotech/view_article.php?article_id=103122

Virtual Worlds Review. (n.d.). Retrieved from http://www.virtualworldsreview.com

VZones. (n.d.). Retrieved November 21, 2007 from http://www.virtualworldsreview.com/vzones

Wagner, M. (2007a, August 21). Five rules for bringing your real-life business into Second Life. *InformationWeek*. Retrieved August 22, 2007, from http://www.informationweek.com/showArticle.jhtml?articleID=201500141

Wagner, M. (2007b, December 7). Second Life residents to get calls from the real world. *InformationWeek*. Retrieved December 7, 2007, from http://www.informationweek.com/showArticle.jhtml;jsessionid=D0UJGWOJENP0MQSNDLRCKHSCJUNN2JVN?articleID=204702181&queryText=Second+Life+residents+to+get+calls

Wagner, M. (2007c, August 2). Second Life voice set to leave beta. *InformationWeek*. Retrieved December 7, 2007, from http://www.informationweek.com/story/showArticle.jhtml?articleID=201202659

Werribee, E. (2007, February 10). *US presidential candidate John Edwards launches campaign in SL*. Retrieved November 28, 2007, from http://www.slnn.com/article/edwards08

What is online (or "cyber") harassment? (2006, May). *Second Opinion Police Blotter*. Retrieved December 16, 2007, from http://secondlife.com/newsletter/2006_05/html/police_blotter.html

What is a virtual world? (n.d.). Retrieved November 21, 2007, from http://www.virtualworldsreview.com/info/whatis/shtml

Wilde, O. (1921). *Intentions* (14th ed.). London: Methuen & Co.

Wong, G. (2007, March 9). Second Life's looming tax threat. *CNNMoney.com*. Retrieved March 13, 2007, from http://money.cnn.com/2007/03/02/technology/sl_taxes/index.htm

Young, J. R. (2007, May 18). Case Western Reserve U. builds virtual campus to woo prospective students. *The Chronicle of Higher Education*, p. A29.

Chapter VIII
Web 2.0, Virtual Worlds, and Real Ethical Issues

Sue Conger
University of Dallas, USA

ABSTRACT

Social networking sites, enabled by Web 2.0 technologies and embodied in role-playing virtual worlds, are gaining in popularity and use both for recreational and business purposes. Behavioral controls can be regulated through program code restrictions, rules of conduct, and local norms. Most vendor hosts of virtual worlds use code restrictions sparingly, restricting only overtly illegal activities. Otherwise, all worlds publish some form of rules of conduct and rely on the development of in-world local norms to regulate behavior. As a result, many unethical forms of behavior have arisen, including griefing, fragging, and industrial espionage. There is no sure method of solving the unethical forms of behavior unless strong social norms develop; therefore, users must take precautions when acting in virtual worlds to understand how to avoid or deflect virtual attacks of different types.

INTRODUCTION

Web 2.0 technologies enable more complex Internet capabilities than ever before. Sites such as *Second Life* (http://www.secondlife.com), *World of Warcraft* (http://www.worldofwarcraft.com), MySpace (http://www.myspace.com), and Zwinky (http://www.zwinky.com) are all examples of types of massive multiplayer online role-playing games (MMORPGs or abbreviated RPGs; MMORPGs, 2007). RPGs all have some common characteristics: a persistent environment that can be shaped by the player who assumes an identity for the game; the player's avatar, that is, his or her identity for the game; and a role that may be self-defined or taken from some book, movie, or other motivator, for example, a fantasy environment.

An avatar is a "graphical image that represents a person as on the Internet" ("Avatar," 2008).

Avatars can be human, animal, or fantasy, depending on the game and the player's disposition. Avatars can be gendered or genderless, dressed or nude, representative of the real-life persons they portray or not. In reality, an avatar is a fancy cursor that provides an alter ego for the participant. Individuals in the games are encouraged to take on an avatar that is consistent with the artificial world context and, therefore, different from the real-world person. RPGs present themselves as harmless, fun, interesting, and benign, but all is not perfect in paradise and artificial worlds are no different.

On one hand, RPGs are harmless when the individual player conforms to the environment's rules of conduct (ROCs), that is, behaves morally. On the other hand, there is no requirement for morals or good behavior in most RPGs. Furthermore, the ROCs and therefore the definition of moral behavior differs within each world. The rise of real-world socially and ethically indefensible behavior has skyrocketed in virtual environments. For instance, Linden Lab, the developer of *Second Life*, now has a police blotter to report *Second Life*'s numerous crimes of the day (http://secondlife.com/community/blotter.php).

Web 2.0 technologies, in enabling artificial worlds, also enable problematic behavior. Crimes in RPGs are called "griefing." Griefs such as rape, murder, theft, beatings by gangs, and other activities that are illegal in the real world have all found their way to virtual environments (Holahan, 2006; Lynn, 2007). Some *Second Life* residents call for Linden Lab, the vendor host organization, to monitor the environment more closely or to use technology to prevent such behaviors. The issues involved in taking no action vs. taking action, and the morality of the parties involved all are developed below. These actions are analyzed through the lens of ethics, the study of moral systems. In this chapter, the moral codes are defined by the codes of conduct within and for each virtual world by its vendor hosts. The ethical analysis uses ethical theories to describe real behaviors

in virtual worlds and their defensibility vis-a-vis different systems of ethical thinking. In the next section, Web 2.0 technologies that enable virtual environments are identified. Then, virtual-environment research is summarized to develop characteristics of individuals who participate in RPGs. Next, several taxonomies of virtual behavior are analyzed to develop a model of virtual-world behavior. From the model, we then develop ethical concerns relating to behaviors in virtual worlds. Implications for individual gamers, game creators, companies, and researchers are developed in the last section.

WEB 2.0 TECHNOLOGIES

Web generations usually are identified by specific software standards like HTML (hypertext markup language) that characterized the beginning of Web 1.0. Web 2.0, however, is not identified by a software standard. Rather, Web 2.0 is characterized as the application of technologies that enable specific interactive capabilities such as coproduction, social networking, and unprecedented forms of communication, with user control and syndication of Web content. Examples of these actions are user-controlled communications of wikis, book reviews on Amazon.com, sharing of activities on MySpace, island development in *Second Life*, and syndications via YouTube video, blogs, and RSS (really simple syndication).

Many technologies enable Web 2.0 capabilities such as Flash, XML (extensible markup language), AJAX (asynchronous JavaScript and XML), mashups, RSS, and interactive applications ("MUD," 2007). Some people agree that Web 2.0 does not exist because there is no standard and no standard technology. Nevertheless, activities enabled by Web 2.0 technologies are paradigmatically different enough from early Web applications to warrant the term. Web 2.0-enabled activities, then, include any sites that provide social networking, environmental experiences, or syndication of news, music, audio, video, or text.

VIRTUAL WORLDS

Virtual worlds are one form of social networking Web 2.0 application. Originating as text-based virtual environments in the 1970s (Bartle, 1990), virtual worlds developed into sophisticated multiuser domains or dungeons (MUDs, 2007; Bartle; Raymond, 2000); multiuser social hacks, habitats, or hallucinations (MUSHs; "MUSH," 2007); and massively multiuser online role-playing games (Hendrickson, 2007a; "MMORPGs," 2007).

There are currently over 1,500 active virtual worlds (*ActiveWorlds*, 2007; Hendrickson, 2007b; "Virtual Worlds List," 2007) classified loosely into specializations for exploring, building, shopping, socializing, and gaming. Many of these worlds are fantasy worlds in which users select a role or avatar that acts for them in-world. An example of a fantasy world is *World of Warcraft*. Some virtual worlds, such as *Second Life*, which has a three-dimensional first-person perspective, are more realistic and contemporary: in essence, an analog to real life. Regardless of the type of virtual world, there are three types of controls over behavior:

- Laws of code (Lessig, 1999)
- Rules of conduct (Foo & Koivisto, 2004)
- Local norms (Foo & Koivisto)

Laws of code refer to restrictions through programming code that are placed on behaviors by the world's creators. For instance, a request to "camp," that is, to sit on another's avatar and kill it every time it comes to life, either can earn points as in *World of Warcraft*, or be prevented, losing points. A program receives the request and responds to the camping request by rewarding, thwarting, or preventing the behavior all through program code. Laws of code are applied to all world citizens without any other considerations such as status, number of points, and so forth.

ROCs are explicit written guidelines for behavior, or a moral code of conduct, to which virtual-world users agree as a condition of world access. ROCs differ across virtual worlds and are mostly permissive rather than restrictive, allowing behaviors the code authors feel are consistent with in-world behaviors. ROCs are followed to the extent that an individual is motivated to follow them, and to the extent that the forbidden behaviors become known to the world creators and are punished or modified in some way. While ROCs are meant to guide behavior, they are rarely imbedded in code that actually prevents transgressions, primarily because the vendor is unlikely to be able to anticipate all possible ways to circumvent the ROCs. Thus, ROCS differ from laws of code in that code directs behaviors while ROCs advise acceptable behaviors.

Local norms are the social contracts that are forged as a result of implicit or explicit agreement on accepted behavior (Donaldson & Dunfee, 1994). In virtual worlds, local norms result from in-world participants' discussions of accepted behavior coupled with reactions to inappropriate behavior that are capable of changing the behavior of the transgressors. In virtual worlds, the negotiation of a social contract is an on-going activity that takes place within in-world groups who may participate in or witness some issue that violates someone's sense of correct behavior.

From these definitions, problem behaviors in virtual worlds may or may not ever become norms unless they are managed through code. ROCs may be violated without the violation becoming known to the creators because the harmed person does not report the transgression. Also, depending on the volume of transgressions, not all may be punished or modified, thereby giving implicit acceptance to the behavior.

Rule through norms is equally problematic. In addition to the difficulty of achieving a local norm from millions of people across many cultures, there is no reward (or punishment) for following (or breaking) a local norm. Some individuals want to create or enforce local norms that mirror their view of accepted behavior in real life. These people are viewed as whining, having a misunderstanding of virtual-environment norms, or just taking the virtual world experience too seriously (Foo & Koivisto, 2004; Yee, 2007). These others typically are gamers who hop from one environment to the next seeking new experiences. Gamers who live by the code of one environment, say, *World of Warcraft*, will violate behavioral norms if they use the same behavior in *Second Life*. So, there is a clash of cultures that is part of the issue in defining ethical behavior in virtual worlds. On one hand, some citizens believe the virtual world should mirror real-world mores and culture. On the other hand, some citizens believe the worlds should be fantasies where many real-life unaccepted behaviors add to the experience.

RPG PARTICIPANT CHARACTERISTICS

Bartle (1991) defined four groups of characteristics that he believed defined virtual gamers and their motivations. Groups, categorized by the type of card in a deck, are hearts, or socializers; spades, who are explorers; diamonds, achievers; and clubs, killers. In Bartle's characterization, socializers seek interaction experiences with other players, viewing the game as a venue for socializing.

Explorers are individuals who seek information, shortcuts, secret means of navigation, and so on, which separates them from their game peers as they are more knowledgeable of game minutia. Achievers are those who seek the highest score, sometimes using means that may transgress the ROCs of the world. Score in a virtual world such as *Second Life* relates to amassing technical skills for purposes of bombarding other avatars with flying objects or increasing attention or traffic for a portion of the site.

The killers are those who are thrilled with causing others grief (hence the term *griefing*), not with focusing on the game or achievement (Bartle, 1991). From these four groups, Bartle hypothesized that achievers and killers (diamonds and clubs) would be the most likely to cause problems for other players.

Although widely accepted, Bartle's (1991) work when empirically tested is not a perfect description of gaming player characteristics. Yee's (2007) evaluation of Bartle's grouping yielded only three overarching groupings of behavior into which he categorized 10 different factors.

Yee's (2007) achievement grouping contains elements of diamonds, spades, and clubs from Bartle's (1991) characterizations. An achiever is interested in knowing more than others to excel at the game (diamonds) while taking a mechanical interest to the extent that it contributes to excelling (spades), with a subgoal of competition and the domination of other players (clubs). The social components in Yee's grouping give detail to Bartle's characterization of a socializing heart. Yee's immersion component has an element of knowledge seeking (spades) and socializing in terms of avatar characteristics (hearts), but identifies role-playing, escapist subcomponents as new constructs. Since Yee's work does not include any of the factor numbers or how he developed the overarching groups, the accuracy of this characterization requires further research.

Weaknesses of the research aside, Yee seems to have tapped some important distinctions between player and participant groups that can explain their different actions and reactions with respect to unethical behavior.

ETHICALITY OF VIRTUAL BEHAVIOR

Behaviors causing problems in virtual worlds sometimes mirror those in real life such as murder, rape, stealing, and assault. These behaviors are grouped under the term *griefing* to describe unacceptable, and sometimes unethical, behavior. In this section, griefing is defined and a list of common complaints is detailed. From these, we discuss the ethicality of the behaviors, relating them to the ethicality of the real-life behaviors they mirror.

Griefing is defined as intentional harassment (Warner & Raiter, 2005) that has three aspects:

1. "The griefer's act is intentional
2. It causes other players to enjoy the game less
3. The griefer enjoys the act" (Foo & Koivisto, 2004, p. 2)

Enjoyment of the griefer is critical in this definition and is used by virtual-world creators as a reason to not take action if they are unable to verify that the griefing was enjoyment as opposed to gaining points within a game. The general question is whether or not it is unethical to deprive another person of enjoyment of a virtual environment. A related question is whether behaviors that are rewarded (via points, tokens, or other means) in some virtual worlds can be held to a different standard in other virtual worlds.

Second Life garners significant attention in the U.S. media partly because so many corporations have built islands and conduct business in-world. Griefs such as rape, harassment in many forms, and stealing are common *Second Life* occurrences. According to *Second Life*'s police blotter, only the most recent 25 transgressions and actions taken are shown, but they are representative of *Second Life* problems (see *Second Life* police blotter for more detail).

Offenses that would be felony crimes in real life have consequences that are less than would occur if the same offense were committed in real life. Assault and public nudity are in this category. However, offenses considered severe in-world, such as spamming, prim littering (leaving an object on someone else's land), and crashing regions, get longer suspensions.

Not all of these offenses are considered griefing. Swearing, slowing a region's operating speed, spamming, unwanted advertisements, inappropriate language, and harassment have been included in various griefing definitions (Bakioglu, 2007; Foo & Koivisto, 2004; Giles, 2007; Yee, 2006). The two virtual-only offenses—prim littering and crashing regions—have real-world analogs in littering and ruining property. It appears that the severity of punishment for the digital offenses relates more to the level of inconvenience to recuperate from them than to their overt severity.

Other examples of potentially unethical behaviors are expanded and discussed, beginning with virtual actions with real-world consequences. Real-world actions demonstrate the mental impacts of immersive virtual worlds.

In China, a man was murdered because he was believed to have stolen a valuable virtual sword from a virtual world (Warner & Raiter, 2005). Stealing, which is not forbidden in *World of Warcraft*, usually is met with virtual retribution through beatings and stealing back the taken item. The violence of the game carried into real life is inexcusable from an ethical perspective. The murder in China, indefensible from any moral stance, shows an extreme of emotion that the immersive experience can provoke.

In another incident, 13-year-old Megan Meier committed real-world suicide after first being befriended then receiving abusive remarks from a MySpace acquaintance thought to be a boy who turned out to be the parent of an ex-girlfriend (Leonard, 2007). Megan Meier's suicide, while complicated because of her prior psychological problems, shows another extreme of emotion possible from virtual entanglements. The adult first lured Megan into a relationship then turned and verbally abused her. As a consequence of her upset at being jilted, she hanged herself. The adult(s) involved have no moral or ethical justification for the original deception, the false content, or the mean-spirited abuse.

These unethical behaviors—killing in China and harassment on MySpace—that caused tragic real-world behaviors relate to single incidents at the moment. These events are probably harbingers of future acts as more people engage in virtual worlds.

Also in China, low-pay employees are paid to play *World of Warcraft* in 12-hour shifts to find virtual gold, which is sold outside of the game to players who gain stature within the game for their gold (Siegal, 2005; Warner & Raiter, 2005; Yago, 2006). Typically, players are paid between 500 to 800 Yuan (US$70 to US$112 as of March 1, 2008) per month while the company makes as much as $27,000 per month from their gold-getting labor (Siegal, 2005; Yago, 2006). The labor is usually continuous killing of a virtual entity to gain points that translate to virtual gold. The wages paid to the gold miners are unethically low since the minimum wage in China is about US$180 per month (Cartman, 2008; Vashtar, 2006). Paying low wages for personal gain violates tenets of justice, equity, virtue, and deontological (i.e., duty and rights) ethics in depriving the miners their just due for their work. If these companies were to pay their workers the money they actually earn, it would be an acceptable form of virtual business. Because the companies are not paying a fair wage, they are unethical in their employee treatment. However, this type of unethical behavior is a by-product of the virtual worlds that also might take place in a real-life company doing something similar. The issues of unjust pay are not only in the virtual world.

Identity theft can occur to an individual or on a large scale to individuals or companies. In either case, the action is wrong because identity thieves can ruin the victim's good name, slander the victim's character, and cause the victim loss of all credibility. Furthermore, the losses can easily carry over from a virtual world into the real world when the theft occurs to an individual in a company setting (both virtually and in real life) or to a company known by the same name in both virtual and real life.

In one incident in *Second Life*, a "breached database included unencrypted names and addresses, and the encrypted passwords and encrypted payment information of all Second Life users" (Kirkpatrick, 2006, p. 1). Identity theft violates most ethical tenets, with neither means nor ends defensible. It involves injustice to the victim, brutish and unvirtuous action by the thief, and subsequent untruthfulness of all uses of the avatar or company after the theft. Therefore, while theft of objects might be accepted in some virtual worlds, identity theft is neither justifiable nor an accepted ROC in many environments. The environments in which theft of avatars is accepted seem targeted toward younger participants who are in a game environment (cf. Paizo, 2007), and it is part of the thrill of the game.

Identity is an issue in Web 2.0 technologies since verification of identity is difficult, if not impossible. Web 2.0 technologies enable the posting and control over content, but as Wikipedia found several times in the last 5 years, false information by unqualified people can be the result. Some worlds have begun a form of verification activity (R. Linden, 2007), but they cannot guarantee that identity theft has not occurred.

Another ethical issue is deceptive research. In one case, researchers sought to determine the limits of endurance of griefing in virtual environments. The researchers' avatars grief other avatars with ill-mannered behavior then ask how they felt about the invasion (Simonite, 2007). Such deceptive research violates several ethical tenets. Truthfulness is crucial to Nicomachean (i.e., ethical systems based on virtuous behavior) and teleological ethics (i.e., ethical systems based on utilitarian ends justifying means) as a general good and also is important in dealing with others. It should be feasible to do research with more truthfulness than shown by those who grief others to test what behaviors they can get away with (Acronym, 2007). Furthermore, since it is possible to do lasting psychological harm in virtual worlds, such deceptive research is unethical in and of itself.

Public outcries about virtual behaviors are both a form of sense making and a norm-formation activity for those initiating the complaints. Some people who admit to bad behavior in virtual worlds argue that their victims take themselves too seriously and are not open-minded about game behavior (PN, 2006). *Second Life* is particularly interesting in this regard because it supports both real-life and game-world metaphors. Corporate islands add etiquette and behavioral norms beyond those of *Second Life*, building real-world cultures and norms into their virtual analogs. Yet, when one first enters *Second Life*, the whole world is available, including games, adult entertainment, and other nonwork activities. Arguments about behavior to some extent are evidence of a clash of these and other game metaphors.

With this metaphoric clash in mind, we examine whether there are any universally proscribed behaviors that apply to both real and virtual worlds. Extreme behavior, such as murder and rape, can highlight contradictions that help us to better understand the issues.

Murder in virtual worlds is sometimes called "fragging," an action within a virtual game that temporarily erases another player from the game. Murder is permanent erasure. In this discussion, we move from fragging to more severe forms of erasing another person from the virtual world to discuss its ethicality. Fragging is not ethically defensible from several perspectives. According to teleological ethics, actions are ethical to the extent that the outcome is ethical; in vernacular, the ends justify the means. Murder, unless explicitly rewarded by the virtual world as accepted behavior, is not defensible since the victim is injured, even if momentarily. The more severe the fragging, the less defensible the act. Examples of more severe fragging incidents are crashing an entire server (in *Second Life*, this is 16 acres of

islands and thousands of people) or permanently destroying one or more persons' presences. The fragging committed by the Chinese gold miners is not of peoples' avatars but of virtual avatars, and thus, does not fall under this discussion.

Fragging and murder also violate ethical tenets from a Nicomachean (i.e., virtuous behavior) perspective as being an undesirable brutal act. In addition, several of Ross's deontological tenets (that is, ethical systems based on rights and duties) relating to beneficence (help others) and maleficence (harm others) are violated (Cooley, 2007). Thus, fragging and/or murder from the relatively harmless momentary killing to the permanent deletion of an avatar or property would be considered unethical behavior unless specifically allowed by the ROCs of the virtual world.

Real-life murde is a complicated social phenomenon. Governments commit murder sometimes justified as for the greater good such as capital punishment or murder during war. Governments also commit murder without justification such as Uganda's murders of tens of thousands of people under Idi Amin. Without global reprisals and outrage against his behavior, the world implicitly accepted those murders.

Fragging and murder in a virtual world differ from murder in real life because the dead can come back to active life. Virtual death is a temporary, albeit complete, interruption of one's virtual experience. The duration of virtual death varies from seconds to rounds of a game to the next log-in. In some virtual worlds, death requires creation of a new avatar, and possibly acquisition of a new network address.

Thus, murder can be viewed as, if not morally acceptable, at least accepted in practice in some situations. But, until the real world proscribes all murder, it is likely to continue in virtual worlds.

This leads to a discussion of another felonious behavior in real life that translates to virtual life. In 1993, Julian Dibbell raised questions about rape in virtual life that "changed a database into a community" (Dibbell, 1993). The rape occurred in the famous MUD LambdaMOO (a MOO is an object-oriented MUD), run by Xerox Parc, on an autumn night with not only the participants but also an audience of about 10 other people. For several days after the event, a discussion list for social issues relating to LambdaMOO was inundated with requests for justice relating to the rape and discussion on what that meant. An in-world 3-hour meeting convened to determine an equitable outcome. At the end of the meeting, which petered out after the rapist appeared and sat in a corner talking to himself, one of the Xerox "wizards" permanently "toaded" the rapist, Mr. Bungle, thereby removing all evidence of his existence. Several weeks later, a Dr. Jest entered the space and led members to believe he was the incarnation of Mr. Bungle (Dibbell, 1993). Upon learning of this event and studying the conversation logs, Archwizard Haakon, also known as Pavel Curtis, created a system for world voting on social issues that bound the technical architects to take the approved actions.

Morality of virtual rape and any attendant mental damage to the victim is difficult to justify on any grounds. Ethical theories of justice and virtue are violated by acts of rape as are deontological tenets of duty that relate the goodness of action to its outcomes. Justice is violated both because of the inequity of the act of rape in imposing one's will or power on another, but also because there is no restitution or reduction of the inequity before, during, or after the act. From a virtue perspective, virtual rape is a brutish, incontinent act. In Ross's deontological theory, maleficence, justice, and restitution are all violated (Cooley, 2007).

Several important themes arose from the LambdaMOO event. First, it is clear that events in a virtual world are "neither exactly real nor exactly make-believe, but [they are] profoundly, compellingly, and emotionally meaningful" (Dibbell, 1993, p. 4). The psychological state that comes with immersion seems to make the virtual real, or at least real to the participant.

Second, the voting mechanism Curtis put into place made LambdaMOO the most democratic world on earth by having binding votes on the governing technicians. Through this action, Curtis used a law of code, in this case, a voting system, to provide a forum for social contract formation and, thus, formation of ethical norms of behavior for LambdaMOO.

Third, the "meme-scape" was "too slippery" to support decisive action exactly because of the rift between the real and the virtual (Dibbell, 1993, p. 7). A meme is "a unit of cultural information, such as a...practice or idea, that is transmitted verbally or by repeated action from one mind to another" ("Avatar," 2008); for instance, " an Internet meme is...the propagation of a digital file or hyperlink from one person to others using methods available through the Internet (for example, email, blogs, social networking sites, instant messaging, etc.)" ("Internet Meme, 2008 p. 1"). The historic development of human cognition from mimetic skill to language and to external symbolic expression (Donald, 1993) appears to be insufficient to reconcile the complexities of virtual engagement that all take place in the mind. The democratic voting system of LambdaMOO is a real-world construction imposed on the virtual world. Perhaps virtual constructions more appropriate to virtual existence require further cognitive evolution to allow us first to articulate, then to govern interior experiences emanating from virtual activities.

The mental engagement that is part of the virtual-world immersion experience causes participants to feel as if the events are real, at least cognitively real. As a result, murder, while condoned in some virtual worlds, may have profound and lasting effects in worlds in which murder is not condoned (Lee & Oh, 2007). Similarly, rape, especially when witnessed and violent in its characterizations, might have lasting effects on the victims. Both types of actions are considered unacceptable in real-life analog environments, such as *Second Life*, while murder is condoned or part of the game in other virtual worlds. Virtual rape is ethically indefensible, but essentially ungovernable.

INTELLECTUAL PROPERTY AND WEB 2.0

So far, this chapter has focused on individual behaviors that are enacted against or toward another individual or set of individuals. Another issue relating to ethics and virtual worlds is one in which intellectual property (IP) is made available on a virtual-world site, and there is a lack of protections for controlling that IP.

IP refers to any property that is covered by copyright laws, such as ideas, Web site design and content, or inventions. Copyright laws give one the right to control access, reproduction, distribution, and creation of derivative works of the copyrighted material ("What is Copyright?" 2008). Two actions are recommended for copyrighted material on the Internet: display of the copyright symbol and/or word with date on every page, and registration of copyrighted material with the U.S. Copyright Office. Both display and registration assume that the owner, in fact, owns outright all material—text, graphics, icons, photos, diagrams, and so forth—on the site. If that is not the case, the copyright will not be honored in the event of litigation. Furthermore registration is not strictly required, but without registration with the Copyright Office within 90 days of a site's publishing, remedies in litigation would be limited to actual damages suffered, something that is difficult to prove ("Copyright Web Site," 2008).

Companies building virtual worlds own the intellectual property that forms and controls their part of the world. In virtual worlds such as *Second Life*, buyers of in-world property specifically are ceded ownership rights to their own property. Protection through copyright laws should then apply.

Problems arise when individuals transgress copyrighted virtual space in some way. Transgressions might take forms such as prim littering (leaving software artifacts on someone else's property), spamming, malicious destruction of virtual objects, or even deleting or stealing of documents and other property. Copyright protection, while giving the weight of the law, does not protect against these violations physically. As a result, security, integrity, and availability are the responsibility of the owning corporation.

To protect IP then, companies have to develop both copyright protection and their own security to protect IP in virtual worlds. This need is no different than that of any other Web site development, except that companies' Web sites might not have been a target but their virtual-world properties may be. Therefore, security becomes more extensive and expensive.

IP law is a Western legal creation that, while enjoying similarity of adoption across the Western world, is not universally recognized. U.S. conflicts with China and India over copyrighted materials attest to this lack of universal recognition (IFLA, 2008). Therefore, transgressions that are benign, such as taking of content that is victimless, are viewed in those countries as a form of flattery; the more the copying, the greater the flattery.

Forms of industrial espionage have been found in *Second Life* (Au, 2007). Script code that takes interactions and communicates them outside of the virtual world is found on business island sites. Having transferred the contents of communications to another location, all in-world communication on spied-on sites is taken. While most activities are likely banal, companies that wholly move their communications activities to *Second Life* and other virtual worlds must exhibit constant quality and integrity assurance on all forms of the underlying code and scripts as well as the database data populating the site. The prevalence of spy code in virtual worlds is unknown but should be assumed to be pervasive. Spying as described in this case is clearly unethical from deontological (i.e., rights and duties), teleological (i.e., ends utility), and Nicomachean (i.e., virtuous acts) perspectives.

There is no simple solution to the issues of universal recognition of intellectual property rights since both forms of legal recognition and nonrecognition are steeped in sociopolitical systems that transcend the Internet. As globalization increases, the more homogenized the world will become. Yet, with one third of the world not recognizing intellectual property as a protectable commodity, it is unclear how this issue will be resolved.

DISCUSSION AND IMPLICATIONS

Virtual worlds can be viewed as a type of social experiment where cross-cultural, cross-generational norms emerge within the virtual realm. To the extent that players have experience of other virtual realms that may condone behaviors viewed as unacceptable or unethical in their present world, social behavioral norms may clash. Furthermore, norm development must somehow be transmitted memetically throughout a virtual world to achieve consensus for adoption. In a world like *Second Life* where many users confine their activity to corporate islands or other restricted areas, such norm transmission is unlikely.

On one hand, a virtual world allows escape from daily existence so that a player might act out fantasy behavior or try on personas that differ wildly from daily life. One example is the character Wilde Cunningham, the avatar of a group of people with cerebral palsy (H. Linden, 2004). As Wilde demonstrates, by allowing freedom of movement to run, fly, and ride speedboats by people confined to wheelchairs, *Second Life* liberates them from their real-life limitations.

On the other hand, virtual escape provides an outlet for aggressions that might be suppressed in real life, leading to griefing behaviors of all types.

As there is no lasting penalty for norm transgressions, there is little motivation for a gamer to comply with stated or developing norms. Gamers who move between environments will suffer some cultural clash from the differing behavioral norms and would be likely griefers in real-world analog environments.

Eugene Kaspersky, president of Kaspersky Lab, a leader in antivirus, antiphishing, and antispam software, identifies three characteristics of the Internet that seem to motivate hacker and other unethical behaviors: low risk, easy opportunity, and inability to personalize the victim (Kaspersky, 2007). These characteristics also apply to virtual worlds and seem to make these venues susceptible to all forms of unethical real-world behaviors.

The implications of griefing activity and the difficulties of developing social norms means that participants in virtual-world activities should arm themselves with methods of escaping from griefing activity: teleporting in *Second Life*, and hiding or preventing communication in other worlds. Also, griefing, like other Internet-based crime, is expected to increase as the number of participants in virtual worlds increase. Therefore, to completely avoid griefing, one should avoid virtual worlds that condone personally unacceptable behaviors. While this may seem like desperation in not working to change the behavior, the reality is that, at least for some time, the options of fight or flight will prevail. Trying to reason with someone who is violating one's personal space in some way may be futile, and opting out may be the only viable option.

For virtual-world developers, the experiences to date show that unethical and unacceptable behaviors will occur in virtual worlds unless prevented. While few people expect a perfect world experience, a world without crimes against persons, such as griefing, murder, and rape, could be prevented through code. Perhaps it is time for such prevention.

Future research could provide better understanding of the personalities attracted to different types of virtual worlds, the effectiveness of different methods in preventing unwanted behaviors, and a more accurate count of the incidence of such behaviors. This idea could be coupled with a virtual-world rating system that provides guidelines on the types of behaviors allowed and practiced in-world. By understanding personality types, such a rating site might channel people to one or another type of virtual world that meets their goals for the game. Then, griefers might have their own world where they can harass each other without reprisal.

Research on the effectiveness of prevention methods might help the cognitive development needed to understand and control behaviors in virtual worlds such that separation is not necessary and that a new world order of cooperation might be feasible. By having a more accurate count of the incidence of griefing and the specific nature of the various types of griefing, individuals seeking to engage in virtual-world activity can be forewarned about the environment they are entering. To this end, a publicly available rating system might be developed to provide virtual-world rankings on various world characteristics.

For companies seeking to develop a virtual presence for the conduct of business, security that prevents griefers from entering or changing the environment should be developed. Individuals using the world should be required to have a log-on and password authentication scheme or more stringent authentication scheme to further prevent unwanted access. For all individuals working, socializing, or entertaining themselves in a virtual world, care should be taken not to encourage griefing behaviors and to report griefing to the software providers.

CONCLUSION

Virtual worlds have been characterized as our future habitats and a way to bring multiple cultures and generations together in virtual work environments. However, like real life, virtual worlds are not perfect and are subject to many of the same unacceptable and possibly unethical activities. The two main approaches to preventing unethical and unacceptable behaviors are to code the environments in a manner that prevents their occurrence or to provide a means for developing virtual-world norms. Most virtual-world creators have opted for the latter approach: to have the norms evolve as the world evolves.

REFERENCES

Acronym, M. (2007). Serious grief. *New Scientist, 195,* 52-53.

ActiveWorlds. (2007). Retrieved April 4, 2008, from http://www.activeworlds.com/tour.asp

Au, W. J. (2007). Spy game. *New World Notes.* Retrieved April 4, 2008, from http://nwn.blogs.com/nwn/2007/02/spy_game.html

Avatar. (2008). *Dictionary.com.* Retrieved March 2, 2008, from http://dictionary.reference.com/browse

Bakioglu, B. (2007). Textual poaching of digital texts: Hacking and griefing as performance narratives of Second Life. In *Creativity, ownership, and collaboration in the digital age.* Cambridge, MA: MIT.

Bartle, R. (1990). *Interactive multi-user computer games.* Muse Ltd.

Bartle, R. (1991). *Hearts, clubs, diamonds, spades: Players who suit MUDs.* Retrieved April 4, 2008, from http://www.mud.co.uk/richard/hcds.htm

Cartman, E. (2008). Chinese wage-price spiral now fully underway. *WordPress*. Retrieved April 4, 2008, from http://cartmanist.wordpress.com/2008/02/28/chinese-wage-price-spiral-now-fully-underway

Cooley, K. (2007). *Sir David Ross's pluralistic theory of duty (the beginnings)*. Retrieved April 4, 2008, from http://www.manitowoc.uwc.edu/staff/awhite/ken95.htm

Copyright Web site. (2008). *Benedict.com*. Retrieved April 4, 2008, from http://www.benedict.com/Digital/Web/WebProtect.aspx

Dibbell, J. (1993). A rape in cyberspace or how an evil clown, a Haitian trickster spirit, two wizards, and a cast of dozens turned a database into a society. *The Village Voice*. Retrieved April 4, 2008, from http://www.villagevoice.com/specials/0543,50thdibbell,69273,31.html

Donald, M. (1993). Precis of origin of the modern mind: Three stages in the evolution of culture and cognition. *Behavioral and Brain Sciences, 16*, 737-791.

Donaldson, T., & Dunfee, T. W. (1994). Toward a unified conception of business ethics: Integrative social contracts theory. *The Academy of Management Review, 19*, 252-284.

Foo, C. Y., & Koivisto, E. M. I. (2004). Defining grief play in MMORPGs: Player and developer perceptions. In *International Conference on Advances in Computer Entertainment Technology (ACE)* (pp. 245-251).

Giles, J. (2007). Serious grief. *New Scientist, 195*, 52-56.

Hendrickson, M. (2007a). 34 more ways to build your own social network. *TechCrunch.com*. Retrieved April 4, 2008, from http://www.techcrunch.com/wp-content/white_label_social_networking_solutions_chart2.html

Hendrickson, M. (2007b). Virtual world hangouts: So many to choose from. *TechCrunch.com*. Retrieved April 8, 2008, from http://www.techcrunch.com/2007/08/05/virtual-world-hangouts-so-many-to-choose-from

Holahan, C. (2006, November 21). The dark side of Second Life. *BusinessWeek*.

IFLA. (2008). Some myths about intellectual property. *IFLA.org*. Retrieved April 4, 2008, from http://www.ifla.org/documents/infopol/copyright/ipmyths.htm

Internet meme. (2008). *Wikipedia*. Retrieved March 2, 2008, from http://en.wikipedia.org/wiki/Internet_phenomenon

Kaspersky, E. (2007). The cybercrime arms race. In Kaspersky Lab (Ed.), *What lies ahead*. Dallas, TX: Kaspersky Lab.

Kirkpatrick, M. (2006). Metaverse breached: Second Life customer database hacked. *TechCrunch.com*. Retrieved April 4, 2008, from http://www.techcrunch.com/2006/09/08/metaverse-breached-second-life-customer-database-hacked

Lee, O., & Oh, J. (2007). The impact of virtual reality functions of a hotel Website on travel anxiety. *CyberPsychology & Behavior, 10*, 584-586.

Leonard, C. (2007). Town shuns Mo. family after MySpace hoax. *USA Today*. Retrieved April 4, 2008, from http://www.usatoday.com/news/nation/2007-12-06-internet-death_N.htm

Lessig, L. (1999). *Code and other laws of cyberspace*. New York: Basic Books.

Linden, H. (2004). The nine souls of Wilde Cunningham, part I. *SecondLife.Blogs.com*. Retrieved April 4, 2008, from http://secondlife.blogs.com/nwn/2004/12/the_nine_souls_.html

Linden, R. (2007). Identity verification comes to Second Life. *blog.SecondLife.com*. Retrieved April 4, 2008, from http://blog.secondlife.

com/2007/08/29/identity-verification-comes-to-second-life

Lynn, R. (2007, May 4). Virtual rape is traumatic, but is it a crime? *Wired.*

Massive multiplayer online role-playing games (MMORPGs). (2007). *Wikipedia.* Retrieved April 4, 2008, from http://en.wikipedia.org/wiki/MMORPG

MUD. (2007). *Wikipedia.* Retrieved April 4, 2008, from http://en.wikipedia.org/wiki/MUD

MUSH. (2007). *Wikipedia.* Retrieved April 4, 2008, from http://en.wikipedia.org/wiki/MUSH

Paizo. (2007). *Avatar theft will not be tolerated.* Retrieved April 4, 2008, from http://paizo.com/paizo/messageboards/community/offTopic/avatarTheftWillNOTBeTolerated&source=rss

PN. (2006). *A special message from PN, authorized by Mudkips Acronym and N3X15.* PN Dept. of Covert Affairs and the Raid Council. Retrieved April 4, 2008, from http://www.freewebs.com/patrioticnigras/literature/declaration.html

Raymond, E. S. (2000). The jargon file. *ManyBooks.net.* Retrieved April 4, 2008, from http://manybooks.net/titles/raymondericetext-02jarg422.html

Siegal, R. (2005). *Paying real money to win online games.* Retrieved April 4, 2008, from http://www.npr.org/templates/story/story.php?storyId=5032947

Simonite, T. (2007, November 2). Anti-social bot invades Second Lifers' personal space. *New Scientist, 16.*

Vashtar, S. (2006). Economics unbound rising wages in China. *BusinessWeek.* Retrieved April 4, 2008, from http://www.businessweek.com/the_thread/economicsunbound/archives/2006/03/rising_wages_in.html

Virtual worlds list. (2007). *Virtual Worlds Review (VWR).* Retrieved April 4, 2008, from http://www.virtualworldsreview.com/info/categories.shtml

Warner, D. E., & Raiter, M. (2005). Social context in massively-multiplayer online games (MMOGs): Ethical questions in shared space. *International Journal of Information Ethics, 4.*

What is copyright? (2008). *FindLaw.com.* Retrieved April 4, 2008, from http://smallbusiness.findlaw.com/copyright/copyright-basics/copyright-defined-overview.html

Yago, G. (2006). The real price of virtual gold. *MTV News.* Retrieved April 4, 2008, from http://www.mtv.com/overdrive/?id=1545907&vid=120059

Yee, N. (2006). The psychology of massively multi-user online role-playing games: Motivations, emotional investment, relationships, and problematic usage. In R. Schroder & A. S. Axelsson (Eds.), *Avatars at work and play: Collaboration and interaction in shared virtual environments* (pp. 187-207). London: Springer-Verlag.

Yee, N. (2007). Motivations of play in online games. *CyberPsychology and Behavior, 9,* 772-775.

Chapter IX
Bringing Real Justice to Virtual Worlds:
World of Warcraft and Second Life

Hunter W. Jamerson
Law Clerk to the Honorable Michael C. Allen, Judge, 12th Judicial Circuit of Virginia, USA

ABSTRACT

The purpose of this chapter is to advise developers, content providers, end users, legislators, and business managers about the challenges and ramifications of conducting business in virtual worlds. The chapter examines crime in virtual worlds, as well as evaluates the current status of property rights (real, actual, and intellectual), and suggests changes to the existing legal structure in order to confront virtual crime. Recommendations to the business manager are also included in this chapter.

INTRODUCTION

Virtual worlds offer a host of opportunities for the Web 2.0 ideal of disseminating information to the masses. Indeed, virtual worlds offer means for collaboration with like-minded individuals; association with other users thousands of miles, national borders, and continents away; unique opportunities for user development of content and applications; and even virtual economies, market systems, means of purchase, sale, trade, and auction that operate according to the same market forces we encounter in the real world. At its best,

a virtual world aspires to be the total package: a conception of the world that users want to create for themselves, having total control over every aspect of the virtual society; they are self-governing, self-sufficient, and self-creating.

Unfortunately, the full promise of virtual worlds has not yet been achieved. Just as our real-world society contains corruption, violence, and bad elements, virtual worlds suffer from their share of transgressions, too. Just as our real society has developed rules and regulations, powers of authority, and means of enforcement, virtual worlds must confront the same issues and resolve them in order for their societies to function without constant interruption from online evildoers. Resolution of these issues in virtual worlds is a matter of significant discussion. What are the rules and who makes them? What authority determines when a rule has been broken? What penalties exist for breaches of the stated regulations and what means are there to enforce those penalties? At what point does a bad act rise to the level that it is no longer appropriate for virtual justice to take the place of real-world law?

Virtual worlds are a place for fun and games, a place for exchanging information and ideas, a place for creativity and development, and even a place for business and profit. Virtual worlds are also a place ripe for abuse and exploitation. Serious issues arise in virtual worlds that profoundly affect game play, the user experience, the rights of the content provider, and the legal and social norms of these virtual worlds. It became obvious in 1993 with the first recorded virtual rape that just because you are online does not mean you are safe from real-world vices.

Today, user experiences are affected by transgressions both minor and extremely serious. Thug behavior and assault are common within today's virtual worlds. Worse, child exploitation, indecency, and pornography have found niches in virtual worlds. Property rights have come into question: What intellectual property protections do end users have for their creations? How do property rights deal with virtual personal property? What rights do content providers have over their own proprietary material? Beyond these property questions, what kinds of tax implications arise when dealing with virtual economies? If virtual worlds seek to provide users with a total virtual reality experience, then these real questions must be answered.

This chapter examines the challenges that virtual worlds have in creating their virtual reality. In particular, attention will be given to two of the most sophisticated virtual worlds—Linden Lab's *Second Life* and Blizzard Entertainment's *World of Warcraft*—and the means by which those companies have addressed some of these issues. Examples of the complications of virtual worlds are illustrated, at times showing the nature of virtual crimes committed through these infrastructures and at times showing the off-line consequences of virtual-world activity. Finally, recommendations are offered for business managers and governments to address the challenges facing virtual worlds. These recommendations are for legislators, content providers, and content users as a means to improve the virtual-world experience and make it safer, more profitable, more just, and more ideal.

VIOLENT CRIME AND PECUNIARY CRIME

As early as 1993, it was clear virtual worlds were fair game for some of society's most vile acts. In the virtual world LambdaMOO, a female user's avatar was raped. Julian Dibbell later chronicled the event in an article titled "A Rape in Cyberspace, or How an Evil Clown, a Haitian Trickster Spirit, Two Wizards, and a Cast of Dozens turned a Database into a Society," published in *The Village Voice* (*Wikipedia*, 2008). According to "A Rape in Cyberspace":

The "cyberrape" was performed by an avatar named Mr. Bungle (after the band of the same name). This user behind the avatar ran a "voodoo doll" subprogram that allowed him to make actions that were falsely attributed to other characters in the virtual community. These actions, which included describing sexual acts that characters performed on each other, went far beyond the community norms to that point and continued for several hours. (p. 1)

LambdaMOO users were alarmed at this behavior, viewed by the online community as sexual predator activity. Discussion ensued within

LambdaMOO regarding what community standards should be enforced within the online society (*Wikipedia*, 2008). The LambdaMOO incident raised questions of how best to regulate virtual worlds and where to draw the line between the real and the virtual.

A decade after the first virtual-world rape came the first virtual-world-motivated murder. *Legend of Mir 3*, according to BBC News, is a fantasy world where players can role-play a range of character classes, including warriors, wizards, and priests. Qiu Chengwei, a longtime player of *Legend of Mir 3*, had spent months to acquire a dragon sabre, an exceptionally rare item in the game. Chengwei loaned the sword to fellow player Zhu Caoyuan. Instead of using the sword and then returning it, however, Caoyuan sold the sword for about US$900 through an online auction. In retaliation for the loss of his dragon sabre, Chengwei fatally stabbed Caoyuan in a real-world act of murder. Chinese police had informed Chengwei that China has no laws that covered theft of an in-game item and told him that the item was not actual property ("Game Theft Led to Fatal Attack," 2005).

Other virtual criminal activity has blurred the line between virtual worlds and real-world legal systems. In May 2007, the *Washington Post* reported that

authorities in Germany announced that they were looking into an incident involving virtual abuse in Second Life after receiving pictures of an animated child character engaging in simulated sex with an animated adult figure. Though both characters were created by adults, the activity could run afoul of German laws against child pornography, prosecutors said. (Sipress, 2007, p. A01)

According to the same article, in another *Second Life* incident, one user found herself the unwilling neighbor of an especially sordid underage sex club. "Tons of men would drop in looking for sex with little girls and boys. I abhorred the club," wrote the user on a Second Life blog....She even tried to evict the club by buying their land. (Sipress, 2007, p. A01)

Another increasingly problematic crime in virtual worlds is gold harvesting and money laundering. In some cases, sweatshop operations play online games for the sole purpose of gathering as much of the in-game currency as possible. Once the gold or other currency is farmed, the currency is then sold at online auctions for real-world profit and traded to the purchaser inside the virtual world (or not; who are you going to complain to if the illegitimate transaction falls through?). Another possible danger in this scenario is the security concern of having your identity and credit card information in the hands of a company with little or no oversight and regulation. Identity theft is a real concern when dealing with unsupervised enterprises.

According to the gaming blog Kotaku, the Symantec Corporation has issued a report warning of money laundering concerns in *World of Warcraft* and *Second Life*, stating that these virtual worlds are "being targeted by organized criminals to launder money and spread key loggers and ID harvesters" ("Virtual Worlds Target for Money Laundering," 2007, p. 1). With so little oversight of transactions within these virtual worlds and no automatic reporting to government regulators, the report warns that

a criminal enterprise could open several thousand [massive multiplayer online role-playing game] accounts. Each could be used to trade with other players in the purchase or sale of in-game assets, the funds from which would ultimately be withdrawn from the accounts. Since thousands of accounts may engage in millions of transactions, each with small profits or losses, it would be difficult to trace the true source of the funds when they are withdrawn. (p. 1)

CIVIL LIABILITY IN VIRTUAL WORLDS

Theft in virtual worlds is so prevalent that South Korea has established an entire police division to handle crimes within virtual worlds. In fact, of the 40,000 cyber crimes reported in the first half of the year 2003, 22,000 of those crimes had to do with online gaming (Ward, 2003). So was the stolen dragon sabre actually a theft of property? According to Dr. Roger Leng, a lecturer on criminal law at the University of Warwick, the dragon sabre absolutely represented stolen property (Ward). Dr. Leng maintains,

It's certainly possible to steal intangible property. It's possible to steal any form of property right that is not represented by tangible objects. In law a bank account is a credit balance. It's not a pile of money that can be stolen even though it is not representing anything physical. (p. 1)

In Mark Ward's (2003) BBC News article "Does Virtual Crime Need Real Justice?" he recounts Stanford University technology law expert Jennifer Granick's stance on this issue:

One problem she sees is that the auction sites and online stores that sell characters, money and artifacts from games are not good guides to the actual value of the goods in question. A player keen to advance a character they have invested hours of time to develop may be happy to splash out hundreds of pounds on a particular item, but the man on the street is unlikely to share this view. (p. 1)

While the legal definitions of property may have room for even virtual conceptions, it is clear that the reality of dealing with virtual property is much more complex. Certainly, valuation is difficult when appraising property in virtual worlds. Also, documentation and chain of possession may be difficult to prove without backed-up secure server data. Still, some people will place hundreds or thousands of dollars of value on their virtual property, and it often reflects massive investments of time, money, and creative energy on the part of the user.

The freedom of creativity given to *Second Life* users has resulted in some terrific artistic creations. In fact, some real-world premier fashion designers have taken their art to *Second Life*, developing exquisite garb for *Second Life* avatars (Lavallee, 2007). Whether or not such creations retain copyright protection, however, is a matter of debate. In the real world, fashion creations are in an intellectual property gray area, with legislation pending to give limited-term copyright protection to the art of fashion design (Carey, 2007).

So, too, in *Second Life*, such creations find halfhearted protection. *Second Life*'s "Terms of Service" assigns all intellectual property rights to their end-user creators; however, that has not stopped some users from "Photoshopping" the designs of other users or simply stealing merchandise from *Second Life* clothing stores (Lavallee, 2007; O'Toole, 2007). Notably, *World of Warcraft* has taken the opposite view in its "Terms of Service" with regard to the user's rights to virtual property: Users "have no interest, monetary or otherwise, in any feature, content or availability of World of Warcraft" or in "any Game Data" associated with the virtual world (Warnecke, 2007, p. 2).

Of particular interest to companies considering doing business in virtual worlds is the case of *Habbo Hotel*. According to BBC News ("Virtual Theft Leads to Arrest," 2007), a group of Dutch teenagers were arrested for stealing US$6,000 worth of virtual furniture, bought with real money, from other users of the virtual world *Habbo Hotel*. In explaining the theft, a spokesman for Sulake, the company that operates *Habbo Hotel*, explained, "The accused lured victims into handing over their Habbo passwords by creating fake Habbo websites" (p. 1).

The actions of the Dutch teenagers constitute a theft of actual property. Moreover, they stole the property through key-logging software in violation of antihacking laws. While the furniture stolen may simply have been a digital image, it has real-world value. That furniture cost real-world currency to create, it carries real-world tax consequences, and it was purchased with real-world dollars. Just because it was stolen in a virtual world does not excuse the actual act of theft. The *Habbo Hotel* furniture is actual property and its owners deserve appropriate, actual legal protections.

The *Wall Street Journal* ("Business Needs to Prepare for Virtual Crime," 2007) provides a candid assessment of the *Habbo Hotel* incident and its impact on companies seeking to do business in virtual worlds:

[I]t's just a matter of time until virtual crime becomes an issue that all businesses have to deal with....We're not saying that this should prevent companies from moving into online services or that it will slow the rate that customers adopt them, but its something worth thinking about today. After all, victims will blame the company that provides the service, no matter who's at fault in the theft. (p. 1)

REGULATION AND TAXATION OF VIRTUAL WORLD COMMERCE

Virtual worlds might contain a complete virtual reality simulation of life off line, but they still operate in the real world, which means they are still bound by legislation and the tax code. Increasingly, the legal world has been examining virtual worlds and the relationship between the content provider and the end user. Most often, this relationship is defined by the terms-of-service (TOS) contract agreed to by the end user upon installing software from the content provider. While this is a prime opportunity for rules and regulations of the virtual world to be established and explained, it is also an opportunity for the content provider to attempt to limit the rights of the end user. Recent court decisions have called into question

the terms-of-service agreement that Linden Lab has used with its *Second Life* software.

In the wake of *Comb v. PayPal Inc.* (2002), which refused to enforce an arbitration clause in PayPal's TOS agreement, a federal court in Pennsylvania considered a similar case against Linden Lab (O'Toole, 2007). Judge Eduardo C. Robreno ruled against Linden Lab in the case of *Bragg v. Linden Research Inc.* (2007; Linden Research, Inc. and Linden Lab are used interchangeably), finding as in *Comb* that compelling arbitration was inappropriate and that the case should proceed to federal court for trial (O'Toole).

Judge Eduardo Robreno's holding in *Bragg v. Linden Research Inc.* (2007) states,

Taken together, the lack of mutuality, the costs of arbitration, the forum selection clause, and the confidentiality provision that Linden unilaterally imposes through the TOS demonstrate that the arbitration clause is not designed to provide Second Life participants an effective means of resolving disputes with Linden. Rather, it is a one-sided means, which tilts unfairly, in almost all situations, in Linden's favor. As in Comb, through the use of an arbitration clause, Linden "appears to be attempting to insulate itself contractually from any meaningful challenge to its alleged practices." (p. 611)

BNA's technology law blog has a clear account of some of the deficiencies in the TOS agreement as cited by Judge Robreno.

- **Lack of mutuality:** The TOS gave Linden Research the right to terminate users "for any reason or no reason," the right to invoke several one-sided remedies to protect its own rights, and the right to modify the TOS at any time, including the arbitration provision (O'Toole, 2007, p. 1).
- **Business realities:** Judge Robreno said that Linden Research made no showing that such

a one-sided agreement was necessary to conduct its business (O'Toole, 2007, p. 1).

In light of *Bragg v. Linden Research Inc.* (2007) and *Comb v. PayPal* (2002), virtual-world content providers must now seriously consider how they craft their TOS agreements. While retaining as many rights as possible and limiting liability are in the corporate interest, these interests will be balanced by courts when weighing the rights of the end user and a doctrine of fairness. Suddenly, legal regulation of virtual worlds is a reality.

Internet tax consequences are currently under congressional consideration, and even virtual worlds may not be a safe place to hide. As Daniel Terdiman (2005) writes for News.com, "If you are a hard-core player of Virtual Worlds like World of Warcraft, Second Life, EverQuest or There, United States Internal Revenue Service (IRS) form 1099 may someday soon take on a new meaning for you" (p. 1). Indeed, as University of Texas School of Law tax professor Bryan Camp explains, Section 61 of the Internal Revenue Code (26 U.S.C. § 61, 2008) clearly states that all income "from whatever source derived" is taxable (Terdiman, p. 2).

This unwelcome news has significant ramifications for content providers and end users. For end users, it means that content providers may be sending them IRS 1099 forms in the future, which are applicable when earning nonemployee income from companies or institutions, whether or not the assets earned are converted into cash (Terdiman, 2005). To clarify, this means that when you make a sale in your virtual store in *Second Life* then whether or not you convert the Linden dollars you earned into U.S. dollars, the gain in your assets is taxable either way.

The idea that the IRS would be interested in small-shop assets like those in *Second Life* may seem far-fetched, but as Dan Miller, a senior economist with the Congressional Joint Economic Committee, explains, "Given growth rates of 10 to 15 percent a month, the question is when, not

if, Congress and the IRS start paying attention to these issues" (Terdiman, 2005, p. 1). Such tax ramifications also mean that content providers must plan to keep closer tabs on virtual-world transactions. Monitoring the virtual macroeconomic data is not going to be enough as content providers will be expected to record every transaction and be prepared to report that data to tax regulators.

RECOMMENDATIONS

This section recommends several changes in the behavioral models for business managers as they relate to virtual worlds. Certainly, virtual worlds cannot continue to function usefully in the lawless environment in which they currently operate. With an awareness of problem areas and a dedicated effort to improve the environment for all participants, virtual worlds can fulfill their purpose as a safe haven for all seeking the benefits of collaboration, association, integration, dissemination, and commercialization, all from the living room sofa.

USE OF END-USER LICENSE AGREEMENTS AS DIFFERENTIATORS

End-user license agreements are typically seen as compilations of all the limitations upon the user when interacting with a technology platform. In Web 2.0, however, user-created content and improvement to the experience should be promoted whenever possible. Two of the largest massive multiplayer online role-playing games (MMORPGs) have approached this concept very differently. *World of Warcraft* has adopted an extremely restrictive terms-of-use policy while *Second Life* has given broad ownership rights to the end user.

Blizzard Entertainment's (2007) "*World of Warcraft*, End User License Agreement" states that users "have no interest, monetary or otherwise, in any feature of content contained in the Game." Furthermore, Blizzard Entertainment makes clear that the user does not even hold title to his or her own account; users simply subscribe for the privilege of use: "All rights and title in and to the Program and the Service (including without limitation any user accounts, titles, computer code, themes, objects, characters, character names...) are owned by Blizzard or its licensors" (p. 1).

This agreement bars many of the principles Web 2.0 has generated. Users have no legal creative control, ability to contribute to the platform, or ability to collaborate on changes to the interface. Such restrictions may be necessary to prevent abuse of the gaming platform in a 10-million-user virtual world considering the challenges of gold farming, mediation of property disputes between users, and corporate liability (Warnecke, 2007). Unfortunately, as Warnecke explains, "there is an inevitable friction between denying users property protection while encouraging them to invest substantial time in developing their world" (p. 2).

One of the most significant differentiating factors of Linden Lab's *Second Life* is its allowance for the end user to retain intellectual property and content-creation rights. *Second Life*'s TOS states that users "retain any and all applicable copyright and other intellectual property rights" (Linden Lab, 2008, p. 1). Some limitations do remain, however, as Warnecke (2007) explains: "Linden Lab still owns all the underlying data and disclaims any liability for deletion" (p. 2).

Retaining copyright and intellectual property rights is a major attraction for Web 2.0 users. MMORPGs can capitalize on the creative spirit of Web 2.0 users by adopting such open-minded end-user license agreements in order to differentiate themselves from the more dated model of content management being employed currently in *World of Warcraft*. Blizzard Entertainment's

model seems likely to give way to the *Second Life* model in the future.

ENSURE LEGAL COMPLIANCE IN EVERY JURISDICTION IN WHICH YOU OPERATE

When *Second Life* shut down all in-game gambling operations and adopted a blanket antigambling policy, many of its users felt that the crackdown was too heavy handed. Users who had worked to develop game content to provide means of gambling and had invested time and money (both real and virtual) into their *Second Life* casinos were scorned by having their items deleted without compensation. The broader *Second Life* community, however, was better off under the new terms of service. The burden should be on the developer to ensure that content in the virtual world and services available in the virtual world are in line with generally applicable law. While it is up to the individual user to ensure that his or her actions are lawful, the content provider should ensure, as much as reasonably possible, that functions available in the virtual world are lawful.

Linden Lab responded exactly as all virtual-world managers should when confronted with a question from a user in whose jurisdiction online gambling was lawful, as reported on the *Second Life* blog of the avatar Robin Linden (2007):

I live somewhere where online gambling is not illegal. Does this policy apply to me? *It does. This policy applies to all users of Second Life. However, it isn't intended to necessarily describe what is or isn't legal for any particular resident or in any particular place. Rather, it describes what Linden Lab believes it must do in order to maintain an atmosphere in which all applicable laws are respected, as well as the U.S. credit card association and other relevant rules and guidelines.* (p. 2)

Business managers cannot get themselves into the habit of trying to gerrymander terms of service to fit the laws of each jurisdiction. Developers should apply strict legal standards in order to minimize risk of liability from user activity within the virtual world.

BEWARE LEGAL AND REGULATORY IMPACTS OF TERMS-OF-SERVICE CONTRACTS

Courts have come down very sternly against companies for having overly broad and burdensome TOS contracts. The BNA E-Commerce and Tech Law Blog probably sums it up best when giving advice to the corporate counsel of virtual-world companies:

Bragg v. Linden Research, Inc. also contains lessons for attorneys drafting online Terms of Service agreements. A fair reading of this case and Comb should lead counsel to reign in their natural impulse to write every single deal point in favor of their client and against the user. (O'Toole, 2007, p. 1)

Content providers must strike a middle ground with end users in determining the parameters of TOS agreements. While it may be in the company's best interest to retain all rights and privileges and limit the recourse of end users as much as possible in order to maintain maximum control over virtual-world content and regulation, such restraints must also be reasonable and lawful.

Interestingly, Linden Lab is the only virtual-world provider to grant its users property rights within the virtual world (Linden, 2007). Nonetheless, because Linden Lab did not have a more narrowly tailored TOS agreement and overzealously curtailed the rights of end users, the court in *Bragg v. Linden Research Inc.* (2007) was no more forgiving than the court in *Comb v. PayPal* (2002). As a result, Linden Lab will have to defend its TOS in federal court, not just in arbitration hearings.

Similarly, the burden of potentially dealing with tax consequences of virtual-world economic activity will be massive. Content developers must consider what resources will be necessary in the future to track, collect, and report data regarding every virtual transaction that takes place through their software. The IRS will not accept burden to the content developer as an excuse should they decide the day has come to regulate virtual-world transactions. As the virtual-world economy continues to grow, tax regulation becomes even more likely.

CONSIDER THE RISKS OF VIRTUAL-WORLD COMMERCE CAREFULLY

Virtual worlds present a terrific opportunity for companies seeking new markets and means of marketing. Product placement and brand identity are extremely valuable marketing devises, and virtual worlds offer means for early adopters to make a big splash in a blue ocean. "Second Lifers" can view products in virtual stores and may then decide to drive down their real-life streets to make the purchase. Even if they just buy products with Linden dollars and stash it in their inventory to take home to their own island, businesses still make real money after the currency exchange.

Such profit, real or virtual, is not without risk. As with any e-commerce mechanism, there is an inherent risk of hacking. While cyber-crime laws may deter hackers from attacking virtual stores, the openness of *Second Life* software makes it a prime haven for evildoers to take a crack at exploiting the code. Recovery can be extremely difficult if your virtual inventory is lost, and the cost of litigation to prove the real value of your lost merchandise may prove greater than the value of the product in the first place. This is not to say there is not good value to be found in being a player in the virtual marketplace. The market is quickly growing and more and more users are becoming comfortable with the virtual transaction system. The prudent early adopter, however, will carefully assess risk before plunging into the virtual market.

RECOGNIZE THE LIMITATIONS OF IN-WORLD SOLUTIONS

Philip Rosedale, the creator of *Second Life*, has said, "We need to create tools as a platform that will allow people to self govern" (Dubner, 2007, p. 1). In fact, Rosedale has gone even further in disputing that the laws of multiple countries should govern *Second Life*, stating "in the ideal case, the people who are in Second Life should think of themselves as citizens of this new place and not citizens of their countries" (Sipress, 2007, p. A01). While it is certainly a noble goal for users to self-govern, developing their own systems of rules and social norms as the content develops and increases exponentially simply leaves too much room for exploitation.

It might be appropriate for users to self-govern themselves in some instances, but certainly not in all. In *World of Warcraft*, for example, if a player on one server earns a reputation as a ninja, that is, the player steals items that cannot be traded once picked up when he or she had not won the right to those items, then the self-regulation of the community on that server will swiftly carry out justice. That player will likely be banned from his or her guild, the player's reputation will preclude him or her from easily finding groups for quests, and he or she may ultimately be forced to apply for a server transfer to start building a new reputation elsewhere. In a situation such as this, self-regulation is effective. There was no need to involve Blizzard and tie up its resources to resolve the situation, and it would be appropriately handled inside the virtual world. However, virtual resolution is not always the appropriate solution.

What about the gold-farming company that employs children at ruthless wages to mindlessly play *World of Warcraft* in Shanghai sweatshops for hours so that the gold earned can be sold through come-and-go Web sites for profit outside of Blizzard's control (Hoyle, 2006)? How can an in-game resolution resolve that? How can an in-game solution control a user having an illicit conversation with a child in *Second Life*? How can online justice resolve the tragedy of the Megan Meier suicide and the harassing comments of a mother toward an innocent child ("Parents: Cyber Bullying Led to Teen's Suicide," 2007)? How can online justice appropriately punish child pornography disseminated through social networking? Sure, accounts can be suspended or banned, but this does effectuate a just response.

At some point, real-world law and real-world law enforcement must take over where the limits of virtual justice have been reached. It is an enviable goal that the worst offenses in virtual societies should be bullying behavior, but the reality is that some virtual crime is real crime, too, and must be treated that way. Subpoenas must be obeyed, server data must be backed up and stored, and proactive reporting to proper authorities must be done.

EXPAND THE COMPUTER FRAUD AND ABUSE ACT AND ESTABLISH UNIFORM LEGISLATION

Most computer crimes in the United States that are prosecuted are done under the Computer Fraud and Abuse Act. Codified at 18 U.S.C. §1030 (2008), this act makes many acts of computer hacking and fraud criminal offenses punishable by fine and imprisonment. Most often in the United States, this statute is used to prosecute crimes against financial institutions or fraud schemes designed to steal consumer financial and identification data. If cyber crime is to be effectively combated in the United States, then the Computer Fraud and Abuse Act must be expanded in order to prosecute crimes of significant copyright infringement, theft of virtual property, and theft of user names and passwords.

Furthermore, cyber-crime legislation must be made uniform across national borders. What is currently an illegal act in Germany or Belgium may not be an illegal act in the United States or China. In order for effective enforcement, clarity of law, and maximum protection of the consumer, all countries whose citizens participate in Web 2.0 technologies should adopt the most stringent available cyber-crime laws.

CONCLUSION

Virtual worlds have a lot of real problems: antisocial behavior, virtual crime, property right infringement, and economic subversion. However, virtual worlds also have a lot of real promise. Since content and business practices are still in the development stages, virtual worlds have the advantage of flexibility in their response to problems. Because of the unique nature of virtual worlds, the dedicated user base is often self-governing and can resolve minor virtual-world issues without having to involve the resources of the developers.

Increasingly, however, virtual worlds are becoming high-profit, high-stakes ventures, and content providers and legislators are beginning to recognize the need for meaningful real-world supervision. To Linden Lab or Blizzard Entertainment, virtual worlds are not just fun and games. To the more than 40,000 users, both individual and corporate, who turned a real-world profit last year through virtual economies, virtual worlds represent a lucrative marketplace where appropriate regulation and oversight is necessary to ensure the smooth flow of commerce. To the proud end user who has created his or her own content through artistic and technical ability, that virtual creation has real value. To the gamer that has spent months of mastering complex mathematical coefficients, building social networks through teamwork and

guilds, perfecting skills and strategies, all to attain a one-of-a-kind item in a virtual world, that property has real value.

Whether you are selling furniture to furnish virtual hotel rooms or designer clothes to keep avatars PG rated, whether you are a raiding an undead fire-mage avatar named Melquiades or just play the auction house for profit, virtual worlds hold real value. It is crucial that subversive, criminal, and exploitative activity not tarnish this experience. By implementing these recommendations, business managers will be better able to safeguard their proprietary content, protect their vested interest in virtual property, operate lawfully and legitimately, and ensure that other users do so as well.

Some may argue that online theft is simply part of the cost of playing. We must recognize, however, that virtual-world commerce is real (and taxable) commerce, virtual-world property is actual property, and virtual-world ideas in *Second Life* are intellectual-property ideas in our first lives that must be protected under copyright laws. While there is some assumption of risk of damages from "griefing" in virtual worlds, no one should have to assume risk to property they own, in which they have invested real-world dollars, and for which they may derive real-world profit.

Web 2.0 has driven technology to the point that it can now reasonably emulate the real world in its entirety. The promise of total integration, maximum collaboration, and a playground for invention, creation, and innovation can be fulfilled in virtual worlds. Complex issues must still be addressed in order to achieve this promise. Society remains a long way from the average man on the street accepting the real value of a virtual sword as a legitimate property right. For the people for whom the idea does not sound so unreasonable, however, legislatures must provide a rational system of rules and enforcement.

While transactions in *Second Life* and *World of Warcraft* are not being targeted for their tax consequences yet, we would be naïve not to be preparing for the day when IRS 1099 forms have to be filed for our *Second Life* sales. Perhaps most importantly, content providers and end users must work together with governments across the globe to ensure that privacy rights are protected, children are protected, and the rule of law is obeyed within virtual worlds. A number of important conversations are in order to ensure that our second lives seem as normal as our first.

REFERENCES

18 U.S.C. §1030. (2008).

26 U.S.C. § 61. (2008).

Blizzard Entertainment. (2007). *World of Warcraft, end user license agreement.* Retrieved May 15, 2008, from http://www.worldofwarcraft.com/legal/eula.html

Bragg v. Linden Research Inc., 487 F. Supp. 2d 593, 611 (E.D. Pa. May 30, 2007).

Business needs to prepare for virtual crime. (2007). *Wall Street Journal.* Retrieved May 15, 2008, from http://blogs.wsj.com/biztech/2007/11/19/business-needs-to-prepare-for-virtual-crime

Carey, E. (2007). *Copyright protection in the fashion industry: Legislative solutions.* Unpublished undergraduate thesis, Virginia Commonwealth University.

Comb v. PayPal Inc., 218 F. Supp. 2d 1165 (N.D. Cal. 2002).

Dubner, S. (2007). Philip Rosedale answers your Second Life questions. *New York Times.* Retrieved May 15, 2008, from http://freakonomics.blogs.nytimes.com/2007/12/13/philip-rosedale-answers-your-second-life-questions

Game theft led to fatal attack. (2005). *BBC News.* Retrieved May 15, 2008, from http://news.bbc.co.uk/go/pr/fr/-/1/hi/technology/4397159.stm

Hoyle, B. (2006). Gamers' lust for virtual power satisfied by sweatshop workers. *The Times.* Retrieved May 15, 2008, from http://technology.timesonline.co.uk/tol/news/tech_and_web/article648072.ece

Lavallee, A. (2007). Now, virtual fashion. *Wall Street Journal.* Retrieved May 15, 2008, from http://online.wsj.com/public/article/SB115888412923570768-HtFYrBweWp-F25yJkL0CdXvkFRkY_20070922.html

Linden, R. (2007). *Anti-gambling policy update: FAQ.* Linden Lab. Retrieved May 15, 2008, from http://blog.secondlife.com/2007/08/09/anti-gambling-policy-update-faq

Linden Lab. (2008). *Second Life terms of service agreement.* Retrieved May 15, 2008, from http://secondlife.com/corporate/tos.php

O'Toole, T. (2007). Arbitration clause in Second Life Terms of Service found unconscionable. *BNA E-Commerce and Tech Law Blog.* Retrieved May 15, 2008, from http://pblog.bna.com/techlaw/virtual_games/index.html

Parents: Cyber bullying led to teen's suicide. (2007). *ABC News.* Retrieved May 15, 2008, from http://abcnews.go.com/GMA/Story?id=3882520

Sipress, A. (2007). Does virtual reality need a sheriff? *Washington Post.* Retrieved May 15, 2008, from http:www.washingtonpost.com/wp-dyn/content/article/2007/06/01/AR2007060102671_pf.html

Terdiman, D. (2005). IRS taxation of online game virtual assets inevitable. *ZDNet News.* Retrieved May 15, 2008, from http://news.zdnet.com/2100-1040-6140298.html

Virtual theft leads to arrest. (2007). *BBC News.* Retrieved May 15, 2008, from http://news.bbc.co.uk/go/pr/fr/-/1/hi/technology/7094764.stm

Virtual worlds target for money laundering. (2007). *Kotaku.* Retrieved May 15, 2008, from http://kotaku.com/gaming/crime/virtual-worlds-target-for-money-laundering-302660.php

Ward, M. (2003). Does virtual crime need real justice? *BBC News*. Retrieved May 15, 2008, from http://newsvote.bbc.co.uk/mpapps/pagetools/print/news.bbc.co.uk/1/technology/3138456.stm

Warnecke, M. (2007). Will the rise of virtual worlds turn EULAs into marketing opportunities? *BNA E-Commerce and Tech Law Blog*. Retrieved May 15, 2008, from http://pblog.bna.com/techlaw/virtual_games/index.html

Wikipedia. (2008). Retrieved May 15, 2008, from http://en.wikipedia.org/wiki/A_Rape_in_Cyberspace

Section V
Theoretical and Educational Perspectives of Web 2.0

Chapter X
Activity Theory Approaches for Authentic Web 2.0 Learning

Tom Reinartz
University of Minnesota, USA & Capella University, USA

ABSTRACT

This chapter discusses activity theory approaches to authentic online learning through Web 2.0 media tools and practices. With the proliferation of Web 2.0 software, many have access to the tools, but it is more difficult to harness the power in them toward authentic and meaningful action. Activity theory provides a lens to examine the "unit of activity" as a way to describe, analyze, and understand activity en route to learning goals. The first part of this chapter briefly defines activity theory and its main tenets, and the last few sections specifically address learning in authentic situations and developing authentic communities. Web 2.0 tools and practices allow learners to be engaged in content-related challenges using the tools as mediating devices and therefore facilitating more authentic and successful learning trajectories.

INTRODUCTION

Oftentimes, educational media tools and technologies provide opportunities for teachers to design rich interactive learning experiences, but just as often they are too prohibitive to integrate into practice either because the cost of the tools or the cost of the training is out of reach (Moser, 2007). Even when conditions are conducive to appropriating media tools for instructional pur-

poses, many teachers do not adopt constructivist approaches to learning though they are considered best practices for higher order thinking and learning in media-rich environments (Ertmer, 2005). Today's media-tool landscape, by contrast, represents a unique period in the continued movement to integrate and design new media tools and practices toward effective and meaningful teaching and learning. At the center are today's tools, dubbed Web 2.0, that offer educators opportunities to easily implement rich interactivity and participation to foster meaningful learning without excessive overhead.

The term *Web 2.0*, originally coined by Dale Daugherty and made popular by O'Reilly Media International, is essentially meant to capture an idea rather than any particular media tool or technology. Though the meaning is difficult to capture and continues to change, at its most basic level it means that participants in the new media Internet landscape are now afforded more opportunities to create, change, control, and participate with the media rather than acquiring information from it (Boutin, 2006; Madden & Fox, 2006; O'Reilly, 2005). The tools and practices afforded by the Web 2.0 concept, along with an increasingly information-rich 21st-century world, furthermore demand instructional design strategies, practices, and models that are able to capture the potential that these accessible, adaptable, and growing list of tools offer (Kaiser Foundation, 2005; Reigeluth, 1999).

Reigeluth's 1999 contention that the paradigm of instructional design "needs to be changed" continues to be a response to a "new science of learning" (p. 19) that represents a move away from knowledge acquisition models to those that are more participatory, flexible, emerging, and codesigned. He states that current paradigms of training and education are "counterproductive for meeting the emerging needs of the information age," and the new paradigm requires "a shift from teacher initiative, control, and responsibility to shared initiative, control, and responsibility. It requires a shift from de-contextualized learning to authentic meaningful tasks" (p. 19). Reigeluth's assessment of the field of instructional design in 1999 has fueled the emergence of new frameworks for learning in subsequent years that has created a healthy tension between designing instruction before learning and instructional designs that accommodate and support learners during and throughout the learning process. Accommodating

learners en route to their goals requires support for learning in context-specific situations in ways that question and transform traditional instructional models. Because of the abundance, ease of use, and flexibility, today's Web 2.0 tools and practices have the potential to bring us closer and perhaps beyond Reigeluth's nearly-decade-old call for a new learning paradigm.

While many have focused on the changing landscape, definition, and the abundant, ever-evolving Web 2.0 tools (Alexander, 2006; Driscoll, 2007; O'Reilly, 2005; Seitzinger, 2006), this chapter attempts to ground and guide the discussion of Web 2.0 media tools toward effective and meaningful use through activity theory. It is argued that the seemingly boundless growth of Web 2.0 tools and concepts requires a robust theoretical lens like activity theory that can potentially augment the understanding about how to harness them toward meaningful authentic learning.

BACKGROUND: ACTIVITY AND GENRE THEORIES

Though there is no easy definition or description of activity theory, it essentially provides a rich descriptive and analytic lens for complex learning environments, especially those that are mediated by tools including anything from computers to pencils (Jonassen, 2000; Nardi, 1996). Activity theory can be difficult to understand because activity systems are both nouns and verbs. That is, activity systems are things, but they are not stationary; rather, they change, grow, and overlap, and some are nested within other activity systems. They resist easy definition because activity systems change from moment to moment. Moreover, they cannot remain stationary if they are to be worthwhile constructs for examining human activity and learning. Hyysalo (2005) offers a rare succinct definition stating that activity theory's concepts "bring to the fore the ways that imaginative work and material resources are transformed into outcomes," including artifacts and collaborative work (p. 19).

Activity theorists further contend that the entire context of a learning situation is important since little if any human action takes place independent of surrounding contextual elements. In this sense, examination of the activities and practices with Web 2.0 tools using activity theory is an ideal approach since it can capture the entire learning process including the learners, the media, and the interactions between, among, and within the entire learning environment. Activity theorists are therefore concerned with the whole system of activity with which participants are engaged, which includes the mediating tools, the goals and objectives of the individuals and community participants engaged in that activity, how their objectives transform over time, how labor or work is divided, and how rules are followed and negotiated (Engestrom 1987, 2001; Nardi, 1996). Figure 1 graphically represents activity theory and the dynamic interactions between and among learners in media-rich environments.

The goal in any activity system is to transform the object (objective) into an outcome. The outcome is derived from the movement, motivation, and activity generated from and during that effort.

Examining computer-mediated environments using this holistic approach centers on the belief that meaning is located in the relationship among the components in the entire system of activity including the subjects and their motives, available tools, negotiated rules, divisions of labor, and representative communities. In this way, these "units of activity" are dynamic, shaped by the purposes, tools, and motivation of the learners involved.

For example, in a traditional classroom learning environment or system, students come to understand the relationships among all system components including the tools, communities, rules, and division of labor as they progress toward their learning objectives. Their learning objectives presumably include attaining good grades, learning content material, advancing to higher level courses, gaining employment, and so forth. Progressing from one course to another does not necessarily disturb students' understanding or equilibrium as they carry the cultural, historical residue of how to learn from one learning system to the next. Because each learning system in schools typically shares tools, rules, divisions of labor, objects, and notions of community, there are few systemic obstacles that challenge students' understanding about how to

Figure 1. Basic activity theory concepts

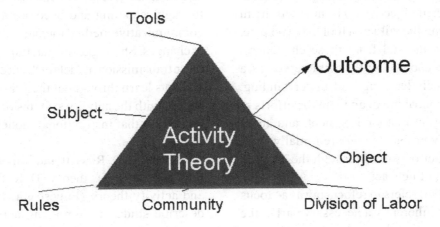

learn. Though seemingly ideal, the challenges learners often encounter are often the locations where learning occurs.

These challenging obstacles have been called many things including breakdowns, contradictions, tensions, disturbances, discoordinations, dilemmas, and "double binds," and they serve to disrupt learning understanding and equilibrium (Bodker, 1996; Engestrom, 2001; Roth, 2004). The breakdowns can nevertheless be considered worthwhile bumps in the road because they provide the means for learners to change, grow, and otherwise transform as they move toward their objectives. When new tools are introduced into the learning environment, for example, students may initially experience a double-bind situation that challenges their understanding about how to move forward toward their objectives. They must first negotiate the double-bind or tension before moving ahead to new activity en route to their objectives. Though perhaps initially challenged and even frustrated with the tensions, students who successfully move through them and refocus their activities essentially move toward "expansive learning" and "transformation" (Engestrom).

An instructor who uses a Web 2.0 tool like a wiki for collaborative responses and posting, for example, may disrupt student understanding about the practice of course participation. Here, students must negotiate the challenges posed by the new tool and refocus their efforts through new participatory practice and activity in order to proceed to their objectives. The new activity in this case is using the wiki as a tool to participate. In these situations and from those challenges, students learn about how the wiki serves as a mediator of their learning and understanding, about how to contribute to and join the efforts of the community in that environment, and about how temporary problems that are initially challenging can later be solved through the creation and refocusing of new activity.

Bodker (1996) refers to refocusing as a "focus shift," and it is inherently a necessary part of the transformational process in any activity system as learners work through the system through a series of breakdowns or contradictions to redirect their effort and focus on new activity. This new unit of activity is a combination of the "given new" and the "created new" as students who effectively cope and negotiate the contradiction or double bind move toward new activity (Engestrom, 1987). Once the contradictions are internalized and operationalized, learners can embrace and handle larger problems that emerge out of the activity as new objects and new activity. For example, learning how to use the wiki to post responses initially requires knowledge about how to edit and post. Once that knowledge is operationalized, students can refocus their efforts toward other activities including collaborating with others, higher level responses and posts, and posting video or audio responses, along with other kinds of activities that wikis afford.

Tensions can also emerge from the cross-purposes of competing activity systems. Evan's (2003) study, for example, demonstrated the resiliency of a "transmission and deficit" model often used for classroom communication. Using an activity theory framework for description and analysis, Evans examined the interactions and activity systems of students and their instructors in a writing course. She found that, in part, "transmission models" of instruction that students learn are resilient and derived from their personal school history. The system is then carried on through schooling and becomes a predominant communicative method for many teacher-student exchanges. She suggests that, though used often, these transmission models or "genre systems" that students learn throughout the years of schooling collide with the activity systems of teachers who do not use that instructional model for teaching writing.

Similarly, D. Russell and Yanez (2003) used both genre systems theory (D. R. Russell, 1997) and activity theory (Engestrom, 1987, 2001) to describe students' competing activity systems encountered when taking a required history course. In D. Russell and Yanez' study, students who understood history to be factual had difficulty understanding the activity system of their history teachers who regarded history as a means to "critically interpret." Here, one former genre system of social action, "understanding history as a collection of facts," collided with another genre system of social action, "history as critical interpretation." Each system has its own set of understood and practiced social actions and tools that mediate the activities in each separate activity and genre system, and in this case, students encountered both competing activity and genre systems. Students who encountered tension between competing systems encountered past, present, and/or future sets of social actions or genres that competed and caused tensions or double-bind situations. Nevertheless, the students who successfully negotiated those challenges, by the end, experienced meaningful and transformative learning (p. 355, 356).

Similarly, Lundell and Beach (2003) used activity theory to examine activity systems of students' writing dissertations and found that students encountered multiple competing activity systems en route to completing their doctoral degrees. The purposes, objectives, activity and genre systems of departments, graduate schools, advisors, and the job market all forced students to cope with contradictions or double binds, triggered when competing activity systems collided. Lundell and Beach and D. Russell and Yanez (2003) suggest that this double bind between one activity system and another can be explained in part through the intertextual links among activity systems mediated through genre systems, where each activity system inherently has its own genre that includes norms, expectations, rules, culture, and historical traditions. The social actions of each genre then become the tools used to mediate the activity within each system. When social actions of competing genres collide, tensions emerge, but they are necessary tensions that require further

participation and negotiation to move toward new activity and subsequent meaningful and transformative learning.

For students and teachers who use Web 2.0 tools and practices for learning, the tensions associated with the transmission model of learning provide important insight into how or even if they are used. Berge and Muilenburg (2001), for example, suggest that the resiliency of the transmission model for communication poses barriers for students who learn online. Much of computer-mediated communication in online courses occurs between students rather than between students and teachers. In many online courses, for example, collaboration is set up between and among students, with teachers monitoring rather than directing their interactions. Students entering into these environments must therefore shift their understanding from a transmission model to one that harnesses energy from other students, or the learning community. One problem and potential barrier, Berge and Muilenburg suggest, is that students may not know the importance of developing a community in these environments, and then fail to invest the required energy to participate in a way that would strengthen it.

Defining genre systems as social actions facilitates and informs the examination of competing activity systems. Social actions are the internal-level (D. Russell & Yanez, 2003) tools used to mediate an entire set of historical cultural norms and expectations. They allow things to get done in these systems, but also potentially constrain what is possible. Social actions mediated over time become so resilient that when faced with competing systems, they cause tension, disturbances, double binds, reverberations, and/or contradictions. Students must learn to cope with and negotiate them in order to change, transform, and therefore learn as successful negotiation of these challenges results in expansive learning or culturally new patterns of activity (Engestrom, 2001).

Eliminating the many tensions and double-bind situations is therefore not a necessary goal; rather, the necessary challenge becomes understanding the complexity and interplay created by the tensions while harnessing the energy created in a way that "invigorates system dynamics and learning" (Barab, MaKinster, & Scheckler, 2004, p. 82). So, successful negotiation of the complexities, challenges, and tensions associated with how wikis or any Web 2.0 tool or practice works can actually serve as a catalyst for practices and understanding that students often consider personally transformative, meaningful, and therefore authentic (Wenger, 1998).

These studies help frame how schooling and learning can be seen as social-action genre systems and how they are experienced and practiced throughout our lives. The tensions that result when the practiced social actions collide with tools or social actions of other activity and genre systems are tempting to avoid, but necessary to encounter. An analysis of these genre and activity systems, moreover, may help explain how in spite of the access to Web 2.0 tools, many educators or organizations have yet to adopt and use them for more authentic, engaging teaching and learning practices (Estabrook, Witt, & Rainie, 2007; Madden & Fox, 2006).

Nevertheless, there are signs that some of the barriers that thwart their use are beginning to diminish. A recent survey given by the Pew Internet & American Life Project suggests that "more people turn to the Internet than consult experts or family members to provide information and resources" (Estabrook et al., 2007). Students are using the Internet to communicate in different ways and more often than ever before (Kaiser Foundation, 2005). The mediating tools like Facebook and MySpace are becoming a new genre of social action that potentially challenge the genre-system resiliency associated with how people have learned in school. With social activity mediated though Internet communities and Web 2.0 tools, a potentially new genre system of social action has already been created that allows learners to enter into dialogue, and negotiate meaning

and activity with greater ease. As such, educators are in a unique position to take advantage of these new genres of social action, and can more readily consider designing activities for authentic learning trajectories.

DESIGNING FOR AUTHENTIC ACTIVITIES

Rather than teacher-centered or learner-centered formulas for instructional design, activity-centered designs focus on the constantly changing unit of activity. This whole unit or

constellation of factors is qualitatively different from that of its components. It is the composite that students and teachers experience; it is the composite which they interact with, not each of the ingredients taken one at a time; and it is that composite that we should be studying (Salomon as cited in Hewitt, 2004, p. 214)

Salomon suggests that the lens of analysis encompasses the entire system of action rather than isolated, discrete, or narrow lenses focused on constructs stripped from the contexts in which they are found. In this way, an activity theory lens is useful for capturing, discussing, and designing learning environments that are essentially authentic in that they represent contexts for user activity and interaction that are complex, ill-structured, and similar to those encountered in real-world situations.

Though authentic learning has been difficult to define, it has nevertheless prompted educators and instructional designers to create the conditions and learning environments that represent real-world situations in some way (Barab, Squire, & Dueber, 2000). Newmann, Secada, and Wehlage (1995) suggest that these environments be designed to include construction of knowledge, disciplined inquiry, and value beyond school. Others put forth models of authentic learning with similar epistemologies including situated learning and cognitive apprenticeships (Brown, Collins & Duguid, 1989), anchored instruction (Cognition and Technology Group at Vanderbilt [CTGV], 1992), problem-based learning (Hmelo, 1999; Savery & Duffy, 1995), goal-based scenarios (Shank & Clearly, 1995), and computer-supported intentional learning environments (CSILEs; Bereiter & Scardamalia, 1989). Together, these learning models have similar features and epistemologies that offer active learning around problem solving in contexts that mirror those that students will most likely encounter throughout their lives. In these environments, the emphasis centers on how learners regulate learning with their peers and with tools to both acquire and apply content knowledge. The goal is to transfer those understandings to future ill-structured problems and environments.

Barab et al. (2000) suggest that these theories have given rise to what Radinsky, Bouillion, Lento, and Gomez (2001) label "simulated" and "participatory" environments. Essentially, the simulated approach includes the practices and tools closest to what would be experienced in real-world situations, but they are guided and observed in controlled environments. In this way, they can only approach authenticity. Participatory designs, by contrast, are those that are located in the actual context, so they offer the closest proximity to the tasks and challenges of the intended environment; however, these are not always practical and are difficult to implement.

Perhaps the models or designs that best approach and perhaps even mirror authenticity are those that are designed en route or during the learning process. Barab et al. (2000) argue that

authenticity lies in learner-perceived relations between practices they are carrying out and the use value of these practices. Although educators can seed learning environments using tasks that are similar to those tasks that are being carried out by real world practitioners, they cannot guaran-

tee the "buy-in" of the learner. Barab et al. deny the legitimacy of preauthentication and instead conceive authenticity as an emergent process that occurs as individuals engage in practices of value to themselves and to a community of practice. (p. 38)

Barab et al. (2000) therefore attempt to advance the coevolutionary model that "places authenticity not in the learner, the task, or the environment, but in the dynamic interactions among those various components" (p. 38). That is, "authenticity is manifest in the flow itself, and is not an objective feature or any one component in isolation" (p. 38). Instead, the tasks and objectives associated with the unit-of-learning activity coevolve with all stakeholders in the process. It is therefore a more dynamic and authentic environment with potential significance and meaning to all involved.

In addition to and beyond participation, engagement, and en route models for authentic learning, Collis and Moonen (2006) propose using a contribution model where learners are active contributors to the process. They suggest that learners and instructors can coconstruct understanding as the course progresses and reflect on their process through the use of technology tools. In these environments, learners are able contribute their own experiences and use the Internet like a library, contributing information and media that inform others. Perhaps the contributing-student model of authentic instruction can actually be realized through the tools, practices, ubiquity, and ease of Web 2.0 tools.

Finally, Kaptelinin and Nardi (2006) suggest that recent trends in interaction design go beyond cognitive models to include affective, emotional, experiential, performance, and intelligent designs (see also Fogg, 2000; Kuutti, Iacucci, & Iacucci, 2002; McCarthy & Wright, 2004; Norman, 2004; Picard, 1997; Pink, 2006). Kaptelinin and Nardi contend that we are moving toward more collaborative uses of technology with groups and the larger society, varied virtual and physical contexts, and an expanded set of activities that require a collaborative approach to their design. In other words, the entire community of learners should be involved in the process of design and the iterative process of constructing and reconstructing the object and unit of activity.

To examine these media tools and practices more thoroughly, schools and organizations could implement activity theory as their tool or lens of choice for examination of sociocultural practices evident in their learning systems. Activity theory focuses on "activities in which people are engaged, the nature of the tools they use in those activities, the social and contextual relationships among collaborators in those activities, the goals and intentions of those activities, and the outcomes or objects of those activities" which, in the end, are all attributes of emerging authentic environments (Jonassen, 2000, p. 109). That is, an activity theory lens can be used as the descriptive and analytic handle necessary for observing how authentic practices and changing social actions emerge through Web 2.0 technologies.

DESIGNING FOR AUTHENTIC COMMUNITIES

J. Brown and Duguid (2000) remind us that in the age of information, learning is also an "identity forming, social act" (p. 140) and that what is needed is not more knowledge, but people to "assimilate, understand, and make sense of it" (p. 121). Like authentic activity, authentic communities defy instructional designs that are prescribed by a required curriculum. Rather, they grow and coalesce en route to purpose and meaning as can be seen in Facebook, the current Web 2.0 choice for many creating personal communities. Though the site continues to be developed, its initial design was to be a simple student and staff directory. As of July 2007, however, it has grown to be the largest social networking site with an education focus (Philips, 2007). Rather than follow

a prescribed trajectory of how it was to be used for social networking, its growth and popularity came from its collaborative en route use.

There is much written about the energy created by learning communities developed across computer-mediated environments. For example, Wang, Sierra, and Folger (2003) examined the extent to which participation, shared identity, and the establishment of a social network created a learning community through computer-mediated communications. Students used chat sessions associated with the live webcasts most often as they afforded the students an opportunity to interact with the instructor and other students. The authors also found that higher performing groups used nicknames to refer to their teams, and that it helped build online camaraderie. In addition, public posting of feelings of respect and appreciation fostered an environment of inclusion and trust.

These new kinds of online communities include names like communities of practice (Wenger, 1998), networks of practice (J. Brown & Duguid, 2000), communities of purpose (Schlager & Fusco, 2004), protocommunities (Hewitt, 2004), and sociotechnical interaction networks (STINs; Kling & Courtright, 2004). Barab et al. (2004) provide a clear and helpful definition that describes these communities as "persistent, sustained social network(s) of individuals who share and develop an overlapping knowledge base, set of beliefs, values, history, and experiences focused on a common practice and/or mutual enterprise" (p. 55). Lave and Wenger (1991) suggest that communities of practice have histories, cultural identities, interdependence among members, and mechanisms for reproduction" (p. 55). Hara adds that communities of practice "are informal networks that support professional practitioners to develop shared meaning and engage in knowledge building among the members" (as cited in Kling & Courtright, p. 104). Barab and Duffy (2000) characterize communities of practice as "self organizing, and cannot be designed *prima facie*. They grow, evolve, and change dynamically, transcending any particular member and outliving any particular task" (Kling & Courtright, p. 106).

Schlager and Fusco (2004) further suggest that communities of practice have been documented in many professional and craft workplaces, but seem to be rare in school environments. Though they may exist in schools, Wenger (1998) suggests that these communities most likely do not exist within the formal curricular and organizational framework that most schools embody. Instead, he states that communities of practice can "sprout" in schools "in spite of the curriculum" and that "the learning that is most personally transformative turns out to be the learning that involves membership in these communities of practice" (p. 6). In other words, Wenger suggests that the kinds of communities that are most transformative are those that gather and socialize during passing time or once "the bell rings," when, ironically, the formal schooling process has ended for the hour or for the day.

These kinds of places are similar to what Oldenburg (1997) calls "third places": places characterized as "the core settings of informal public life" that are "happily anticipated," and away from the "first place" home and "second place" work environments where people spend a majority of their time (p. 16). The people that meet in these third places, moreover, are groups who negotiate meaning; preserve, create, and share knowledge; and mutually support the development of individual and group identities. Riel and Polin (2004) further suggest that traditional classrooms cannot develop rich participatory practices necessary for communities of practice or third places because they are "weighed down by the burden of a prescribed curriculum, constrained by the limitations of age and ability grouping, and with compulsory attendance…lack the defining characteristics of a cohesive community" (p. 22).

What seems to be important here is that few of these communities are formally designed or at least resist formality in some way. Instead, they exist independently of prescribed curricular aspirations; the activities within them are motivated through the recursive practices of negotiating meaning, creating and sharing knowledge en route, and building individual and group identity. In other words, the most meaningful communities may not be part of anyone's intentional learning objectives, yet they are, as Wenger (1998) suggests, potentially the most personally transformative.

Authentic learning environments seem to therefore require authentic communities of learning. Like Barab et al. (2000), Engestrom (2001) posits that computer-mediated learning environments be developed as they unfold, and that they often require support en route to outcomes with "more capable peers." He states that in

important transformations of our personal lives and organizational practices, we must learn new forms of activity which are not yet there. They are literally learned as they are being created. There is no competent teacher. Standard learning theories have little to offer if one wants to understand these processes. (p. 138)

Web 2.0 tools and practices like wikis, Facebook, MySpace, and even Twitter offer possibilities for generating these kinds of communities in order to augment learning in authentic ways that mirror both real-world communities and authentic learning and problem-based situations. Because many of these Web 2.0 communities already exist, they are already social-action genre systems ready to be adopted and adapted for use in educational settings.

FUTURE TRENDS

Today's conditions for learning suggest that learning environments be designed to accommodate the need for participation, creation, and collaboration. Designs that accommodate the en route interactions of learners seem to represent authentic and real-world learning more than the prescriptive authentic instructional designs provided by school or classroom environments. More importantly, these emergent environments are collaborative and participatory, and are therefore potentially more personally transformative, meaningful, and motivating while fostering higher ordering thinking and problem solving essential to real-world applications and success (Barab et al., 2000; Newmann et al., 1995; Radinsky et al., 2001; Sfard, 1998; Wenger, 1998).

With open access to source code, abundant and changing Web 2.0 and mobile tools, and the attitudes about sharing knowledge and ideas, today's media environments provide innovative ways to think, create, and use media dynamically. The latest iteration of Web 2.0, for example, appears as mashups that mix Web 2.0 media tools together for even more dynamic activity (Merrill, 2006; Lackie & Terrio, 2006). The fact that the definition of Web 2.0 continues to change while defying definition perhaps best represents the dynamic nature of these units of activity and bodes well for their continued evolution and use. As Lorenzo, Oblinger, and Dziubna (2007) suggest, Web 2.0 tools and practices have already changed what it means to be Net savvy.

With any introduction of new media tools, it is important to consider not only their ease of use and accessibility, but how user purposes and objectives contribute to their evolution into meaningful, authentic cultural practices. Web 2.0 tools provide accessibility, ease of use, and rich possibilities for learning, and therefore a realistic platform for sustainability and growth.

CONCLUSION

This chapter discussed the teaching and learning possibilities with Web 2.0 tools and practices along with the lens of activity theory to help describe and examine the learning environments that emerge from them. The new instructional-design paradigm is upon us as authentic activity models move from providing learners with systematic knowledge-acquisition models for learning to providing learners with learning-environment accommodations that range from the people in those environments to the tools and resources that learners find in them (see Hannafin, Land, & Oliver, 1999). Today, our cultural and societal conditions, norms, and practices demonstrate movement away from previously valued systems of interactions that are logical, linear, and sequential (see Pink, 2006). In the new learning environments, knowledge is not delivered nor acquired; rather, it unfolds during the process through participation, construction, and collaboration (Kosma, 2000; Land, 2000; Reigeluth, 1999).

The new paradigm of instructional design and learning furthermore decenters the role of teachers, instructional designers, and even computers as purveyors of information, contexts, and formulas for learning. Today's tools and practices create cocollaborators and designers out of teachers and students in participatory contexts. Rather than regarding learners as passive, empty vessels or blank slates, they prompt learners into active roles in learning processes as learners appropriate knowledge about what and how they learn. It is, according to Hannafin, Hannafin, Hooper, Rieber, and Kini (1996), more about the process than outcomes; the process requires learners to be more actively involved decision makers, knowledge builders, and designers rather than receivers of information in order to experience higher level and meaningful learning. To access these dynamic, collaborative, and contributory processes, activity theory provides a useful lens to better analyze and describe the complexity of learners in action with others and with media while proceeding on their learning trajectories. Moreover, Web 2.0 tools and practices associated with them allow students and teachers to engage in tensions that are centered on content-related challenges while generating new social-action genres and practices.

REFERENCES

Alexander, B. (2006, March/April). Web 2.0: A new wave of innovation for teaching and learning? *Educause Review*, pp. 33-44.

Barab, S., & Duffy, T. (2000). From practice fields to communities of practice. In D. Jonassen & S. Land (Eds.), *Theoretical foundations of learning environments* (pp. 25-55). Mahwah, NJ: Lawrence Erlbaum Associates.

Barab, S., MaKinster, J., & Scheckler, R. (2004). Designing system dualities: Characterizing an online professional development community. In S. Barab, R. Kling, & J. Gray (Eds.), *Designing for virtual communities in the service of learning* (pp. 53-90). New York: Cambridge.

Barab, S., Squire, K., & Dueber, W. (2000). A co-evolutionary model for supporting the emergence of authenticity. *Educational Technology Research and Development, 48*(2), 37-62.

Bereiter, C., & Scardamalia, M. (1989). Intentional learning as a goal of instruction. In L. B. Resnick (Ed.), *Knowing, learning, and instruction* (pp. 361-391). Hillsdale, NJ: Lawrence Erlbaum.

Berge, Z., & Muilenburg, L. (2001). Obstacles faced at various stages of capability regarding distance education in institutions of higher learning. *Tech Trends, 46*(4), 40-45.

Bodker, S. (1996). Applying activity theory to video analysis: How to make sense of video data in HCI. In B. Nardi (Ed.), *Context and consciousness: Activity theory and human computer interaction* (pp. 147-174). Cambridge, MA: MIT Press.

Boutin, P. (2006). Web 2.0: The new Internet boom does not live up to its name. *Slate*. Retrieved March 15, 2008, from http://www.slate.com/id/2138951

Brown, A., Collins, A., & Duguid, P. (1989). Situated cognition and the culture of learning. *Educational Researcher, 18*, 32-42.

Brown, J., & Duguid, P. (2000). *The social life of information*. Boston: Harvard Business School Press.

Collis & Moonen. (2006). The contributing student: Learners as co-developers of learning resources for reuse in Web environments. In D. Hung & M. S. Khine (Eds.), *Engaged learning with emerging technologies* (pp. 49-67). The Netherlands: Springer.

Cognition and Technology Group at Vanderbilt (CTGV). (1992). The Jasper experiment: An exploration of issues in learning and instructional design. *Educational Technology Research and Development, 40*(1), 65-80.

Driscoll, K. (2007, May/June). Collaboration in today's classrooms: New Web tools change the game. *Multimedia & Internet Schools*, pp. 9-12.

Engestrom, Y. (1987). *Learning by expanding*. Orienta-Konsulti. Retrieved March 15, 2008, from http://communication.ucsd.edu/MCA/Paper/Engestrom/expanding/toc.htm

Engestrom, Y. (2001). Expansive learning at work: Toward an activity theoretical reconceptualization. *Journal of Education and Work, 14*(1), 133-156.

Ertmer, P. (2005). Teacher pedogological beliefs: The final frontier in our quest for technology integration? *Educational Technology Research and Development, 53*(4), 25-40.

Estabrook, L., Witt, E., & Rainie, L. (2007). *Information searches that solve problems: How people use the Internet, libraries, and government agencies when they need help*. Retrieved March 15, 2008, from http://www.pewinternet.org/pdfs/Pew_UI_LibrariesReport.pdf

Evans, K. (2003). Accounting for conflicting mental models of communication in student-teacher interaction: An activity theory analysis. *Writing Selves/Writing Societies*. Retrieved March

15, 2008, from http://wac.colostate.edu/books/selves_societies

Fogg, B. J. (2000). Persuasive technologies and Net smart devices. In E. Bergman (Ed.), *Information appliances and beyond: Interaction design for consumer products* (pp. 335-360). San Francisco: Morgan Kaufmann.

Hannafin, M., Hannafin, K., Hooper, S., Rieber, L., & Kini, A. (1996). Research on and research with emerging technologies. In D. Jonassen (Ed.), *Handbook of research for educational communications and technology* (pp. 378-402). New York: Simon and Schuster.

Hannafin, M., Land, S., & Oliver, K. (1999). Open learning environments: Foundations, methods, and models. In C. Reigeluth (Ed.), *Instructional design theories and models: A new paradigm of instructional theory* (Vol. 2, pp. 115-140). Mahwah, NJ: Lawrence Erlbaum Associates.

Hewitt, J. (2004). An exploration of community in a knowledge forum

classroom: An activity system analysis. In S. Barab, R. Kling, & J. Gray (Eds.), *Designing for virtual communities in the service of learning* (pp. 210-238). New York: Cambridge.

Hmelo, C. E. (1999). Problem based learning: Effect on the early acquisition of cognitive skill in medicine. *Journal of Learning Sciences, 7*(2), 173-208.

Hyysalo, S. (2005). Objects and motives in the product design process. *Mind Culture and Activity, 12*(1), 19-36.

Jonassen, D. (2000). Revisiting activity theory as a framework for designing student centered learning environments. In D. Jonassen & S. Land (Eds.), *Theoretical foundations of learning environments*. Mahwah, NJ: Lawrence Erlbaum Associates.

Kaiser Foundation. (2005). *Generation M: Media in the lives of 8-18 year-olds*. Retrieved March 15, 2008, from http://www.kff.org/entmedia/entmedia030905pkg.cfm

Kaptelinin, V., & Nardi, B. (2006). *Acting with technology: Activity theory and interaction design*. Cambridge, MA: MIT Press.

Kling, R., & Courtright, C. (2004). Group behavior and learning in electronic forums. In R. Kling, J. Gray, & S. Barab (Eds.), *Designing for virtual communities in the service of learning* (pp. 91-119). Cambridge, United Kingdom: Cambridge University Press.

Kosma, R. (2000). The relationship between technology and design in educational technology research and development: A reply to Richey. *Educational Technology Research and Development, 48*(1), 19-21.

Kuutti, K., Iacucci, G., & Iacucci, C. (2002, October 13-16). Acting to know: Improving creativity in the design of mobile services by using performances. In *Proceedings of the Fourth Conference on Creativity and Cognition* (pp. 95-102). Loughborough, United Kingdom.

Lackie, R., & Terrio, R. (2006, July/August). Mashups and other new or improved collaborative social software tools. *Multimedia and Internet @ Schools*, pp. 12-15.

Land, S. (2000). Cognitive requirements for learning with open ended learning environments. *Educational Technology Research and Development, 48*(3), 61-78.

Lave, J., & Wenger, E. (1991). *Situated learning: Legitimate peripheral participation*. Cambridge, United Kingdom: Cambridge University Press.

Lorenzo, G., Oblinger, D., & Dziubna, C. (2007). How choice, co-creation, and culture are changing what it means to be Net savvy. *Educause Quarterly, 1*, 6-12.

Lundell, D., & Beach, R. (2003). Dissertation writers' negotiations with competing activity systems. In Bazerman & Russell (Eds.), *Writing selves/writing societies* (pp. 483-514). Retrieved March 15, 2008, from http://wac.colostate.edu/books/selves_societies

Madden, M., & Fox, S. (2006). *Riding the waves of "Web 2.0."* Retrieved March 15, 2008, from http://www.pewinternet.org/pdfs/PIP_Web_2.0.pdf

McCarthy, J., & Wright, P. (2004). *Technology as experience.* Cambridge, MA: MIT Press.

Merrill, D. (2006). *Mashups: The new breed of Web app.* Retrieved March 15, 2008, from http://www.ibm.com/developerworks/library/x-mashups.html

Moser, F. Z. (2007). Faculty adoption of educational technology. *Educause Quarterly, 1*, 66-69.

Nardi, B. (1996). Studying context: A comparison of activity theory, situated action models, and distributed cognition. In B. Nardi (Ed.), *Context and consciousness: Activity theory and human computer interaction.* Cambridge, MA: MIT.

Newmann, F., Secada, G., & Wehlage, G. (1995). *A guide to authentic instruction.* Madison, WI: Wisconsin Center for Educational Research.

Norman, D. (2004). *Emotional design: Why we love (or hate) everyday things.* New York: Basic Books.

Oldenburg, R. (1997). *The great good place.* New York: Marlow.

O'Reilly, T. (2005). *What is Web 2.0?* Retrieved March 15, 2008, from http://www.oreillynet.com/pub/a/oreilly/tim/news/2005/09/30/what-is-web-20.html

Philips, S. (2007). A brief history of Facebook. *Guardian Unlimited.* Retrieved March 15, 2008, from http://www.guardian.co.uk/technology/2007/jul/25/media.newmedia

Picard, R. (1997). *Affective computing.* Cambridge, MA: MIT Press.

Pink, D. (2006). *A whole new mind: Why right-brainers will rule the future.* New York: Penguin.

Radinsky, J., Bouillion, L., Lento, E., & Gomez, L. (2001). Mutual benefit partnership: A curricular design for authenticity. *Journal of Curriculum Studies, 33*(4), 405-430.

Reigeluth, C. (1999). What is instructional design theory and how is it changing? In C. Reigeluth (Ed.), *Instructional design theories and models: A new paradigm of instructional theory* (Vol. 2, pp. 5-30). Mahwah, NJ: Lawrence Erlbaum Associates.

Riel, M., & Polin, L. (2004). Online learning communities: Common ground and critical differences in designing technical environments. In S. Barab, R. Kling, & J. Gray (Eds.), *Designing for virtual communities in the service of learning* (pp. 16-52). New York: Cambridge.

Roth, W. M. (2004). Activity theory and education: An introduction. *Mind Culture and Activity, 11*(1), 1-8.

Russell, D., & Yanez, A. (2003). *"Big picture people rarely become historians": Genre systems and the contradictions of general education.* Retrieved March 15, 2008, from http://wac.colostate.edu/books/selves_societies

Russell, D. R. (1997). Rethinking genre in school and society: An activity theory analysis. *Written Communication, 14*, 504-554.

Savery, & Duffy, T. (1995). Problem based learning: An instructional model and its constructivist framework. In B. Wilson (Ed.), *Constructivist learning environments: Case studies in instructional design* (pp. 135-148). Englewood Cliffs, NJ: Educational Technology Publications.

Schlager, M., & Fusco, J. (2004). Teacher professional development, technology, and communities of practice: Are we putting the cart before the horse? In S. Barab, R. Kling, & J. Gray (Eds.), *Designing for virtual communities in the service of learning* (pp. 120-153). New York: Cambridge

Seitzinger, J. (2006). Be constructive: Blogs, podcasts, and wikis as constructivist tools. In *Learning solutions: Practical applications of technology for learning.* Elearning Guild.

Sfard, A. (1998). On two metaphors for learning and the dangers of choosing just one. *Educational Researcher, 27*, 4-13.

Shank, R., & Cleary, R. (1995). *Engines for education.* Mahwah, NJ: Lawrence Erlbaum.

Wang, M., Sierra, C., & Folger, T. (2003). Building a dynamic online learning community among adult learners. *Education Media International, 40*(1-2), 49-61.

Wenger, E. (1998). *Communities of practice: Learning, meaning and identity.* Cambridge, MA: Cambridge University Press.

Section VI
Glossary and Web 2.0 Tutorial

Glossary

3-D Internet: See *Virtual Worlds*.

Activity Theory: Activity theory provides a rich descriptive framework through which a person can classify an activity as it pertains to working toward an objective or goal. Activity theorists contend that the entire context of a learning situation is important and should be accounted for since little, if any, human action takes place independent of surrounding contextual elements.

Asynchronous JavaScript and XML (AJAX): AJAX is a development technique used on Web sites that combines the use of JavaScript and XML (extensible markup language) to create a more interactive user experience. The concept is to separate the user interface from data in order to be able to exchange data with the server without having to refresh the entire user interface. As a result, the Web page becomes more responsive. AJAX is a key part of Web 2.0 because of its ability to greatly improve the user interface of applications and make them more dynamic.

ATOM: ATOM is a publishing format that is similar to RSS (really simple syndication), but is more robust and flexible. It is based on XML and, while not as widely used as RSS, is gaining market adoption. Like RSS, ATOM is part of Web 2.0 because of its ability to exchange data in a structured but easily consumable manner between applications.

Avatar: An avatar is a graphical representation of a person in a virtual world setting, such as *Second Life*. Avatars can be human, animal, or fantasy depending on the game and player's disposition. Avatars can be gendered or genderless, and representative of the real-life participant or not. Practically speaking, an avatar is a fancy cursor that provides an alter ego for the participant.

Best Practice: Best practice is the belief that there is an appropriate action or pattern to be followed that will consistently lead to the best possible desired outcome, therefore minimizing problems and avoiding unforeseen complications.

Blog: See *Weblog*.

Botnets: Botnets are networks (or groups) of security-compromised computers known as zombies. Botnets are used in spamming (mass junk e-mail distributions), in focused attacks to steal data, or as client-naïve instruments in denial-of-services (DoS) attacks.

Business to Consumer (B2C): B2C refers to a business interacting with its customers on the Internet, also known as the retailing side of e-commerce. Other types of interactions include business to business (B2B), which refers to the interaction of a business with other businesses or business partners.

Cascading Style Sheets (CSS): CSS is used to describe the presentation of a document written in HTML (hypertext markup language) or XML. For each style that is defined in the markup language, CSS tells the client how to display that style. For example, CSS would define that the Header style should be displayed in a bold 12-point font.

Collaboration: Collaboration is defined by Merriam-Webster's Online Dictionary (n.d.) as "to work jointly with others or together especially in an intellectual endeavor." Collaboration is about more than one person (a team, a group, etc.) working together toward a common goal.

Collective Intelligence: Collective intelligence refers to any system that attempts to tap the expertise of a group, rather than an individual, to make decisions. Technologies that contribute to collective intelligence include collaborative publishing and common databases for sharing knowledge.

Cracker: Also known as a "black hat," it refers to a person who illegally compromises the security of a computer system or network to reach a malicious end.

Cross-Site Request Forgery (CSRF): Similar to cross-site scripting (XSS), in CSRF, unauthorized (or forged) commands from a user are transmitted to or from a trusted Web site. This type of attack takes advantage of the trust between the user and Web site.

Cross-Site Scripting (XSS): XSS involves the injection of malicious code into a Web page viewed by others. There are several types of XSS attack methods; however, the common denominator is that the user's browser always executes code that it is not authorized to execute or is destructive or compromising.

Enterprise 2.0: Enterprise 2.0 is a recently identified term that is used to refer to the application of Web 2.0 and social networking concepts in an enterprise business context.

Extensible Markup Language (XML): XML is a programming language that allows a developer to define content and specific tags that surround the content. Like HTML, the content can be formatted through the use of tags. However, XML also allows the programmer to create his or her own tags and then find and manipulate content through the tags that are associated with the content.

Folksonomy: Folksonomy is a taxonomy where the tags and categorization of data are created and updated in a dynamic way by the consumers of the content. Folksonomies are part of Web 2.0 because they give the responsibility of creating the tags and associating them with the content to the users of the system.

Fragging: Fragging is to "kill" a player in a virtual world, with the player being able to "respawn" or come back to life a short time later. It is an action within a virtual game that temporarily erases another player from the game.

Griefing: Griefing is unacceptable, and sometimes unethical, behavior in a virtual world. In order for something to be considered griefing, the act must (a) be intentional, (b) cause other players to enjoy the game less, and (c) provide the griefer enjoyment. Typical acts of griefing in a virtual world, such as *Second Life*, might include murder, theft, or beatings by gangs.

Hacker: A hacker is someone who creatively manipulates computer code or procedures to achieve a desired outcome, generally a mischievous or malicious one.

Hypertext Markup Language (HTML): HTML has been around since the creation of the Internet. This language is used to create and format the content that is included on Web pages.

Identify Theft: Identity theft occurs when a criminal uses another person's personal information, without that person's knowledge, to take on that person's identity and commit fraud. It can occur on an individual or on a large scale to individuals or companies. Identity thieves can ruin the victim's good name, slander the victim's character, and cause the victim loss of credibility and/or property.

Instant Messaging: Instant messaging is a form of real-time communication that allows short text messages to be sent from one computer user to another across a computer network. Instant messaging allows people to communicate faster than e-mail and slightly less synchronously than a phone call. Instant messaging software also displays presence information, which is a user's status regarding whether the person is available for conversation or away from the machine.

JavaScript: JavaScript is a cross-platform scripting language that can be used in a server or client environment to manipulate data and objects. It is most commonly used for client-side Web development to create a more dynamic user experience with a Web page.

JavaScript Object Notation (JSON): JSON is a lightweight computer data interchange format. It is a subset of the JavaScript programming language and is commonly used within AJAX as an alternative to using XML.

Malware: Malware is malicious software that damages and degrades a user's computer. Malware is usually installed without the computer user's consent or knowledge.

Marketing 2.0: Marketing 2.0 is being used to describe the impact Web 2.0 has had on the discipline of marketing. Companies are finding and leveraging the many uses of Web 2.0 technologies to successfully connect, communicate, and collaborate with their consumers.

Mashups: Mashups are Web sites or applications that take multiple data sources and bring them together to provide specialized or situational value. Mashups are part of Web 2.0 because of their ability to let regular users create valuable situational applications without having to perform extensive application development.

Massively Multiplayer Online Role-Playing Game (MMORPG or MMOG): An MMORPG is an online virtual game, such as *World of Warcraft* or *Second Life*, that supports thousands or tens of thousands of players at the same time.

Message Boards: Message boards are online discussion forums that let users post topics and responses in a threaded conversation format.

Metaverse: The Metaverse is one of the worlds described in Neal Stephenson's science-fiction novel, *Snow Crash*, published in 1992. The Metaverse is Stephenson's concept of how an online, virtual space might evolve in the future. This concept has inspired many online virtual worlds today.

Online Community: An online community is a group of people with common interests who use an electronic medium (Internet, phone, e-mail, instant messaging) as their primary means of facilitating communication and collaboration.

Phishing: Phishing involves Web sites that look legitimate, but are facades developed to acquire credit card numbers, passwords, social security numbers, and other personal data.

Podcast: A podcast is a radio-style broadcast that is recorded and made available for users to download onto their computer, iPod, or MP3 player. Users generally find and subscribe to podcasts on Web sites as a method to keep up with the information being disseminated on the site. Podcasts are a very valuable tool to both mobile and office workers because they provide the ability to access audio information (e.g., presentations) at the convenience of the listener. Podcasts are part of Web 2.0 because of their ability to be easily created and disseminated by users without costly equipment or extensive experience.

Really Simple Syndication (RSS): RSS is a method for publishing information in a structured "feed" format (usually in XML). This allows clients and other software applications to subscribe to and receive timely information updates. Many people use feed readers to subscribe to a number of Web sites and have the updates aggregated into a single interface. RSS is part of Web 2.0 because of its ability to exchange data in a structured but easily consumable manner between applications.

***Second Life*:** *Second Life* is an Internet-based virtual world developed by Linden Lab (Linden Research, Inc.) that is a massive multiplayer online game. *Second Life* enables its users to interact with each other through motional avatars, providing an advanced level of social network service.

Semantic Web: The Semantic Web refers to a vision for the Web to become a medium for machines to be able to understand, relate, and compile information without human intervention.

Simple Object Access Protocol (SOAP): SOAP is the common protocol used for Web services remote procedure calls. It mainly exchanges data formatted in XML standards between computer systems.

Social Bookmarks: Social bookmarks allow users to centrally store, organize, share, and tag links to Web pages in a central place. These bookmarks are usually shared publicly and allow users to more quickly find information by searching other user's social bookmarks.

Social Branding: Companies can create a page for their brand or product on an existing social networking Web site. This allows the brand to interact with others on the site, including, but not limited to, making connections with others, allowing site participants to join brand groups, fostering blogging about the brand, displaying brand information, and promoting the brand.

Social Graph: The social graph refers to a visual mapping of all of our social interactions and connections as human beings. As opposed to having connections to others maintained on a Web-site-by-Web-site basis, it has been proposed that there be one open social graph created to manage connections between anyone and everyone.

Social Network: A social network is a grouping of personal relationships that each of us establishes. As opposed to other types of networks, the value of a social network is not in the nodes of the network, which in this case are people, but in the relationships themselves. Social networking, therefore, is the act of building one's social network.

Social Network Analysis (SNA): SNA is a way of identifying and understanding social linkages and relationships between people. Through the understanding of these relationships, we can then assess information flows and communication breakdowns in a social network.

Social Software: Social software is the use of technology, and more specifically computer software, to support the process of social networking. It is important to note that the software itself is not performing the activity of social networking. The software is simply being leveraged to support and facilitate the creation and maturation of relationships between individuals, otherwise known as social networking.

Tags: Tags are keywords that users of a particular application can associate with a piece of content in that application. For example, if a user is posting a blog entry about what he or she ate for breakfast, that entry might be tagged with the keywords *orange juice*, *toast*, *breakfast*, and *eggs* so that other users searching on those keywords will find the blog entry. Users can also tag content created by others.

Value-Chain Members: Value-chain members can be businesses or individuals that make up a value chain. A value chain is a set of businesses, people, processes, and information that, linked together, provide value to customers.

Videocasts: Also known as video podcasts, they provide information to viewers by playing a recorded audio or video file.

Virtual Worlds: Sometimes called digital worlds, they are computer-based simulated environments, usually modeled after the real world and accessed through online interfaces. They are inhabited by users in the form of avatars, two- or three-dimensional graphic characters that may resemble humans, animals, or imaginative creatures that take on fanciful names.

Web 2.0: Web 2.0 refers to a style or method for combining existing technologies to empower people. Web 2.0 is a technology concept, unlike social networking (which is a sociology concept). The premise behind Web 2.0 is the use of the Internet as a platform.

Web 2.0 Marketing Mix: The Web 2.0 marketing mix leverages Web 2.0 technologies to enable consumers to participate in each p of the traditional "four p" marketing mix (price, product, promotion, and placement).

Web 3.0: Web 3.0 is a term used to describe the future iteration of the World Wide Web. If the current state is Web 2.0, then the future must be Web 3.0.

Weblog (Blog): A blog is a Web site that is essentially a journal posted on the Web. The most common uses for the journal are either personal publishing, or commentary or news on a particular topic. Blogs are part of Web 2.0 because they enable common users to publish their thoughts and have their voice heard without the need to know how to program Web pages.

Web Services: Web services are software systems that make it easier for different computer systems to communicate with one another in order to pass information or conduct transactions. For example, a retailer and supplier might use Web services to communicate over the Internet and automatically update each other's inventory systems.

Widget: A widget is a small application that can be embedded on different Web pages. The content in widgets can include blogs, live discussions, bookmarks to other Web sites, webcasts, video, games, and more.

Wikis: Wikis are server software that allow for one or more users to work together to create and edit content. Many wikis serve as a place for multiple people or communities to come together to collaborate on a particular topic. Wikis are part of Web 2.0 because of their ability to facilitate collaboration between users.

World of Warcraft: *World of Warcraft* is a massively multiplayer online role-playing game in which the participants assume the role of a specific predefined character, are restricted by rules, and progress through a series of competitive events (e.g., fighting monsters) to a predefined goal. This progression through events requires interactions, and perhaps even teaming up with other players to successfully accomplish the events in the game. By successfully accomplishing events, players are rewarded with in-game money, items, experience, and reputation.

XML Poisoning: XML poisoning is the corruption (or poisoning) of XML data during transmission between client and server in such a way as to disrupt the processing of the information. The effect of the poisoning can range from denial of service, where the targeted server is bombarded with spurious requests that will, in effect, bring the server down or render it nonfunctional, to compromised confidential information.

Social Software and Web 2.0 Technology Tutorial

ABSTRACT

This tutorial will provide the reader with a more in-depth understanding of the technologies associated with Web 2.0. MBA students from the Robins School at the University of Richmond are recognized for their overall contributions to this tutorial and to the particular sections indicated.

WEBLOGS (BLOGS)

Joe Biedenharn,

Jeff Snyder, Alex White

History of Weblogs (Blogs)

Back in the earliest days of the Internet, weblogs (World Wide Web logs or journals, also referred to as blogs) were simply lists of Web links that afforded early Internet users easy access and navigation to new Web sites. In 1992, Internet pioneer Tim Berners-Lee actually developed and maintained the first-ever weblog known as the What's New Page, available at http://www.unc.edu/~zuiker/blogging101 (Zuiker, 2004). As the World Wide Web continued to expand, blogs evolved as Web page authors began to filter content to their particular points of interest. In 1994,

Justin Hall created Justin's Home Page (http://www.links.net/vita/web/original.html), which is generally considered one of the first filtered blogs (Zuiker). By late 1997, blogs began to resemble their current format in that posts were now dated, filtered, and personalized. In the minds of many blog creators, the interactivity of their Web sites distinguished them from the more standard Web pages that only allowed users one dimensional access to content. The early 1990s evolution of blogs led Jorn Barger to coin the term *weblog* as a description of the postings to his Robot Wisdom Web site (http://www.robotwisdom.com/#top; Blood, 2000). Weblog, or blog for short, is now the universally accepted name for all Web sites that feature postings displayed in reverse chronological order.

While blogs experienced significant content refinement in the 1990s, growth was relatively modest; there were only 23 known blogs in existence at the beginning of 1999 (Blood, 2000). Contrast this to 2006, in which there were an estimated 50 million blogs, with new blogs coming online every second (Tapscott & Williams, 2006). This explosive growth can be attributed to two main factors: the debut of free blog-creation Web sites and users' desire for more interactive, unfiltered content. In July 1999, the launch of Pitas allowed bloggers a free and easy way to design a weblog (Blood). Shortly after the launch of Pitas, Blogger was created, and the steady growth of blogs exploded with hundreds of blogs popping up seemingly overnight (Blood).

While the ease of use of these free tools undoubtedly played a huge role in blog development, the growth explosion of blogs cannot be fully explained by functionality improvements alone. Users' desire for unfiltered, peer-posted media content supported the tremendous growth of blogs in areas such as politics, sports, and entertainment. Aliza Risdahl (2007), author of the book *Ecommerce*, believes that the explosive growth of blogs at the turn of the century can be attributed in part to users' desire to post articles and opinions concerning the latest news on the 2000 presidential election and the Iraq war. One significant event that contributed to the legitimacy of blogs as a reliable source for news and current events was the Monica Lewinsky scandal. Internet blogger Matt Drudge was the first to break the story that President Bill Clinton was reportedly having an affair with White House intern Monica Lewinsky (Whitworth, 2008). The tremendous growth of blogs in the early 21st century seems to support the view of TakingITGlobal (http://www.takingitglobal.org) founder Michael Furdyk when he states, "Our generation really doesn't trust the media and advertising as much as we trust peer to peer opinion and social networks" (Tapscott & Williams, 2006).

Over just 15 years, blogs have evolved from a few Internet sites containing Web links to a network of over 50 million sites that allow users to gather information and post opinions on any and all subjects. Current trends seem to indicate that more and more news and entertainment will come from peer sources, such as blogs, rather than traditional sources such as newspapers and television. While the history of blog growth has been profound, the ease of blog creation and users' clear desire for more peer-created and interactive content indicates that blogs will become more and more prevalent.

Current Trends

Blogs are used in a wide variety of applications throughout everyday life. Blogs can be used to connect and correspond with friends and colleagues on sites like MySpace (http://www.myspace.com); keep up to date and discuss the latest sports, business, and political news on Technorati (http://technorati.com); or communicate about work-related happenings and business issues with senior executives and coworkers in a corporate or business setting. While all of these applications have become increasingly prevalent in recent years, sites such as MySpace and Technorati have enjoyed more relative growth and adoption than corporate blogs. Consider the following: In 2006, MySpace had 80 million members and experienced year-over-year site growth of 752% (Granneman, 2006). While growth was not quite as spectacular at Technorati, it was still significant; quarter-on-quarter site traffic increased by roughly 150% during the first half of 2007 (Sifrey, 2007). This is in stark contrast to the growth of the corporate blog, as only 6% of Fortune 500 companies reported that they kept and maintained a blog in 2006 (Nail, 2006). In order to explain the reasons behind these growth statistics, it is necessary to explore these major trend differences from a demographic and perceived-value perspective.

According to Tapscott and Williams (2006), young people born between 1977 and 1996 choose to interact online as content creators. These so-called "N-Geners" believe that blogs and social networking sites are valuable because they allow individuals to communicate using "unfiltered self-expression" (Tapscott & Williams, pp. 52-53). While critics argue that all of these blog choices and opinions lead to oversaturation in the market, young people seem to like the amount of choices and interactivity that the current blogosphere provides. With roughly 73% of bloggers under 30 years old, statistics from the Communication Initiative Network (2006) seem to support this claim.

Unlike young Internet bloggers, most corporations simply cannot express how their internal blogs add value. Research compiled at the Porter Novelli Institute reveals that 63% of corporate respondents started their company blog with no specific need or purpose in mind. Not surprisingly, corporate respondents reported a low level of usage on their blogs as 71% stated they were not pleased with the number of postings (Reicherter & Nail, 2006).

In an effort to assist corporations in unlocking the value of blogs, Gartner researchers have offered three main suggestions. First, identify a point of focus for the blog and then work to understand the current bloggers and etiquette within the particular environment. Second, keep expectations at a reasonable level. While blogging can act as a low-cost supplement to other forms of communication, it is not a replacement. Finally, keep in mind that creating and maintaining an effective blog does require a fair amount of skill and effort. Be realistic about your company's abilities, and if necessary, do not hesitate to outsource initial blog hosting efforts (Valdes, Austin, & Drakos, 2007).

While current trends indicate that blogs are growing much more rapidly in the social networking and media sphere, corporate blogs will not lag behind forever. As N-Geners continue to age and advance in their careers, their preference and familiarity with personal blogging will lead to a natural extension into their work life. In addition, blogs are less costly and easier to use than many other communication tools. Because of this, corporations will continue to unlock the value of blogs by developing a more focused approach, managing expectations, and gaining expertise. Current growth trends and adoption by young users indicate that blogs will continue to be more and more accepted as an effective, low-cost communication tool.

Business Applications

Although the concept of blogging is considered a recent trend in communications and social networking, many firms have begun researching, investing in, and implementing blogging capabilities in order to effectively communicate with their stakeholders. Blogs enable the "voice" of a company's leadership, its brands, or its interests to be accessible to a wide and varied audience. In general, three distinct types of blogs have been found to be most pervasive in practical application: internal blogs, external blogs, and interest-driven blogs.

Internal blogs are those that have been created through internal development practices in an effort to conjoin disparate employee bases around concepts, work streams and processes, or idea generation. According to Mann (2006), firms have recently begun assessing an internal blog posting capability through three approaches: universal, targeted people, and targeted project. Universal internal blogs are created by the firm, are inwardly facing to the employee base, and ask the universe of employees to contribute to the internal blog process (Mann). Examples of this may include the encouragement of nonbusiness-activities blogs or rumor-mill blogs. Any employee may contribute to the blog, while additional employees assist in answering the outstanding questions presented via the blog.

Targeted-people and targeted-project internal blogs are similar to each other in that only a select few individuals may initiate and contribute to the blog. Targeted-People blogs can be typically seen through a firm's senior management espousing company values, mission, and mission goals (Mann, 2006). For example, Pfizer, Inc. conducts an internal blog in an effort to pool its internal communication policy, offering the latest company news, changes to its policies, or direction from the top. Employees may contribute to the blog, but may not initiate new blogs.

Targeted-project blogs tend to be similar to targeted-people blogs, but focus on specific elements of the firm's current business environment (Mann, 2006). Examples of this may include the construction of a new building, the status of a new R&D (research and development) project, or the implementation of enterprise-wide software. These types of blogs allow employees to ask questions and receive answers related to projects, thus raising the level of common knowledge amongst the employee base.

Mann (2006) insists that highly successful internal blogs, such as learning diaries, rumor-mill blogs, and job blogs, promote the general well-being of the employee base. These blogs elevate understanding of particular topics, diffuse rumors, and enhance human resource capabilities that drive comprehension of job roles and accountabilities (Mann). Prentice (2007), however, indicates that employees may still be hesitant to contribute in a forthcoming manner due to personal intellectual property. Employees' desire to ask questions or to "stick their necks out" through the blog may be restricted as employees may feel that their postings could reveal too much information about their capabilities or their worth.

The United States Government's Disaster Management Techniques are an example of a practical business application for internal blogs. Vining (2007) identified that blogs can assist disaster management officials in assessing damage and fatality counts. The previous process for collating this information was through a standard paper-based process. Reports were manually handwritten and sent in to a central processing office, where officials gathered, analyzed, and developed holistic assessments based upon these reports. Using blogs, disaster management officials are now able to quickly post their accounts of the disaster, provide up-to-date assessments of the information, and quickly turn around critical direction to officials who are at the disaster. These blogs' speed, accuracy from first-hand accounts, and chronology provide a much more efficient mechanism for delivering information internally to the disaster management officials.

External blogs are those that outwardly face the general Web community. These blogs are developed by a firm in an effort to both inform and persuade stakeholders regarding company values and brands. Southwest Airlines maintains an outwardly facing blog that provides a sense of community to its users (*Southwest Airlines Blog Website*, 2008). A recent blog (dated February 17, 2008) was written by Southwest's public relations (PR) coordinator, and refers to Valentine's Day travel. Through this blog, the firm's PR coordinator presented a contest to the blog community to share its thoughts about Valentine's Day travel. The best written blog, as voted by the blog community, would win a prize. Clearly, this external-facing blog from Southwest provides a sense of community for those that fly the airline, while engaging the customer and providing a sense of closeness to the brand.

Similarly, Glenfiddich ("Glenfiddich Runs Blog as Part of Online Consumer Loyalty Club," 2006) developed a whisky blog to augment the online presence of the brand. Participants in the blog have exclusive access to specific loyalty-club promotions and are educated about whisky. Targeted to whisky connoisseurs, the blog provides information about whisky-related events with the hope of attracting new customers and rewarding current drinkers. Through this development, Glenfiddich was able to compile a database of over 100,000 drinkers to augment its online marketing efforts.

Outwardly facing blogs that provide information and promotional content may be the most practical use for firms trying to build and/or retain their brand identities. Pinedo and Tanenbaum (2007) discovered that some firms are attempting to communicate critical industry information through blogs. In 2007, Sun Microsystems sent the SEC a blog posting that raised a question regarding the "broadness" of the blogosphere (Pinedo & Tanenbaum). In general, Sun Microsystems wanted to determine whether it could disseminate its company information via its blog while still complying with the SEC regulation FD disclosure requirements (selective disclosure and insider trading). The SEC would not comment whether the blog would be sufficient, but, surprisingly, the SEC responded to the blog via the blog. Clearly, as blogs gain additional attention and become more widely accepted and available, additional SEC regulations and considerations may weigh upon the blogosphere.

The third practical business application of blogs is for special-interest groups. Most often, these blogs represent political, social, or ethnic groups that seek to persuade individuals to see their perspective or persuade government officials to adjust their views or votes. Groups such as RedState.com or BarackObama.com provide blog space for interested parties to view political positions. These special-interest groups often carry large audiences. Mooney (2008) points out that other general blog sites, such as Boing Boing, have audience sizes that are beginning to rival major media outlets. In fact, Boing Boing has a quarter of the registered audience of the *New York Times* online. Technorati compiled a top-100 listing of the most linked information sources, 22 of which are blog sites.

Educational Applications

Educational applications for blogs are less intensive from a control standpoint, but have the most potential upside for learning value. The University of Houston Clear-Lake (2008) posted a Web site that provides educators with facts about blogs, how blogs can be introduced into a learning environment, and how other major educators are capitalizing upon blog capabilities. The site indicates that the major uses of educational blogs include, but are not limited to, the following: content-related blogs, instructional tips for students, course announcements and readings, reflective-writing journals, assignment submission, dialogue for group work, and sharing of course-related documents. Likewise, the commonly used Blackboard system contains a discussion forum for each class. This discussion forum is similar to that of a blog in that students of the class may leave remarks, ask questions, or find answers related to the classroom materials.

If a firm or an educational institution decides to implement an inwardly or outwardly facing blog, the entity is still faced with a major dilemma: control. When the blog space is open, the free form or freelance mechanism for autonomous monologue is inevitable. The control over this form of speech is loose at best. Lundy, Drakos, and Mann (2007) suggest that the firm or institution develop a corporate blogging policy. Such a policy limits risk to the enterprise and, accordingly, should be a subset of an overall communications plan, on which employees should be trained. By putting a blogging policy in place, the firm or institution can highlight the rules of engagement for blogging: what to say, what not to say, grammar choice, and interpretation rules. The firm or institution should minimize the risk of leaking company-sensitive materials or trade secrets while encouraging productivity through blogging, rather than the "blogging down" of the blogosphere.

How to Blog

A main growth driver for blogs over the past several years has been the ease of creation and accessibility of blogs to everyone. Sites such as http://www.blogger.com, http://www.wordpress.

com, and http://www.blogdrive.com enable users to set up a blog in a matter of minutes. Each of these sites takes users through a simple setup process in which the name, format, intended audience (i.e., public or private), and background configuration of the blog are established (Derouin et al., 2008). After several easy steps, bloggers are free to post entries and begin communicating with the world. Some of these Web sites offer free templates and blogging capabilities while others charge a fee for more add-ons and high-tech capabilities. Therefore, whether the blogger is a computer-savvy business person looking to establish a communication link with other like-minded people or a grandmother looking for a better line of communication with her grandson, there is a blog template available that will satisfy those needs.

It is not as easy to maintain an interesting blog as it is to create one. Blogs are designed as a communication tool: a modern-day digital conversation between people across the globe (Mastio, 2007). So the question becomes less about computer savvy and more about communication skills. Anyone can start a blog, but it takes some effort to maintain a successful, engaging blog. For starters, a blogger should "blog about what [she or he] know[s]" (Neal, 2005). Possessing a high level of interest in the subject matter will encourage the blogger to invest time and energy in the conversation (Neal). Successful bloggers such as Matt Drudge of http://www.drudgereport.com and Perez Hilton of http://www.perezhilton.com display a genuine interest and passion for their subject matter, be it politics or celebrities. Hill (2006) recommends writing blogs as if every reader is a paying subscriber and it is the author's job to convince readers to renew their subscriptions. This mindset will compel the author to maintain focus and passion about the blog and its success.

Further, honesty is a key criterion for any interesting conversation. Whether the blogger is a CEO relating a strategic vision to employees or a political guru looking to influence voters, honest communication is necessary to fully engage people in meaningful dialogue (Neal, 2005). Finally, bloggers should continue to explore ways to expand their blogs with knowledge from other resources. Content for blogs may spring from a variety of outlets, so bloggers must be aware of this and maintain a keen focus for additional information (Neal). Developing a successful blog may seem difficult but, in reality, it is as easy as engaging in an honest, dynamic conversation about an area of interest.

Conclusion and Future Trends

Weblogs have forever changed the manner with which people and businesses communicate. In a few short years, the growth of weblogs has signified the benefits of mass collaboration. People want to hear and be heard; they want pertinent, honest information; they require up-to-the-second data; and they want it their way. Blogs can provide all of these benefits and will continue to evolve with the growing demand of global communication.

The future of blogging, and mass collaboration in general, is bright. People will continue to search for ways to customize experiences and information. Highly engaged, Internet-savvy people will look to customize the educational, technological, and business resources they use both at home and at work. Businesses and individuals alike will strive to maintain a constant conversation with people around the globe in order to harness the collective knowledge made available by technology such as weblogs.

Individuals will continue to utilize blogs in order to gain new perspectives and collaborate with like-minded people. People will use IT enhancements and blogs as a means to redefine the marketplace and work environment (Morello & Burton, 2006). As underserved markets such as India and China become more developed, an entire new generation of computer users will emerge and offer bloggers an even larger base from which to gain perspective.

Businesses will utilize blogs to profit from the collective knowledge of the masses rather than simply issuing directives to the masses. As explained by Tapscott and Williams (2006), blogs can serve as means for businesses to "integrate the talents of dispersed individuals." In the years to come, successful businesses will discover ways to benefit from the highly individualized employee (Morello & Burton, 2006) and will realize that the individual, not the manager, will determine the work environment (Morello, 2007). Investors will want direct access to the CEO, CIO, and CFO through blogs. Frequent communication will be the norm, not the exception, as the public demands more dialogue with employers, and weblogs will certainly play an important role in connecting businesses with individuals.

REFERENCES

Blood, R. (2000). Weblogs: A history and perspective. *Rebecca's Pocket*. Retrieved February 9, 2008, from http://www.rebeccablood.net/essays/weblog_history.html

Communication Initiative Network. (2006). *Stats: Age demographics make a difference in blogging*. Retrieved February 16, 2008, from http://www.comminit.com/en/node/243880/36

Derouin, T., et al. (2008). *How to start a blog*. Retrieved February 17, 2008, from http://www.wikihow.com/start-a-blog

Glenfiddich runs blog as part of online consumer loyalty club. (2006, September 3). *New Media Age*. Retrieved from http://blog.glenfiddich.com

Granneman, S. (2006). MySpace, a place without my parents. *Security Focus*. Retrieved February 16, 2008, from http://www.securityfocus.com/columnists/408

Hill, B. (2006). *Blogging for dummies*. Indianapolis, IN: Wiley Publishing.

Lundy, J., Drakos, N., & Mann, J. (2007, June 15). Why your enterprise needs a corporate blogging policy. *Gartner Research*.

Mann, J. (2006, October 24). PCC conference reveals best practices in internal corporate blogging. *Gartner Research*.

Mastio, D. (2007). Blogging: Do try this at home. *Masthead, 59*(3), 12-13.

Mooney, C. (2008, January/February). Blogonomics: Bloggers of the world unite! *Colombia Journalism Review*, pp. 18-19.

Morello, D. (2007, June 4). CIOs and IT leaders: Prepare for the "pull" mind-set of consumer IT. *Gartner Research*.

Morello, D., & Burton, B. (2006, March 27). Future worker 2015: Extreme individualization. *Gartner Research*.

Nail, J. (2006). Five indicators that 2007 will be the year of the corporate blog. *Influence 2.0*. Retrieved February 16, 2008, from http://blog.cymfony.com/2006/08/five_indicators.html

Neal, S. (2005). What about these blogs? *Public Management, 87*(5), 18-21.

Pinedo, A., & Tanenbaum, J. (2007). The danger of blogging. *International Financial Law Review, 26*, 130-131.

Prentice, B. (2007, December 4). Three potential pitfalls of corporate social networking. *Gartner Research*.

Reicherter, B., & Nail, J. (2006). Corporate blog owners report success, but differences in resources devoted to blogs. *Porter Novelli*. Retrieved February 16, 2008, from http://www.porternovelli.com/site/pressrelease.aspx?pressrelease_id=123&pgname=news

Risdahl, A. (2007). *Ecommerce.* Avon, MA: F+W Publications.

Sifrey, D. (2007, April). The state of Technorati. *Silfry's Alerts.* Retrieved February 16, 2008, from http://www.sifry.com/alerts/archives/000492.html

Southwest Airlines Blog Website. (2008). Retrieved February 17, 2008, from http://www.blogsouthwest.com

Tapscott, D., & Williams, A. D. (2006). *Wikinomics.* New York: Penguin Group.

University of Houston Clear-Lake. (2008). *Blogs in education.* Retrieved February 16, 2008, from http://awd.cl.uh.edu/blog

Valdes, R., Austin, T., & Drakos, N. (2007). Corporate blogging. *Gartner Research.* Retrieved February 16, 2008, from http://www.gartner.com

Vining, J. (2007, April 17). Blog/wiki use in disaster management gains credibility. *Gartner Industry Research.*

Whitworth, D. (2008). Oral history: The Monica Lewinsky scandal ten years on. *Times Online.* Retrieved February 16, 2008, from http://women.timesonline.co.uk/tol/ life_and_style/women/relationships/article3185449.ece

Zuiker, A. (2004). Blogs: A short history. *Blogging101.* Retrieved February 14, 2008, from http://www.unc.edu/~zuiker/blogging101

ADDITIONAL RESOURCES

Bloggertalk. (n.d.). Retrieved from http://www.bloggertalk.net

Hill, B. (2006). *Blogging for dummies.* Indianapolis, IN: Wiley Publishing.

How-To Manual. (n.d.). Retrieved from http://www.wikihow.com

McDougall, J. S. (2007). *Start your own blogging business.* Canada: Entrepreneur Press.

Technorati. (n.d.). Retrieved from http://technorati.com

PODCASTS AND VIDEOCASTS

Kristen Booros,
Sean-Thomas Pumphrey,
Kristin Watts

Introduction and History of Podcasts

Podcasts are a relatively new technological phenomenon that has had a huge impact on audio, video, and print media for the public. Podcasts are digital audio recordings, with or without video, that are able to be automatically downloaded using specific software to the users' files (McBride & Wingfield, 2005). This is distinguished from an ordinary audio file that is posted on the Internet and clicked on once or saved manually by the user (McBride & Wingfield). Podcasts were introduced as a cross between a blog and an audio file. A blog is a form of communication in which the creator can post any type of information, from personal anecdotes to current news, for all World Wide Web users to read (Morris & Terra, 2006). A podcast essentially adds an audio file to a blog, which then can be downloaded to a user's PC and then to an MP3 player (Morris & Terra). Podcasts are available to anyone with a computer and the Internet, and can be easily created by following simple steps. They provide greater convenience to consumers and will continue to be used more as the trend for interactive experiences increase in today's society.

Podcasts have an interesting and collaborative history, beginning with a Boston-area television and radio personality, Christopher Lydon (Doyle, 2005). Lydon created a radio program for Boston University called *The Connection*. This program triggered the growth of the operation from US$5 million to US$25 million. After being fired from the radio station because he was unable to manage the rights to his content, Lydon was asked by Dave Winer to write a blog for the first BloggerCon at Harvard in 2003. Lydon was more interested in his voice talent, so Winer compromised and had Lydon record rather than write. This was the first attempt to make an audio blog. Lydon continued, 1 year before the 2004 presidential election, to audio blog in an attempt to stir up additional blogging for the election (Doyle). This audio blog was the first step in the creation of the podcast.

In order to have the audio files automatically updated, the audio blogs needed to be connected with an RSS (really simple syndication) feed. Dave Winer and Adam Curry, previously an MTV host, wrote a software program that would automatically download new files that have been uploaded to a Web site (Haygood, 2007). This advanced podcasting from its audio-blog origin. As new material was downloaded by the creator to a Web site, the RSS feed would pick it up and automatically download it to the personal computer. From here, the user could download the podcast onto an MP3 player and listen. The term *podcasting* was coined in September 2004 (Haygood).

The popularity of podcasts has continued to increase as more individuals and companies become familiar with this new technology and the benefits. There were 4.8 million podcast downloads in 2005, increasing from only 820,000 podcast downloads in 2004 (Haygood, 2007). Additionally, podcast awareness grew from 22% of Americans in 2006 to 37% in 2007 (Haygood). With a relatively low percentage of Americans who know what podcasts are, there is considerable room for growth. Podcasts can easily be subscribed to from iTunes, through Apple, or through individual Web sites that offer podcasts. In addition to the ease of use and creation of pod-

casts, they are usually free to download. Podcasts have the potential to impact each individual user in a unique way. The development of podcasts in the years to come will be interesting to follow.

Current Trends

There are several current podcasting trends that vary for individual users vs. corporate users. Even though there is a relatively small percentage of the American population who know what a podcast is, there are several trends in force. Generally, podcasts are created for one of four kinds of purposes: (a) personal, (b) art, (c) informative or educational, and (d) performance (Felix & Stolarz, 2006). Videos can be added to the podcast in order to make it a videocast that appeals to the eyes and ears of the listener or watcher. Podcasts are very convenient (McBride & Wingfield, 2005). One can listen to a podcast in a car, on a walk, or at a computer. In addition, podcasts are easy to find on the Internet, covering a variety of topics and interests for all listeners of all ages. The podcast topics can range from learning Spanish to a personal travel journal account. They are also easy to create without the use of expensive equipment. The opportunities and cost-saving benefits of podcasts are left to the imagination of the individual and corporate users.

Personal podcasts are left up to each individual designer or author of the information and what one wishes to share on the World Wide Web. These podcasts can usually be placed in one of the following categories: diary podcasts, documentary work, media fact checking, informational, educational, religious, or entertainment (McBride & Wingfield, 2005). Podcasts have the ability to truly be personalized by an individual.

Corporate trends for podcasts include informing employees, boards and shareholders, and consumers. Podcasts are an inexpensive yet high-impact form of audio content that can be utilized by corporations large and small to train and give information to their employees (Latham

& Lundy, 2006). Employees are able to retain more information by listening to this type of media and then being able to listen again when necessary (Latham & Lundy). Another advantage to using this type of application for employees is that podcasts are available on many different portable devices, which enables the user to multitask while listening (Latham & Lundy). Thus, an individual employee could be listening to or watching an instructional podcast while completing the task. This enhances learning capabilities because the employee is actually doing the activity while listening to the instruction instead of just reading the material or listening to a lecture. Podcasts can be used to give information to shareholders who are not in attendance at annual meetings or to help employees understand the format or content of the annual meeting (Felix & Stolarz, 2006). The information can easily be edited so that highly guarded content is not revealed to the public. In addition, corporations can inform consumers about current products and services. For example, General Motors used podcasts to explain and describe new products it was selling (Haygood, 2007). Corporations large and small can easily find benefits to using podcasts as they are easy and economical to create.

Another current trend for podcasting is advertising. Podcasting has allowed advertisers to capitalize using this new technology. Statistics show that US$80 million were invested in podcast advertising in 2006 and that number is expected to increase to approximately US$400 million by 2011 (Haygood, 2007). The use of podcasts is becoming more sophisticated as new companies utilize the software to target consumers (Haygood). Ads will become more personalized and companies are likely to be willing to spend more money if they know their ads are more likely to be seen by one of their target consumers. Of course, this trend may fade if consumers find advertisements to be similar to pop-ups or spam e-mail. There is a wide-ranging future for advertising via podcasts

and true potential for increased profitability using this type of medium for ads.

Business Applications

There are many internal and external business applications for which companies can use podcasting. If used correctly and creatively, these applications will increase corporate productivity, enhance the communication efforts of the company, and create an interactive experience with customers. Since podcasting is relatively inexpensive and easy to use and maintain, the applications for the technology are only limited by the imaginations of the people in control of the podcasting programs within the company. Successful corporate podcasting programs share a common thread: They expand upon the existing culture of the company and are perceived as adding value to employees and consumers.

Internal podcasting gives employees an opportunity to creatively communicate with and learn from one another. Updates on company and industry news can be posted weekly to make sure that all employees are up to date with the current events in the industry. Podcasting also lets employees see and hear directly from top executives within the company. CEO podcasts are an effective way for the top executive to share his or her vision of the company with employees and update them on how that vision has been furthered through the course of business (Sona, 2008). Executives from human resources can also use podcasting to communicate general orientation, benefits packages, training seminars, and best practices with new hires.

Communicating the best practices of a company is an excellent application for podcasting in a business. For example, the top producer in sales each month can post a podcast giving tips and advice on how to increase sales productivity. Top manufacturers within the corporation can share how they increased capacity and reduced the cost of inventory. Human resource managers can share how they increased employee retention while reducing training costs. Using podcasting to effectively communicate the best practices of an organization is an inexpensive and powerful tool that ultimately leads to greater productivity (Miller, 2007).

Another outstanding internal application for podcasting is for seminars. Attending every meeting of a seminar can be next to impossible. Creative companies tape each seminar meeting and post it online in the form of a podcast; some companies edit the recording to include only the highlights in a 15-minute broadcast. Not only is this application a benefit for the employee who attended the conference but could not make a specific meeting, it is also beneficial to the associate who could not make the conference at all. Creative execution of podcasting is also a plus to the business that wants to save on travel costs. After the seminar is over, podcasting can be used to obtain feedback from the attendees on what they learned, and liked and disliked about the event (Dodson, John, & Doughty, 2007).

Obtaining quality, objective feedback and suggestions are excellent internal uses of podcasting. Feedback can be given from employees on essentially every topic that is pertinent to an organization. Feedback and suggestions on the direction of the company, upcoming projects, new product development, and a litany of other items ultimately give each employee a voice and allow them to feel like more of a contributing member to the corporation (Young, 2008).

The internal business applications for podcasting run the gambit from sharing best practices to communicating a vision of the company. Creative and consistent internal use of podcasting can lead to a more effective, knowledgeable, and collaborative organization.

While internal podcasts focus on the employee, external podcasts focus on the customer. Well-organized customer podcasts enable a customer to interact with the corporate brand in a profitable way. External podcasts give the customer a way to relay their thoughts with the company. Podcasting gives the consumer of a company's product or service an excellent avenue to provide feedback and suggestions about how the company can improve (Ochalla, 2008). Effective businesses can utilize this information to make appropriate changes to advance their services.

Since customers know the product or service better than anyone else, many companies use their own customers to champion their products. This podcasting application not only allows loyal customers to form an intimate relationship with the brand, but also gives potential customers who may be immune to normal marketing efforts an opportunity to be introduced to the company by an ordinary person who has benefited from the company's products and services (Salerno, 2005).

Corporate podcasts are an effective way to communicate to customers. Companies whose business depends upon weather conditions (ski slopes, fishing excursions, etc.) can update the customer quickly and correctly, which provides a meaningful interaction with the brand. The customer views this as an added value to the other products the company sells.

Podcasting effectively requires commitment and creativity. Dedication to this technology extends the brand of the company and enhances the experience for both the employee and the customer (Franklin, 2008).

A summary of relevant internal and external business applications is as follows:

Internal Applications
- Updates on corporate and industry trends
- Communication from top executives
- Seminars
- Training
- Suggestions and feedback

External Applications
- Updates on corporate and industry trends
- Customers championing the brand

- Customer interaction
- Customer updates (weather conditions, etc.)
- Suggestions and feedback

Educational Applications

Podcasts are being used as an educational tool both in undergraduate and graduate school. Podcasts enable students to be able to listen to a missed class or get more information on a certain assignment (McBride & Wingfield, 2005). The technology streamlines more information from professors and administrators to the students. Assignments, lectures, and additional material could be automatically uploaded for student use, which would eliminate the need for the student to have to search through school databases or other forms of communication to get the information. This would encourage efficiency and effectiveness within the educational system. Educational uses of podcasts are developing and will most likely be a new creative instructional device used more and more by professors.

Outside of the formal education system, individuals are able to learn almost anything from how to cook a turkey to how to snowboard using a podcast (Morris & Terra, 2006). Podcasts, which can be retrieved from extremely reliable sources, are an educational tool that can be used outside of the classroom. The opportunities are endless and there are many individuals who are not aware that this type of technology could be beneficial. One could also research and teach oneself about a new product he or she is considering purchasing by getting a more one-on-one experience through a podcast than reading it on the Internet or going to the actual store. Podcasting is a new convenience that can be utilized for much more than entertainment. As an educational instrument, podcasting will continue to make a bigger impact as society continues to grasp the full utility that this application holds.

How to Create a Podcast

When creating a podcast, it is important to ensure that you first have the proper software downloaded on your computer. Audacity is the most common software used for digitally recording podcasts (Richardson, 2006). Audacity is a free program that can be used to record, edit, and replay sounds and can convert your sound file into WAV, AIFF, MP3, or OGG formats (Audacity, 2008).

Download the Software

To download Audacity, visit the Audacity Web site at http://audacity.sourceforge.net and download the most recent version. To properly convert your file to MP3 format, you must also download the most recent version of the LAME encoder from http://lame.buanzo.com/ar (Richardson, 2006). When saving the LAME program to your computer, you must remember where you save it because you will be required to find the program once you open the Audacity software. You will then be prompted by WinZip to unzip the LAME file. Unzip the file to finish saving the software to your computer.

Once you have saved the applications to your computer and unzipped the LAME file, you should open Audacity and record a practice file. Once you have recorded the file, select the option "Export as MP3" under the File menu (Richardson, 2006). You will then be prompted to find the location where the encoder is located. At this point, you should locate the file entitled lame_enc.dll. Audacity will then recognize the LAME file as the encoder for saving future sound clips in MP3 format. After saving the test file, you can delete it from your computer if you wish. Simply saving the file using the LAME encoder will enable Audacity to appropriately locate the file when exporting any sound clips into MP3 format.

Record Your Sound File and Save in MP3 Format

After you have downloaded Audacity and LAME and allowed Audacity to appropriately locate the LAME file, you are ready to begin recording your podcast. Before recording, you might want to make an outline of what you want to say (Richardson, 2006; Williams & Tollett, 2007). You may also want to set a predetermined length prior to actually recording (Williams & Tollett). Once you have finished recording, you should listen to the sound file to determine if you approve of the quality of the recording (Richardson). If you would like to edit the sound clip, you can use Audacity to cut out unwanted segments.

To delete a segment in Audacity, first find the segment that you want to edit (Morris & Terra, 2006). Click the Selection tool and click and drag across the unwanted segment. Then, click the segment between the two cuts one time and press the Backspace key. Once you have deleted the segment, review the clip. If you do not like the edit, select "Undo Change of Position Region" under the Edit menu (Morris & Terra). If you like the edit, save your changes. Once you are content with the quality of the sound file, you are ready to share your podcast.

Add an ID3 Tag to Your Podcast

An ID3 tag is a way of identifying an audio file's artist, album, and track title (Morris & Terra, 2006). Adding an ID3 tag to your podcast is important because it allows users to organize and easily locate various podcasts on their MP3 player and recognize which sound clips are playing (Morris & Terra). Creating an ID3 tag is easy in Audacity: Simply choose the "Edit ID3 Tags" option under the Choose Project menu and fill in the fields (Morris & Terra). Audacity will give you the option to automatically create tags when you save a project, so it may be easiest to do so while saving the initial file.

You can also create an ID3 tag in iTunes. Some users prefer to add ID3 tags in iTunes rather than Audacity because iTunes has more options and gives you more flexibility in customizing genres and incorporating artwork (Morris & Terra, 2006). To create ID3 tags in iTunes, simply select "Get Info" from the File menu and enter information into the pertinent fields. You can also add artwork in iTunes by clicking on the Artwork tab and dragging desired art into the Artwork field (Morris & Terra).

Share Your Podcast

You can share your podcast by (a) e-mailing the file directly to a friend, (b) using an RSS feed to save the file to your Web site or blog, or (c) adding your podcast to the iTunes library.

- **E-Mail the File Directly to a Friend.** The simplest way to share your podcast with another individual is to e-mail the file directly to that person. To do this, simply attach the MP3 file to an e-mail and send it to your friend. Your friend can download the file from the e-mail to iTunes to listen to it. However, podcasts are generally intended for a wide audience and it would be tedious to send an e-mail to all of your intended listeners. Accordingly, the following two methods of sharing your podcast are recommended.
- **Use an RSS Feed to Save the File to Your Web site or Blog.** To post the file to your personal Web site or blog, you need to enter XML (extensible markup language) code that indicates the location of the MP3 file (Godwin-Jones, 2005). Typically, such XML code will be in RSS 2.0 format (Godwin-Jones). RSS stands for *really simple syndication* and is a Web content syndication format (Morris & Terra, 2006; Richardson, 2006). Because most podcasters use software to generate RSS 2.0 feeds, it is not necessary to go into detail about how to actually create

an RSS feed. If you would like to learn more about RSS 2.0, please refer to the resources at the end of this section.

Today, blogging software, such as Blogger, can be used to automatically create the RSS feed based upon the title and description that the user enters (Godwin-Jones, 2005). You can also use free Web sites such as Feed 2JS, available at http://feed2js.org/index.php?s=build, or Feedburner.com to build a feed. Once the XML code is generated, the link is published to the Web site and is available to the public (Godwin-Jones).

- **Make the File Available on iTunes:** While iTunes does not host podcast files, you can easily make your podcast available on iTunes once you have created your own RSS feed (Apple, 2008). To make your podcast available on iTunes, you must simply click on the Submit a Podcast icon in the iTunes store. Then, place the link to your podcast in the box and hit Submit. Your podcast will then be available to the public and iTunes will automatically update your podcast once new episodes are made available (Apple).

Conclusion

It is evident that podcasting has a number of uses in everyday life, including creating radio shows for friends, advertising, and making the general public aware of certain issues. Podcasting has a number of business applications as well, including training employees, internal communications, allowing attendees to review annual meetings, and maintaining relationships with customers. Educationally, podcasts can be used in various ways to facilitate and increase learning. Creating a podcast is relatively simple. By following the steps above, one can easily create a podcast from the comfort of home. It is clear that podcasts will have a lasting effect and will continue to be used in classrooms, marketing programs, music downloads, and an expanding set of business ap-

plications. From individual use to the corporate world, the current trends of podcasting and videocasting will be changing as society embraces this new technology.

REFERENCES

Apple. (2008). *FAQs: For podcast makers*. Retrieved February 17, 2008, from http://www.apple.com/itunes/store/podcastingfaq.html

Audacity. (2008). *The free, cross-platform sound editor*. Retrieved February 15, 2008, from http://audacity.sourceforge.net

Dodson, S., John, M., & Doughty, R. (2007, September 18). Link news. *The Guardian*. Retrieved April 29, 2008, from http://educationguardian.co.uk

Doyle, B. (2005). The first podcast. *Econtent, 28*(9), 33.

Farkas, B. (2006). *Secrets of podcasting: Audio blogging for the masses*. Berkley, CA: Pearson Education, Inc.

Felix, L., & Stolarz, D. (2006). *Hands-on guide to video blogging & podcasting*. Burlington, MA: Elsevier, Inc.

Franklin, D. (2008). Web 2.0: High tech and high touch. *Credit Union Management, 31*(2), 38-42.

Godwin-Jones, R. (2005). Emerging technologies Skype and podcasting: Disruptive technologies for language learning. *Language Learning & Technology, 9*(3), 9-12. Retrieved February 15, 2008, from http://llt.msu.edu/vol9num3/emerging

Haygood, D. (2007). A status report on podcast advertising. *Journal of Advertising Research, 47*(4), 518-523.

Latham, L., & Lundy, J. (2006, March 8). Podcasting is a new medium for training and communication. *Gartner Research*.

McBride, S., & Wingfield, N. (2005, October 10). Audio players: As podcasts boom, big media rushes to stake a claim; Clear Channel, networks jump at offering downloads after lessons from rivals; "Is anybody out there?" *The Wall Street Journal*, p. A1. Retrieved February 16, 2008, from http://proquest.umi.com

Miller, R. (2007, April 22). Keeping up with the iPod generation: New media technologies can offer a more effective way to communicate with employees, customers, shareholders and investors. *The Daily Telegraph.* Retrieved April 29, 2008, from http://www.telegraph.uk.co

Morris, T., & Terra, E. (2006). *Podcasting for dummies.* Indianapolis, IN: Wiley Publishing, Inc.

Ochalla, B. (2008). Old dog, new tricks. *Credit Union Management, 31*(2), 46-49.

Richardson, W. (2006). *Blogs, wikis, podcasts, and other powerful Web tools for classrooms.* Thousand Oaks, CA: Corwin Press.

Salerno, F. (2005). Podmarketing. *Direct, 17*(9), 52-53.

Sona, H. (2008). Podcast and blog: The engaging brand. *Strategic Communication Management, 12*(2), 3.

Williams, R., & Tollett, J. (2007). *Podcasting and blogging with GarageBand and iWeb.* Berkeley, CA: Pearson Education, Inc.

Young, S. (2008). Could you podcast? *NZ Marketing Magazine, 27*(1).

ADDITIONAL RESOURCES

Felix, L., & Stolarz, D. (2006). *Hands-on guide to video blogging & podcasting.* Burlington, MA: Elsevier, Inc.

Finkelstein, E. (2005). *Syndicating Web sites with RSS feeds for dummies.* Hoboken, NJ: Wiley Publishing, Inc.

Morris, T., & Terra, E. (2006). *Podcasting for dummies.* Indianapolis, IN: Wiley Publishing, Inc.

Richardson, W. (2006). *Blogs, wikis, podcasts, and other powerful Web tools for classrooms.* Thousand Oaks, CA: Corwin Press.

Stephens, M. (2006). *Web 2.0 & libraries: Best practices for social software.* Chicago: ALA TechSource.

WIKIS

Grant Garcia,
Drew Mann, Mike Matthews

History of Wikis

The first wiki precursor dates back to 1945 when Vannevar Bush published an article explaining his vision of a microfilm hypertext system that he called the "memex" (a blend of the words *memory* and *extender*; Bush, 1945). Another precursor of the wiki concept emerged in 1972 when researchers at Carnegie-Mellon University created the ZOG (an early hypertext system) multiuser database. The ZOG interface consisted of text-only frames; each frame contained a title, a description, a line with standard ZOG commands, and a set of hypertext links leading to other text-only frames (Abrams, 1998).

In 1981, two members of the ZOG team at Carnegie-Mellon spun off a company and developed an improved version of ZOG called Knowledge Management System (KMS), a collaborative tool based on direct manipulation, allowing users to modify the contents of frames, freely intermixing text, graphics, and images, all of which could be linked to other frames (Abrams, 1998). The KMS database was accessible from any workstation on a network and, thus, changes became visible immediately to other users, which enabled multiple users to work concurrently on shared documents and programs.

In 1985, the ZOG system was the model for Janet Walker's Document Examiner, which was created for the operation manuals of Symbolics computers. Document Examiner was then used as the model for the Note Cards system, released that same year by Xerox. Note Cards, a hypertext system, featured scrolling windows for each note card combined with a separate browser and navigator window. Note Cards inspired Bill Atkinson's WildCard, later called HyperCard. In the late 1980s, Ward Cunningham wrote a HyperCard stack that was the impetus to the wiki idea (Cunningham, 2008).

Kent Beck, after obtaining access to Hyper-Card when he joined Apple Computers, introduced HyperCard to Ward Cunningham. Cunningham used HyperCard to make a stack with three kinds of cards: cards for ideas, cards for people who hold ideas, and cards for projects where people share ideas (Cunningham, 2008).

Next, Cunningham made a single card with three fields (name, description, and links) that served all three purposes. The HyperCard fields were WYSIWYG (what you see is what you get) editors; however, linking between multiple cards was still a hassle. Cunningham deserted the regular stack links and instead used search on demand (Cunningham, 2008).

Only through the hypertext capabilities of the World Wide Web was Cunningham's first wiki made possible. In 1990, Tim Berners-Lee of CERN (Centre European pour la Recherche Nucleaire) built the first hypertext browser, which he called WorldWideWeb, and the first hypertext server (info.cern.ch). The next year, Berners-Lee posted a short summary of this project on the alt. hypertext newsgroup, marking the debut of the Web as a publicly available service on the Internet (Abrams, 1998).

Enough momentum generated over the next few years that organizations were forming to capture the power of WorldWideWeb. By April 1994, Mosaic Communications Corporation had changed its name to Netscape and continued development of Netscape Navigator. That same month, CERN allowed anyone to use the Web protocol and code for free (Abrams, 1998). Finally, the stage was set for the appearance of Ward Cunningham's WikiWikiWeb.

In 1994, Ward Cunningham started developing the WikiWikiWeb as a supplement to the Portland Pattern Repository, a Web site that contained documentation about design patterns (Cunningham, 2008).

People, Projects and Patterns, categories Cunningham used to organize his wiki, the WikiWikiWeb, was intended as a collaborative database focused on making the exchange of ideas between programmers easier. Cunningham wrote the software using the Perl programming language. He named it using the Hawaiian word *wikiwiki*, which means *quick*, to avoid calling it quick-Web (Cunningham, 2008).

Cunningham installed a prototype of the software on his company Cunningham & Cunningham's Web site c2.com on November 6, 1994. A few months later, after some initial repository work was completed, Cunningham sent the following e-mail to a colleague, dated March 16, 1995:

Steve—I've put up a new database on my web server and I'd like you to take a look. It's a web of people, projects and patterns accessed through a cgi-bin script. It has a forms based authoring capability that doesn't require familiarity with html. I'd be very pleased if you would get on and at least enter your name in RecentVisitors. I'm asking you because I think you might also add some interesting content. I'm going to advertise this a little more widely in a week or so. The URL is http://c2.com/cgi-bin/wiki. Thanks and best regards.—Ward. (Cunningham, 2008)

On May 1, 1995, Cunningham sent an "Invitation To The Patterns List" to a number of programmers, which caused an increase in participation. The site earned immediate popularity within the pattern community (Cunningham, 2008).

Immediately, clones of the WikiWikiWeb software were developed. Cunningham himself wrote a version of a wiki that could host its own source code, called Wiki Base. Programmers soon started several other wikis to build knowledge bases about programming topics. Popularity continued to grow for wikis in the free and open-source software (FOSS) community. Wikis were ideal for collaborating on, discussing, and documenting software. Being used only by specialists, these early software-focused wikis failed to attract widespread public attention (Cunningham, 2008).

Until 2001, with the introduction to the general public by the success of Wikipedia, wikis were virtually unknown outside of the restricted circles of computer programmers. Since then, wikis have developed by incorporating many of the features used on other Web sites and blogs, including support for various wiki markup styles, editing of pages with a graphical user interface (GUI) editor and WYSIWYG HTML (hypertext markup language), optional use of external editors, support for plug-ins and custom extensions, use of RSS feeds, integrated e-mail discussion, precise access control, and spam protection.

Current Trends

According to the Gartner Hype Cycle, wikis are in the "Trough of Disillusionment," with an estimate of 2 to 5 years until mainstream adoption (Knox et al., 2007) and only 5% to 20% market penetration of the target audience as of mid-2007 (Drakos & Andrews, 2007).

What is the market that wikis are penetrating? Wiki usage can be generally categorized as one of four types (Woods & Thoeny, 2007).

1. **Content-focused** wikis are those that have large amounts of content and are edited by large numbers of people. These wikis should be easy to use and edit.

2. **Process-focused** wikis are often used in business to document or manage a process. Often, notifications are used to let members know of a change or addition that has been made.

3. **Community** wikis are most often used for subject matter that is of interest to a select group of people. Examples might be sport fishing, rock climbing, or *Star Trek*.

4. **Ease-of-use** wikis are simply an easy way to create a Web site. Someone wanting an immediate presence on the Web without the trouble and expense of learning HTML or hiring a Web designer can utilize a wiki. The normal collaboration and open editing are normally disabled with this type of wiki as it is set up as more of a read-only site. The ability to make the wiki private and to lock pages makes this possible.

Content-focused wikis currently rule the wiki world, with Wikipedia at the top of the list. Most people who have no idea what a wiki is have heard of, and have even accessed, Wikipedia. Process-focused wikis are most often seen within organizations and are accessed through a company intranet. Their use is most common among project managers who are running complex projects or processes. Community wikis are often the mom-and-pop type of wikis. Some are very small, such as a wiki for a small town's historical society. Some are quite large with a much more important impact on the world, such as the Wiserwiki, which is an online medical book created by a leading publisher and edited by board-certified physicians from around the world.

A number of free online wikis have become popular. Each of these has subtle differences. They include PBwiki, Wetpaint, Wikia, BluWiki, and XWiki. Some of these wikis use advertising and some simply ask for donations from their users. Some use WYSIWYG text entry and some use more cryptic HTML formatting. Some require the user to download software and some work directly online.

One of the free wikis, Wikia, was founded by Wikipedia's founder, Jimmy Wales. According to Wales, this for-profit wiki company may go public in the future (Hong, 2008). Revenues for this wiki site are generated through advertising.

A search of the most active communities on the Wikia Web site revealed that community wikis seem to be most popular. The top list included wikis on the TV show *24*, astronomy, and the Muppets, as well as seven on *Star Trek* and *Star Wars*. It seems only natural that those who currently gravitate to wikis as a social outlet would be interested in these topics. In fact, none of the top-55 sites seemed to be of any serious substance.

It seems that most business wikis utilize company intranets rather than the Internet. Based on interviews with small businesses in North America and Europe (Brodkin, 2008), one observer predicts that Microsoft's SharePoint collaboration software will continue to dominate the market, and Web 2.0 technologies, including wikis, will make major inroads in companies in 2008.

Numerous government agencies are also using wikis. In early 2008, the U.S. Congress was tallying and tracking earmark spending (known as pork-barrel spending to most) for the Office of Management and Budget. According to *The Washington Post*, over 13,000 earmarks were compiled by various federal agencies in a 10-week period (Barr, 2008). Without the use of a wiki, the process would have taken over 6 months. This is a closed wiki, available only to the 5,500 members who are registered under their federal agencies. Of course, we must ask ourselves if empowering congress to spend tax money faster and more efficiently is a good thing.

Business Applications

As of early 2008, wikis appear to be slowly finding their way into businesses. However, it seems most small business owners and CEOs still do not know what a wiki is other than the popular Wikipedia. A Lexis-Nexis search revealed that most of today's published articles are still written to educate readers as to what a wiki is and how one might be used in a business setting rather than on how businesses are using them and what advantages or gains are being realized. According to a survey by McKinsey, at the close of 2007, approximately one third of businesses were currently using or were planning to use Web 2.0 technologies, including wikis ("Insurer Takes a Bold Leap into Web 2.0," 2007).

Most wikis that find their way into small businesses start from the bottom of the organization, often without the knowledge of upper management. Young employees who are adept at social networking software often start communicating in the workplace through blogs and wikis. These unstructured communication tools form a collaborative work space in these organizations. Upper management is sometimes introduced to these Web 2.0 technologies only after they have become a part of the company workflow through an underground culture.

A small firm interviewed in early 2008 was working from the top to implement wikis from the bottom. The CEO of this 150-person professional services firm met with the firm's 35 20-somethings to get ideas on how the firm might benefit from Web 2.0 technologies. One of the ideas that emerged from that meeting was the use of technology wikis for the firm's knowledge workers. It seemed that most of the company's engineers had notepads, scratch paper, word files, and spreadsheets where they documented ideas and tasks for the projects they work on. Once a project or employee is gone, so are those ideas, at least in any written form. A number of the young, tech-savvy staffers were brought together by the CEO to create wikis for the firm's knowledge management using the underutilized SharePoint software sitting on the firm's server. The wikis were first seeded with some of the firm's existing technical documents that were spread about in different forms. At that point, the hope was that the employees would use this wiki to look up information, add information, supplement current writings, and document new ways of doing things. The CEO openly showed his support of this idea by setting up his own wiki and blog on the company's intranet.

According to McDougall (2007), a firm's underutilization of its wiki capabilities is not uncommon. A recent survey found that one in five companies has wikis available on its server, but they go unused (McDougall). Some firms are taking a proactive approach to this problem. A 32-person law firm in Raleigh, North Carolina, has a contest that provides a US$1,000 reward for the most contributions to its internal wiki (Nussenbaum, 2008). The purpose of this "encouraged collaboration" was to wean the employees off of the less-efficient Lotus Notes communication tools and to have a central repository for everything from contracts to case files.

While most small companies do not seem to be on the wiki path yet, many large technology companies have been using wikis successfully for some time. Sun Microsystems uses wikis across its enterprise. In addition to encouraging its employees to use social networking software, such as Facebook and MySpace, the company encourages its employees to use wikis for collaboration among engineers, systems architects, and marketing people (Cane, 2007). Utilizing a wiki, Cisco has implemented a company-wide forum called I-Zone. This wiki was developed by the company's Emerging Technologies Group and has produced 600 ideas from 10,000 of Cisco's 61,000 employees (Martin, 2008). According to Microsoft, it has over 300,000 blogs and wikis (Hoover, 2007), and Motorola claims 92% of its staff utilizes its intranet Web 2.0 tools, which includes 4,500 internal wikis ("Twenty Great Ideas: Web 2.0," 2007).

One nontechnology company that has successfully deployed Web 2.0 technologies, including wikis, is a European bank, Dresdner Kleinwort Wasserstein (DrKW). In an article on Enterprise 2.0, McAfee (2006) outlines four keys to a suc-

cessful implementation of these technologies based on the DrKW case:

1. **A Receptive Culture:** The DrKW culture was already one of collaboration and cooperation. Any firm with this type of culture should have a leg up on the beginnings of successful implementations of wikis. Most firms who utilize knowledge workers should realize an advantage.

2. **A Common Platform:** DrKW found that using a single platform for wikis allowed for better searches between seemingly disconnected groups within the enterprise. The small engineering firm we spoke of previously has also taken that approach. In its case, mechanical, electrical, and civil engineers' work, while different and performed separately, is connected throughout a project. According to the company's CEO, their knowledge base, likewise, should be connected.

3. **An Informal Rollout:** By their very nature, wikis are informal gatherings of thoughts and information. DrKW decided nothing more than pointing the employees in the direction of the wiki was necessary. It did this through letting a few groups start using the new tools and allowing them to post non-work-related materials, as well.

4. **Managerial Support:** DrKW's management showed its support by being one of the first users of the wiki and encouraging employees to log in and provide updates and additions. In fact, the company's managing director refused to communicate on some issues other than through a wiki he had started. Likewise, the small engineering company's management showed its support through the CEO's personal wiki and blog.

It is clear that large technology companies have made extensive use of Web 2.0 technologies and that wikis can be successfully deployed as a means of collaboration in the workplace. Managers of smaller companies, for the most part, do not seem to know that these technologies exist. However, any business that relies on knowledge workers can reap great benefits from collaboration through wikis.

Educational Applications

The use of wikis in education has become increasing popular among students, teachers, and professors worldwide. Many educators choose to use wikis for multiple purposes such as group projects, homework, and research writing assignments rather than a conventional classroom-assignment approach. Mader (2006) published information about wikis and education on the Web site Using Wiki in Education. According to Mader:

the Wiki is gaining traction in education, as an ideal tool for the increasing amount of collaborative work done by both students and teachers. Students might use a wiki to collaborate on a group report, compile data or share the results of their research, while faculty might use the wiki to collaboratively author the structure and curriculum of a course and the wiki can then serve as part of each person's course web site.

In this context, the wiki serves as an ideal online host for assisting students in completing assignments and collaborating with classmates using their existing Web browsers. The wiki is also useful for teachers and faculty members. Its use allows them to easily edit wiki entries and keep track of recent edits by others. They are also able to document the history of an assignment or project as it is revised.

Wikis have recently become the latest method of online writing, which can be used in conjunction with education for writing-related assignments. With the ease of editing and peer or teacher review, a wiki is a user-friendly choice for completing assignments. Additionally, when students are

writing in a public forum with an audience that includes parents, classmates, and professors, they may be more inclined to work harder, write and revise more carefully, and achieve greater academic competencies.

The process of using a wiki in the classroom setting could potentially replace other collaboration software or network (server) storage systems. Since students would be allowed to use the wiki, and thereby make changes without uploading new documents, the wiki may be a more productive and efficient way to tackle large assignments with lengthy documents.

So how can a wiki be applied to education? Wikis have many uses in education, with some of the most common uses discussed below from the electronic book published on the Web site "Using a Wiki in Education" (Mader, 2006).

1. **Web Site Creation:** Wikis can be used as an easy way to create a personalized Web site, a process that has become part of many courses in secondary and higher education. Some professors require their students to create a Web site as part of the course syllabus, or suggest they create a Web site to showcase their resumes and accomplishments. Students now use free wiki development software as an easy way to fulfill their educational course requirements, and they can make the link to the wiki readily available to other students, professors, and corporate recruiters. Using a wiki also makes Web site creation easier for all students, not just those who have had previous training on technical Web site development. The wiki experience, similar to the blog, can be used in higher education and professional careers, thereby giving anyone with Web proficiency the chance to create, invite friends, and host a page on the Internet.

2. **Project Development and Review:** Students can develop their writing assignments directly on a wiki. The wiki platform allows

the user to write and revise class work within the wiki (with a track-back feature), thus making it an ideal way to complete assignments. The tracking feature allows teachers and professors to follow the students' progress and view edits and previous drafts in the wiki history. Peers may also view the wiki and make suggestions, which can be an easier way to assign peer-review homework. Students may benefit from teacher and peer comments that can be made directly on the wiki. A wiki also serves as an online location, or Web site, to host the students' final work, available for public viewing. This feature on a wiki may also entice students to perform at a higher level, knowing their work may be viewed and critiqued by others.

3.   **Group Work:** Students are frequently assigned projects that require group collaboration. By using a wiki, group members can post their contributions to the group project, easily edit other group members' work, and immediately retrieve documents related to the project. A wiki may eliminate confusion caused by multiple document storing locations, or the common problem of overlapping ideas and additions to a project section. Students can also use the wiki as an online home page, where the sharing of documents and ideas brings the group closer together academically. Teachers and professors then track the progress of group work by using the track-back function and history feature on the wiki. In fact, this manuscript was developed by a group of graduate students with the use of a wiki for group collaboration.

4.   **Group Work Review:** A wiki is an efficient solution for tracking group progress online and from remote locations. Students can save time by reviewing their team members' posts to the wiki and edit the entire project or paper from anywhere they have Internet access. Online collaboration through a wiki may also help teachers and professors construct and monitor group assignments. The group (or class) wiki, which can be set up to allow access by only group members and an administrator, gives students an opportunity to comment on the project and review group work in one convenient online location.

5.   **Research Collection Center:** Wikis allow posting, editing, and sharing of research collected by students. Having this ease of access can help facilitate the sharing of data in group projects and provides a central location to collect students' data and research rather than storing data on each individual computer and sharing through a chain of e-mails. A wiki could also replace existing methods of online research collection such as a college or university server. Data collection tools specific for wikis are readily available, with JotSpot (http://www.jot.com) being an innovative solution for this concept.

6.   **Sharing of Classroom Experiences:** Web sites such as Rate My Professors and Rate My Teachers allow students to review college professors and high school teachers. The use of a wiki may replace these Web sites as a place where students can post comments on their course experiences and rate the perceived quality of instruction they have experienced. Students will then be able to add comments and reply to these posts with ease on the wiki. Educators may find that sharing classroom teaching strategies and techniques may be more efficient and may reach a larger audience through a wiki focused on classroom experience. In addition, teachers and professors could post syllabus updates, take-home exams, and final course evaluations on a wiki.

7.   **Group Presentations:** Students now have the ability to give a presentation through use of a wiki. Many classrooms are equipped with hardware to display computer presentations, thus making it easy for a student

to project the wiki from the Internet onto a whiteboard or screen. In these wiki presentations, the wiki can be used in place of conventional presentation software such as Microsoft PowerPoint.

Previous education issues that were prohibitive to adult learning can also be reconciled by using a wiki. Adult education uses include literacy campaigns, distance learning for commuter students, and secure collaboration for graduate education. The campaign for adult literacy is a perfect example of how individual adults may have some experience with a computer but lack sufficient reading skills. Or, in some cases, they may not have both a computer and reading skills, in which case using a wiki could be an opportunity for adults to become both literate and proficient at using a computer.

In addition to the multiple uses of wikis in general education, there are also specific examples of wikis currently in use in the classroom or in undergraduate and graduate course work. Professors can create a course syllabus, course schedule, and course Web site through the use of a wiki. This concept may be especially beneficial for professors who frequently update course information or the course syllabus, and may reduce the need to physically print new handouts for each update.

There has been a rapid increase in recorded uses of educational wikis in colleges and universities around the United States. Psychology students at Brown University used a wiki to track and collect data for certain human behaviors, which were then recorded as journal entries on the wiki (Mader, 2006). Students at Pennsylvania State University use wikis to post class notes and blog about classroom experiences (Mader). Similarly, students at the State University of New York used a wiki for exchanging feedback on classroom assignments, and completed collaborative writing projects on the wiki (Mader). An information technology class at the University of Richmond had students create a wiki and collaborate on a group project by posting assignments and individual parts on the wiki for peer and professor review.

Many other uses of a wiki have yet to be implemented; however, educators should consider creating and using a wiki if they are looking for a safe way to increase student engagement in classroom assignments, promote accountability and collaborative editing during group projects, and finally, showcase students' work in a single online location. These are just a few of the many examples of the potential for educational wikis to be used around the world.

Conclusion and Future Trends

Whether it is to collaborate on a class project, brainstorm ideas with people around the world, or record family history, wikis will continue to manifest themselves in educational, business, and personal settings. For now, Wikis have found a permanent place in online communities and, as popularity continues to grow, there is little stopping the wiki from overtaking blogs and current online collaboration software.

Wikis will continue to develop as a personal and organizational online tool. Social wikis and wiki innovations continue to develop at an overwhelming rate. Wiki innovations such as Swicki, a collaborative search engine offering impressive detailed searches, and WikiHow, a social wiki offering thousands of how-to answers to its users, make the possibilities for wiki usage seem endless. Other wiki developments like WikiDocs and WikiTrails help users navigate around wiki pages. Wiki Widgets provides small objects such as calendars, video clips, and audio that can be added to an existing wiki page. The usage patterns and trends among users attract increasing innovation and attention to the capabilities of wikis.

Another future trend of wiki use will most certainly include e-commerce and e-business in Web 2.0. Already visible in the wiki community, advertising will continue to play a vital role in marketing to wiki users and to support keeping new wiki accounts free to users of hosted wikis. Collaborative wiki technology is also spreading to small and medium-sized businesses as a way to market, advertise, and interact with the public. One company, Des Moines, Iowa-based CustomerVision, released RapidWiki, which is designed to get small to medium businesses up and running with dynamic Web sites that look and feel more like forums than brochures (Cohen, 2007). Business owners know they need to keep up with emerging online trends, wikis included. "It's time to go beyond static Web sites," said Cindy Rockwell, president and CEO of CustomerVision, one of the most innovative wiki marketing companies (Cohen). Market penetration has certainly taken place in online social communities like MySpace and Facebook, and there is plenty of evidence that wikis are next on the horizon for companies involved in e-commerce.

Before long, there will even be applications where wiki and video come together to make TV IV, an online compendium of television knowledge that anyone can edit. The world of wikis has a lot to offer and many other variations of the wiki are going online every day.

Wikis are sure to play a significant role in the emergence of Web 2.0, and their applications will continue to develop in business, education, and government, and in online communities. The explosion in popularity of wikis has led to multiple variations, and the number of ways wikis are being offered has grown at an explosive rate. Wikis are a great tool that can help people learn and communicate in a safe, collaborative setting, and the future for wikis is very bright. The time and place is now for wikis, and it will be interesting to watch carefully as the future for wikis unveils itself in the coming years.

REFERENCES

Abrams, M. (Ed.). (1998). *World Wide Web: Beyond the basics*. Upper Saddle River, NJ: Prentice Hall.

Barr, S. (2008, January 28). Agencies share information taking a page from Wikipedia. *The Washington Post*.

Brodkin, J. (2008). Microsoft SharePoint will "steamroll" Web 2.0 market, plus eight more predictions from Forrester. *Network World, Inc.* Retrieved March 10, 2008, from http://www.networkworld.com/news/2008/013008-forrester-predictions.html

Bush, V. (1945, July). As we may think. *The Atlantic Monthly*. Retrieved March 10, 2008, from http://www.theatlantic.com/doc/194507/bush

Cane, A. (2007). Doing what comes naturally. *Financial Times*, 4. Retrieved on March 10, 2008, from http://search.ft.com/ftArticle?queryText=%22doing+what+comes+naturally%22&aje=false&id=071120000504&ct=0&nclick_check=1

Cohen, N. (2007). Wiki engines begin to drive small business. *eCommerce Times*. Retrieved March 10, 2008, from http://www.linuxinsider.com/story/59049.html

Cunningham, W. (2008). *Cunningham & Cunningham, Inc.* Retrieved March 3, 2008, from http://www.c2.com

Drakos, N., & Andrews, W. (2007). Hype cycle for the high performance workplace: Wikis. *Gartner Research*.

Hong, S. (2008). For-profit Wikia eyes IPO in longer term. *Dow Jones Newswires*.

Hoover, J. (2007, September 24). Social networking: A time waster or the next big thing in collaboration? *Information Week*, p. 40.

Insurer takes a bold leap into Web 2.0. (2007, November 2). *Life Insurance International*.

Knox, R., et al. (2007). Hype cycle for the high performance workplace. *Gartner Research*.

Mader, S. (2006). Ways to use wiki in education. In S. Mader (Ed.), *Using wiki in education: A wiki based book.* Retrieved April 21, 2008, from http://www.wikiineducation.com/display/ikiw/home

Martin, R. (2008, January 28). Cisco's emerging collaboration strategy. *InformationWeek*, p. 30.

McAfee, A. (2006). Enterprise 2.0: The dawn of emergent collaboration. *Sloan Management Review*, 26.

McDougall, P. (2007). 5 tips to make wikis sticky. *InformationWeek*, p. 26.

Nussenbaum, E. (2008). Tech to boost teamwork. *Fortune Small Business, 18*(1).

Twenty great ideas: Web 2.0. (2007, September 17). *InformationWeek 500*, p. 97.

Woods, D., & Thoeny, P. (2007). *Wikis for dummies.* Indianapolis, IN: Wiley Publishing, Inc.

ADDITIONAL RESOURCES

Huettner, B., & James-Tanny, C. (2007, January). Using wikis. *Intercom, 54*(1), 20-24.

Notari, M. (2006). How to use a wiki in education: Wiki based effective constructive learning. *Proceedings of the International Symposium on Wikis* (pp. 131-132).

Parker, R., & Cho, J. (2007). Wiki as a teaching tool. *Interdisciplinary Journal of Knowledge and Learning Object, 3.*

Richardson, W. (2006). *Blogs, wikis, podcasts, and other powerful Web tools for classrooms.* Thousand Oaks, CA: Corwin Press.

Tapscott, D., & Williams, A. (2008). *Wikinomics: How mass collaboration changes everything.* New York: Penguin Group.

Woods, D., & Thoeny, P. (2007). *Wikis for dummies.* Indianapolis, IN: Wiley Publishing, Inc.

VIRTUAL WORLDS

David Esposito,
Brian Hoade, Cuyler Lovett

History of Virtual Worlds

Since their introduction in 1974, virtual worlds have moved from being solely used for entertainment purposes to being innovative tools in business and education. Currently, virtual worlds are used for everything from training business employees and virtual classrooms, to reaching new audiences through advertising. Analysts believe that virtual worlds will become even more important in the near future through the world of communication. Understanding how to use virtual worlds will be an important step, not only for individuals, but also for businesses and other organizations.

Virtual worlds began with Steve Colley's *Maze War* in 1974 (Terdiman, 2006). The original program was a three-dimensional depiction of a maze through which the player tried to navigate. The game design was improved by using serial ports to put multiple players in the game. These other players were depicted as eyeballs. Finally, the programmers added the ability to shoot at other players to score points (Colley, 2008).

Today's online virtual world's most recognizable ancestor is the multiuser dungeon or dimension (MUD; Nguyen, 2008). These were text-based multiuser role-playing games. The earliest code was written in 1978 by Roy Trubshaw, a University of Essex student, and resulted in a game with a set of interconnected rooms in which users could move through and chat with other users. Similar to the virtual worlds of today, this MUD had no objective and no score. A landmark came in 1980 when the English MUD developers were able to use an experimental packet-switching system to link up with ArpaNet in the United States and get the first American players to log on. This took off and is still running today as *British Legends* under a license to CompuServe (Bartle, 1990). MUDs have since included graphics and real-time action instead of text.

Massive multiplayer online role-playing games (MMOGs) developed from these original MUDs (Terdiman, 2008) include persistent, virtual-world games like *Ultima Online* and *EverQuest* (Patrizio, 2001). *EverQuest*, launched by Sony in 1999, became the most popular MMOG game between 2000 and 2004 (Woodcock, 2008), but this position has since been ceded to *World of Warcraft* ("Top 10 Most Popular MMO Games," 2007).

As the MMOGs developed, another kind of interactive online program for multiple users was being developed by Lucasfilm. The result, *Habitat*, is arguably the first online social virtual world (Farmer, 2008). A pilot of the program was developed in 1988 by Chip Morningstar, Douglas Crockford, and F. Randall Farmer named *Quantum Link* for the Commodore 64 computer system. The program consisted of regions through which players could move their avatars, or online representations of themselves. The game also featured "ghosts," which could move around the regions and become avatars. The program was released in 1988 as *Club Caribe* in the United States and *Fujitsu Habitat* in Japan, both of which were somewhat popular. A refined version of this program was released by CompuServe in 1995 as *WorldsAway*. *WorldsAway* later became *VZones*, taking on the name and format it carries to this day.

VZones essentially resembles a series of online chat rooms where avatars, all facing forward, speak to one another in dialogue boxes (*VZones Website*, 2008). The game features two separate online communities: *NewHorizone* and *Dreamscape*. *NewHorizone* utilizes realistic cartoon people as avatars and real-world settings, including various cities around the world. *Dreamscape* has a fantasy element, and avatars can look gothic or fairy-like.

From the relatively simple worlds used as games and chat rooms, the virtual-world industry has come a long way in recent years, seeing many advances that have transformed the nature of virtual worlds. The next progression from *VZones* was the virtual world *There*. *There* takes the social aspect of programs like *VZones* and incorporates them into a more realistic, three-dimensional world. First tested in 2001, *There* is a three-dimensional virtual world that was launched in 2003 ("History Timeline," 2008). *There* markets itself as an online hangout that allows users to explore the virtual world, interact with other users, and play games ("What is There? Makena Technologies, Inc.," 2008).

Moove Online is an online virtual world released by the German company Moove in 2001. The focus of this virtual world is social networking and chatting ("3D Avatar Chat in Virtual Worlds," 2008). The program is supported through peer-to-peer connections, and interaction is conducted by visiting other users' houses, which are also customizable. On average, *Moove* users tend to be older than those of other virtual worlds, with many users over the age of 40 ("Moove," 2008).

The Sims Online debuted on December 17, 2003 (Becker, 2003). This was an online version of the all-time best-selling computer game *The Sims*, created by video game developer Electronic Arts (EA). The online version allowed players to play against each other. *The Sims Online* required players to buy packaged software and then pay US$10 per month to participate online. Upon its release, *The Sims Online*'s reception was disappointing. Much of this was attributed to the required monthly fee and a mismatch with its target customers (Ratan, 2003).

First developed in 1994, *Active Worlds* has existed in various forms and under various names, with its most recent version in 2002. While it allows users to chat, the emphasis in *Active Worlds* is on building and creating worlds and visiting those built and created by others ("Home of the 3D Chat, Virtual Worlds Building Platform," 2008). Consistent with this emphasis, users have even established a builders' academy to teach other users how to build structures and accomplish a variety of technical effects (*SW City Builders Academy*, 2008). *Active Worlds* likely has the most realistic and visually impressive three-dimensional graphics of any of the virtual worlds.

Released in its current form in the summer of 2003, *Second Life* won a place among *Time Magazine*'s best inventions of 2002 ("2002 Best Inventions, Robots & Tech, 3-D Online Environment," 2002). The site has grown to become the most popular, widely used, and cutting-edge virtual world. It is widely considered the benchmark, reflecting both the potential of virtual worlds and signaling a possible demise in their popularity (Ward, 2007). *Second Life* is the most realistic and comprehensive virtual world available. The breadth of activity and the expanse of its user base make *Second Life* truly unique. It shows the potential of virtual worlds that was only suggested by earlier programs. Some have argued that *Second Life* allows users who face impediments in real life to more easily connect with others, thereby allowing them to develop social skills for real life (Terdiman, 2005). While many virtual worlds allow and encourage commerce with virtual versions of currency, *Second Life* has taken this idea to a new level by utilizing its currency, the Linden Dollar (Dubner, 2007). The Linden Dollar is exchangeable for real currencies through a resident-to-resident exchange facilitated by Linden Labs ("Terms of Service," 2008). This means that people and companies are able to make real money in *Second Life*. Companies have flocked to *Second Life* in search of a new channel for marketing (Siklos, 2006). The ability to buy, sell, and develop land attracts online investors (Craig, 2006). Until early 2008, *Second Life* even featured banks where users could invest Linden Dollars (Cavalli, 2008).

A little over a year since a Gartner analyst suggested that *Second Life* had reached the peak of inflated expectations, *Second Life*'s potential remains uncertain (Reuters, 2007). The history of virtual worlds provides little guidance as the dynamics of *Second Life* are radically different from MUDs, MMOGs, and even more recent virtual worlds aimed at social networking and exploring a virtual environment. Interestingly, as *Second Life* has become the premier online virtual world, others have been developed to cater to particular niches of various segments of society.

First launched in 2004, *Kaneva* offers users a more conservative version of *Second Life*. *Kaneva*'s emphasis is on business and social networking (Jana & McConnon, 2007). The environment in *Kaneva* is much more controlled. Users are limited in their options for self-expression and the extent to which they can affect their surroundings. While *Second Life* offers users entrance to another world, *Kaneva* promotes itself as an extension of this world. Avatars are limited to human forms and there are none of the unrealistic or fantasy elements that are available in *Second Life*. *Kaneva* strives to deliver a virtual world experience to the suburban user, offering a world more suited to that user's needs and tastes.

Current Trends

In recent years, virtual worlds have become increasingly relevant to recreational, business, and educational users. These new worlds have made interaction with people in different areas of the world possible over the Internet through the use of each user's avatar. However, much has changed since the introduction of *Second Life* in 1991 (Tuft, 2007). Seventeen years later, virtual worlds are far less clumsy and capable of much more than just avatar interaction. The current trends existing in virtual worlds exemplify a world of promise, but these do not come without problems (Dredge, 2007).

The virtual world now has a myriad of applications ranging from gaming to in-world entrepreneurship. The business world has seen opportunity for brand recognition and marketing, not just in worlds like *Second Life*, but also in regular gaming ("Youniversal Branding: Part 1,"

2006). Also, companies have found ways to cut costs of training and other activities through use of virtual worlds ("It's Not All Fun and Games," 2006). The educational arena has found uses in virtual worlds from training to the creation of online classrooms accessible to people around the world. A quick visit to *Second Life* reveals educational tools, such as access to books and even language lessons. Of course, the social network aspect of virtual worlds still remains the focus of these sites. Even social networking, however, has led to financial opportunity as people create commerce in these parallel worlds, creating real value (Tuft, 2007). *Second Life* and other sites have created a lucrative professional world for those who have taken advantage of these opportunities to earn a very comfortable real-world living (MacMillan, 2007).

Many current trends look promising for the future of virtual worlds. Perhaps the most important is the proposed introduction of numerous new virtual worlds in the upcoming year (Dredge, 2007). This will mean increased competition and improved interfaces as companies will be forced to consistently advance and adapt to stay relevant in the virtual-world market. In the business world, companies are using virtual worlds for many things.

- As a training ground for employees to cut costs and improve productivity (Dredge, 2007)
- To send mock-ups and drawings to other offices and companies in other locations ("It's Not All Fun and Games," 2006)
- To view proposed marketing and branding ideas in a three-dimensional space (Carr, 2007)
- To have virtual premieres for clothing, movies, television, and so forth (Carr)

Education has also found a niche in the virtual world by utilizing the ability to connect people from across the world and set up areas where dif-

ferent resources for learning can be accessed from a computer. Some of the educational applications are as follows:

- Virtual classrooms (Nesson, Nesson, & Koo, 2006)
- In-world language lessons and classes (*Suffern Middle School in Second Life*, 2008)
- Access to resources in a 3-D environment (Levine, 2008)
- Creation of real-world experiences for a relatively low price through marketing and branding experience, creation of engineering projects, and practice running a business (Beller, 2007; Dartmouth College, 2005; Idaho State, 2007; BBC News, 2007)

There is also the social aspect where people can interact through their avatars (Tuft, 2007). Younger generations seem to be leading the way in virtual worlds because of their familiarity with the Internet. All these new and savvy users will be looking for the best platform that will drive innovation in all virtual worlds. Business and educational applications of virtual worlds will be discussed in more depth in following sections.

While virtual worlds have created many trends that are positive, there are still many problems that exist. Problems with the capability of the worlds to support the number of users that are visiting the sites cause slowdowns and other hindrances that make it more difficult to use these worlds. Other problems also exist, such as the difficulty in making communication between tech-savvy and regular people less "geeky," difficulty in getting around, and "griefers" who cause problems for users in the world (Dredge, 2007). It is increasingly difficult to police these sites internally as they grow larger and grow in value. A June 2007 estimate indicated that the market was already worth more than US$1 billion (Tuft, 2007). Additionally, there are safety issues for the population at large. The government has taken an interest in whether or not these communities might become or already are a breeding and meeting ground for terrorists (Nickson, 2008). The answer to these current problems will drive future trends in virtual worlds and help to shape virtual worlds' capabilities and limitations.

It is still early in the development of virtual worlds and the technology is still in its relative infancy. However, many expect it to take shape as quickly as the Internet did. Companies such as IBM, Coca-Cola, Toyota, and other heavyweights are putting money into creating better applications and opportunities within virtual worlds (LaMonica, 2007). With technology advancing faster than ever before, and many new virtual worlds on the horizon, the explosion could arrive very quickly. Looking at current trends and identifying the problems facing these virtual worlds will help companies and individuals to be prepared for what is to come.

Business Applications of Virtual Worlds

The increasing numbers of users have led to greater opportunities for businesses in the virtual world. There are opportunities for companies to increase their brand recognition, cut costs in training and real-time information transfer, and facilitate employee communication. Companies need to be careful, however, understanding the landscape and what opportunities are present to make the leap into virtual worlds profitable. While many believe that virtual worlds will become increasingly business friendly (LaMonica, 2007), many still heed caution for businesses ready to enter the market (Broersma, 2007). The pitfalls range from security issues to investment risks. Analyzing these pitfalls is imperative before a company enters the virtual world.

The most used and obvious business application of virtual worlds is branding and marketing. Just as in the real world, marketing opportunities are everywhere in virtual worlds because they

parallel the real world. Companies utilize this platform to get their name out to new customers (especially teens) and to reach markets that are more dependent on computers than on television for entertainment ("It's Not All Fun and Games," 2006). Companies have also realized that operating in a virtual world is similar to operating in the real world ("Youniversal Branding: Part 1," 2006). Creating a store in a virtual world and leaving it has not proven successful, and companies are realizing they need to run these stores in similar ways to the real world (Carr, 2007). An advantage is that the cost of creating campaigns, store space, and other types of advertising in virtual worlds is exceedingly less expensive than in the real world. It also allows service industries such as hotels and architects to show clients or potential clients what structures will look like (Carr). Even though a company may be reaching only a niche market for now, it is doing so for a much lower cost.

Companies with multiple offices can also cut costs by displaying real-time information and modeling products in virtual worlds. Meetings can be held online, helping to eliminate travel costs for clients and customers. Being able to post designs in a virtual world and allowing clients or other offices to view them can cut down on the costs associated with sending items, while allowing for better representations of products ("It's Not All Fun and Games," 2006). While the meeting functions may not be as advanced as teleconferencing and its brethren, the ability to display objects in 3-D can be a huge advantage.

Training has become a much bigger part of the business use of virtual worlds. Any company can take advantage of the cheap costs associated with virtual worlds and supplement its business online. This allows employees to interact with equipment and processes that are costly to provide in real life. It also allows employees to see exactly how processes work and are created ("It's Not All Fun and Games," 2006). Travel costs associated with training may also be substantially reduced or almost eliminated through the use of virtual worlds. Keeping costs down while providing the best possible training is a definite bonus for companies that maintain a presence in a virtual world.

Most companies face the questions of whether they should enter a virtual world and whether entry is worth the costs. While the amount of potential profit from a virtual world is low, the cost of entry is almost nonexistent. Gartner predicts that, by 2011, 80% of individual Internet users and Fortune 500 companies will be in virtual worlds ("Gartner says 80 Percent of Active Internet Users will have a 'Second Life,'" 2007). This presents a large opportunity for companies looking to enter now and be forerunners in this technology. There is much speculation that Google's entry into the virtual world is imminent (Pasick, 2007). Many believe that Google's entrance and the combination of a virtual world with its Google Earth function could be a boon to businesses looking for more profitability and opportunity in virtual worlds. Some useful applications in *MyWorld* (the proposed name of Google's virtual world) are real-time information on city buildings and residents of buildings, among many others. People also expect the usability of *MyWorld* to be much better than that of existing worlds such as *Second Life* since Google plans to build off of its already existing technologies (Smith, 2007).

The business applications of virtual worlds are growing daily and companies need to look at the risk and reward of entering the market. Based on estimates, it appears that sometime in the future, almost everyone will be involved in virtual worlds, and companies need to prepare for that. Judging by the explosion of past technologies, the time when virtual worlds become more profitable could come sooner than expected. However, companies need to weigh the cost savings of being present in a virtual world now with the money to be invested while waiting for a truly integrated and easily navigable virtual world.

Educational Applications

Education is one sector that has gotten remarkable use out of virtual worlds. Educational institutions at all different levels have found the value in utilizing the ability to connect people from across the world and interact with various resources. The advantages and uses that virtual worlds offer to educational institutions have only been touched upon, but have already been used across the world. *Second Life* alone has been used by institutions of higher education all across the globe, including Penn State, Columbia University, Duke University, the University of Sydney, and the University of Edinburgh, among others (Harris, Lowendahl, & Zastrocky, 2007).

Virtual worlds are being used for all different types of educational purposes, not just by elite educational institutions. Some educational institutions have utilized virtual worlds in order to create virtual classrooms. For example, one middle school has used *Second Life* as a venue to practice foreign language skills by having an Italian class meet in a virtual café to practice ordering from a menu. Simply by using headsets, *Second Life* enables students to practice their foreign language skills in a virtual café environment while, in reality, these students could be on the other side of the world (*Suffern Middle School in Second Life*, 2008). Another example of using *Second Life* as a classroom is Harvard Law School, which actually holds all course lectures in a virtual classroom in *Second Life* (Nesson et al., 2006). Other universities such as Emory University have also used *Second Life* to hold conferences (Levine, 2008).

The Otis College of Art and Design features a class where students actually create art projects in *Second Life* using the proprietary software to generate different art scenes. The class was split into teams who met in *Second Life* at a scheduled time, developed their themes by communicating, and then started to build their art projects.

In addition to classroom uses, a number of researchers have used virtual worlds to model human behavior. For example, following the outbreak of a virtual disease in the MMOG *World of Warcraft*, scientists now point to virtual worlds as environments to carry out experiments on human behavior in epidemic situations. When an outbreak occurred in this virtual world, epidemiologists were surprised by how closely the behavior of online avatars paralleled that of humans in real life. Some players altruistically helped infected players, while some players, once inflicted, tried to pass the disease on deliberately. Running such a disease simulation in a virtual world may provide insight that is otherwise unavailable. Epidemics are usually available for study only after the fact and many simulated scenarios limit human behavior to a mathematical model or ignore it completely ("Virtual Game is a 'Disease Model,'" 2007).

Another educational aspect of educational virtual worlds is their similarity to real-world institutions. *Second Life*'s economy, for example, is so large that it can reasonably be compared to that of a small country dependent on tourism. Economists have found that studying the growing economies of these virtual worlds can be a useful learning tool and a realistic model of a real-world economy (Beller, 2007).

In addition to classroom applications and behavioral models, virtual worlds have also proven to be useful as training tools. For example, Dartmouth College has used *Second Life* to create an immersive multiuser environment to train emergency responders. This is a virtual prototyping experiment used for emergency response simulation that is funded by the U.S. Department of Homeland Security (Dartmouth College, 2005). Another interesting educational use for virtual worlds is run by the Institute of Rural Health at Idaho State University, which is using a multiuser immersive environment to host virtual tabletop exercises in bioterrorism and preparedness (Idaho State University, 2007).

The educational sector has found tremendous uses for virtual worlds today, from hosting classes, conferences, and training programs to using virtual worlds as venues to test economic and human behavioral models. Educational institutions are finding all sorts of uses for virtual worlds that were never before possible. The possibilities seem endless in an environment that makes communication broader and more interactive than ever.

How to Participate in Virtual Worlds

Getting started is similar in all virtual worlds. Life begins with an e-mail address. Users generally use e-mail addresses or other names as user names. Users then enter information and may take steps to customize their avatars, connect with a particular community, or add money to their accounts. Nearly all sites offer basic membership for free, but also offer premium services for a monthly charge, usually around US$10. The registration process of *Second Life* serves as a good example because it is similar to that of other virtual worlds, is very user friendly, and is the most popular.

A good place to start is to use a search engine to enter the name of the virtual world, in this case, *Second Life*. Upon arriving at the site, a user is first presented with the option of joining a community, such as Ben & Jerry's, Dublin in SL, and Scion. This step may be skipped and the user may go straight to Linden Lab's Orientation Island. This walks the user through the process of picking out a name and entering his or her birth date and e-mail address. For those wary of unsolicited spam or simply wishing to maintain their total anonymity, the process can be started by creating a false e-mail address for their *Second Life* personality.

After this step, the user chooses from among 12 default avatars to represent them in virtual space. Next, the user is prompted to enter his or her real name. Interestingly, the terms and conditions specify that users must agree to provide "true, accurate, current and complete information," and to maintain and update this information as it changes ("Terms of Service," 2008). The user must then enter a password. Following these steps, the user must then check his or her e-mail for a link to *Second Life*, which will be sent after the registration is complete. The user must then install the software, which will download to the Programs folder on the computer and automatically install a *Second Life* shortcut on the desktop if the user wishes.

After everything downloads, the user is ready to log in. At this point, the user may make certain modifications, including setting up the VoIP (voice over Internet protocol) option, and is now free to explore *Second Life*.

Conclusion and Future Trends

One thing that is for certain is that virtual worlds will continue to grow in the future. It appears that they will multiply at an incredible rate in 2008, with many new worlds launching then. Additionally, users around the world appear to be multiplying. Entire markets like China seem to be opening up to the idea of virtual worlds (Dredge, 2007). However, while virtual worlds do expect to continue growth in the future, there are a few questions surrounding their future. Who will be using them? How will they be using them? Which virtual worlds will be the major players of the future?

Corporate users are expected to grow as more than 80% of the Global 1000 are expected to have a presence in at least one virtual world by the end of 2011 (Abrams, 2007). However, the question to consider is how corporations will decide to use virtual worlds in the future. As virtual-world technology progresses and access improves, virtual worlds will become an increasingly pervasive part of the Web. As this advancement continues, the potential for businesses to take advantage of this new marketplace will only grow. Businesses will be able to use virtual worlds to transform customer

experiences, improve business processes, drive collaboration, enrich commerce and transactions, and enable 3-D modeling and simulations so that they can better understand their markets (Parris, 2007). With all of the advantages that virtual worlds offer modern companies, it seems advantageous for companies to at least test the waters. Whether organizations find themselves in industries that are using virtual worlds or not, it is relatively cheap to enter one such as *Second Life* to explore the possibilities (Abrams).

Companies that are considering entering virtual worlds must consider how they want to do so. While many companies have unsuccessfully entered them for advertising purposes (Dredge, 2007), there are other options for using virtual worlds internally that appear to be productive. While virtual worlds such as *Second Life* and *There* have created a thriving public environment, there is an increasing demand for that same type of virtual world on a more secure and private level (Fenn, Harmo, Prentice, Raskino, & Cearley, 2008). Some companies have found that meetings in *Second Life* (or their own private virtual worlds) have increased productivity and saved money (Dredge). Research indicates that by 2012, 70% of organizations will use private virtual worlds to support internal collaboration and social interaction. Some even expect that, as organizations make the move to private worlds, their presence in public virtual worlds will decline, decreasing demand for the public worlds (Fenn et al.).

Another consideration for the future of virtual worlds is who the major players will be. While *Second Life* may have been the first big virtual world, it may not be the leader in the years to come. In fact, in April 2007, *Second Life* was not even listed as a top-10 most popular virtual world, as measured by percentage of traffic or market share of visits. One of the reasons for *Second Life*'s decline is that newer virtual worlds are coming out that are easier to use and, accordingly, have a larger potential customer base (Kharif, 2007).

Some of the major virtual worlds that seem to be taking over, such as *Club Penguin, Webkinz,* and *Habbo Hotel,* have targeted teenage users (Dredge, 2007). *Second Life* currently offers a richer creative environment than most other sites, but, if organizations are looking to reach a younger demographic, virtual worlds such as *There, Kaneva,* and *Laguna Beach* are also options (Abrams, 2007).

Another threat to *Second Life* and other current virtual worlds will be incoming competition from already existing technology companies. Many of these companies are trying to offer a virtual world in combination with their current services. For example, a company like MySpace may incorporate a virtual world so that its users can create avatars and virtual houses instead of standard profiles. Google may be looking to incorporate a virtual world with functions like Google Earth, building a virtual world based on a real one. A startup company, Weblo, has already been successful with a similar project (Kharif, 2007). Big names like Microsoft, Google, and Yahoo! may be looking to get a piece of the virtual-world pie, and it seems likely that they will take these virtual worlds to a whole new level.

Overall, virtual worlds are a new phenomenon that will only continue to spread across the globe. As new users continue to enter these worlds and new applications are developed, it seems impossible to predict the potential impact that virtual worlds will have on businesses, consumers, and industry in the future. It appears that we are only scraping the surface at this point and that improved technology in the future is likely to create virtual worlds that will, in one way or another, become a part of everyday life.

REFERENCES

2002 best inventions, robots & tech, 3-D online environment. (2002). *Time.* Retrieved February 22, 2008, from http://www.time.com/time/2002/inventions/rob_environment.html

3D avatar chat in virtual worlds. (2008). *Moove Online.* Retrieved February 12, 2008, from http://www.moove.com

Abrams, C. (2007). Three ways that Second Life can add real benefits for Web businesses, despite the negative hype. *Gartner Media.*

Bartle, R. (1990). *Early MUD history.* Retrieved February 13, 2008, from http://www.mud.co.uk/richard/mudhist.htm

Becker, D. (2003). "Sims Online" off to a slow start. *CNET News.com.* Retrieved February 17, 2008, from http://www.news.com/Sims-Online-off-to-slow-start/2100-1040_3-982673.html

Beller, M. (2007). *The coming Second Life business cycle.* Retrieved February 13, 2008, from http://www.mises.org/story/2640

Broersma, M. (2007). Virtual worlds pose business risk says Gartner. *TechWorld.* Retrieved February 12, 2008, from http://www.techworld.com/security/news/index.cfm?newsID=9765&pagtype=samechan%20-%2056k%20%E2%80%93

Carr, D. F. (2007). Second Life: Is business ready for virtual worlds? *Baseline Magazine.* Retrieved February 11, 2008, from http://www.baselinemag.com/c/a/Projects-Management/Second-Life-Is-Business-Ready-For-Virtual-Worlds/1

Cavalli, E. (2008). Second Life bans traditional banking. *Wired Blog Network.* Retrieved February 12, 2008, from http://blog.wired.com

Colley, S. (2008). Stories from the maze war 30 year retrospective: Steve Colley's story of the original maze. *Digibarn Computer Museum.* Retrieved February 13, 2008, from http://www.digibarn.com/history/04-VCF7-MazeWar/stories/colley.html

Craig, K. (2006). Second Life land deal goes sour. *Wired News.* Retrieved March 10, 2008, from http://www.wired.com

Dartmouth College. (2005). Synthetic environments for emergency response simulation. Retrieved February 20, 2008, from http://www.ists. dartmouth.edu/projects/seers/misc.php

Dredge, S. (2007). 20 trends defining virtual worlds in 2007. *Tech Digest.* Retrieved February 22, 2008, from http://techdigest.tv/2007/10/20_ trends_defin.html

Dubner, S. J. (2007). Philip Rosedale answers your Second Life questions. *New York Times: Freakonomics Blog.* Retrieved March 10, 2008, from http://freakonomics.blogs.nytimes. com/2007/12/13/philip-rosedale-answers-your-second-life-questions/?scp=1-b&sq=Philip+Ro sedale+answers+your+Second+Life+questions &st=nyt

Farmer, F. R. (2008). Social dimensions of habitat citizenry. *Electric Communities.* Retrieved February 12, 2008, from http://www.crockford. com/ec/citizenry.html

Fenn, J., Harmo, T., Prentice, S., Raskino, M., & Cearley, D. (2008). Predicts 2008: Emerging trends expand collaboration and human performance. *Gartner Media.*

Gartner says 80 percent of active Internet users will have a "Second Life" in the virtual world by the end of 2011. (2007). *Gartner Media.* Retrieved February 12, 2008, from http://www.gartner. com/it/page.jsp?id=503861

Harris, M., Lowendahl, J. M., & Zastrocky, M. (2007). Second Life: Expanding higher education e-learning into 3D. *Gartner Media.* Retrieved February 20, 2008, from http://www.gartner. com/resources/149800/149847/second_life_expanding_higher_149847.pdf

History timeline. (2008). *There.com.* Retrieved February 12, 2008, from http://therehistory.wetpaint.com/page/00+Early+History

Home of the 3D chat, virtual worlds building platform. (2008). *Active Worlds.* Retrieved February 13, 2008, from http://www.activeworlds.com

Idaho State University. (2007). Training in a large scale massive virtual environment. Retrieved February 20, 2008, from http://www.isu.edu/irh/ IBAPP/simulations.shtml

It's not all fun and games. (2006). *Business Week.* Retrieved February 13, 2008, from http://www. businessweek.com/magazine/content/06_18/ b3982007.htm

Jana, R., & McConnon, A. (2007). Digital suburbia: Kaneva aims to bring social networking to a relatively cautious, upscale crowd. *BusinessWeek.* Retrieved February 22, 2008, from http://www. businessweek.com/technology/content/apr2007/ tc20070416_936979.htm

Kharif, O. (2007). Virtual world gold rush? *Business Week.* Retrieved February 22, 2008, from http://www.businessweek.com/technology/content/may2007/tc20070522_380944.htm

LaMonica, M. (2007). Wanted: Applications for virtual worlds. *CNET News.com.* Retrieved February 12, 2008, from http://www.news.com/8301-10784_3-9730918-7.html

Levine, A. (2008). NMC teachers buzz: Check out student art projects at Otis Island. *NMC Campus Observer.* Retrieved February 18, 2008, from http://sl.nmc.org/2008/02/17/otis-student-art

MacMillan, D. (2007). Virtual world rich list. *Business Week.* Retrieved February 11, 2008, from http://images.businessweek.com/ss/07/04/0416_ richlist/index_01.htm?chan =technology_ special+report+--+virtual+life_virtual+life

Moove. (2008). *Virtual Worlds Review.* Retrieved February 12, 2008, from http://www.virtualworld-sreview.com/moove

Nesson, C., Nesson, R., & Koo, G. (2006). *CyberOne: Law in the court of public opinion.* Retrieved February 20, 2008, from http://blogs. law.harvard.edu/cyberone

Nguyen, B. (2008). Linux dictionary. *Matisse/ Linux Dictionary V. 0.16.* Retrieved February

12, 2008, from http://www.tldp.org/LDP/Linux-Dictionary/html/index.html

Nickson, C. (2008). Terrorists using virtual worlds to plan? *Digital Trends*. Retrieved February 17, 2008, from http://news.digitaltrends.com/news/story/15686/terrorists_ using_virtual_worlds_to_plan

Parris, C. (2007). Do better business in 3D. *Business Week Online*. Retrieved February 22, 2008, from http://www.businessweek.com/technology/content/may2007/tc20070501 _526224.htm?chan=top+news_top+news+index_technology

Pasick, A. (2007). Doors open on Google virtual world(s)? *Reuters Online*. Retrieved February 18, 2008, from http://blogs.reuters.com/mediafile/2007/10/24/doors-to-open-on-google-virtual-worlds

Patrizio, A. (2001). Gamers jump on online bandwagon. *Wired*. Retrieved February 22, 2008, from http://www.wired.com/culture/lifestyle/news/2001/10/47181

Ratan, S. (2003). Sims flop dogs game developers. *Wired*. Retrieved February 22, 2008, from http://www.wired.com/gaming/gamingreviews/multimedia/2003/05/58749

Reuters, A. (2007). Gartner says Second Life hype near peak. *Reuters Second Life News Center*. Retrieved February 22, 2008, from http://secondlife.reuters.com/stories/2007/01/04/gartner-says-second-life-hype-near-peak

Siklos, R. (2006). A virtual world, but real money. *New York Times*. Retrieved February 22, 2008, from http://www.nytimes.com/2006/10/19/technology/19virtual.html? ex=1318910400&en=75ee308b86b461aa&ei=5088&partner=rssnyt&emc=rss

Smith, T. (2007). Google's virtual world could be business answer to Second Life. *Information Week*. Retrieved February 17, 2008, from

http://www.informationweek.com/blog/main/archives/2007/09/googles_virtual.html

Suffern Middle School in Second Life. (2008). Retrieved February 20, 2008, from http://rama-poislands.edublogs.org

SW City Builders Academy. (2008). Retrieved February 12, 2008, from http://www.swcity.net/academy/index.php

Terdiman, D. (2005). Second Life teaches life lessons. *Wired News*.

Terdiman, D. (2006). Newsmaker: A brief history of the virtual world. Interview of Bruce Damer. *CNET News.com*. Retrieved February 12, 2008, from http://business2-cnet.com.com/A-brief-history-of-the-virtual-world/2008-1043_3-6134110.html

Terdiman, D. (2007). The future is here: Google Earth meets virtual worlds. *CNET News.com*. Retrieved February 14, 2008, from http://www.news.com/8301-13772_3-9793643-52.html

Terdiman, D. (2008). "Hello Kitty" MMO goes into beta. *CNET News.com*. Retrieved February 12, 2008, from http://www.news.com/8301-13772_3-9871891-52.html

Terms of service. (2008). *Second Life*. Retrieved February 22, 2008, from http://secondlife.com/corporate/tos.php

Top 10 most popular MMO games. (2007). *Videogamesblogger*. Retrieved February 12, 2008, from http://www.videogamesblogger.com/2007/06/14/top-10-most-popular-mmo-games-list.htm

Tuft, M. (2007). Virtual world, real millions. *BBC News*. Retrieved February 13, 2008, from http://news.bbc.co.uk/1/hi/business/6708417.stm

Virtual game is a "disease model." (2007). *BBC News*. Retrieved February 13, 2008, from http://news.bbc.co.uk/2/hi/health/6951918.stm

VZones Website. (2008). Retrieved February 12, 2008, from http://www.vzones.com/about.htm.

Ward, M. (2007). A very real future for virtual worlds. *BBC News*. Retrieved February 22, 2008, from http://news.bbc.co.uk/2/hi/technology/7144511.stm

What is there? Makena Technologies, Inc. (2008). *There.com*. Retrieved February 12, 2008, from http://www.there.com

Woodcock, B. (2008). *MMOG chart post by SirBruce*. Retrieved February 12, 2008, from http://www.mmogchart.com

Youniversal branding: Part 1. (2006). *Trendwatching.com*. Retrieved February 11, 2008, from http://www.trendwatching.com/trends/youniversalbranding.htm

ADDITIONAL RESOURCES

Cheng, J. (2007). *Google testing "My World" for launch later this year*. Retrieved February 22, 2008, from http://arstechnica.com/news.ars/post/20070924-google-testing-my-world-for-launch-later-this-year.html

Donath, J. (2008). Giving avatars emote control. *Harvard Business Review, 86*(2), 31.

Graves, L. (2008). A second life for higher ed. *U.S. News & World Report, 144*(2), 49-50.

Levine, A. (2006). Our movie "NMC Campus: Seriously Engaging." *NMC Campus Observer*. Retrieved February 20, 2008, from http://sl.nmc.org/2006/06/12/seriously-engaging-movie

Muve Forward. (2007). *Educationally relevant virtual trends for 2008*. Retrieved February 22, 2008, from http://muveforward.blogspot.com/2007/12/educationally-relevant-virtual-world.html

Robbins, S., & Bell, M. (2008). *Second Life for dummies*. Indianapolis, IN: Wiley Publishing, Inc.

SOCIAL NETWORKS

Kim Baker, Iryna Butler

History of Social Networking

Electronic social networks have become a part of everyday life. Online communities help millions of people instantly connect with former classmates, communicate, find friends or people with the same interests, exchange information, establish business networks, and even share views. Social networking has integrated with day-to-day activities to the point that we now live in a real-time global society.

The first online social network, SixDegrees.com, was established in1997 (Boyd & Ellison, 2007). This Web site combined the ability to create a profile, send an instant message, and create a circle of friends on one Web site. The concept that all things are within "six degrees of separation" was behind this innovative idea. The site attracted many users. A number of sites similar to SixDegrees.com were introduced to the public in the late 1990s to early 2000s, including LiveJournal, Asian Avenue, BlackPlanet, and LunaStorm. Most of these Web sites targeted certain demographic groups.

MySpace was launched in 2003 by the company eUniverse. Its user base grew exponentially within just a couple of years, transforming the Web site into the most popular online social networking community in the United States. Most teenagers opened profiles on MySpace because of the site's lenient age policy. By 2006, MySpace had more than 20 million users. It was acquired by News Corporation for US$580 million in July of 2005 (Rosebush, 2005).

Facebook, another popular social networking Web site, was founded by a former Harvard student who used it as a tool to reconnect with former classmates. It was launched in February of 2004 (Yadav, 2006). Soon Facebook became a popular social network for college students in the United States. Initially, to join the network, a person was required to have an active college e-mail address. In 2006, the network extended to high school students and some larger companies. Now, anyone age 13 or older can join the network.

LinkedIn is a professionally oriented social networking site. It was founded in 2003 by Reid Hoffman and Konstantin Guericke. The site applied the concept of social networking, initially used primarily by youths in a casual context, and made it relevant to adults seeking career growth. LinkedIn tries to help people connect with others who might help their careers ("How LinkedIn Broke Through," 2006).

Other popular social networking sites include Furl, Spurl.net, Shadows, Scuttle, Yahoo! My Web 2.0, Ma.gnolia, Digg, StumbleUpon, and reddit.

Current Trends

Recently, MySpace went international and launched its Web sites in Europe, Asia Pacific, and South America. Last year, the Web site added the ImageShack application, which simplified the way videos are compressed and uploaded. MySpace also elected to become part of OpenSocial, a network that enables third-party programmers to build platforms to take advantage of the Web site's user base. The site is now in the process of adding new products to its portfolio to make users' communication more dynamic. Photobucket is going to be integrated with the MySpace platform at the beginning of 2008 ("Photobucket to Launch New Applications on MySpace," 2008). With the help of Photobucket, users will be able to change their photo images and customize and personalize their digital identity more easily than before.

Facebook became part of OpenSocial a few months prior to MySpace. You can now mash Facebook with other applications. As a result of launching a developer platform, the Web site drew many new users. Facebook recently introduced a Spanish version of its site. The new user-friendly Extended Profile application allows members to clean up their cluttered pages and move seldom-used profiles and applications to the extended profile.

LinkedIn is used by professionals across various industries. It enables professionals to network, stay connected, and tap into one another's list of contacts. The site takes advantage of word-of-mouth and personal references to foster career growth and enables users to stay in touch with other professionals that they may have worked with in the past. The site is more than a job search Web site like Monster.com ("How LinkedIn Broke Through," 2006). Rather than focusing on individual jobs, it focuses on people. The site does, however, provide expanded tools for job hunters and employment recruiters for a fee (Fitzgerald, 2007). LinkedIn has recently begun adding more features to enable users to customize their profiles with a personal touch. In 2007, *LinkedIn* doubled its membership from 9 to 18 million users and continues to add 25 new members every minute (Dye, 2007).

Business Applications

As previously stated, MySpace is a member of OpenSocial. By integrating new applications into MySpace, businesses will gain instant exposure to million of customers (Olsen, 2008). If the application becomes popular, the programmer or business can sell advertisements and collect profits. For example, MySpace will let developers sell advertisements, products, and sponsorships on the specially assigned pages and collect 100% of the revenue generated from the ads.

Since Facebook became open, more than 168,000 developers joined its platform to evaluate and create new applications. Such applications as Top Friends, Fun Wall, Super Wall, and others became widely used on the Web site, generating profits for the creators. For example, Top Friends, used by over 2 million members, is currently valued at over US$29 million. Companies like iLike.com, a music-sharing start-up, and Slide. com, a photo-sharing service, helped Facebook attract more users and market their services at the same time.

Facebook also allows businesses to create profiles. In addition, third parties can now sell advertisements directly on the Facebook member's page using "hypertargeting." This system analyzes users' tastes and preferences and automatically advertises products that might be interesting to the user. By attaching advertisements to news feed stories and social ads, businesses can promote their services (Morin, 2007). Companies can also run surveys targeting specific demographics, which is very helpful when conducting marketing research.

Many employers use social networking sites such as Facebook and MySpace to research potential candidates. Likewise, some interviewees are researching employers and interviewers, which creates some controversy but is becoming a tactic with widening popularity.

LinkedIn's user base has grown considerably. The company expects 2008 revenue from its fee-based subscriptions and advertising to reach between US$50 million and US$100 million. The more users are on the site, the more useful it is to its members as networks deepen and extend farther. The site has been continuing to grow in popularity and new features have been added to enrich the experience (Ricadela, 2007).

Educational Applications

From the standpoint of education, both Facebook and MySpace help students to create and innovate. Even though Facebook opened its network to virtually anyone, the majority of Facebook and MySpace members are either high school or college students. Students currently use technology to create and customize their profile pages, identify new trends, and apply existing knowledge. The main purpose of social networking is communication and collaboration. Students are socially engaged through virtual communities and learn how to build social networks. Students are also able to access, convert, and retrieve digital data, helping them learn to organize and evaluate information.

Facebook developers are now developing educational applications for Facebook. In the fall of 2007, Stanford's computer science department introduced a new course called *Create Engaging Web Applications Using Metrics and Learning on Facebook (Eldon, 2007). In this course, students develop new applications for Facebook and analyze how such applications are used by users.*

LinkedIn offers academic institutions a way to stay connected with alumni, build recruitment efforts, and increase marketing profiles. College students may be encouraged by the career services center to use the tool to build networks for their careers and learn from people in various fields about areas of interest to help guide them in their professional job search.

How to Use Social Networking

Anyone 14 years or older can become a member of MySpace. By providing general information, age, name, and a valid e-mail address, one can create his or her own MySpace account. MySpace members can customize their profiles, upload pictures, write blogs and comments, send e-mails and instant messages, download music, and interact with friends and acquaintances. As a member you can also invite friends to join the network, view profiles of your friends, and much more. Many users have public pages, but you can also make your page private. The service is free.

Facebook enables anyone 13 years or older to open an account. Similar to MySpace, Facebook members provide information about themselves prior to joining the Web site. Currently, users can store up to 1 GB of information for free. Some Facebook applications are targeted for specific age groups. For example, calendar applications can be used to organize everyday activities. With the help of the Courses application, users can create study groups by knowing who is signed up for a specific academic course. The Skype application allows phoning service for free over the Internet.

LinkedIn membership is free for professionals. Registration is easy and takes just a few minutes. Once members, users can personalize their settings to facilitate different kinds of exchange with other users such as those regarding job referrals, questions about their place of employment, or industry experience. The site is professionally based, and the information posted is career focused in nature. This is the primary difference between LinkedIn and other social networking sites. Resumes can be uploaded and users create a network with other members to build their reach into the corporate world. Members are invited to join other members' lists of contacts, and may accept or decline. The site offers job search information and enables people to stay connected.

Conclusion and Future Trends

With a huge variety of online communities and the rise of *Second Life* as a virtual alternative to social networking, it is difficult to predict how the world of social networking will unfold. There will likely be more collaboration and integration of various applications within communities and Web sites. In the future, Web sites like MySpace and Facebook may become wholesale retailers of various applications and features, providing users with multiple options with just a single click.

Sites geared toward professionals and career networking are also likely to grow in popularity. As people continue to work at more corporations throughout their lifetime, sites such as LinkedIn

will be instrumental in keeping networks alive. Professional associations, boards of directors, and other advisory committees may be sourced more heavily from social networking sites, and headhunters and recruiters are likely to rely on sites such as LinkedIn more to source job candidates.

REFERENCES

Boyd, D. M., & Ellison, N. B. (2007). Social network sites: Definition, history and scholarship. *Journal of Computer-Mediated Communication, 13*(1), article 11. Retrieved from http://jcmc.indiana.edu/vol13/issue1/boyd.ellison.html

Dye, J. (2007). LinkedIn Corporation. *EContent, 30*(10), 42-43.

Eldon, E. (2007). *Facebook to take over Stanford classroom.* Retrieved February 19, 2008, from http://venturebeat.com/2007/09/10/facebook-to-take-over-stanford-classroom

Fitzgerald, M. (2007). Let's get together making contacts with social nets. *Inc., 29*(8), 54-55.

How LinkedIn broke through. (2006, April, 10). *BusinessWeek Online*, p. 12. Retrieved February 19, 2008, from http://www.businessweek.com/technology/content/apr2006/tc20060410_185842.htm?chan=search

Morin, D. (2007). *Introducing Facebook ads.* Retrieved February 19, 2008, from http://developers.facebook.com/news.php?blog=1&story=52

Olsen, S. (2008). *MySpace gets social with developers.* Retrieved February 20, 2008, from http://www.news.com/8301-10784_3-9865741-7.html

Photobucket to launch new applications on MySpace. (2008). *Business Wire.* Retrieved February 19, 2008, from http://www.forbes.com/businesswire/feeds/businesswire/2008/02/07/businesswire20080207006073r1.html

Ricadela, A. (2007). LinkedIn reaches out. *BusinessWeek Online*, 20.

Rosebush, S. (2005). *MySpace growing even faster since acquisition.* Retrieved February 20, 2008, from http://www.businessweek.com/the_thread/dealflow/archives/2005/11/myspace_growing.html

Yadav, S. (2006). *Facebook: The complete biography.* Retrieved February 16, 2008, from http://mashable.com/2006/08/25/facebook-profile

ADDITIONAL RECOURSES

Abba, J. (2007). *I'm on LinkedIn: Now what??? A guide to getting the most out of LinkedIn.* Silicon Valley, CA: ebook.

Allen, S. (2008). *LinkedIn for dummies.* Indianapolis, IN: Wiley Publishing, Inc.

Facebook. (n.d.). Retrieved from http://www.facebook.com

Facebook factsheet. (n.d.). Retrieved from http://richmond.facebook.com/press/info.php?factsheet

MySpace. (n.d.). Retrieved from http://www.myspace.com

Social Networking Developers. (n.d.). Retrieved from http://developers.facebook.com/get_started.php

Tylock, J. (2007). *LinkedIn personal trainer.* Tylock and Company.

Veer, E. A. Vander, & Veer, E. Vander. (2008). *Facebook: The missing manual.* Pogue Press.

SOCIAL NETWORKS: BOOKMARKS

History of Social Bookmarking

Social bookmarking is an easy way to tag, organize, and manage electronic information with the help of metadata (keywords). Bookmarks provide an alternative way of searching the Web based on popularity rather than algorithm-based systems such as Google. Sites of interest are bookmarked, which is the equivalent of adding it to a favorites list that is organized by category. Once a bookmark is created, it is tagged with descriptions and keywords for future retrieval and can be shared with friends or other members of the network interested in the topic.

ITList was a pioneer in electronic bookmarking. Launched in 1996, it rapidly became popular among users, who could store and share a collection of favorite Web sites and selected information in the assigned folders. Bookmarking Web sites like Backflip, Blink, and Clip2 appeared over the next couple of years but did not attract enough users to continue to compete.

In 2003, the social bookmarking phenomenon was introduced to the mainstream public by del.icio.us, an open-ended system where users choose what information to save. With the help of tags, members of del.icio.us could assign a name to a bookmark, store it, create categories, and share information with other users. Like prior bookmarking programs, del.icio.us is free. The bookmarks can be instantly accessed anywhere in the world by accessing the Internet.

In 2005, Yahoo! acquired del.icio.us for approximately US$30 million (Norton, 2006). While del.icio.us is arguably the most popular, other widely used social bookmarking sites include Furl, Spurl.net, Yahoo! My Web 2.0, Ma.gnolia, Digg, StumbleUpon, and reddit.

Current Trends

Originally created to help users organize information on the Web, social bookmarks have recently been integrated with social networking sites such as Facebook, enabling multiple Web sites to be easily accessible from one place and shared with friends. When researching a specific topic, Word and Excel files can be uploaded to del.icio.us and tagged accordingly to keep information centrally located and not tied to a hard drive or personal server. By creating a shortcut on a computer desktop, individuals can also view all the saved bookmarks through a browser. Bookmarks can be made public, semiprivate (allowing access only to specific users), or completely private. The del. icio.us homepage also provides members with a list of the most popular and recently posted items. These additional features make del.icio.us more attractive for users and businesses.

Business Applications

Businesses can use del.icio.us by creating an account with shared information on particular topics. If a team is working on a project involving research, each team member can bookmark pages that he or she finds interesting and the entire team can access them. Users can also collect publicly available information on their competitors by tagging articles in del.icio.us.

Del.icio.us is highly beneficial to online publications, journalists, and media professionals who access and source from popular information. Because this group of professionals deals with an overwhelming amount of information on a regular basis, social bookmarks can organize articles and press releases in a preferred order with just a few clicks (Angelotti, 2008). For example, in August 2007, the BBC News Web site started tagging its news links and sports overviews using del. icio.us.

Marketers can also bookmark their company's Web site to create interest in and awareness of their products and services. Bookmarking a corporate Web site and tagging it with keywords enables the site to be more easily found by others interested in the category.

Sites such as YouTube also have links where video clips can be automatically added to various bookmarking sites to foster viral marketing. As new media outlets continue to appear on the Web, bookmarking will continue to become a more popular feature.

Educational Applications

Students typically work on several computers to conduct their research including in libraries, homes, dorms, classrooms, and so forth. With the help of del.icio.us, students can tag and save information to easily retrieve it from any location. Groups can be formed for classes and information can be saved in a single location for both professors and students to access. Both the professor and the students can enrich the collected information by posting updated research findings in one place.

How to set up a Del.icio.us Account

Del.icio.us is very user friendly. To set up an account with del.icio.us, follow these simple steps:

1. Go to http://www.del.icio.us and click "Get started."
2. Create a user name and password.
3. Del.icio.us requires e-mail verification: You will be notified via e-mail to confirm registration.
4. A customized Web page, for example, http:// del.icio.us/student, will be automatically created in your account.
5. To post a link, click the "post" link on your del.icio.us page, tag it, and save it.

Conclusion and Future Trends

Social bookmarking organizes and customizes information on the Web. It has been successfully integrated with numerous businesses and scholastic applications. Some consider social bookmarking the next stage in Web searches ("Top 10 Ways to Use del.icio.us," 2008). With so much information available on the Web, social bookmarks create a meaningful way to both locate information and share it with others. In the near future, social bookmarking sites are likely to offer more personalized and customizable features and become more heavily integrated with electronic devices and other technology applications (Mac-Manus, 2007).

REFERENCES

About del.icio.us. (n.d.). Retrieved February 20, 2008, from http://del.icio.us/about

Angelotti, E. (2008). *Del.icio.us/pointer*. Retrieved February 20, 2008, from http://www.poynter.org/column.asp?id=122

MacManus, R. (2007). *10 more future Web trends*. Retrieved February 20, 2008, from http://www.readwriteweb.com/archives/10_more_future_web_trends.php

Norton, Q. (2006). *I want to build something that grows*. Retrieved February 20, 2008, from http://www.guardian.co.uk/media/2006/jan/26/newmedia.technology1

Top 10 ways to use del.icio.us. (n.d.). Retrieved February 20, 2008, from http://www.lifehack.org/articles/technology/top-10-ways-to-use-delicious.html

ADDITIONAL RESOURCES

Social Bookmarking Creation Tools

del.icio.us: http://www.del.icio.us

Digg: http://digg.com

Furl: http://www.furl.net

Ma.gnolia: http://ma.gnolia.com

reddit: http://reddit.com

Spurl.net: http://www.spurl.net

StumbleUpon: http://stumbleupon.com

Yahoo! My Web 2.0: http://myweb2.search.yahoo.com

SOCIAL NETWORKS: TAGGING

History of Tagging

Tagging evolved as a method of organizing the vast quantity of information on the Web. Its origins are highly interrelated with social bookmarking and collaborative Web sites. Tagging uses keywords to categorize information. Blog posts, Web sites, articles, and photographs are given keywords, which are assigned by the users themselves rather than through a hierarchical system. This enables users to retrieve information more easily and share information with other users interested in the same category. Sites such as Flickr and del.icio.us were among the first to popularize this feature (Gordon-Murnane, 2006).

Current Trends

Over the last several years, tagging has become a critical component in collaborative Web 2.0 applications, and its usage spans widely across the Internet. Bookmarking sites, which are gaining in popularity, and tagging go hand in hand (Conley, 2005). As online media has become more prevalent, sites such as Technorati have come to rely on tags to filter the information (Roush, 2005). Debates about the quality of the tags have increased as their use has grown. However, many agree that tags provide a critical step in organizing the information on the Web that mirrors the rapid changes in content that is available (Ojala, 2007).

Business Applications

A business with an online presence can benefit from tags to help drive awareness and interest within its category by directing those interested in its product or service toward its URL (uniform resource locator). Tags can also facilitate e-commerce by directing people interested in the keyword categories to the right place (Koeppel, 2007).

Social networking sites, bookmarking sites, and online media sites use tags to manage the vast quantity of information within their platforms and connect people with common interests. Tags are invaluable and inextricably linked to prevailing Web 2.0 technologies.

Educational Applications

Because tags organize large quantities of information, academic institutions can apply the technology to their services. Libraries can tag information for easy retrieval and, as mentioned previously, classes can use tags to facilitate exchange and class discussion on bookmarking sites such as del.icio.us by tagging content and information.

How to Create Tags

Social bookmarking, social networking, and photo-sharing sites prompt users to tag the images or content that they have uploaded or linked. The keywords should be simple phrases that describe the information. This helps users easily find the information at a later date and enables others interested in that category to find it with keyword searches. Any number of tags can be used on a single image or piece of information. Users can use their discretion about what keywords to list as their tags. There are no official guidelines on what is appropriate. Tags on information posted on many Web sites can also be updated to maintain relevancy (Roush, 2005).

Conclusion and Future Trends

Tagging is an extremely useful method of organizing various forms of information. It is expected that new applications for the technology will be developed as the information age continues to drive the need for users to filter the noise. Tagging might be applied within the workplace to increase productivity and efficiency. For example, tags may be applied to e-mail messages to enable easy retrieval. Advertisers will also likely use tagging to specifically direct their messages to target audiences with a high interest in their products or services. Tagging is a broadly applicable technology that will continue to be utilized more as a larger volume of information is shared and referenced.

REFERENCES

Conley, L. (2005). *Web* graffiti *2. Fast Company, 100.*

Gordon-Murnane, L. (2006). Social bookmarking, folksonomies, and Web 2.0 tools. *Searcher, 14*(6), 26-38.

Koeppel, P. (2007). Technically speaking. *Retail Merchandiser, 47*(6), 30-31.

Ojala, M (2007). *Web 2.0* and value-added indexing. *Online, 3,* 31.

Roush, W. (2005). Tagging is it. *Technology Review, 108*(6), 21-22.

ADDITIONAL RESOURCES

125 social bookmarking sites: Importance of user generated tags, vites, and links. (n.d.). Retrieved from http://www.searchenginejournal.com/125-social-bookmarking-sites-importance-of-user-generated-tags-votes-and-links/6066

Smith, G. (2008). *Tagging: People powered metadata for the social Web.* New Riders Press.

SOCIAL NETWORKS: PHOTO SHARING

History of Photo Sharing

The first photo-sharing sites originated during the mid to late 1990s, primarily from online services that offered finished prints from digital photographs. Services have evolved to include more advanced features like photo editing, purchasing image-based products, public and private file sharing, and community-oriented Web sites with broad networking opportunities. Some services are subscription based and some are free (Beardi, 2000).

Flickr, which was acquired by Yahoo! in 2005 for US$35 million, is one of the most popular photo-sharing Web sites. The company was founded in 2002 by two entrepreneurs attempting to build Game Neverending, a game based on social interactions. In 2003, struggling as a start-up to raise money and stay in business, the team decided to turn the original site into a photo-sharing portal by revamping the gaming interface to incorporate photos. Today, Flickr is considered one of the best photo-sharing sites on the Web (Fitzgerald, 2006).

Flickr is an international site that is available in eight languages, so photos can be shared globally. Every hour, upward of 4,000 photos are added to the site, creating an incredible wealth of visual information and connectivity.

Business Applications

Photo sharing is a way for people to visually stay connected and learn from one another. While initially a consumer technology, there are several applications and benefits within an enterprise. In a business setting, photo sharing is a useful tool for sharing information and learning from external sources. Photo sharing can also help to develop relationships within the workplace, which is particularly important as businesses become more global and employees are scattered around various offices with few ways to feel connected. Photo sharing can be limited to private communities, so employees can post photographs from local events to share with colleagues firm-wide and facilitate exchange without broadcasting the images publicly. Posting images also offers glimpses of personality and coworkers can learn about each other in ways they might not otherwise be able to within the confines of their cubicle walls. Photo sharing can be a useful tool for collaboration, communication, and cultural initiatives, especially in large organizations. In addition, photo-sharing Web sites can also be helpful research tools because images can be sorted based on various geographies and categories. For example, a professional could learn about a new venue for meetings by surfing images posted by other participants without actually visiting the locations. These images could be shared with other decision makers within the firm to help discussion.

From a technical point of view, there are also benefits to using photo-sharing sites such as Flickr within an enterprise. Many corporations house headshots and other photographic records that take up server space. Rather than maintaining photo files on company servers, they can be posted to photo-sharing sites to free up bandwidth and also provide a common place for retrieval that is easy to access for employees within the organization.

Educational Applications

Learning institutions can use photo-sharing Web sites to share visual knowledge about cities of interest, news, events, people, and organizations (Sinclair, 2006). Photographs facilitate learning and, in today's changing society where youth may learn best through active engagement, photo sharing can be an instrumental tool in bringing information to life and drawing students into the subject at hand. Educators, teachers, and students can share information with each other and with other schools across the globe by posting photographs and sharing experiences. Researchers at the University of Washington have even tapped into Flickr to create three-dimensional models of famous landmarks (Greene, 2007).

Libraries are becoming increasing supporters of photo-sharing sites such as Flickr that enable users to share knowledge and experience with one another. By tagging photos accurately, the images can be catalogued for users to make accessing information simple. Recently, the Library of Congress decided to share archived images on the site (Gordon & Stephens, 2006).

How to Share Photos

If you already have a Yahoo! account, you will just need to create a Flickr user name and password. If you are not yet registered with Yahoo!, you must set up an account, which is free of charge and requires some basic registration information. This service provides 100 MB of photo storage monthly. If you need additional space, you can upgrade to a paid subscription that costs approximately US$24.95 per year.

You can participate in Flickr in a number of ways. Photos can be private or shared publicly with the broad Flickr user base. It is easy and fast to upload photos, and it can be done in numerous ways.

1. E-mail photos from a mobile phone.
2. Upload directly to the Flickr Web site.
3. Export large volumes of photos from programs such as iPhoto.
4. Use a dedicated program called Flickr Uploadr.
5. Link from third-party programs, such as Shutterfly and Snapfish.

The site offers various features that facilitate community. There are groups that can be joined based on common interests. The site includes a blog with photography-related news, such as Polaroid's recent decision to stop producing instant film. Your account can be customized to create a personality profile, and you can create a buddy list to instantly be connected to photographs from friends and family. Products and reprints can also be ordered using posted images.

Once photos are posted, they can be organized into various libraries and tagged with keywords to help make them easier to locate. Tags are keywords that help organize and identify photos of interest. Descriptions of the photos can be added to provide context to the image for others that view the images. The site provides specific guidelines and photos can only be posted for personal use. Any commercial-based photos result in account termination.

The site is facilitated by tagging photos. These keywords help organize and identify photos of interest.

Conclusion and Future Trends

Peer-to-peer photo sharing has taken basic photo storage and finishing to an interactive level that facilitates learning and social interaction. Future programs will likely have additional features that make the experience richer, more engaging, and more collaborative. Features such as photo retouching or playful Photoshop elements might be added to the functionality. Users may be able to add more in-depth stories to their photos to help bring them to life with words. Schools, businesses, and institutions are likely to continue to use photo-sharing sites to build relationships and share information.

REFERENCES

Beardi, C. (2000). Photo sites bulk up amid surge in interest. *Advertising Age, 71*(8), 40-50.

Fitzgerald, M. (2006). How we did it. *Inc., 28*(12), 116-118.

Gordon, R. S., & Stephens, M. (2006). Priceless images: Getting started with Flickr. *Computers in Libraries, 26*(10), 44-45.

Greene, J. (2007). Building a 3D world one snapshot at a time. *BusinessWeek, 4060*, 74.

Sinclair, M. (2006). What is Flickr? *Creative Review, 26*(6), 39-41.

ADDITIONAL RESOURCES

Bausch, P., & Bumgardner, J. (2006). *Flickr hacks: Tips and tools for sharing photos online.* O'Reilly Media, Inc.

Giles, R. (2006). *How to use Flickr: The digital photography revolution.* Course Technology PTR.

Howard, D. M. (2003). *Sharing digital photos: The future of memories.* Redmond, WA: Microsoft Press.

King, J. A. (2007). *Digital photo projects for dummies.* Hoboken, NJ: Wiley Publishing Inc.

Story, D. (2007). Great Flickr add-ons. *Macworld, 24*(11), 80-81.

Wilkinson, D. (2007). *Flickr mashups (programmer to programmer).* Indianapolis, IN: Wiley Publishing, Inc.

dotPhoto: http://www.dotphoto.com

faces.com: http://www.faces.com

Fotki: http://www.fotki.com

MyPhotoAlbum: http://www.myphotoalbum.com

Pixagogo: http://www.pixagogo.com

SmugMug: http://www.smugmug.com

TopTenREVIEWS: http://photo-sharing-services-review.toptenreviews.com

Webshots: http://www.webshots.com

Zoto: http://www.zoto.com

SOCIAL NETWORKS: MASHUPS

Tim Davis

History of Mashups

Mashups came into prominence with the advent of Web 2.0 and the increasing collaboration on the Internet. Mashups are essentially a content aggregation technology that combines and draws on the functionality of diverse applications into one integrated tool that is browser compatible. Typically, mashups rely on information from public Web sites as well as private applications.

Mashups began with programmers using a technique called "screen scraping," where a computer program parses the program from an application or a Web site and tries to discover the advanced programming interface (API), which is the interface that programmers use to modify an application. This was a tedious and often ineffective process, yet it was the only way that programmers could create mashups since no companies had their APIs open for programmers to tinker with. Google was one of the first big companies to open its API when it opened Google Maps. This was a momentous occasion for mashups since the programmers finally had access to the API. Prior to this, many programmers did not want to take the time to attempt screen scraping, so they did not create mashups. Other mapping applications, such as MapQuest, followed suit and opened up their APIs as well (Fagan, 2007).

Currently, mashups have entered into a new era of use for nonprogrammers with the advent of technology such as Microsoft Popfly and Yahoo! Pipes, which allow nonprogrammers to create mashups (Fagan, 2007). Before these, mashups were largely the domain of programmers who knew enough about the code of the applications to be able to write the transition codes to create the mashups.

Current Trends

Mashups were at the peak of inflated expectations in the Gartner "Hype Cycle for E-Commerce" in 2007, which means that they are likely in the trough of disillusionment right now. Yet, Gartner places mashups as a technology that will be adopted in the mainstream in less than 2 years. It is listed as a technology with a high benefit in a short time frame, making it ideally suited for tactical uses by businesses to solve discrete problems. It does not have the same strategic benefit as some of the transformational technologies, but it certainly can solve any number of tactical problems.

Although mashups began primarily as a consumer tool in mashing various applications at a user's whim, especially with the advent of Microsoft Popfly and Yahoo! Pipes, the current trend is shifting toward enterprise and commercial use of the mashups. Businesses are adopting mashups to solve discrete, tactical problems in an increasingly diverse number of ways. Companies are using mashups to give a more interactive and easy user experience on their Web sites, as well as to improve their Web store offerings. This increased use of business-to-consumer mashups is a trend that will likely continue into the future. Though less

utilized at the moment than business-to-consumer and consumer-to-consumer mashups, business-to-business mashups will increasingly be used to allow businesses to compare products and have a more interactive experience, much like businesses provide the service to their customers. Enterprise use of mashups will increase significantly as some of the enterprise mashups mature and companies get a better idea of how they can leverage the technology to meet their needs.

Business Applications

Both businesses and government agencies have been utilizing mashups as a way to integrate diverse applications into a single collaborative, user-friendly application. Mashups can be created for nearly anything by combining two or more existing applications, so businesses have a wide variety of possibilities in utilizing mashups (Brodkin, 2007). A few of the examples below demonstrate innovative ways that companies have been using mashups.

Government agencies are increasingly using mashups as they learn to harness the mass collaboration that Web 2.0 offers. For example, the Environmental Protection Agency (EPA) created a mashup known as the Environmental Land-Use Control Web Ring. The EPA uses the mashup to track contaminated sites by combining various state and federal environmental databases that track contaminated sites. Also, the military is using a business intelligence mashup to track defective Humvee batteries that might cause the vehicle to explode. Once a defective battery is found, all of the contracts and orders are consolidated so that all of the Humvees from the same batch can be fixed quickly (Havenstein, 2007). The Air Force also used mashups to streamline their decision-making process for construction on their bases, allowing it to view the posts centrally with live video footage and access many years of construction information. This led to US$5 million a year in savings in decision-making costs for a one-time cost of less than US$1 million.

Businesses have been using mashups to combine internal data with external applications in a number of innovative ways. The most common business use of mashups is to leverage mapping technologies (Dearstyne, 2007). One excellent example is a real estate company that combined its data application with VoIP to make what is known as a VoIP-data mashup (Reed, 2007). This mashup recognized the house that people were calling to inquire about and gave the callers the option to take a virtual tour of the house on a cell phone and to examine the particulars (price, square footage) of the house as well. The real estate agent also received an e-mail notification of the interested buyer and could call and arrange a live tour (Reed).

Although most mashups now combine external and internal applications, there is also the possibility of integrating legacy applications with new applications in a mashup. This allows all of the information from the legacy system to be combined with the new system into one application. Although there are numerous problems with writing translation code to combine the two applications, businesses have been doing this, particularly when the legacy systems contain a large amount of important data.

For a business, mashups provide a way to quickly aggregate multiple sources of content and present it in an easily understandable way (Trombly, 2007). This can lead to quicker time to market and reduced development costs as public applications are leveraged instead of needing to be developed. However, this approach can reduce the thoroughness and longevity of the application. Therefore, businesses need to examine what their needs are with regard to the application before attempting to do a mashup.

In addition to creating mashups for their own tactical use, companies such as Google have opened up their APIs for various proprietary applications in the hopes of getting new ideas. Opening up its API allows Google to leverage its technology in a way that it never could have done on its own. All of the programmers who tinker with Google's technology create new innovations in a shorter amount of time. They are leveraging all of the minds on the Web to improve an application and to create innovations that drive future change within the company. Yet, many companies are afraid to release their APIs due to the fact that they cannot control the direction of the applications once they do. However, releasing the API to their applications may allow certain companies to leverage the innovation on the Web into new and innovative ideas.

Educational Applications

With applications like Microsoft Popfly and Yahoo! Pipes available for free, there are numerous educational opportunities to learn about mashups. Both Microsoft and Yahoo! offer this free service along with tutorials and frequently asked questions (FAQs) about creating your own diverse types of mashups. In addition, the user community offers feedback and support as well as showcasing their diverse mashups. This creates a user-friendly, collaborative environment for students to learn about mashups.

There are many diverse data mashups that students can use or create to assist in their projects and other schoolwork. A few intriguing ones will be described briefly. A particularly useful ability of mashups for students is the ability to mash up all of their favorite RSS feeds into one RSS feed. This would allow students to keep track of topics of interest from diverse sources without having to constantly keep visiting the other resources. If they failed to visit the news Web site, it would download automatically into their mashup RSS feed. This provides a valuable tool for keeping up with current events.

Additionally, many data mashups provide an integrated way to do research. For example, a mashup combining MapQuest with an image search would enable students to look up their school or other schools on the map and also see any pictures that came up. They could likewise look up other places in the world and see the corresponding images alongside a map of where the location is. This represents an interactive way of learning that places heavy emphasis on visuals. This can be a more effective way of learning.

An interesting anthropological project for students would be to create what is known as an "autobiogeography." An autobiogeography combines one's autobiography with mapping software to show an interactive map of your life. You can pick discrete events, like places you have traveled to, or any other combination of events. Students could also create an autobiogeographical resume, where it shows everywhere they worked in the past.

How to Create Mashups

1. To begin, create a Windows Live ID account (http://get.live.com).
2. Sign into Microsoft Popfly (http://www.popfly.com).
3. Download Microsoft Silverlight.
4. Click "Create Stuff," then select "Mashup" from the drop-down menu.
5. Click "Images and Video," then select "Live Image Search" from the drop-down menu and drag it onto the screen.
6. Click "Display," then select "Carousel" and drag it onto the screen.
7. Click the wrench on the "Live Search" box and type "Vincent Van Gogh" into the query box.
8. Click on the wrench again to zoom back out.
9. Click on the blue circle on "Live Image Search" and connect it to "Carousel."
10. Click "Preview" to see what the mashup looks like.
11. Click "Save" to save the mashup.

Conclusion and Future Trends

A key trend in mashups is in the increasing use of mapping technologies. Ever since Google released the API to Google Maps, huge numbers of mashups have been created. Due to the popularity of the mapping mashup and the ease of creating one now that Google's API is open, more and more people are requesting that better public data be released, which has largely been the domain of geographical information systems (GISs) in the past. The demand for GIS has gone up significantly as more and more businesses and consumers have demanded more accurate data. In the future, the demand for readily available geographical information will drive a spike in GIS data, provide more useful and accurate mashups, and provide consumers with much more accurate information to help their decision making. Businesses will begin using this data to get more accurate geographical views of their share of the market and potential customers.

Some companies are opening up their APIs like Google did with Google Maps. Immediately after Google opened up its API, AOL's MapQuest, Yahoo! Maps, and Microsoft Virtual Earth all quickly opened theirs as well. Since Google was the first one to open its API, it has much more visibility on the Web through these mashups than its competitors. It is likely that other Web applications will open up their APIs so that people can create mashups for them. Just as with the mapping technology, many innovative mashups will spawn from the opening up of APIs. Yet, this is often proprietary information for the companies, and they lose control over how their products are implemented once they release the APIs (Gerber, 2006). Therefore, the potential of their products being used in ways they did not imagine may have a chilling effect on the release of APIs. Yet, it is likely that the trend of opening the API will continue, especially as competitors begin to do it. This presents an interesting conflict between the desire for innovation and the free flow of information, and the desire of companies to own their intellectual property (Johnson & Wilcox, 2007). However, it seems like many companies are realizing that by giving up some of their intellectual property, they can leverage the innovation of millions of users and create even more useful intellectual property as a result (Tapscott & Williams, 2006).

Additionally, mashups will likely be used increasingly in wireless applications. As the emphasis shifts from wired technology to wireless technology, mashups will increasingly be used in all kinds of consumer products, such as cell phones and GPS (Global Positioning System) devices ("The World on Your Desktop," 2007). Users often have innovative ideas about what applications would be most useful for their devices, and companies that can leverage their users' innovation to create useful applications and mashups will likely do well. The problem now is that most of the technology is locked, so it cannot be modified at all. In the future, applications might open up their technology for tinkering and create new mashups for many types of wireless devices.

REFERENCES

Brodkin, J. (2007). Strategic technologies for 2008. *Network World, 24*(40), 3-4.

Dearstyne, B. (2007). Blogs, mashups, & wikis oh my! *Information Management Journal, 41*(4), 24-33.

Fagan, J. (2007). Mashing up multiple Web feeds using Yahoo!Pipes. *Computers in Libraries, 27*(10), 10-17.

Gerber, R. S. (2006). Mixing it up on the Web: Legal issues arising from Internet "mashups." *Intellectual Property & Technology Law Journal, 18*(8), 11-14.

Havenstein, H. (2007). Military, oil firm use BI to avoid disaster. *Computerworld, 41*(40), 8.

Hype cycle for e-commerce (2007). *Gartner*.

Johnson, M. J., & Wilcox, P. A. (2007). The world of connected things. *The Journal of Government Financial Management, 56*(4), 48-53.

Reed, B. (2007). VoIP applications seem to be branching out. *Network World, 24*(43), 14.

Tapscott, D., & Williams, A. D. (2006). *Wikinomics*. New York: The Penguin Group.

Trombly, M. (2007). Mashups bring added dimension to Web services. *Securities Industry News, 19*(11), 1-16.

The world on your desktop. (2007). *The Economist, 384*(8545), 15-20.

ADDITIONAL RESOURCES

Blogger's Guide to Mashups: http://blog.sherifmansour.com?p=187

Chicago Crime Block: http://chicago.everyblock.com/crime

Google Mashups: http://editor.googlemashups.com

Housing Maps: http://www.housingmaps.com

IBM's Guide: http://www.ibm.com/developerworks/views/xml/libraryview.jsp?search_by=The+ultimate+mashup+semantic+Web

Labnotes: http://blog.labnotes.org/2006/07/11/scraping-with-style-scrapi-toolkit-for-ruby/

Microsoft Popfly: http://www.popfly.com

Programmable Web: http://www.programmableweb.com/mashups

Yahoo! Pipes: http://pipes.yahoo.com

WEB CONFERENCING AND ELECTRONIC MEETINGS

Kostadin Bisharov,
Meghan Blake, Melanie Riera

History of Web Conferencing

Web conferencing can trace its roots back before the Internet and World Wide Web to a computer-based education system called PLATO. Wooley (1994, ¶ 1) states that "the PLATO system pioneered online forums and message boards, emails, chat rooms, instant messaging, remote screen sharing, and multiplayer games, leading to the emergence of what was perhaps the world's first online community."

In the 1960s, Professor Don Bitzer created the PLATO system at the University of Illinois. PLATO gained more popularity throughout the 1970s as new features were added. PLATO Notes, released in 1973, is the equivalent of what we know today as online message boards. That same year, the PLATO system added Talkomatic, which "transmitted characters instantly as they were typed instead of waiting for a complete line of text" (Wooley, 1994, ¶ 25). Talkomatic allowed for multiple users to chat as a group and was the equivalent of today's chat rooms. This was a big success and led to the development of TERM-talk, a program that allowed two people to converse and one person to page another person while not having to stop whatever he or she was doing. This can be seen as today's instant messaging. In addition, there was a feature that allowed for a user to switch to monitor mode, whereby one person could view another's screen (the equivalent of today's remote screen sharing). PLATO Personal Notes came soon after, which is the same as e-mail.

As a result of overcrowding, trying to sort through Notes became more difficult because of the amount of information and the limited number of Notes files. This led to the develop-

ment of Group Notes, which was an extension of the original Notes. Group Notes users could now create their own private Notes files with no set limit. In addition, users were able to organize notes by category.

PLATO's community started off small with academics, but later grew to include business, government, and military, in which PLATO was marketed as a training tool (Wooley, 1994). With the increased number of users, PLATO experienced many of the well-known problems that plague our online communities today, for example, a person pretending to be a woman when the user is actually a man, or posting inappropriate comments in Note files. No one had ever experienced this before and there was some uncertainty until social norms could be established (Wooley).

The PLATO system has had a huge impact on the development of software and programs that we have today. Some of the descendants of PLATO include Lotus Notes, DEC Notes, NetNotes, and WebNotes. After the World Wide Web became a viable option for collaboration, companies attempted to use conferencing software that was originally designed to run on internal company software by modifying it for the Web. However, the results were not perfect, and it was not until the mid-90s that Web conferencing software was available (Roberts, 2004). The software developed (based on a centralized structure) included Backtalk, Web Crossing, Podium, TALKaway, and PlaceWare.

Another form of conferencing software called groupware, which was not based on a centralized structure, allowed for additional options such as document sharing and scheduling (Roberts, 2004). Some of groupware's products included Lotus Domino, Oracle InterOffice, WebShare, and Livelink. Of special note is GroupSystems, formerly known as Ventana, which was influential in the development of group software and recognized by Gartner Inc. "as the world leader in Group Intelligence and Innovation" (GroupSystems, 2008). In 1989, it created the group decision support system (GDSS) category. GroupSystems released GSI WorkGroup and Meeting Room in 1992. These software programs "are still the most full featured team collaboration products for face-to-face meetings on the market today" (GroupSystems).

Interestingly, as the price of personal computers went down, more and more file sharing occurred on a peer-to-peer basis and this culminated in the Napster phenomenon. Peer-to-peer "began to be seen as the way to host Web conferencing, rather than through a single server" (Roberts, 2004, ¶ 23). Some of the groups that offered the peer-to-peer concept to Web conferencing included Groove, WiredRed, and NextPage.

Web conferencing has been evolving for decades and can be defined today as a collaborative way to interact over a network in real time and can take place in peer-to-peer meetings or one-to-many presentations (Mann, 2007). At a minimum, a Web conferencing product should offer presentation delivery, desktop or application sharing, text chat, shared whiteboard, and basic security. However, additional features are available and can greatly enhance the Web conferencing experience. These include integrated public switched telephone network audio, integrated VoIP, audio, videoconferencing, file sharing, application and document sharing, remote control, archiving, feedback, polling, e-learning facilities, and advanced security (Mann).

Current Trends

Currently, some of the developing trends in Web conferencing include the increased use of VoIP and video, the incorporation of features to support e-learning, the movement toward document-centric conferencing, and changes in deployment models (Smith, 2008).

Most companies use telephone bridges for the audio part of the Web conference. However, there is an increasing demand for VoIP because it is controlled by the Web conferencing product.

Using VoIP allows for on-screen control of the speaker as well as eliminating the need to pass out bridge numbers and PIN codes (Mann, 2007). In terms of the visual component of Web conferencing, with increasing bandwidth capabilities it is becoming more feasible to use webcams to enhance the experience of participants.

There are three deployment options for Web conferencing applications: the software-as-a-service (SaaS) model, on-premise model, and blended model. The SaaS model means the user accesses the software through the Internet from the vendor's system. The on-premise model means that the user has bought the license to use the software and installs it on his or her system. The blended model is a combination of the SaaS and on-premise model (Mann, 2007). The majority of companies are using the SaaS deployment model; however, it is likely that more companies will turn to the on-premise deployment model because of cost and security concerns. Microsoft will be coming up with a new on-premise version of Live Meeting, which is expected to boost the transition to on-premise models (Mann).

Another important development in Web conferencing is the transformation to a standard (used by all employees) rather than a specific point solution for select users. Mann (2007) believes that by "2010, web conferencing will be available to 75% of corporate users as a standard facility, alongside e-mail, presence, calendaring, IM and other collaborative facilities" (p. 5).

Other factors supporting the trend toward Web conferencing as a standard are cost savings and environmental concerns. Companies can measure hard ROI (return on investment) by reducing the amount of travel employees take. Meetings can take place anywhere and include participants from all over the world. In addition, with the current concerns about the environment, some companies are citing "green" reasons for the increased use of Web conferencing in reducing carbon emissions due to travel (Smith, 2008).

Business Applications

Numerous business applications exist in which electronic meetings are being used as a part of Web conferencing. Through electronic meetings, corporations are able to increase collaboration at all levels, which is becoming crucial to attaining high performance. Mann (2007) states that this technology can increase shared information among colleagues and business partners, provide the ability to work on more projects simultaneously, and increase overall impact. Polls, testing, and chat features can also offer advantages beyond physical meetings (Mann). In the near future, electronic meetings will become a customary tool for all employees (Smith, 2008).

A Chicago-based check-cashing company, Barr Management, uses Web conferencing to train affiliates, customers, and vendors located throughout the country. Specifically, Web conferencing enables remote vendors, such as Western Union, to train Barr Management employees on things such as new wire procedures. Barr Management believes that Web conferencing provides additional functionality that was not included in instant messaging, a tool it were using prior to implementation. Web conferencing allows Barr Management to communicate in real time with other companies that are not on its LAN (local area network) and provides a remote-control capability to increase efficiency in the software training process ("Barr Management Deploys WiredRed's e/pop Web Conferencing," 2004).

Pulse Inc. is a company that supplies healthcare providers with a complete solution to automate the record-keeping process. Headquartered in Wichita, Kansas, Pulse Inc. utilizes Web conferencing to enable employees to communicate with each other in real time between four offices. Physicians nationwide use its Patient Relationship Management (PRM) System and Electronic Health Records (EHR) software to improve patient care, while at the same time improving their bottom line. Pulse uses Web conferencing

to train customers and help them troubleshoot the PRM and EHR software issues much more quickly than before having Web conferencing ability. Through Web conferencing, Pulse is able to better train customers using the application and desktop-sharing feature, and troubleshoot PRM and EHR software issues as they arise in a swift and efficient manner ("E/pop Web & Video Conferencing Simplifies Training and Company Communications at Pulse, Inc.," 2007).

Tindall Corporation, headquartered in Spartanburg, South Carolina, designs, manufactures, and erects concrete systems for various types of construction projects, ranging from parking decks at universities to prison cells throughout the United States. The company has held numerous electronic meetings where employees are able to share Outlook calendar functions and PowerPoint presentations dynamically. The engineering team is able to share drawings with others who may not even have the software installed on their own desktops. The company expects to save US$200,000 in travel costs per year since installing Web conferencing. As a result, Tindall Corporation has received a very quick return on their investment ("Tindall Invests in e/pop Web Conferencing to Cut Business Travel Expenses in Half," 2005).

Educational Applications

Web conferencing has many educational applications. However, it is mainly used in online distance education, which has evolved into an extremely convenient way for working people to continue their education. Some people may be hesitant to engage in this style of education because they fear it may not be interactive enough. However, advancements made in video or Web conferencing applications have made online distance education much more engaging. With a Web conferencing format, students can ask questions in real time, build relationships, meet with professors, and be mentored online directly, much as they would through face-to-face meetings on campus in order to gain a better understanding of the material.

One very good example of Web conferencing being used for educational purposes is the incorporation of Macromedia Breeze in the Academy of Art University. It has integrated different multimedia applications to enhance the interaction among the students, making the e-learning more similar to real life at schools. However, there was an issue to be resolved: "how to duplicate the rite of passage all graduate school students must go through when presenting thesis proposals and completing projects in front of their professors" (Shaeffer, 2005). The university's reputation depended on finding a solution to this problem.

Within only 6 months of being used, Web conferencing was proving effective. Scheduled Web-based meetings helped students experience the process and pressure of presenting in front of a live faculty audience. The online students present their work via a Breeze videoconference before a panel of professors seated in a specially equipped conference room. Video images of the students and their work appeared on a big screen for discussion, and a final review decision greatly enhanced the experience (Shaeffer, 2005).

After the success of online reviews, the academy is finding new ways to use Web conferencing. For example, a blog-like journal allows graduate students to conduct weekly videoconferences and chat sessions with advisors. Students and their mentors also use the Breeze whiteboard feature to regularly critique work in progress. Another use is an online multimedia presentation designed for the orientation of new faculty hires. Video-enabled online marketing events are utilized for recruiting new students. Recruiters are set up with microphones and cameras to display art samples and answer prospective student questions (Shaeffer, 2005).

Web conferencing provides a solution for students who cannot leave their homes with an educational experience comparable to what they might have in a classroom. Baltimore County's Home and Hospital Center in Bare Hills has eight full-time teachers who interact with students using Web conferencing to teach classes such as history, algebra, geometry, and physics. It provides education for Baltimore County students who are unable to attend school for at least 4 weeks due to physical or emotional crisis, medical condition, expulsion, or administrative transfer from their home schools (Dawson, 2007).

Web conferencing is also used in Kent College Preparatory School. The college adopted WiredRed's e/pop Web conferencing software. It enhanced relations in both education and business to easily communicate complex topics and eliminate unnecessary travel. Web conferencing allows the boarding students to communicate securely with their parents and friends, as well as improve the learning experience and collaboration for the students by enabling off-site teachers and speakers to lead a lesson without being physically in the classroom. It allows arranging virtual classrooms with other schools and colleges both in the United Kingdom and the rest of the world. This can be very beneficial: "Imagine having a French lesson with students in a Paris classroom helping the students in Kent" ("E/pop® Web & Video Conferencing Brings Kent College Pembury's Staff, Students and Parents Together," 2006).

Conclusion and Future Trends

The market for Web conferencing is still crowded by numerous vendors, resulting in increased mergers and acquisitions to capture market share. However, there will only be a handful of leaders and as of now they include Microsoft, IBM, Cisco, and Adobe. We will see differentiation strategies from these vendors, such as pricing or ease of use. Nevertheless, companies will first look to the vendor that supports their e-mail infrastructures—demonstrating favorability for collaboration platforms—for enhancing Web conferencing capabilities (Mann, 2007). In fact, Mann states that "by 2010, 60% of companies using web conferencing will acquire this capability as part of a larger suite of applications, rather than from a specialist vendor" (p. 2).

An important ongoing trend to acknowledge is the mixture of unified communications and collaboration technology and its impact on Web conferencing. For example, many Web conferencing programs and audio products have been merged into one offering. In addition, "instant messaging clients can launch conferences, and presence engines are 'surfacing' availability information within web conferencing products" (Smith, 2008, p. 3). Storage and discussion features are being added to Web conferencing products, which are muddying the distinction between "team workspaces and group decision tools" (Smith, p. 3).

Gartner estimates that in 2007, the Web conferencing market was worth US$1.13 billion and will increase to US$1.37 billion by 2008. Revenues are forecasted to grow at a 19.5% compound annual rate (Smith, 2008). There is no doubt that Web conferencing will become an integral part of a company's collaborative environment. According to Gartner's hype cycle, it is only about 2 years from mainstream adoption. With globalization, Web conferencing has and will open the door for many to interact with others throughout the world who may not have been able to before in both a business and educational sense. As Tapscott and Williams (2006) state, Web conferencing is another way in which the collaborative spirit will increasingly grow.

REFERENCES

Barr Management deploys WiredRed's e/pop Web conferencing to support corporate training initiatives. (2004). *WiredRed Software*. Retrieved February 16, 2008, from http://www.wiredred. com/appstory_barrmgmt.html

Dawson, C. (2007). With Web conferencing, homebound students are keeping up. *ZDNet Editor*. Retrieved February 17, 2008, from http:// education.zdnet.com/?p=787

E/pop® Web & video conferencing brings Kent College Pembury's staff, students and parents together. (2006). *WiredRed Software*. Retrieved February 17, 2008, from http://www.wiredred. com/downloads/appstory_kentcollege.pdf

E/pop Web & video conferencing simplifies training and company communications at Pulse, Inc. (2007). *WiredRed Software*. Retrieved February 16, 2008, from http://www.wiredred.com/appstory_pulse.html

GroupSystems. (2008). *History: Group collaboration and Web meetings software*. Retrieved March 1, 2008, from http://www.groupsystems. com/history

Mann, J. (2007, February 17). Magic quadrant for Web conferencing. *Gartner, Inc.*

Roberts, L. (2004). History of Web conferencing: Multi-function conferencing comes of age. *Web Conferencing Zone*. Retrieved February 17, 2008, from http://www.web-conferencing-zone. com/history-of-web-conferencing.htm

Shaeffer, J. R. (2005). Using Macromedia Breeze, we've elevated our program to a whole new level. *Academy of Art University*. Retrieved February 17, 2008, from http://www.adobe.com/cfusion/ showcase/index.cfm?event=casestudyprint&casestudyid=92699&loc=en_us

Smith, D. M. (2008). Key issues for Web conferencing. *Gartner Inc*. Retrieved February 17, 2008, from http://www.gartner.com/resources/154100/154170/key_issues_for_web_conferenc_154170.pdf

Tapscott, D., & Williams, A. D. (2006). *Wikinomics: How mass collaboration changes everything*. New York: Portfolio (member of Penguin Group Inc).

Tindall invests in e/pop Web conferencing to cut business travel expenses in half. (2005). *WiredRed Software.* Retrieved February 16, 2008, http://www.wiredred.com/appstory_tindall.html

Wooley, D. (1994). *Plato: The emergence of online community.* Retrieved February 16, 2008, from http://thinkofit.com/plato/dwplato.htm

ADDITIONAL RESOURCES

http://thinkofit.com/webconf/index.htm

http://www.web-conferencing-zone.com

208

Compilation of References

18 U.S.C. §1030. (2008).

26 U.S.C. § 61. (2008).

Acronym, M. (2007). Serious grief. *New Scientist, 195*, 52-53.

Active World's educational universe. (n.d.). Retrieved November 26, 2007, from http://www.activeworlds.com/edu/awedu.asp

ActiveWorlds. (2007). Retrieved April 4, 2008, from http://www.activeworlds.com/tour.asp

Alexander, B. (2006, March/April). Web 2.0: A new wave of innovation for teaching and learning? *Educause Review*, pp. 33-44.

All the virtual news that fits. (2006, October 16). *Wired*. Retrieved September 1, 2007, from http://www.wired.com/techbiz/media/news/2006/10/71954

Alter, A. (2007, August 10). Is this man cheating on his wife? *Wall Street Journal*, p. 1.

Alter, A. E. (2007, August 23). A second life: 10 Web 2.0 Apps CIOs personally use. *CIO Insight*. Retrieved August 27, 2007, from http://www.cioinsight.com/print_article2/0,1217,a=213943,00.asp

American Bar Association Legal Technology Resource Center. (2008). *Text messaging and the importance of a records retention policy.* Retrieved February 25, 2008, from http://meetings.abanet.org/ltrc/index.cfm?&data=20080204#E6AADE50-02C7

American Marketing Association. (2007a). *Beyond Marketing 2.0: Harnessing the power of social media for marketing campaign results.* Retrieved December 28, 2007, from http://www.marketingpower.com/aevent_event1221988.php

American Marketing Association. (2007b). *Dictionary of marketing terms.* Retrieved October 15, 2007, from http://www.marketingpower.com/mg-dictionary-view1876.php

Athavaley, A. (2007, June 20). A job interview you don't have to show up for. *The Wall Street Journal*, p. D1.

Au, W. J. (2007). Spy game. *New World Notes*. Retrieved April 4, 2008, from http://nwn.blogs.com/nwn/2007/02/spy_game.html

Avatar. (2008). *Dictionary.com*. Retrieved March 2, 2008, from http://dictionary.reference.com/browse

Baker, S. (2006, November 15). IBM on Second Life: More than PR. *BusinessWeek*. Retrieved September 1, 2007, from http://www.businessweek.com/the_thread/blogspotting/archives/2006/11/ibm_on_second_1.html?chan=search

Bakioglu, B. (2007). Textual poaching of digital texts: Hacking and griefing as performance narratives of Second Life. In *Creativity, ownership, and collaboration in the digital age.* Cambridge, MA: MIT.

Barab, S., & Duffy, T. (2000). From practice fields to communities of practice. In D. Jonassen & S. Land (Eds.), *Theoretical foundations of learning environments* (pp. 25-55). Mahwah, NJ: Lawrence Erlbaum Associates.

Barab, S., MaKinster, J., & Scheckler, R. (2004). Designing system dualities: Characterizing an online professional development community. In S. Barab, R. Kling, & J. Gray (Eds.), *Designing for virtual communities in the service of learning* (pp. 53-90). New York: Cambridge.

Barab, S., Squire, K., & Dueber, W. (2000). A co-evolutionary model for supporting the emergence of authenticity. *Educational Technology Research and Development, 48*(2), 37-62.

Bartle, R. (1990). *Interactive multi-user computer games.* Muse Ltd.

Bartle, R. (1991). *Hearts, clubs, diamonds, spades: Players who suit MUDs.* Retrieved April 4, 2008, from http://www.mud.co.uk/richard/hcds.htm

Barton, B. (2006). Ratings, reviews, and ROI: How leading retailers use customer word of mouth in marketing and merchandising. *BazaarVoice.* Retrieved April 15, 2008, from http://www.jiad.org/vol7/no1/barton/bv-wom-wp-oct06.pdf

Basiat, S. (2007, November 4). *Library allows students to pay fines in Second Life.* Retrieved November 28, 2007, from http://www.slnn.com/article/library-fine-paying-machine

Beaudoin, J. (2007). *Web 2.0 for marketers ebook review on Web 2.0 portals.* Retrieved November 26, 2007, from http://www.web20portals.com/web-20-marketing/web-20-for-marketers

Bell, L., Pope, K., Peters, T., & Galik, B. (2007, July/August). Who's on third in Second Life? *Online, 31*(4), 14-19.

Bereiter, C., & Scardamalia, M. (1989). Intentional learning as a goal of instruction. In L. B. Resnick (Ed.), *Knowing, learning, and instruction* (pp. 361-391). Hillsdale, NJ: Lawrence Erlbaum.

Berge, Z., & Muilenburg, L. (2001). Obstacles faced at various stages of capability regarding distance education in institutions of higher learning. *Tech Trends, 46*(4), 40-45.

Big Sky Brands. (2007). *MySpace.* Retrieved November 26, 2007, from http://www.myspace.com/bigsky-brands

Blizzard Entertainment. (2007). *World of Warcraft, end user license agreement.* Retrieved May 15, 2008, from http://www.worldofwarcraft.com/legal/eula.html

Bock, W. (2006). *Larry Ellison and the network computer that wasn't.* Retrieved December 30, 2007, from http://www.mondaymemo.net/031103feature.htm

Bodker, S. (1996). Applying activity theory to video analysis: How to make sense of video data in HCI. In B. Nardi (Ed.), *Context and consciousness: Activity theory and human computer interaction* (pp. 147-174). Cambridge, MA: MIT Press.

Boutin, P. (2006). Web 2.0: The new Internet boom does not live up to its name. *Slate.* Retrieved March 15, 2008, from http://www.slate.com/id/2138951

Bragg v. Linden Research Inc., 487 F. Supp. 2d 593, 611 (E.D. Pa. May 30, 2007).

Brandon, J. (2007). *Q&A with the forefather of hacking.* Retrieved December 24, 2007, from http://www.pcmag.com/print_article2/0,1217,a=213916,00.asp

Brandon, J. (2007, May 2). The top eight corporate sites in Second Life. *Computerworld.* Retrieved November 19, 2007, from http://www.computerworld.com

Brenner, B. (2007). *Black hat 2007: Estonian attacks were a cyber riot, not warfare.* Retrieved December 30, 2007, from http://searchsecurity.techtarget.com/originalContent/0,289142,sid14_gci1266728,00.html

Brenner, B. (2007). *How Russia became a malware hornet's next.* Retrieved December 30, 2007, from http://searchsecurity.techtarget.com/originalContent/0,289142,sid14_gci1275987,00.html

Brighton, G. (2005). Flickr kills trendspotting. *PSFK.* Retrieved September 27, 2007, from http://psfk.com/2005/03/flickr_kills_co.html

Broersma, M. (2007, August 12). *Virtual worlds pose business risks.* Retrieved October 11, 2007, from http://www.washingtonpost.com/wp-dyn/content/article/2007/08/13/AR2007081300007.html

Brown, A., Collins, A., & Duguid, P. (1989). Situated cognition and the culture of learning. *Educational Researcher, 18*, 32-42.

Brown, J., & Duguid, P. (2000). *The social life of information*. Boston: Harvard Business School Press.

Browning, J. (2007). Adopting a blogging policy could limit your exposure to legal risk. *Houston Business Journal*. Retrieved February 25, 2008, from http://houston.bizjournals.com/houston/stories/2007/05/28/smallb2.html

Bugeja, M. J. (2007a, November 12). Second Life, revisited. *The Chronicle of Higher Education*. Retrieved November 12, 2007, from http://chronicle.com/weekly/v54/i12/12c00101.htm

Bugeja, M. J. (2007b, September 14). Second thoughts about Second Life. *The Chronicle of Higher Education*. Retrieved September 14, 2007, from http://chronicle.com/weekly/v54/i03/03c00101.htm

Bughin, J., & Manyika, J. (2007). *How businesses are using Web 2.0: A McKinsey global survey*. Retrieved April 19, 2008, from http://www.mckinseyquarterly.com/article_page.aspx?ar=1913&pagenum=1

Burns, E. (2007, May 4). *Second Life users top 1.3 million in March*. Retrieved December 6, 2007, from http://www.clickz.com/3625769/print

Business needs to prepare for virtual crime. (2007). *Wall Street Journal*. Retrieved May 15, 2008, from http://blogs.wsj.com/biztech/2007/11/19/business-needs-to-prepare-for-virtual-crime

Capps, B. (2007, May 28). How to succeed in Second Life. *Advertising Age, 78*(22), 6.

Carey, E. (2007). *Copyright protection in the fashion industry: Legislative solutions*. Unpublished undergraduate thesis, Virginia Commonwealth University.

Carnevale, D. (2007, July 13). Colleges find they must police online worlds. *The Chronicle of Higher Education*, p. A22.

Carpenter, P. (2007). *The current and future state of Second Life*. Retrieved February 15, 2008, from http://www.computerworld.com/blogs/node/5426

Carr, D. F. (2007, March 1). Second Life: Is business ready for virtual worlds? *Baseline*. Retrieved March 4, 2008, from http://www.baselinemag.com/c/a/Projects-Management/Second-Life-Is-Business-Ready-For-Virtual-Worlds

Carter, B. (2007, October 4). Fictional characters get virtual lives, too. *The New York Times*. Retrieved November 12, 2007, from http://www.nytimes.com/2007/10/04/arts/television/04CSI.html?_r=1&ex=1192161600&en=6994ec8ad88ab2d8&ei=5070&oref=slogin

Cartman, E. (2008). Chinese wage-price spiral now fully underway. *WordPress*. Retrieved April 4, 2008, from http://cartmanist.wordpress.com/2008/02/28/chinese-wage-price-spiral-now-fully-underway

CBS mobile launches widget to promote new animated series. (2007). *MuseStorm*. Retrieved December 28, 2007, from http://www.musestorm.com/site/jsp/spotlight/1042.jsp

Charlesworth, A. (2006, December 19). Circuit City and IBM launch 3-D Web store. *ITNews*. Retrieved December 7, 2007, from http://www.itnews.com.au/Tools/Print.aspx?CIID=70445

Claburn, T. (2007). *Hacker profile becomes more social, adds women*. Retrieved December 24, 2007, from http://www.informationweek.com/shared/printableArticle.jhtml?articleID=205101618

classroom: An activity system analysis. In S. Barab, R. Kling, & J. Gray (Eds.), *Designing for virtual communities in the service of learning* (pp. 210-238). New York: Cambridge.

CNN enters the virtual world of Second Life. (2007, November 12). Retrieved November 12, 2007, from http://www.cnn.com/2007/TECH/11/12/second.life.irpt/index.html?iref=newssearch

Coca-Cola. (2007, April 16). *Coca-Cola launches competition to design online "virtual thirst" coke machine*.

Retrieved October 14, 2007, from http://www.virtual-thirst.com/virtualthirst-socialmediarelease.html

Cognition and Technology Group at Vanderbilt (CTGV). (1992). The Jasper experiment: An exploration of issues in learning and instructional design. *Educational Technology Research and Development, 40*(1), 65-80.

Collaboration. (n.d.). *Merriam-Webster's Online Dictionary*. Retrieved December 15, 2007, from http://www.m-w.com/dictionary/collaboration

Collis & Moonen. (2006). The contributing student: Learners as co-developers of learning resources for reuse in Web environments. In D. Hung & M. S. Khine (Eds.), *Engaged learning with emerging technologies* (pp. 49-67). The Netherlands: Springer.

Comb v. PayPal Inc., 218 F. Supp. 2d 1165 (N.D. Cal. 2002).

Cooley, K. (2007). *Sir David Ross's pluralistic theory of duty (the beginnings)*. Retrieved April 4, 2008, from http://www.manitowoc.uwc.edu/staff/awhite/ken95.htm

Copyright Web site. (2008). *Benedict.com*. Retrieved April 4, 2008, from http://www.benedict.com/Digital/Web/WebProtect.aspx

Craig, K. (2006, February 8). Making a living in Second Life. *Wired*. Retrieved November 12, 2007, from http://www.wired.com/gaming/virtualworlds/news/2006/02/70153

Cross, R., Abrams, L., & Parker. (2004). A relational view of learning: How who you know effects what you know. In M. L. Conner & J. G. Clawson (Eds.), *Creating a learning culture: Strategy, technology, and practice* (pp. 152-168). Cambridge University Press.

Davis, P. (2007, August 10). "Second Life" avatar sued over virtual sex device. *USA Today*. Retrieved December 7, 2007, from http://www.usatoday.com/tech/webguide/internetlife/2007-08-10-virtual-sex-lawsuit_N.htm

Del Conte, N. T. (2006, November 14). *Dell to see PCs on Second Life*. Retrieved December 8, 2007, from http://www.pcmag.com/article2/0,1895,2059016,00.asp

Dell, K. (2007, August 20). Second Life's real-world problems. *Time, 170*(8), 49.

Dibbell, J. (1993). A rape in cyberspace or how an evil clown, a Haitian trickster spirit, two wizards, and a cast of dozens turned a database into a society. *The Village Voice*. Retrieved April 4, 2008, from http://www.villagevoice.com/specials/0543,50thdibbell,69273,31.html

Disabled could think their way around "Second Life." (2007, November 27). Retrieved December 8, 2007, from http://www.news.com

Donald, M. (1993). Precis of origin of the modern mind: Three stages in the evolution of culture and cognition. *Behavioral and Brain Sciences, 16*, 737-791.

Donaldson, T., & Dunfee, T. W. (1994). Toward a unified conception of business ethics: Integrative social contracts theory. *The Academy of Management Review, 19*, 252-284.

Driscoll, K. (2007, May/June). Collaboration in today's classrooms: New Web tools change the game. *Multimedia & Internet Schools*, pp. 9-12.

Dubner, S. (2007). Philip Rosedale answers your Second Life questions. *New York Times*. Retrieved May 15, 2008, from http://freakonomics.blogs.nytimes.com/2007/12/13/philip-rosedale-answers-your-second-life-questions

Engestrom, Y. (1987). *Learning by expanding*. Orienta-Konsulti. Retrieved March 15, 2008, from http://communication.ucsd.edu/MCA/Paper/Engestrom/expanding/toc.htm

Engestrom, Y. (2001). Expansive learning at work: Toward an activity theoretical reconceptualization. *Journal of Education and Work, 14*(1), 133-156.

Enright, G. (2007). *Web 2.0 vulnerabilities to watch for*. Retrieved July 22, 2007, from http://www.computerworld.com/action/article=9027342

Ertmer, P. (2005). Teacher pedagological beliefs: The final frontier in our quest for technology integration? *Educational Technology Research and Development, 53*(4), 25-40.

Estabrook, L., Witt, E., & Rainie, L. (2007). *Information searches that solve problems: How people use the Internet, libraries, and government agencies when they need help.* Retrieved March 15, 2008, from http://www.pewinternet.org/pdfs/Pew_UI_LibrariesReport.pdf

Evans, K. (2003). Accounting for conflicting mental models of communication in student-teacher interaction: An activity theory analysis. *Writing Selves/Writing Societies.* Retrieved March 15, 2008, from http://wac.colostate.edu/books/selves_societies

Evans-Correia, K. (2007, August 23). *Second Life job fairs boost IT prospects.* Retrieved December 8, 2007, from http://searchcio.techtarget.com/originalContent/0,289142,sid19_gci1269191,00.html?trac=NL-48&ad=601108&asrc=EM_NLN_2046654&uid=3195005

Evers, J. (2007). *Hacking for dollars.* Retrieved December 24, 2007, from http://www.news.com/2102-7349_3-5772238.html

Evers, J. (2007). *The security risk in Web 2.0.* Retrieved July 17, 2007, from http://news.com.com/2102-1002_3-6099228.html

Fanning, E. (2007). *Editor's note: Security for Web 2.0.* Retrieved July 17, 2007, from http://www.computerworld.com/action/article=283283

Fogg, B. J. (2000). Persuasive technologies and Net smart devices. In E. Bergman (Ed.), *Information appliances and beyond: Interaction design for consumer products* (pp. 335-360). San Francisco: Morgan Kaufmann.

Foo, C. Y., & Koivisto, E. M. I. (2004). Defining grief play in MMORPGs: Player and developer perceptions. In *International Conference on Advances in Computer Entertainment Technology (ACE)* (pp. 245-251).

Foster, A. L. (2007, July 13). The death of a virtual campus illustrates how real-world problems can disrupt online islands. *The Chronicle of Higher Education*, p. A22.

Foster, A. L. (2007, June 11). MIT's virtual dormitories for freshmen. *The Chronicle of Higher Education.*

Retrieved December 8, 2007, from http://chronicle.com/wiredcampus/index.php?id=2143?=atwc

Foster, A. L. (2007, September 21). Professor Avatar. *The Chronicle of Higher Education*, pp. A24-A26.

Foster, A. L. (2007, July 6). Virtual worlds as social-science labs. *The Chronicle of Higher Education*, pp. A25-A27.

Freed, J. (2007, April 4). Best Buy offers help in "Second Life." Retrieved December 9, 2007, from http://www.msnbc.msn.com/id/17953078

Game theft led to fatal attack. (2005). *BBC News.* Retrieved May 15, 2008, from http://news.bbc.co.uk/go/pr/fr/-/1/hi/technology/4397159.stm

Gartner says 80 percent of active Internet users will have a "second life" in the virtual world by the end of 2011. (2007, April 24). Retrieved December 6, 2007, from http://www.gartner.com/it/page.jsp?id=503861

Gaudin, S. (2007, June 18). *Rivals face off in Enterprise 2.0 debate.* Retrieved February 15, 2008, from http://www.informationweek.com/news/showArticle.jhtml?articleID=199905148

Germain, J. M. (2007). *IT security and the no good, very bad Web app nightmare.* Retrieved December 24, 2007, from http://www.technewsworld.com/story/60208.html

Giles, J. (2007). Serious grief. *New Scientist, 195*, 52-56.

Gillen, P. (2007, May 7). Giving Second Life a first chance. *B to B, 92*(6), 13.

Glaser, M. (2006, October 23). *Wired, CNET, Reuters agog over Second Life.* Retrieved December 8, 2007, from http://www.pbs.org/mediashift/2006/10/virtual_journalismwired_cnet_r.html

Gogoi, P. (2007). Retailers take a tip from MySpace. *Business Week.* Retrieved April 15, 2007, from http://www.businessweek.com/bwdaily/dnflash/content/feb2007/db20070213_626293.htm?chan=search

Guiragossion, L. (2007, October 29). A thousand ways to widget in the age of Web 2.0 marketing. *Web 2.0 Marketing.* Retrieved December 28, 2007, from http://web2pointzeromarketing.blogspot.com

H&R Block launches first virtual tax experience in Second Life. (n.d.). Retrieved December 9, 2007, from http://www.hrblock.com/presscenter/articles/secondrelease.jsp

Habitat. (n.d.). *Wikipedia.* Retrieved November 21, 2007, from http://en.wikipedia.org/wiki/Habitat_(video_game)

Hamblen, M. (2007). *Second Life for a Cisco virtual press conference: Fly on over!* Retrieved November 21, 2007, from http://blogs.computerworld.com/node/6496

Hannafin, M., Hannafin, K., Hooper, S., Rieber, L., & Kini, A. (1996). Research on and research with emerging technologies. In D. Jonassen (Ed.), *Handbook of research for educational communications and technology* (pp. 378-402). New York: Simon and Schuster.

Hannafin, M., Land, S., & Oliver, K. (1999). Open learning environments: Foundations, methods, and models. In C. Reigeluth (Ed.), *Instructional design theories and models: A new paradigm of instructional theory* (Vol. 2, pp. 115-140). Mahwah, NJ: Lawrence Erlbaum Associates.

Harkin, F. (2007). *Virtual style? In another life.* Retrieved February 15, 2008, from http://www.ft.com/cms/s/0/733d2398-05a6-11dc-b151-000b5df10621.html

Hayes, G. (2007). *A video comp of major brands in Second Life.* Retrieved December 28, 2007, from http://www.youtube.com/watch?v=tEGHJuCbGdo

Hendrickson, M. (2007). 34 more ways to build your own social network. *TechCrunch.com.* Retrieved April 4, 2008, from http://www.techcrunch.com/wp-content/white_label_social_networking_solutions_chart2.html

Hendrickson, M. (2007). Virtual world hangouts: So many to choose from. *TechCrunch.com.* Retrieved April 8, 2008, from http://www.techcrunch.com/2007/08/05/virtual-world-hangouts-so-many-to-choose-from

Hewitt, J. (2004). An exploration of community in a knowledge forum

Hillis, S. (2007, October 10). Open borders sought for virtual worlds. *Boston.com Business.* Retrieved October 11, 2007, from http://www.boston.com/business/technology/articles/2007/10/10/second_life_ibm_in_open_borders_for_virtual_worlds/?rss_id=Boston+Globe+--+Technology+stories

Hmelo, C. E. (1999). Problem based learning: Effect on the early acquisition of cognitive skill in medicine. *Journal of Learning Sciences, 7*(2), 173-208.

Hof, R. (2006). *Second Life's first millionaire.* Retrieved February 15, 2008, from http://www.businessweek.com/the_thread/techbeat/archives/2006/11/second_lifes_fi.html

Hof, R. D. (2006, May 1). Virtual world, real money. *BusinessWeek*, pp. 72-82.

Holahan, C. (2006, November 21). The dark side of Second Life. *BusinessWeek.*

Holden, R. (2006, December 6). *Cisco gets a Second Life.* Retrieved December 8, 2007, from http://www.thestreet.com/pf/newsanalysis/second-life/10326341.html [Note: Virtual reporter Robert Holden is known in the real world as Robert Holmes.]

Holohan, C. (2006, November 21). The dark side of Second Life. *BusinessWeek.* Retrieved December 8, 2007, from http://www.businessweek.com/print/technology/content/nov2006/tc20061121_727243.htm

Hoover, J. N. (2007, May). Wells Fargo taps Web 2.0. *Wall Street & Technology, 25*(5), 25.

Hoyle, B. (2006). Gamers' lust for virtual power satisfied by sweatshop workers. *The Times.* Retrieved May 15, 2008, from http://technology.timesonline.co.uk/tol/news/tech_and_web/article648072.ece

Hyysalo, S. (2005). Objects and motives in the product design process. *Mind Culture and Activity, 12*(1), 19-36.

Iamigor. (2006, August 2). *Tea partay*. Retrieved October 15, 2007, from http://www.youtube.com/watch?v=PTU2He2BIc0

IBM CEO sets sights on the 3-D Internet. (2006, November 14). Retrieved December 7, 2007, from http://www-03.ibm.com/press/us/en/photo/20632.wss

IBM Global Services. (2006). *Expanding the innovation horizon: Global CEO study 2006*. Retrieved December 15, 2007, from http://www-935.ibm.com/services/us/gbs/bus/html/bcs_ceostudy2006.html

IBM introduces video game to help university students develop business skills. (2007, November 6). Retrieved March 2, 2008, from http://www.03.ibm.com/press/us/en/pressrelease/22549.wss

IBM. (2007, May 15). *Live IBM sales people to staff new virtual IBM business center*. Retrieved October 15, 2007, from http://www-03.ibm.com/press/us/en/press-release/21551.wss

IFLA. (2008). Some myths about intellectual property. *IFLA.org*. Retrieved April 4, 2008, from http://www.ifla.org/documents/infopol/copyright/ipmyths.htm

InnoCentive. (2008). Retrieved February 15, 2008, from http://www.innocentive.com

Internet meme. (2008). *Wikipedia*. Retrieved March 2, 2008, from http://en.wikipedia.org/wiki/Internet_phenomenon

Ives, B. (2007, December 1). More Web 2.0 stories, part two: Procter and Gamble embraces the wisdom of the Web for new product ideas. *The FASTForward Blog*. Retrieved December 28, 2007, from http://www.fastforwardblog.com/2007/12/01/more-web-20-stories-part-two-proctor-gamble-embraces-the-wisdom-of-the-web-for-new-product-ideas

Jacoby, C. J. (2007). E-discovery update: Discovery of ephemeral digital information. *Law and Technology Resources for Legal Professionals*. Retrieved February 25, 2008, from http://www.llrx.com/columns/fios19.htm

Jana, R. (2006, August 23). Starwood Hotels explore Second Life first. *BusinessWeek*. Retrieved December 9, 2007, from http://www.businessweek.com/innovate/content/aug2006/id20060823_925270.htm

Jana, R. (2006, June 27). American Apparel's virtual clothes. *Business Week*. Retrieved September 26, 2007, from http://www.businessweek.com/innovate/content/jun2006/id20060627_217800.htm

Jaokar, A. (2006, October 25). *Ajit Jaokar's mobile Web 2.0 blog: The widget widget Web*. Retrieved October 12, 2007, from http://www.web2journal.com/read/289798.htm

Jerney, J. (2007, January 23). Even experts have difficulty understanding Web 3.0. *The Daily Yomiuri (Tokyo)*, p.18.

Jonassen, D. (2000). Revisiting activity theory as a framework for designing student centered learning environments. In D. Jonassen & S. Land (Eds.), *Theoretical foundations of learning environments*. Mahwah, NJ: Lawrence Erlbaum Associates.

Kaiser Foundation. (2005). *Generation M: Media in the lives of 8-18 year-olds*. Retrieved March 15, 2008, from http://www.kff.org/entmedia/entmedia030905pkg.cfm

Kaptelinin, V., & Nardi, B. (2006). *Acting with technology: Activity theory and interaction design*. Cambridge, MA: MIT Press.

Kaspersky, E. (2007). The cybercrime arms race. In Kaspersky Lab (Ed.), *What lies ahead*. Dallas, TX: Kaspersky Lab.

Kharif, O. (2007). Retail 2.0. *Business Week: Innovation*. Retrieved April 15, 2007, from http://www.businessweek.com/innovate/content/jan2007/id20070131_360739.htm?chan=search

Kiley, D. (2007). Using bad news to a brand's advantage. *Business Week*. Retrieved November 14, 2007, from http://www.businessweek.com/the_thread/brandnewday

Kimban, D. (2007, November 19). *Small country has big plans for Second Life*. Retrieved November 29, 2007, from http://www.slnn.com/article/serbia-island

Kirkpatrick, D. (2007, March 23). Coldwell Banker's Second Life. *Fortune*. Retrieved December 9, 2007, from http://money.cnn.com/2007/03/22/technology/fastforward_secondlife.fortune/index.htm

Kirkpatrick, D. (2007, January 8). Second Life to go open source. *Fortune*. Retrieved September 3, 2007, from http://money.cnn.com/2007/01/07/technology/secondlife.fortune/index.htm

Kirkpatrick, D. (2007, January 23). Second Life: It's not a game. *Fortune Small Business*. Retrieved September 3, 2007, from http://smallbusiness.aol.com/start/startup/article-partner/_a/second-life-its-not-a-game/20070130134209990001

Kirkpatrick, M. (2006). Metaverse breached: Second Life customer database hacked. *TechCrunch.com*. Retrieved April 4, 2008, from http://www.techcrunch.com/2006/09/08/metaverse-breached-second-life-customer-database-hacked

Kling, R., & Courtright, C. (2004). Group behavior and learning in electronic forums. In R. Kling, J. Gray, & S. Barab (Eds.), *Designing for virtual communities in the service of learning* (pp. 91-119). Cambridge, United Kingdom: Cambridge University Press.

Konrad, R. (2007, August 2). Second Life bans gambling. *ABC News*. Retrieved December 7, 2007, from http://abcnews.go.com/Technology/wireStory?id=3438941

Kosma, R. (2000). The relationship between technology and design in educational technology research and development: A reply to Richey. *Educational Technology Research and Development, 48*(1), 19-21.

Kraft Foods. (2007). *Kraft foods goes digital to unveil more than 70 new products in first-ever virtual supermarket in Second Life*. Retrieved October 12, 2007, from http://www.kraft.com/mediacenter/country-press-releases/us/2007/us_pr_04192007.htm

Krazit, T. (2006, November 14). Dell sets up "Second Life" shop, offers PCs to residents. Retrieved December 8, 2007, from http://news.zdnet.com/2100-9595_22-6135497.html

Kuutti, K., Iacucci, G., & Iacucci, C. (2002, October 13-16). Acting to know: Improving creativity in the design of mobile services by using performances. In *Proceedings of the Fourth Conference on Creativity and Cognition* (pp. 95-102). Loughborough, United Kingdom.

Lackie, R., & Terrio, R. (2006, July/August). Mashups and other new or improved collaborative social software tools. *Multimedia and Internet @ Schools*, pp. 12-15.

Land, S. (2000). Cognitive requirements for learning with open ended learning environments. *Educational Technology Research and Development, 48*(3), 61-78.

Laningham, S. (2006). *developerWorks interviews: Tim Berners-Lee*. Retrieved December 15, 2007, from http://www.ibm.com/developerworks/podcast/dwi/cm-int082206.html

LaPlante, A. (2007, February 3). Second Life lessons: Cisco, IBM pace corporate push into virtual worlds. *InformationWeek*. Retrieved December 8, 2007, from http://www.informationweek.com/news/showArticle.jhtml?articleID=197001839&pgno=1&queryText=

Lavallee, A. (2007). Now, virtual fashion. *Wall Street Journal*. Retrieved May 15, 2008, from http://online.wsj.com/public/article/SB115888412923570768-HtFYrBweWpF25yJkL0CdXvkFRkY_20070922.html

Lave, J., & Wenger, E. (1991). *Situated learning: Legitimate peripheral participation*. Cambridge, United Kingdom: Cambridge University Press.

Law library/court rules. (n.d.). *LexisNexis Applied Discovery*. Retrieved February 25, 2008 from http://www.lexisnexis.com/applieddiscovery/lawLibrary/courtRules.asp

Lee, O., & Oh, J. (2007). The impact of virtual reality functions of a hotel Website on travel anxiety. *CyberPsychology & Behavior, 10*, 584-586.

Lenssen, P. (2005). *Samy, their hero: Interview*. Retrieved December 29, 2007, from http:blogoscoped.com/archive/2005-10-14-n81.html

Leonard, C. (2007). Town shuns Mo. family after MySpace hoax. *USA Today*. Retrieved April 4, 2008, from http://www.usatoday.com/news/nation/2007-12-06-internet-death_N.htm

Lessig, L. (1999). *Code and other laws of cyberspace.* New York: Basic Books.

Lilley, A. (2007). *Is Web 3.0 a brand relaunch just like Kylie's new look?* Retrieved April 28, 2008, from http://www.guardian.co.uk/media/2007/oct/15/monday-mediasection8

Linden Lab. (2008). *Second Life terms of service agreement.* Retrieved May 15, 2008, from http://secondlife.com/corporate/tos.php

Linden, H. (2004). The nine souls of Wilde Cunningham, part I. *SecondLife.Blogs.com.* Retrieved April 4, 2008, from http://secondlife.blogs.com/nwn/2004/12/the_nine_souls_.html

Linden, R. (2007). *Anti-gambling policy update: FAQ.* Linden Lab. Retrieved May 15, 2008, from http://blog.secondlife.com/2007/08/09/anti-gambling-policy-update-faq

Linden, R. (2007). Identity verification comes to Second Life. *blog.SecondLife.com.* Retrieved April 4, 2008, from http://blog.secondlife.com/2007/08/29/identity-verification-comes-to-second-life

Lorenzo, G., Oblinger, D., & Dziubna, C. (2007). How choice, co-creation, and culture are changing what it means to be Net savvy. *Educause Quarterly, 1,* 6-12.

Lundell, D., & Beach, R. (2003). Dissertation writers' negotiations with competing activity systems. In Bazerman & Russell (Eds.), *Writing selves/writing societies* (pp. 483-514). Retrieved March 15, 2008, from http://wac.colostate.edu/books/selves_societies

Lynn, R. (2007, May 4). Virtual rape is traumatic, but is it a crime? *Wired.*

MacKinnon, R. (2005). *Chinese bloggers: Everybody is somebody.* Retrieved February 15, 2008, from http://rconversation.blogs.com/rconversation/2005/11/chinese_blogger_1.html

Madden, M., & Fox, S. (2006). *Riding the waves of "Web 2.0."* Retrieved March 15, 2008, from http://www.pewinternet.org/pdfs/PIP_Web_2.0.pdf

Mamberto, C. (2007). Instant messaging invades the office: Companies say it spurs broader collaboration—and scares some bosses. *Wall Street Journal Online.* Retrieved February 25, 2008, from http://online.wsj.com/article/SB118523443717075546.html

Maney, K. (2007, February 4). The king of alter egos is surprisingly humble guy. *USA Today.* Retrieved November 19, 2007, from http://www.usatoday.com/tech/news/2007-02-04-second-life-rosedale_x.htm

Markoff, J. (2006). *Entrepreneurs see a Web guided by common sense.* Retrieved April 28, 2008, from http://www.nytimes.com/2006/11/12/business/12web.html?_r=1&oref=slogin

Massive multiplayer online role-playing games (MMORPGs). (2007). *Wikipedia.* Retrieved April 4, 2008, from http://en.wikipedia.org/wiki/MMORPG

McAfee, A. (2006). *The trends underlying Enterprise 2.0.* Retrieved February 15, 2008, from http://blog.hbs.edu/faculty/amcafee/index.php/faculty_amcafee_v3/the_three_trends_underlying_enterprise_20

McAfee, A. (2006). Enterprise 2.0: The dawn of emergent collaboration. *MIT Sloan Management Review, 4*(3), 21-28.

McAfee, A. (2006). *Enterprise 2.0, version 2.0.* Retrieved December 15, 2007, from http://blog.hbs.edu/faculty/amcafee/index.php/faculty_amcafee_v3/enterprise_20_version_20

McAfee, A. (2007). *How to hit the Enterprise 2.0 bullseye.* Retrieved December 15, 2007, from http://blog.hbs.edu/faculty/amcafee/index.php/faculty_amcafee_v3/how_to_hit_the_enterprise_20_bullseye

McCarthy, J., & Wright, P. (2004). *Technology as experience.* Cambridge, MA: MIT Press.

McConnon, A. (2007, June 14). IBM's management games. *BusinessWeek.* Retrieved September 26, 2007, from http://www.businessweek.com/print/technoloyg/content/jun2007/tc20070613_838152.htm

McConnon, A. (2007, August 13). Just ahead: The Web as a virtual world. *BusinessWeek*, pp. 62-63.

McConnon, A. (2007, August 13). The name of the game is work. *BusinessWeek*. Retrieved March 5, 2008, from http://www.businessweek.com/innovate/content/aug2007/id20070813_467743.htm

McKenzie, H. (2007, April). Hype sparks rash of 3-D world launches in Asia. *Media*, p. 5.

McMillan, R. (2007). *Researchers: Web 2.0 security seriously flawed.* Retrieved December 24, 2007, from http://www.pcworld.com/printable/article/id,131215

Mellor, C. (2008). Sub-prime crisis god news for legal discovery software. *Techworld*. Retrieved February 25, 2008, from http://www.techworld.com/storage/news/index.cfm?newsid=11042

Merrill, D. (2006). *Mashups: The new breed of Web app.* Retrieved March 15, 2008, from http://www.ibm.com/developerworks/library/x-mashups.html

Millions of Us. (2007). Retrieved October 12, 2007, from http://www.millionsofus.com

Mollman, S. (2007). *Second Life's 2ⁿᵈ value: Testing ideas.* Retrieved February 15, 2008, from http://edition.cnn.com/2007/BUSINESS/09/16/second.life

Moore, J. (2006). *Five reasons why...* Retrieved October 16, 2007, from http://brandautopsy.typepad.com/brandautopsy/2006/08/five_reasons_wh.html

Mootee, I. (2004). *High intensity marketing.* Canada: SA Press.

Morath, E. (2007, January 26). Automakers connect with hip, young buyers in virtual world. *Detroit News Online.* Retrieved January 29, 2007, from http://www.detnews.com/apps/pbcs.dll/article?AID=20070126

Moser, F. Z. (2007). Faculty adoption of educational technology. *Educause Quarterly, 1,* 66-69.

MUD. (2007). *Wikipedia.* Retrieved April 4, 2008, from http://en.wikipedia.org/wiki/MUD

MUSH. (2007). *Wikipedia.* Retrieved April 4, 2008, from http://en.wikipedia.org/wiki/MUSH

Naone, E. (2007, November/December). Financial woes in Second Life. *Technology Review, 110*(6), 13.

Nardi, B. (1996). Studying context: A comparison of activity theory, situated action models, and distributed cognition. In B. Nardi (Ed.), *Context and consciousness: Activity theory and human computer interaction.* Cambridge, MA: MIT.

Naylor, D. (2007, May 17). Virtual environments create their own legal problems. *New Media Age*, p. 17.

Needle, D. (2006, October 11). *Sun finds a home in Second Life.* Retrieved December 7, 2007, from http://www.internetnews.com/dev-news/article.php/3637411

Newmann, F., Secada, G., & Wehlage, G. (1995). *A guide to authentic instruction.* Madison, WI: Wisconsin Center for Educational Research.

Nichols, S. (2006, November 14). IBM to fund "3-D Internet" project. *ITNews.* Retrieved December 7, 2007, from http://www.itnews.com/au/Tools/Print.aspx?CIID=68316

Noguchi, Y. (2005, November 22). Self 2.0: Internet users put a best face forward. *Washington Post*, p. A01. Retrieved December 6, 2007, from http://www.washingtonpost.com/wp-dyn/content/article/2005/11/21/AR2005112101787.html

Norman, D. (2004). *Emotional design: Why we love (or hate) everyday things.* New York: Basic Books.

O'Reilly, T. (2005). *What is Web 2.0: Design patterns and business models for the next generation of software.* Retrieved July 1, 2007, from http:www.oreilly.net.com/lpt/a/6228

O'Reilly, T. (2006). *Web 2.0 compact definition: Trying again.* Retrieved December 15, 2007, from http://radar.oreilly.com/archives/2006/12/web_20_compact.html

O'Toole, T. (2007). Arbitration clause in Second Life Terms of Service found unconscionable. *BNA E-Commerce and Tech Law Blog.* Retrieved May 15, 2008, from http://pblog.bna.com/techlaw/virtual_games/index.html

Oldenburg, R. (1997). *The great good place.* New York: Marlow.

Orlowski, A. (2005). *Web 2.0 worm downs MySpace.* Retrieved July 17, 2007, from http://www.theregister.co.uk/2005/10/17/web20_worm_knocks_out_myspaces/print.html

Page, J. (2007, May 24). *Tiny island nation opens the first real embassy in virtual world.* Retrieved November 22, 2007, from http://technology.timesonline.co.uk/tol/news/tech_and_web/article1832158.ece

Paizo. (2007). *Avatar theft will not be tolerated.* Retrieved April 4, 2008, from http://paizo.com/paizo/messageboards/community/offTopic/avatarTheftWillNOTBeTolerated&source=rss

Parents: Cyberbullying led to teen's suicide. (2007). *ABC News.* Retrieved May 15, 2008, from http://abcnews.go.com/GMA/Story?id=3882520

Philips, S. (2007). A brief history of Facebook. *Guardian Unlimited.* Retrieved March 15, 2008, from http://www.guardian.co.uk/technology/2007/jul/25/media.newmedia

Picard, R. (1997). *Affective computing.* Cambridge, MA: MIT Press.

Pink, D. (2006). *A whole new mind: Why right-brainers will rule the future.* New York: Penguin.

PN. (2006). *A special message from PN, authorized by Mudkips Acronym and N3X15.* PN Dept. of Covert Affairs and the Raid Council. Retrieved April 4, 2008, from http://www.freewebs.com/patrioticnigras/literature/declaration.html

Radinsky, J., Bouillion, L., Lento, E., & Gomez, L. (2001). Mutual benefit partnership: A curricular design for authenticity. *Journal of Curriculum Studies, 33*(4), 405-430.

Rangaswami, M. R. (2006). *The birth of Enterprise 2.0.* Retrieved February 15, 2008, from http://sandhill.com/opinion/editorial.php?id=98

Raymond, E. S. (2000). The jargon file. *ManyBooks.net.* Retrieved April 4, 2008, from http://manybooks.net/titles/raymondericetext02jarg422.html

Reibstein, D. (2007). *Word of mouth wisdom.* Retrieved April 15, 2008, from http://blog.shop.org/index.php?s=Reibstein

Reigeluth, C. (1999). What is instructional design theory and how is it changing? In C. Reigeluth (Ed.), *Instructional design theories and models: A new paradigm of instructional theory* (Vol. 2, pp. 5-30). Mahwah, NJ: Lawrence Erlbaum Associates.

REPERES Second Life. (2007). Retrieved October 12, 2007, from http://www.reperes-secondlife.com

Riel, M., & Polin, L. (2004). Online learning communities: Common ground and critical differences in designing technical environments. In S. Barab, R. Kling, & J. Gray (Eds.), *Designing for virtual communities in the service of learning* (pp. 16-52). New York: Cambridge.

Riley, D. (2007, December 5). *You're not in the USSR any more: Estonia opens an embassy in Second Life.* Retrieved December 8, 2007, from http://www.techcrunch.com/2007/12/05/youre-not-in-the-ussr-any-more-estonia-opens-an-embassy-in-second-life

Rizova, P. (2006). Are you networked for successful innovation? *MIT Sloan Management Review, 47*(2), 49-55.

Robinson, K. (2007, September 1). Virtual worlds: Another world, another business. People are using avatars to develop businesses and have fun in virtual worlds such as Second Life. *The Banker.* Retrieved November 12, 2007, from http://proquest.umi.com.proxymu.wrlc.org/pqdweb?index=0&did=1334571311&SrchMode=1&sid=1&Fmt=3&VInst=PROD&VType=PQD&RQT=309&VName=PQD&TS=1197220110&clientId=31813

Rogers, D. (2008). A search for balance in the discovery of ESI since December 1 2006. *Richmond Journal of Law*

& Technology. Retrieved May 5, 2008, from http://law.richmond.edu/jolt/v14i3/article8.pdf

Rose, F. (2007). How Madison Avenue is wasting millions on a deserted Second Life. *Wired Magazine.* Retrieved November 12, 2007, from http://www.wired.com/techbiz/media/magazine/15-08/ff_sheep?currentpage=all

Roth, W. M. (2004). Activity theory and education: An introduction. *Mind Culture and Activity, 11*(1), 1-8.

Row, H. (2006). *DoubleClick touchpoints survey IV: How digital media fit into consumer purchase decisions.* Retrieved April 19, 2007, from http://www.doubleclick.com/insight/pdfs/dc_touchpointsIV_0611.pdf

Russell, D. R. (1997). Rethinking genre in school and society: An activity theory analysis. *Written Communication, 14*, 504-554.

Russell, D., & Yanez, A. (2003). *"Big picture people rarely become historians": Genre systems and the contradictions of general education.* Retrieved March 15, 2008, from http://wac.colostate.edu/books/selves_societies

Rymaszewski, M., Au, W. J., Wallace, M., Winters, C., Ondrejka, C., & Batsone-Cunningham, B. (2007). *Second Life: The official guide.* Hoboken, NJ: John Wiley & Sons, Inc.

Savery, & Duffy, T. (1995). Problem based learning: An instructional model and its constructivist framework. In B. Wilson (Ed.), *Constructivist learning environments: Case studies in instructional design* (pp. 135-148). Englewood Cliffs, NJ: Educational Technology Publications.

Schlager, M., & Fusco, J. (2004). Teacher professional development, technology, and communities of practice: Are we putting the cart before the horse? In S. Barab, R. Kling, & J. Gray (Eds.), *Designing for virtual communities in the service of learning* (pp. 120-153). New York: Cambridge

Second Life lets CDC be everywhere—all at once. (n.d.). Retrieved December 6, 2007, from http://www.cdc.gov/about/stateofcdc/everywhere/secondLife.htm

Second Life. (2008). Retrieved February 15, 2008, from http://secondlife.com/whatis/economy-market.php

Seitzinger, J. (2006). Be constructive: Blogs, podcasts, and wikis as constructivist tools. In *Learning solutions: Practical applications of technology for learning.* El-earning Guild.

Sfard, A. (1998). On two metaphors for learning and the dangers of choosing just one. *Educational Researcher, 27*, 4-13.

Shah, S. (2006). *Top 10 Web 2.0 attack vectors.* Retrieved July 17, 2007, from http://www.net-security.org/article.php?id=949&p=1

Shank, R., & Cleary, R. (1995). *Engines for education.* Mahwah, NJ: Lawrence Erlbaum.

Siegal, R. (2005). *Paying real money to win online games.* Retrieved April 4, 2008, from http://www.npr.org/templates/story/story.php?storyId=5032947

Simonite, T. (2007, November 2). Anti-social bot invades Second Lifers' personal space. *New Scientist, 16.*

Sipress, A. (2007). Does virtual reality need a sheriff? *Washington Post.* Retrieved May 15, 2008, from http:www.washingtonpost.com/wp-dyn/content/article/2007/06/01/AR2007060102671_pf.html

Smagg, C. (2007). *15 golden rules for Web 2.0.* Retrieved October 12, 2007, from http://visionarymarketing.wordpress.com/2007/07/03/web20

SMSs to surpass 2 trillion messages in major markets in 2008. (2007). *Cellular-News.* Retrieved February 25, 2008, from http://www.cellular-news.com/story/28126.php

Sponder, M. (2007, March 29). *Pontiac Second Life case study.* Retrieved December 7, 2007, from http://www.webmetricsguru.com/2007/03/pontiac_second_life_case_study.html

Spring 2007 survey: Educators in Second Life. (2007). Retrieved November 27, 2007, from http://www.nmc.org/news/nmc/sl-educator-survey

Steel, E. (2006). Web-page clocks and other "widgets" anchor new Internet strategy. *Wall Street Journal*. Retrieved November 12, 2007 from http://marcomm201. blogspot.com/2006/11/marketing-widgets-you-saw-it-here-first.html

Stein, R. (2007, October 6). Real hope in a virtual world. *Washington Post*, p. A01.

Stephens, R.(2007). *P&G Web 2.0 success story*. Retrieved December 27, 2007, from http://www.rtodd.com/collab-orage/2007/11/pg_web_20_success_story.html

Sun Microsystems takes a leap into virtual world Second Life. (2006, October 10). Retrieved December 7, 2007, from http://www.sun.com/smi/Press/sunflash/2006-10/sunflash.20061010.2.xml

Sussman, B. (2007). Teachers, college students lead a Second Life. *USA Today*. Retrieved December 7, 2007, from http://abcnews.go.com/print?id=3439059

Tapscott, D., & Williams, A. (2006). *Wikinomics: How mass collaboration changes everything*. New York: Portfolio.

Technorati. (2007). Retrieved December 28, 2007, from http://technorati.com

Terdiman, D. (2005). IRS taxation of online game virtual assets inevitable. *ZDNet News*. Retrieved May 15, 2008, from http://news.zdnet.com/2100-1040-6140298.html

Terdiman, D. (2006, October 26). Reuters' "Second Life" report talks shop. *CNET News.com*. Retrieved December 8, 2007, from http://www.news.com/Reuters-Second-Life-reporter-talks-shop/2008-1043_3-6129335.html

Terret, B. (2007). Brand in good Web 2.0 project shock. *Noisy Decent Graphics*. Retrieved December 28, 2007, from http://noisydecentgraphics.typepad.com/de-sign/2007/11/brand-in-good-w.html

The logic of blogs and wikis in the enterprise. (2005). *The Gilbane Report, 12*(10). Retrieved February 25, 2008, from http://gilbane.com/gilbane_report.pl/104/Blogs__Wikis_Technologies_for_Enterprise_Applica-tions.html

U.S. House of Representatives Committee on the Judiciary. (2006). *Federal rules of civil procedure*. Retrieved February 25, 2008, from http://judiciary.house.gov/me-dia/pdfs/printers/109th/31308.pdf

Understanding hype cycles. (n.d.). Retrieved December 15, 2007, from http://www.gartner.com/pages/story.php.id.8795.s.8.jsp

United States Department of Justice. (1999). *U.S. Department of Justice proposed findings of fact*. Retrieved February 25, 2008, from http://www.justice.gov/atr/cases/f2600/2613-1.htm

University of California at Berkeley's School of Information Management and Systems. (2003). *How much information?* Retrieved January 2, 2008, from http://www2.sims.berkeley.edu/research/projects/how-much-info-2003/execsum.htm

Valdes-Dapena, P. (2006, November 18). *Real cars drive into Second Life*. Retrieved December 7, 2007, from http://www.cnn.com/2006/AUTOS/11/17/2nd_life_cars/index.html

Vashtar, S. (2006). Economics unbound rising wages in China. *BusinessWeek*. Retrieved April 4, 2008, from http://www.businessweek.com/the_thread/econom-icsunbound/archives/2006/03/rising_wages_in.html Virtual worlds list. (2007). *Virtual Worlds Review (VWR)*. Retrieved April 4, 2008, from http://www.virtualworld-sreview.com/info/categories.shtml

Vielle, T. (2007). IBM avatar commercial. *SL Universe*. Retrieved December 31, 2007, from http://sluniverse.com/php/vb/showthread.php?t=2797

Vijayan, J. (2007). *Six ways to stop data leaks*. Retrieved July 17, 2007, from http://computerworld.com/action/ar-ticle=285138

Villafania, A. (2007, November 26). *Arroyo activates virtual self in Second Life*. Retrieved December 7, 2007, from http://technology.inquirer.net/infotech/infotech/view_article.php?article_id=103122

Virtual theft leads to arrest. (2007). *BBC News*. Retrieved May 15, 2008, from http://news.bbc.co.uk/go/pr/fr/-/1/hi/technology/7094764.stm

Virtual Worlds Review. (n.d.). Retrieved from http://www.virtualworldsreview.com

Virtual worlds target for money laundering. (2007). *Kotaku*. Retrieved May 15, 2008, from http://kotaku.com/gaming/crime/virtual-worlds-target-for-money-laundering-302660.php

VZones. (n.d.). Retrieved November 21, 2007 from http://www.virtualworldsreview.com/vzones

W3C (World Wide Web Consortium) Advisory Committee. (2007). *Semantic Web activity statement*. Retrieved December 16, 2007, from http://www.w3.org/2001/sw/Activity.html

Wagner, M. (2007, August 21). Five rules for bringing your real-life business into Second Life. *InformationWeek*. Retrieved August 22, 2007, from http://www.informationweek.com/showArticle.jhtml?articleID=201500141

Wagner, M. (2007, December 7). Second Life residents to get calls from the real world. *InformationWeek*. Retrieved December 7, 2007, from http://www.informationweek.com/showArticle.jhtml;jsessionid=D0UJGWOJENP0MQSNDLRCKHSCJUNN2JVN?articleID=204702181&queryText=Second+Life+residents+to+get+calls

Wagner, M. (2007, August 2). Second Life voice set to leave beta. *InformationWeek*. Retrieved December 7, 2007, from http://www.informationweek.com/story/showArticle.jhtml?articleID=201202659

Walker, A. (2005). *How and why hackers want to get inside your machine*. Retrieved December 24, 2007, from http://www.informit.com/articles/printerfriendly.aspx?p=425380

Wallop, H. (2007). Cadbury plans Wispa revival. *Telegraph*. Retrieved November 28, 2007, from http://www.telegraph.co.uk/news/main.jhtml?xml=/news/2007/08/18/nwispa118.xml

Wang, M., Sierra, C., & Folger, T. (2003). Building a dynamic online learning community among adult learners. *Education Media International, 40*(1-2), 49-61.

Ward, M. (2003). Does virtual crime need real justice? *BBC News*. Retrieved May 15, 2008, from http://newsvote.bbc.co.uk/mpapps/pagetools/print/news.bbc.co.uk/1/technology/3138456.stm

Warnecke, M. (2007). Will the rise of virtual worlds turn EULAs into marketing opportunities? *BNA E-Commerce and Tech Law Blog*. Retrieved May 15, 2008, from http://pblog.bna.com/techlaw/virtual_games/index.html

Warner, D. E., & Raiter, M. (2005). Social context in massively-multiplayer online games (MMOGs): Ethical questions in shared space. *International Journal of Information Ethics, 4*.

Waters, J. K. (2007). *Web 2.0 entails "sleeping giant" security risk*. Retrieved December 24, 2007, from http://www.adtmag.com/print.aspx?id=21499

Web 2.0. (2007). *Wikipedia*. Retrieved September 15, 2007, from http://en.wikipedia.org/wiki/Web_2.0, http://en.wikipedia.org/wiki/American_Express

Wendland, M. (2008). Most text messages just vanish. *Detroit Free Press Online*. Retrieved February 25, 2008, from http://www.freep.com/apps/pbcs.dll/article?AID=/20080125/COL11/801250422/1081/COL

Wenger, E. (1998). *Communities of practice: Learning, meaning and identity*. Cambridge, MA: Cambridge University Press.

Werribee, E. (2007, February 10). *US presidential candidate John Edwards launches campaign in SL*. Retrieved November 28, 2007, from http://www.slnn.com/article/edwards08

What is a virtual world? (n.d.). Retrieved November 21, 2007, from http://www.virtualworldsreview.com/info/whatis/shtml

What is copyright? (2008). *FindLaw.com*. Retrieved April 4, 2008, from http://smallbusiness.findlaw.com/

copyright/copyright-basics/copyright-defined-overview.
html

What is online (or "cyber") harassment? (2006, May).
Second Opinion Police Blotter. Retrieved December 16,
2007, from http://secondlife.com/newsletter/2006_05/
html/police_blotter.html

Wikipedia. (2008). Retrieved February 15, 2008, from
http://www.wikipedia.org

Wilde, O. (1921). *Intentions* (14th ed.). London: Methuen
& Co.

Wong, G. (2007, March 9). Second Life's looming tax
threat. *CNNMoney.com.* Retrieved March 13, 2007, from
http://money.cnn.com/2007/03/02/technology/sl_taxes/
index.htm

Yago, G. (2006). The real price of virtual gold. *MTV
News.* Retrieved April 4, 2008, from http://www.mtv.
com/overdrive/?id=1545907&vid=120059

Yee, N. (2006). The psychology of massively multi-user
online role-playing games: Motivations, emotional
investment, relationships, and problematic usage. In R.
Schroder & A. S. Axelsson (Eds.), *Avatars at work and
play: Collaboration and interaction in shared virtual
environments* (pp. 187-207). London: Springer-Verlag.

Yee, N. (2007). Motivations of play in online games.
CyberPsychology and Behavior, 9, 772-775.

Young, J. R. (2007, May 18). Case Western Reserve U.
builds virtual campus to woo prospective students. *The
Chronicle of Higher Education,* p. A29.

About the Contributors

P. Candace Deans is on the faculty of the Robins School, University of Richmond. She teaches courses in information technology and international business. Prior to her current position, she served on the faculty at Thunderbird Global School of Management and Wake Forest University. She received her PhD from the University of South Carolina and her undergraduate degree from the University of North Carolina, Chapel Hill. She holds masters' degrees from University of Arizona, North Carolina State University, and East Carolina University. Dr. Deans has received several teaching awards. She is a frequent presenter at national and international conferences and she is the author of several books. She has published in journals such as *Journal of MIS* and *Global Information Management*. She currently serves on the editorial board of the *AIMS International Journal of Management*. Her research interests focus on international IT issues.

****

Nadira Ali is a 2008 graduate of the MBA program at the Robins School of Business, University of Richmond. She received her BS degree from Virginia Tech in 2005 with a major in accounting and minor in economics. From there, she pursued a career as an external auditor at Deloitte. Currently, she is employed by Cadmus Communications in the finance department. Her parents immigrated to America from India in 1975. During her spare time, she enjoys playing tennis and basketball.

Richard T. Barnes is a senior project manager for Sungard Higher Education Corporation and is based in the Richmond, Virginia, area. He specializes in managing the implementation of ERP (enterprise resource planning) software for higher education institutions. He has also worked as a corporate trainer and adjunct professor in business and technology. Prior to moving to Richmond, he was a technical account manager with various banking institutions in the New England and Mid-Atlantic regions. After earning bachelor degrees in engineering and computer information science in Michigan, he earned his MBA from the University of Richmond in May of 2004. In September 2004, he earned his project manager professional (PMP) certification.

Samantha C. Bryant has a degree in business information technology from Virginia Tech (2003) and a master's in business administration from the University of Richmond (2007). Ms. Bryant has professional experience in information technology, marketing, and brand management. She currently works in the sales and brand management department of Philip Morris USA developing strategic plans via retail, direct mail, and experiential marketing programs for Marlboro, the top-selling cigarette brand in the world. Ms. Bryant's professional expertise and education fuels her interest in Web 2.0 technologies, particularly their application to the marketing discipline and their effect on consumer behavior.

Peter Burkhardt is a program director for IBM Software Services for Lotus (ISSL). He has spent 12 years as a consultant, working with companies around the world. His area of expertise is collaborative and social software solutions. He holds a bachelor of arts from the University of Richmond and is a frequent guest speaker at the Robbins School of Business. He lives in Richmond, Virginia, with his wife and two children.

Sue A. Conger has a BS in psychology from Ohio State University, an MBA in finance and cost accounting from Rutgers University, and a PhD in computer information systems from the Stern School of Management at New York University. She is the author of several books, including *The New Software Engineering* (1994) and *Planning and Designing Effective Web Sites* (with Richard O. Mason, 1997), and is currently completing *Process Mapping & Management*. Dr. Conger's research interests are ethics and IT, and innovative uses of IT. She is currently on the faculty of the University of Dallas where she manages both information technology and IT service management programs.

David Harrell received his BS in business administration with concentrations in marketing and finance from the University of Richmond. David has professional experience in multichannel retailing, merchandising, demand forecasting, and inventory management. He is currently employed by Circuit City Stores Inc., working at the Richmond, Virginia, headquarters in the merchandising group. David is extremely passionate about the innovation of multichannel customer experiences and the opportunities companies are currently presented with in converting customer feedback into lifetime customer loyalty opportunities.

Carolyn McKinnell Jacobson, PhD, is the director of graduate and adult business programs and professor of information systems at Mount St. Mary's University in Maryland. Previously, she was a professor at Marymount University in Virginia where she served as chair of the Department of Information Systems and Management Science for 6 years. Under her leadership, the department established an undergraduate degree in information systems. Dr. Jacobson has won grants from several organizations including GTE and Verizon. She has also received awards for her scholarship including the AIS Best Educational Paper Award. Her current research interests are in knowledge management, human-computer interaction, and information systems education. She is on the editorial board of the *International Journal of Technology and Human Interaction* and the editorial advisory board for *Advances in Technology and Human Interaction*. Dr. Jacobson is past president of the International Academy for Information Management and currently serves on the Computing Accreditation Commission of ABET, Inc.

Hunter W. Jamerson currently serves as law clerk to the Honorable Michael C. Allen, judge of the 12th Judicial Circuit of Virginia. Hunter received his JD from the University of Richmond's T.C. Williams School of Law in 2008 and his BA from the University of Virginia in 2005. In 2009, Hunter will receive his MBA from the University of Richmond's Robins School of Business. Prior to his judicial clerkship, Hunter served as a summer associate for the Washington, DC, law firm of Cooter, Mangold, Tompert & Karas, as well as the Criminal Appellate Division of the United States Attorney's Office for Washington,

DC. Hunter's research interests include virtual and computer law, international intellectual property issues, and regulatory concerns affecting business today. Currently, Hunter resides in Richmond, Virginia.

Gigi Kelly has over 26 years of information technology experience. Dr. Kelly's expertise is in business processes and change management. Her research focuses on the effective integration of people, technology, processes, and data. She has published in journals such as the *Journal of MIS and Decision Systems Support* and has presented her work at national and international conferences. She teaches courses in process and data management, project management, and the strategic use of information technology. She has taught at the College of William and Mary, the University of Richmond, and the University of Virginia, and has been recognized for her teaching excellence.

Bryan Kimes has 10 years of experience in litigation support and technology. Bryan is currently manager of legal technology and practice support at Altria Client Services Inc. The opinions expressed in his chapter are solely those of the author and are not intended to reflect the positions of Altria Client Services Inc. or any of its affiliates.

Tom Reinartz has 14 years of teaching experience, including teaching English at Rosemount High School, new media design and development at the University of Minnesota, and instructional design for online learning at Capella University. He has presented at a variety of national and international conferences including AECT, Ed-Media, AERA, and IVLA. His research interests include collaboration and community building in online learning environments, activity theory and cognitive tools, new media design and development, and open-source software initiatives. Dr. Reinartz received his PhD from the University of Minnesota in learning technologies.

Index

A

Activity and Genre Theories 132
AJAX 60
Anything 2.0 7
attackers, what are their motivations 61
attackers, who are they 61
authentic activities, designing for 136
authentic communities, designing for 138

B

blogs 76
buying guides 23

C

civil procedure, federal rules of 71
collaboration 4
Computer Fraud and Abuse Act 126
customer experience 24

E

e-discovery, background 69
end-user license agreements, as differentiators 123
enterprise 1.0 to 2.0, evolution from 45
Enterprise 2.0 7
enterprise 2.0, communication and participation 49
enterprise 2.0, employees and the workforce 48
enterprise 2.0, implications for international business 53
enterprise 2.0, managers 47
enterprise 2.0, open innovation 51
enterprise 2.0, organization 46
enterprise 2.0, organizational challenges for 52
enterprise 2.0, project management 50

enterprise 2.0, why ? 54
enterprise 2.0 erganization, and the impact of virtual worlds 52

F

feedback, integrating into business functions 25
Flickr (tagging) 34

I

IM applications 75
in-world solutions, limitations of 126

L

legal compliance, ensured in all jurisdictions 124

M

marketing, the four Ps 31
message boards, customer reviews on 22

P

participant input 24
pecuniary crime 119

R

retail, implications for 24
retail industry, the 20
RPG, participant characteristics 108

S

Second Life 83
Second Life (virtual world) 31
Second Life, business in 86